D1603954

FROM SAFETY TO SUPEREGO

To Anne-Marie

FROM SAFETY TO SUPEREGO
Selected Papers of Joseph Sandler

Edited by

JOSEPH SANDLER

Freud Memorial Professor of Psychoanalysis in the University of London

THE GUILFORD PRESS
New York   London

© 1987 The Guilford Press
A Division of Guilford Publications, Inc.
200 Park Avenue South, New York, N.Y. 10003

Printed in the United States of America

Last digit is print number: 9 8 7 6 5 4 3 2 1

Library of Congress Cataloging in Publication Data

Sandler, Joseph.
  From safety to superego.

  (The Guilford psychoanalysis series)
  Bibliography: p.
  Includes index.
  1. Psychoanalysis. I. Title. II. Series.
RC504.S29 1987   616.89'17   86-26990
ISBN 0-89862-327-8

Contents

Acknowledgments

The number of people who played some part in the production of the papers that constitute this book is vast, and so what follows is only a partial acknowledgment of my debt to all those who helped in the creation of the individual papers and their presentation in this volume. I owe most of all to Anna Freud, who in 1956 invited me to participate in the work of the Hampstead Clinic (now the Anna Freud Centre), and to take charge of the project known as the Hampstead Index. In spite of occasional differences of opinion about theoretical matters she and Dorothy Burlingham gave me and my colleagues in the Index Group unwavering support in our work.

My next acknowledgment must surely go to my coauthors in the papers contained in this collection—Rose Edgcumbe, Christopher Dare, Alex Holder, Walter Joffe, Maria Kawenoka-Berger, Hansi Kennedy, Dale Meers, Humberto Nagera, Lily Neurath, and Bernard Rosenblatt. The work we did together, not only in the writing of the papers, but also in the discussions which led to them, was a source of very great pleasure and stimulation. There were other colleagues in the Index research groups who also contributed substantially to the formulations contained in this volume. Some wrote papers of their own describing Index work, while others participated in the writing of papers not contained in this volume. Of those who were staff members or students at the Clinic, I will mention only Sheila Baker, Agi Bene-Moses, Marion Burgner, Eleanor Dansky, Irme Elkan, Elsa First, Max Goldblatt, Sara Rosenfeld, Anneliese Schnurmann, and John Sigal. A number of visitors from abroad contributed as well—Kurt Eissler, Marjorie Harley, Irving Janis, and Albert Solnit.

For the typing of innumerable drafts of the papers before publication, thanks go first and foremost to Trudi Dembovitz and Doreen Ross. The collation and integration of the original articles into a book proved to be an extremely difficult task, but I was fortunate in having the superb help of Hannah Groumi and Michele Morowitz at the Sigmund Freud Center of the Hebrew University during my tenure there as Freud Professor from 1979 to 1985. On my return to London,

I was able to complete the work with the help of the word-processing efforts of Bryony Tanner. The references were put in order through the meticulous work of Jane Pettit.

Many of the papers contained in this volume first appeared in a two-volume Italian edition of collected papers published by Boringhieri under the title *La Ricerca in Psicoanalisi*. That edition was prepared by my good friend Paolo Coen-Pirani, and my indebtedness to him is substantial. I also want to thank Carlo Strenger for the suggestions he made for the organization of the present text. All the papers were first published in mimeographed form at the Hampstead Clinic, but special thanks are due to the Editors of the various journals and symposia reports in which the papers appeared. These include the *Journal of Psychosomatic Research*, the *Ciba Foundation*, the *International Journal of Psycho-Analysis*, the *Psychoanalytic Study of the Child*, the *British Journal of Medical Psychology*, the *Journal of the American Psychoanalytic Association*, the *Bulletin of the Menninger Clinic*, and the *Journal of Child Psychotherapy*.

These testimonials would be grossly incomplete if they did not include an acknowledgment of debt to the members of my family—my wife Anne-Marie and children Trudy, Catherine, and Paul, who suffered over the years from the effects of my psychic withdrawal whenever a paper was brewing. While I cannot say that they did not complain, they showed a degree of forbearance which was beyond the call of duty.

Finally, it gives me pleasure to acknowledge the help we have received, directly or indirectly, from the following sources:

The American Philanthropic Foundation, Philadelphia, PA; Gustave M. Berne Foundation, New York, NY; Lionel Blitzsten Memorial, Inc., Chicago, IL; G. G. Bunzl Fund; H. Daroff Foundation, New York, NY; The Division Fund, Chicago, IL; Herman A. and Amelia S. Ehrmann Foundation, New York, NY; Field Foundation, New York, NY; Ford Foundation, New York, NY; Foundation for Research in Psychoanalysis, Beverly Hills, CA; Foundation for Research in Psychiatry, New Haven, CN; Freud Centenary Fund, London, England; Grant Foundation Inc., New York, NY; The Estate of Flora Haas, New York, NY; Lita Hazen Charitable Fund, Philadelphia, PA; A. and M. Lasker Foundation, New York, NY; Anne Pollock Lederer Research Institute, Chicago, IL; Leslie Foundation, Chicago, IL; John D. and Catherine T. MacArthur Foundation, Chicago, IL; Andrew Mellon Foundation, later Paul Mellon; Walter E. Meyer Research Institute of Law, New Haven, CT; National Institute of Mental Health, Bethesda, MD; New-Land Foundation, New York, NY; Overbrook Fund, New York, NY; Psychoanalytic Research and Development

Fund, New York, NY; William Rosenwald Family Fund, Inc., New York, NY; William Sachs Foundation, New York, NY; J. and M. Scheider Foundation, New York, NY; Philip M. Stern Foundation, Washington, DC; W. Clement and Jessie V. Stone Foundation, Chicago, IL; Taconic Foundation, New York, NY; Lester Tuchman Fund, New York, NY; The Wolfson Foundation, London, England; The Bethlem Royal and Maudsley Hospital Research Fund, London, England.

Foreword

From its beginnings, the evolving structure of psychoanalytic theory has consisted of the cumulated monumental achievement of its founding genius, Sigmund Freud, and of the continuing developmental lines that he foreshadowed, and, at the same time, of the major revisionist and deviationist reconstructive endeavors at the hands of gifted and charismatic followers. Thus, the first generation around Freud was beset with the new directions articulated by such fellow pioneers as Carl Jung, Alfred Adler, Wilhelm Stekel, and Otto Rank. Each of these directions led to a major secession from the psychoanalytic ranks. In three of the instances, the new theories developed into alternative schools of therapy and rival efforts at explanatory psychologies. A generation later, a new set of revisionisms again led to new psychologies (and attendant new directions in therapy) that less clearly set themselves apart from psychoanalysis proper, but rather claimed to be its more "modern" extensions and transformations (hence the group designation, "neo-Freudians"). This was the group of Karen Horney, Erich Fromm, Frieda Fromm-Reichmann, and Harry Stack Sullivan. They set themselves partly outside the main body of psychoanalysis and yet remained to some extent within it.

Overlapping with this "neo-Freudian" generation and extending contemporaneously, but claiming a more central position within the established psychoanalytic vision and a more direct portion of Sigmund Freud's legacy, have been those "movements" (or perspectives) within psychoanalysis that have developed and remained within the body of psychoanalysis as "schools", usually identified by the name of the founder. Thus we have Kleinians, the British Object Relations School (with multiple coalescing founders like Fairbairn, Guntrip, Balint, Winnicott, Bowlby, etc.), Bionians, Lacanians (with their main focus moved outside official psychoanalysis, but with a persisting great influence remaining within), and now Kohutian self psychology. Among these groups there have been efforts to organize politically and administratively outside organized psychoanalysis—the Lacanians are an example—as well as efforts to organize scientifically and educationally within organized psychoanalysis—the Kleinians and Kohutians are good examples. And to add to this sweep of an ever widening array of variant, and varyingly deviant, psychoanalytic perspectives and emphases, a current book entitled "Beyond Freud: A Study of Modern Psychoanalytic Theorists" contains critical, but laudatory, essays on 14 major contemporary theorists, each of them the creator of a distinctive psychoanalytic "point of view" by which he or she is identified—Gill, Mahler, Peterfreund, and Schafer are among the examples.

This proliferation of revisionisms varies from those that are essentially self-contained new psychologies, like self psychology, straining to remain within the body of organized psychoanalysis, to those that essay only to be altered ways of conceptualizing the phenomena—or speaking the language—of psychoanalysis, like Schafer's "action language". A consequence, perhaps inevitable, of all this is that a lesser credit often seems to accrue to those other major theoreticians, of fully equal stature, within our ranks, who just because they are not seen to be centrally revisionist or deviationist become less a focus for a distinctively identified perspective associated with their persona, and of course much less a nidus for the formation of a school or movement. Joseph Sandler is one such major theoretician solidly building within and upon the psychoanalytic mainstream (Hans Loewald and Leo Stone are others), and this book goes a long way in making clear the full scope and stature of his contribution to the ongoing development of our discipline. Set firmly within the Freudian psychoanalytic mainstream and without benefit of the glare accorded by an avowed or acknowledged revisionist perspective or emphasis, Sandler has helped to articulate and guide the gradual evolution of that mainstream. If we but look at it freshly and critically, the theory can be seen today to be really far different from what it was but 30 years ago, during the period of hegemony of the ego-psychology metapsychological paradigm of Hartmann and Rapaport and their many coworkers, when Sandler began his studies of psychoanalysis and his signal contributions to it.

What then are Sandler's contributions to psychoanalysis as I see them expressed in this book? I will group them under two rubrics, methodological and conceptual, and, as such, they become clearly germane to two major interrelated and interdependent facets of our discipline as one of the sciences of man's intelligence. One facet is the scholarly research enterprise by which all science tests its hypotheses and accrues new empirical knowledge, and the other, the theory-building enterprise that generates new conceptualizations, and within those, new propositions and hypotheses to be tested for their fit with clinical data and clinical findings.

Sandler's methodological contributions, so clearly delineated throughout the chapters of this book, consist in his thorough and unrelenting exploitation of the possibilities in the unparalleled data collection of the Anna Freud Centre in the Hampstead Index. By constantly exploring the degree of fit and congruence, or conversely, of discrepancy, between the Index categories that are the working concepts of our general theory of psychoanalysis, and the clinical data from the ongoing psychoanalytic cases at the Anna Freud Centre that were to be indexed in accord with those categories, he again and again exposes the full range of semantic, definitional, and conceptual problems of our science. For psychoanalytic theory has evolved unevenly, with periodic reconceptualizations by Freud and by those who have come after. Often, little attention was given to the need for recasting the frames of reference of older conceptions when new conceptualizations arose. While efforts to formulate new theories resolved certain conceptual problems, they created others not always anticipated, and when older conceptions were made to articulate with newer ways of ordering or comprehending the phenomena, this created unremarked shifts in the meanings and usages of these concepts. Sandler has labeled this the elasticity of our concepts, heuristically useful indeed if fully cognized and understood.

The logical structure of our bodies of concepts and the degree of "goodness of fit" of these concepts to the data have been highlighted by the empirical application of the concepts as Index categories to the cataloguing of the data. In the pursuit of these indexing efforts, Sandler and his many coworkers who have shared in this book have had then to create serial research study groups in efforts to clarify, refine, expand, or better delimit several central concepts of our therapeutic and our theoretic enterprise. Thus, the clinical data of our cases can be better arrayed for systematic study and our clinical findings can become more meaningful, coherent, and fitted to context. Through such efforts the fit between our psychoanalytic data and our psychoanalytic concepts will be reciprocally both illuminated and enhanced.

And it is out of these persistent and painstaking methodological endeavors that the conceptual developments portrayed sequentially in this book have sensibly unfolded. Arrayed logically and chronologically the progression is impressive. It begins with the principle of safety and the striving for a background of safety as the dialectical counterpart to anxiety, the signal of danger when the ego's conditions for safety can not be met. From that develops the full elaboration of the theater of the mind, the conception of the representational world and of the complex self and object representations at play within it, as the ego constantly attempts to balance the press of anxiety and the search for conditions of safety. Considering representations leads inevitably then to issues of the nature and meanings of the varieties of internalizations: incorporations, introjections, and identifications. Here Sandler's formulations, internally consistent and quite persuasive, are not necessarily on all fours with the familiar viewpoints of other contributors to this complex literature. They lead equally to concerns with delineating and differentiating more precisely such quintessential developmental internalizations as superego, ego ideal, and ideal self. Along the way, issues of trauma, of outer event, of strain, and of inner response, emerge while being embedded in larger conceptions of the relation of inner to outer, of psychic reality to material reality, and of the continuum from fantasy to theory to reality.

And in this whole evolving edifice one sees gradually the transition in both concept and language from an economics and dynamics of drives and energies, of discharges and restraining structures, to an economics and dynamics of feeling states reflecting the full range from anxiety, depression, and pain to well-being and safety—employing now in amplified way the original conceptual building blocks of the first formulations in the book. And yet this transformation of psychoanalysis into a psychology which adapts to changes in feeling states has been stepwise accomplished while never losing the vital linkage to issues of instinctual gratification and frustration, which are after all centrally important as the ego balances its conditions of danger and safety and regulates adaptively its feeling states. Yet these issues are no longer bound to an untenable isomorphism between drive pressures and discharges and painful and pleasurable affect states, that is to say, the developmentally earlier psychoanalytic libido-energic model which was Sandler's starting point in his theory building.

And lastly, alongside the transformation of the ego into the organ which regulates feeling states, one need note the elaboration of the basic model of the mind as a whole. Vaguely sketched early in the book via the distinction between the function of fantasying and the mental content of fantasy states, this model is expanded into the full blown conceptualization of the non-experiencing realm of mental functions, dispositions, and capacities and the counterpart experiencing realm of conscious and unconscious mental life. The full panoply of the representational world (the experiencing realm) operates within the constraints and possibilities of the evolutionarily developed and adapted mental apparatus (the non-experiencing realm).

This brief highlighted listing of the main conceptual planks in this book clearly evokes papers and concepts distinctly associated with Sandler and his coworkers for all those who have followed their unfolding contributions over the years. What the book succeeds so well in adding is to show how all these concepts fit together and build into an edifice, representing the gradual but clear transformation of mainstream psychoanalysis from a psychology of drive and of drive discharge and restraint into a full-bodied object-relational perspective. In its focus upon self and object representations and the feeling states reflected in them, this perspective leads ineluctably to an ego transformed into the executive organ of adaptation and management of feeling states. All this, it should be added, has been accomplished without diminishing the powerful role of the drives—our biological heritage—as a major determinant of life satisfactions and frustrations, and therefore of the requirements of adaptation and the conditions of regulation of ego feeling states.

In all these senses, Sandler has taken most seriously the fullest implications of Freud's last great theoretical reconceptualization in 1926 into the functional–structural ego paradigm that became the framework of the ego psychology that we collectively inherited from him. Sandler has enlarged its scope and developed its adaptive potential in ways that Hartmann and Rapaport and their coworkers were not able to do, bound as those workers still were to an energy transformation model of the psychic apparatus (operating by fusion, defusion, and neutralization) that kept affects and behaviors too directly tied to drive and energy dynamics, and thereby insufficiently responsive to the full range and complexity of the human experience. Erikson, in one sense, essayed something more akin to Sandler in his psychosocial elaboration of the psychosexual developmental model of the mind though with a less thorough integration into the totality of the psychoanalytic theoretic and clinical corpus. Sandler's conceptions, on the other hand, remain organically unified, in their developmental progression from the drive–energy model of classical psychoanalysis, to the ego-psychological functional–structural psychoanalytic paradigm, and finally to a responsive ego managing the flux of shifting feeling states under the impact of affectively charged self and object representations. It is a model that stands somewhere at the uncertain intersect of ego psychology, object–relations psychology, and, yes, also self psychology. Perhaps there is even a point here at which various psychoanalytic perspectives, and not only the ego-psychological and the object–relational, can begin to fruitfully coalesce.

I trust that I have made my point persuasively enough. Sandler is indeed a major exponent and architect of the new theoretical structure in which psychoanalysis has by now evolved. It is a developmental transformation that has been less explicitly self conscious and less remarked than its really far-reaching nature has warranted. Sandler's book stands as a telling corrective to that relative unawareness.

Robert S. Wallerstein

Preface

The contents of this volume reflect research and theoretical work in psychoanalysis undertaken in association with a number of colleagues over a period of more than 20 years. The various chapters show the gradual crystallization of a theme that found substantial expression in the papers that have emerged from the research project known as the Hampstead Psychoanalytic Index, described in the Appendix. Essential to the ideas expressed here is the view that psychoanalytic theory has no clear boundaries and that it merges at times into many different aspects of general psychology and the biological sciences. Emphasis is placed on the fact that we relate to the world (including our own selves) by way of mental representations, and that we may modify and distort such representations for purposes of our own. Such purposes are adaptive in the sense that we respond not only to pressures arising from outside ourselves, but also to demands from internal sources. These demands arise not only from the instinctual drives but also from anxiety and pain in its many forms; and in this pain we must include that which arises from wounds to our self-esteem.

Freud was fully aware that his psychoanalytic theories were working models employing constructs that were useful, but that continually had to be reexamined in order to test their usefulness, and to be changed as necessary as psychoanalytic observations and insights increased. Since the earliest days of psychoanalysis its theory has been intimately linked with clinical observations and with the technique of the psychoanalytic method. New clinical findings and insights have been reflected in theoretical changes, and conceptual reformulations have, in turn, affected clinical observation.

Within Freud's lifetime the development of psychoanalytic theory proceeded by leaps and bounds, first in one area of thinking and then in another. While certain of the basic elements of psychoanalysis (e.g., mental conflict and unconscious mental functioning—so-called basic assumptions of psychoanalysis) have remained unchanged, the psychological model of psychoanalysis has undergone substantial modification. However, because theoretical developments did not take place along a single broad front, earlier formulations were not always integrated into later ones. Concepts belonging to a prior phase of development were often retained relatively unchanged and not revised or reformulated. And, it can be said, for a long time the problems raised by such inconsistencies were relatively minor when compared to the major and exciting conceptual developments that characterized Freud's thinking.

Ernst Kris has pointed out that Freud was little concerned with semantics. He remarked (1947), "The correct use of a term had little meaning to him; it was the context that mattered." In addition, Freud had little time to review older concepts carried forward in the tide of his theoretical development. Thus one of his most radical theoretical reformulations was put forward in *Inhibitions, Symptoms and Anxiety*, published in 1926 when he was 70. With Freud's death in 1939, we were left a theory and body of findings of great magnitude. Freud, as well as the growing group of psychoanalytic colleagues in many different countries, did not leave for us a fully worked-out and completely coherent theory of psychoanalysis. What did, and still does, exist was a developing theory, one that could only be fully comprehended if looked at in terms of its history (Sandler, 1983).

After the Second World War, psychoanalysis entered a flourishing period in terms of the number of those engaged in psychoanalytic work and their contributions to psychoanalytic literature. Psychoanalysts other than Freud had, of course, made many significant contributions during his lifetime and—within the general context of Freud's own formulations—postwar developments drew heavily upon and elaborated the work of writers such as Karl Abraham and Sandor Ferenczi. Of special importance for later developments were Anna Freud's *The Ego and the Mechanisms of Defence*, published in 1936, and Heinz Hartmann's *Ego Psychology and the Problem of Adaptation*, which appeared in 1939. These two contributors initiated an important line of development in psychoanalytic thinking in the area of what is generally known as "ego psychology." More recently, there has been special interest in what has been called "self psychology" (Kohut, 1971, 1977), the origins of which can also be traced to the work of Hartmann and other ego psychologists who urged a conceptual distinction between the ego and the self. It will be seen that some of the material in this volume can be regarded as straddling the gap between ego-psychology and self psychology.

Coupled with the further extension and application of psychoanalytic thought has been the distinct awareness of a need in the last 20 or 30 years for the clarification of psychoanalytic concepts. This need arose as part of the process of having to deal with the mushrooming of psychoanalytic literature, with problems of sharpening treatment methods, with growing concern about the assessment of therapeutic results, and with the heightening of interest in child development and psychoanalytic child and baby observation. This book is partly a product of that need. Such clarification is, in my view, a necessary part of the process of theory-making. But because clarification, if it is part of a healthy scientific development, leads to reformulation, it is inevitable that any new propositions put forward must be controversial until their usefulness has been tried and tested. Moreover, as in all fields of science, new theoretical constructions are necessarily provisional, and it will be noticed that some of the formulations made in the earlier chapters have been modified in later ones. The chapters themselves should be treated as reflecting a developing line of thought in the area of the construction of psychoanalytic theory. They represent, in the main, attempts to solve difficulties that arose when existing psychoanalytic concepts were applied to clinical observations obtained from psychoanalytic treatment. The procedure of "indexing," undertaken at Anna Freud's Hampstead Clinic (now the Anna Freud Centre), and described in some detail later in this volume, is one in which theoretical formulations are systematically applied to clinical material. A consequence of this procedure is that areas in which there is an incomplete "fit" between theory and observation are highlighted. This has led to the reformulation and redefinition of certain basic psychoanalytic concepts in the work reported in this book. I hope these efforts have contributed to a more satisfactory level of integration between theory and clinical observation.

The Hampstead Child-Therapy Clinic (now the Anna Freud Centre) was founded in 1947 and was from the beginning under the directorship of Anna Freud, who died in 1982. Accounts of its history and organization have been published elsewhere (see A. Freud, 1970; J. Sandler, 1965; Sandler & Novick, 1968). The clinic has specialized in the psychoanalysis of children, who are seen five times a week, for sessions of 50 minutes each. Treatment in most cases lasts several years. While the majority of children who have been and are being treated at the Clinic present neurotic disturbances of one sort or another, children with other psychological difficulties have also been taken into treatment. A large number of children are in full psychoanalytic treatment at any one time and the documented psychoanalytic material of each has been available for research purposes.

The process of indexing is described in the Appendix. In the Index project the therapist conducting the child's analysis attempts to classify the psychoanalytic material on his or her case under a large number of different headings. The material put under each heading is typed on large index cards, and the appropriateness of the indexing is then discussed in an Index research group. When it is evident that existing theoretical formulations cannot lead to a satisfactory indexing, and that either a new heading is necessary or previous headings and definitions have to be modified, a special Index subgroup is set up to consider the questions involved. At times the work of each subgroup, meeting once or twice a week, involves a complete reconsideration of the relevant literature and a reexamination of previously indexed cases. A number of senior therapists and analysts have been associated with the Index work for many years, while others have spent shorter periods in one or several of the research groups. While each of these groups has worked under my direction, the group members constantly acted as critics, examining the arguments and linking the theoretical ideas with the accumulated clinical material in the Index.

It became clear very early in the work of the Index group that a set of manuals of definitions was necessary in order to assist the therapist in the task of indexing. It was at this point that the problems of integrating psychoanalytic theory and clinical observation came to the fore. Many definitions, which previously had been thought to be satisfactory, now appeared to be ambiguous, and a substantial number of concepts, which had been regularly employed in theoretical discussions of clinical material, were seen to lack sufficient theoretical precision. As a consequence it was found necessary to reexamine a number of these concepts, as described above, and to find formulations that would allow for an adequate description of the clinical material in theoretical terms. Examples of concepts that have had to be reconsidered are the pleasure-principle, the superego and ego ideal, identification, introjection, incorporation, internalization, the ego and the self, mental representation, adaptation, narcissism, fixation and regression, fantasy, mental energy, sublimation, psychological structure, trauma, transference, object relationships, depression, and the general theory of affects.

In these reconsiderations and reformulations of concepts, the products of intensive research and group discussions, it is inevitable that the interests, general scientific approach, background, and creative capacities of the individuals concerned should play an important and significant role. As a result the theories and concepts that have emerged from the various research projects are not necessarily the same as those that a different group of research workers, with different orientation and interests, might have produced. In this regard one cannot say that one theoretical model is "right" and another is "wrong." What one can say, however, is that the test of the value of a theory is the degree to which it can be used to explain and understand the phenomena to which it is related, as well as the extent to which it enables observations that were previously not well understood to be comprehended more clearly. A consequence of more precise understanding is that predictions about a patient's future patterns of behavior and the effect of, for example, environmental experiences in general as well as psychotherapeutic interventions may be made with greater accuracy. In addition, I believe it to be vital that psychoanalytic theory be formulated in such a way that the bridges between psychoanalysis and neighbouring disciplines be widened and their number increased, so that communication between psychoanalysts and workers in related fields may be facilitated, and findings in other areas can in turn influence the theory of psychoanalysis.

While the chapters of this book are based on published papers, many of them reporting work carried out as part of the Hampstead Clinic Index project, they have been organized so that they present the development of a line of thought, and in certain cases repetitive references to Indexing procedures have been eliminated or abbreviated. Apart from this, editorial changes have been minor, and in the few instances where they have been significant, the modifications are indicated. I have added a commentary linking the papers together so that the book is more than the sum of the chapters contained in it.

Joseph Sandler

1

The Background of Safety

Joseph Sandler

This paper was read at the 21st Congress of The International Psychoanalytical Association, held in Copenhagen in 1959, where it received a somewhat less than enthusiastic reception. This was probably because of the perennial fear of many establishment psychoanalysts that the role of the instinctual drives in psychoanalytic theory may be threatened. However, following its publication in the *International Journal of Psycho-Analysis* (Sandler, 1960a), the paper seems to have established itself rather more firmly. In it the importance of the concept of "safety" and the associated "safety principle" is emphasized, and constant reference to the paper is made in the later chapters. The introduction of the notion of safety as a feeling state, quite distinct from feelings of sensual pleasure, foreshadows the later emphasis on the part played by feelings of well-being in the regulation of mental functioning.

Although this paper makes use of the example of perception as an activity that can generate feelings of safety, it should be emphasized that *all* aspects of psychobiological functioning, insofar as they proceed smoothly and harmoniously, can be regarded as generating safety feeling. This point is taken up again later, and the relation between safety feeling and narcissism is discussed and developed in Chapter 12.

Freud distinguished, in *Inhibitions, Symptoms and Anxiety* (1926), between the experience of trauma and that of danger. In the traumatic situation, the ego is helplessly exposed to quantities of excitation that cannot be discharged or in any way controlled. Situations of danger, on the other hand, are those in which the ego anticipates a situation that it cannot master, one that is potentially traumatic. The experience of trauma, that is of helplessness, is the same no matter what the source of the uncontrollable excitation may be, and in the course of development, highly specialized methods are evolved whereby traumatic excitation, the threat of trauma implicit in the

1

danger situation, and the correlated affect of anxiety may be avoided. The source of potentially traumatic excitation may be the id or stimulation of the sense organs. In the earliest undifferentiated phase of development, however, no distinction is made by the infant between excitations arising from different sources.*

Some of the techniques that the ego develops for dealing with potentially traumatic excitation have been studied in detail, in particular the mechanisms of defence. Yet all the functions of the ego that subserve adaptation, including those of the conflict-free sphere (Hartmann, 1939), can be considered as being directed toward the mastery of excitation. I want to single out for discussion one, from some points of view the most important, of the ego's functions through which it controls and contains excitation that might otherwise be traumatic. I refer to the process of *perception* in which unorganized sensations arising from the various sense organs are transformed into organized and structured perceptions. The development of a primitive capacity for perception must clearly precede the differentiation of situations of danger from the experience of trauma.

I should like at this point to summarize my thesis very briefly by saying that the act of perception is a very positive one, and not at all the passive reflection in the ego of stimulation arising from the sense organs; that the act of perception is an act of ego mastery through which the ego copes with the excitation, that is, with unorganized sense data, and is thus protected from being traumatically overwhelmed; that the successful act of perception is an act of integration that is accompanied by a definite *feeling of safety*—a feeling so much a part of us that we take it for granted as a background to our everyday experience; that this feeling of safety is more than a simple absence of discomfort or anxiety, but a very definite feeling quality within the ego; that we can further regard much of ordinary everyday behavior as being a means of maintaining a minimum level of safety feeling; and that much normal behavior as well as many clinical phenomena (such as certain types of psychotic behavior and the addictions) can be more fully understood in terms of the ego's attempts to *preserve* this level of safety.

Following from this I want to put forward, without considering it in detail, the notion of a "safety principle" that mediates the development of the reality principle from the pleasure principle.

It will be remembered that Freud described his view of the perceptual apparatus in his paper on "The Mystic Writing-Pad" (1925a) in which he differentiated "an external protective shield against stim-

---

*Willi Hoffer (personal communication) has suggested that "differentiating state" is a more appropriate description of this early state than "undifferentiated state."

uli," the "surface behind it which receives the stimuli, namely the system Pcpt.–Cs.," and the memory systems that lie behind that, and that permanently record traces of the excitation. In *Beyond the Pleasure Principle* (1920), Freud suggested that perception was not in fact an altogether passive process, and he returned to this suggestion in the "writing-pad" paper and in his paper "Negation" (1925b). Evidence collected over the past 20 or 30 years, particularly from the work of experimental psychologists, fully substantiates the idea that perception is a very active ego process, a part of the ego's essentially integrative activity. It seems clear that there is a very real qualitative difference between incoming sensory stimulation that has passed the external protective barrier, and the percept that we actively construct to modify and confine the sensory excitation. Perception need not, moreover, be tied to states of consciousness, and we can speak of preconscious as well as of unconscious perception.

We know that the act of perceiving constitutes an attempt to add "meaning" to incoming excitation: meaning, that is, in terms of past experience and future activity. We know, too, that instinctual drives and the ideas attached to them (so-called unconscious phantasy) can substantially modify the form and content of our perceptions; that unpleasant and threatening cues can be suppressed and incongruities overlooked in the act of perception.

We can conclude, therefore, that it is not only variation in the quantity of cathexis that modifies the incoming excitation (as described by Freud in his paper "Negation"), but that there is also a *qualitative organizing component,* related to instinctual wishes and to past memories and to the whole body of organized concepts and schemata built up within the ego, that constitutes an internal frame of reference by which the outside world is assessed. This frame of reference is essential to all perception, and its formation is a necessary basis, for example, for successful distinction between "self" and "not-self."

It seems that the central feature of the perceptual process is that it attempts to organize and structure the incoming data from the sense organs. In this the ego deals with incoming stimulation in exactly the same way as it modifies latent dream thoughts and transforms them into manifest content. *There is a "perception work" corresponding to the "dream work."* Indeed, this need not surprise us if we consider that the distinction between the various sources of excitation, between drive excitation and excitation from the real world, is only painstakingly built up in the infant over months and years. That our adult perceptions refer so strikingly to the outside world (I include here the body as part of the outside world), while the demands of the id are not so clearly differentiated, is a result of the necessity during development to abandon the pleasure principle in favor of the reality principle, and the consequent need for reality testing.

When we speak of the cathexis of the external world, or of objects in that world, we mean the cathexis of representations within the ego, representations that have been built up by successive experiences of the real world; experiences, however, that represent reality as distorted by the child's intellectual limitations, by his memories, wishes, and defense mechanisms. As the child matures and achieves successful reality testing, perceptions can be assumed to provide a more and more accurate rendering of real events.

We know, particularly from the work of Piaget, that the young child's perception of his body and of the external world is distorted not only by his needs and fantasies but also by his inadequately developed frame of reference, a frame of reference through whose use sensations are modified into perceptions. The development of the capacity for more refined and valid perceptions goes hand in hand with the development of more accurate reality testing.

We can speak of a successful act of sensory integration as one in which excitation (I speak now of stimulation from any source, from the id or the outer world) is smoothly and effectively dealt with by the ego. I want to suggest that such successful sensory integration is not only accompanied by anxiety reduction, but also contributes to a background feeling within the ego, a feeling that can be referred to as one of safety or perhaps of security. I want to stress the positive character of this feeling (which need not, of course, be conscious). It is a feeling that bears the same relation to anxiety as the positive body state of satiation and contentment bears to instinctual tension. Genetically, this feeling must be a derivative of the earliest experiences of tension and satisfaction. It is a feeling of well-being, a sort of ego tone. It is more than the mere absence of anxiety, and reflects, I believe, some fundamental quality of living matter that distinguishes it from the inanimate. It is a quality of feeling that we can oppose to the affect of anxiety, representing in a sense its polar opposite.

This concept of safety feeling is not, I believe, identical with Federn's concept of ego feeling, thought it may be related to it. The feeling of safety is not connected a priori with ego boundaries or with the consciousness of self, but develops from an integral part of primary narcissistic experience, and must exist in rudimentary form from the time of the earliest experiences of need satisfaction. Later, of course, it becomes attached to different ego activities and structures, and to mental content, and we can postulate safety signals in the same way as we do signals of anxiety. These safety signals are related to such things as the awareness of being protected; for example, by the reassuring presence of the mother. I refer only to a simple background feeling that can be compared to a level of tonus in a resting muscle, and that is as different from atonic feelings of death and emptiness as a healthy muscle is from a denervated one.

I have stressed the positive aspect of this feeling, and its existence as a sort of constant affective background to all our experience. It is normally maintained through regular and effective handling of quantities of incoming excitation by the ego, a process that becomes increasingly automatic as time goes on, but that retains its active character throughout. In sleep, disturbing stimuli from any source may be dealt with by the dream work, and in this sense we can regard the dream not only as the guardian of sleep but also as a perceptual mechanism that maintains the level of safety feeling within the ego.

At any given moment, we are all dealing, in a smooth and integrative way, with the results of stimuli impinging on us from all sides, for example, those arising from the proprioceptors that give us unconscious, or preconscious, information about our posture. This incoming excitation is all organized and dealt with, and we tend only to become aware of it when the sense data do not correspond to our experience and expectation, as when we step into a hole in the dark. We then experience a momentary trauma and a reduction in the level of safety feeling. Normally, however, the experience of our senses is in harmony with what we expect on the basis of our mental model of the external world, with our psychic schemata or frames of reference, and our experience coincides with our expectations.*

Now trauma, danger, and anxiety deriving from any source can reduce the safety level. It would seem that in taking appropriate action resulting in reduction of anxiety, the ego also heightens the level of safety feeling. This leads us to an important theoretical step that is, I believe, thoroughly substantiated by experience. In addition to directly defensive activity aimed at the reduction of anxiety, the ego will attempt to counterbalance the anxiety, so to speak, by heightening the safety level by whatever techniques it has at its disposal. Perhaps the most convenient way of heightening safety feeling is through the modification and control of perception, and I should like to describe a few of the ways in which this can take place.

The classification of these techniques of controlling perception is fascinating topic in itself, but I will only mention here that these methods of perceptual modification seem to fall into two major classes, though, of course, we can classify them in many different ways: those methods that involve modification of the perceptual processes

*Dr. Martin James (personal communication) has pointed out that techniques of scientific research have the same function, that is, to diminish the gap between what is expected on the basis of the theoretical model and actual experience.

within the ego (that is modification of the excitation that has passed the external protective barrier); and those that involve deliberate and purposive behavioral manipulation of the external world so that the sense organs are subjected to altered and different stimulation.

In the first Ernest Jones Lecture (1946), Professor Adrian made a point that is perhaps relevant to the present discussion, as it indicates that the usual distinction between motor behavior and sensory experience can be a misleading one. He suggested that the impulse to a particular piece of behavior was a pattern of nervous activity in the brain that is canceled when the appropriate set of signals arrives at the brain from the motor apparatus. The motor act is controlled through the matching up of the incoming sensations with the pattern of neural disturbance prompting the behavior. We can state this in psychological terms by saying that when perception of the motor activity corresponds with the drive-cathected image of that activity, there will be a corresponding reduction in tension. Thus a simple act of *appropriate* motor activity can itself reinforce the safety feeling simply by virtue of the fact that it is appropriate, that is, that the incoming excitation is smoothly transformed in an unconscious or preconscious manner. From this point of view, incidentally, the fear of loss of motor control and the feeling of being hopelessly overwhelmed by stimulation are more similar than might appear at first sight.

I do not want to enter into the many ways in which the ego controls perception and reinforces its feeling of safety. These range from simple sensory and motor adjustments to those mechanisms that Anna Freud has described so thoroughly in *The Ego and the Mechanisms of Defence* (1936), mechanisms such as denial and ego restriction. In particular I would refer to Miss Freud's Amsterdam Congress paper "Negativism and Emotional Surrender" (1951a), in which she considered certain forms of negativism as being a defense against the threat of primary identification with the love object, "a regressive step which implies a threat to the intactness of the ego. . . . The individual fears this regression in terms of dissolution of the personality, loss of sanity, and defends himself against it by a complete rejection of all objects (negativism)." This is, of course, one form of defense through perceptual control in the sense of the present discussion, and we can understand that the "threat to the intactness of the ego" as the lowering of safety feeling and the experiencing of anxiety consequent on the danger of being traumatically overwhelmed.

Another technique for raising the level of safety feeling at the disposal of the ego is the "hypercathexis" of certain sources of stimulation that lead to secure perceptions. Such hypercathexis enters into much of the behavior that we call regressive, into such normal phenomena as transitional objects and mascots, and is particularly striking in certain psychotic manifestations. I refer to the bizarre posturings and stereotyped movements found in certain forms of schizophrenia, and we may perhaps include such phenomena as echolalia and echopraxia. These can, in part at any rate, be understood as attempts to raise the safety feeling level by gaining a secure source of stable perceptions that correspond to intact object, thing, or movement representations within the fragmented psychotic ego. These perceptions result in an increase in the level of safety feeling, through a hypercathexis of the residual but secure perception. There is recent evidence that the schizophrenic defect involves gross direct perceptual disturbance, and I would suggest that much of the most bizarre and regressed schizophrenic behavior is meaningful if we take the point of view that it represents a desperate attempt to find an 'island' of perceptual security. Those who are familiar with the way in which psychotic children clutch their possessions, hide in corners or under blankets, or perform stereotyped movements, will have been, I am sure, impressed by the panic that these children show when their source of secure perceptions is tampered with (for example, through forcibly restraining a child from carrying out a repetitive movement).

In certain catatonics, the only source of this security may be the perceptual constancy achieved through complete immobility. In this connection I would mention the outstanding work on the ego disturbances of chronic schizophrenia carried out by Freeman and his colleagues in Glasgow, and in particular a paper by Chapman, Freeman, and McGhie (1959), in which they describe some of the responses and comments of a patient who had suffered a catatonic illness. This patient described, in vivid detail, the tremendous efforts he had to make to retain secure sources of perception. To quote: "He appeared to be able to move only after conscious reference to a series of mental pictures of his body," and the authors go on to say: "The performance of any movement disregarding this process of attending to the motor act, aroused in the patient intense fear." Other authors have described similar reactions in catatonic patients, and it would seem reasonable to conclude that the essential ego defect in these patients lies in their disturbed capacity for efficient and automatic organization of their sensory experience into percepts.

I want now, briefly and tentatively, to suggest that we can see, from all of this, the workings of what one might call a "safety principle." This would simply reflect the fact that the ego makes every effort to maintain a minimum level of safety feeling, of what I have called ego tone, through the development and control of integrative processes within the ego, foremost among these being perception. In this sense, perception can be said to be in the service of the safety principle. Familiar and constant things in the child's environment may therefore carry a special affective value for the child in that they are more easily perceived—colloquially we say that they are known, recognizable, or familiar to the child. The constant presence of familiar things makes it easier for the child to maintain its minimum level of safety feeling. And this is a process that is not necessarily identical with the libidinal cathexis of objects as sources of instinctual gratification, though it may often be difficult in practice to discriminate the one from the other. Instinctual drives will always remain the prime motivators of behavior, and although I have, to use Freud's analogy, described a little part of the rider, this does not mean that the horse does not exist.

2

On the Repetition of Early Childhood Relationships

Joseph Sandler

The analysis of the case presented in this chapter illustrates an application in clinical work of the concept of safety and of the safety principle. The discussion of these ideas was introduced in the previous chapter and can be seen to provide a basis for some of the formulations relating to superego functioning put forward in Chapter 3. Some technical problems, related to the so-called negative therapeutic reaction and to countertransference, which are only outlined in this presentation, have undergone further discussion and elaboration in a work on the clinical concepts of psychoanalysis (Sandler, Dare, & Holder, 1973).

Mrs. B was my first psychoanalytic control case, and this account was published some years after her initial analysis ended (Sandler, 1959b). The case was supervised, during the first part of the analysis, by Mrs. Hedwig Hoffer. My experience of Mrs. B's transference and of my own countertransference left a profound impression on me, and brought home very forcibly the way in which early object relationships can be repeated and reexperienced during the course of an analysis.

It is widely accepted nowadays that psychosomatic disturbances have a multiple causation; that genetic and constitutional factors present at birth, as well as later physical and mental experiences, all play important parts on the psychosomatic stage. When, however, one comes to read the script of a psychosomatic drama, it turns out, alas, that each part is written in a different language: the languages of biochemistry and physiology, of endocrinology and genetics, of anatomy and pathology, of sociology and of psychoanalysis may each or all be represented.

Each one of us can understand something of the play's plot, so to speak, by following those actors we understand best. A consequence of this is that we can all get very different impressions of the theme of the play, although these impressions must necessarily be related to one another. And, of course, the actor we understand is for us the most important one on the stage.

In this chapter I shall attempt to demonstrate the way in which the relationships with important figures in early childhood can enter into the formation and perpetuation of some of those physical disorders that we distinguish by the titles of hysteria, neurasthenia, stress disorder, and the like. The subject is exceedingly complex, from both physical and psychological points of view, and remains complex even when seen from the standpoint of psychoanalysis alone. Consequently I shall resist the temptation, as far as I can, to produce more of those generalities that are so characteristic of conferences such as these, and instead to present aspects of the psychoanalysis of a single case. If it does nothing more, I hope that it will demonstrate how the same mechanisms can enter into both psychic and somatic symptoms, and how an apparently stressful situation occuring in the external environment of the patient can in fact be provoked unconsciously by the patient for neurotic reasons. I shall present, if I may pursue my analogy, that part of the patient's drama that is written in the language of psychoanalysis, and I trust that you will forgive me if I describe complex and overdetermined processes in the language that I best understand.

THE PRESENTING PICTURE

Mrs. B came to analysis at the age of 35. Her main complaint that she was unable to have intercourse with her husband because her vagina "went into spasm" and her husband could not achieve penetration. She had been married for 15 years and had succeeded in having intercourse neither with her husband nor with other men. They would attempt intercourse, but she would tense up involuntarily, and however much they tried to force her she could not yield to them. She was having, as she put it, a "cat and dog life" with her husband.

Her symptom was first brought to the attention of the medical profession when, in her late teens, a medical student attempted to have intercourse with her. In spite of her willingness to cooperate, he could not effect penetration, and expressed the view that she was physically deformed. Later the diagnosis of "vaginismus" was made and she underwent a surgical operation that was unsuccessful. She also complained of backache and occasional severe attacks of cramp-like pain in her hands.

Further symptoms related to social anxieties that revealed a marked fear of exposing herself, and she had anxiety dreams that she was walking naked in the street. She also reported work difficulties, mainly revolving around her fear of responsibility and a tendency to become acutely anxious when promoted to a senior position. She had been working in a restaurant, and on being promoted to man-ageress had been so overcome by fear that she managed to engineer herself out of employment.

Mrs. B was an identical twin whose mother had died when she was a few months old. Her father was a chronic alcoholic who left the children to a succession of women, finally depositing them with the maternal grandparents when they were a year old and then committing suicide. Her grandmother was an irritable and aggressive woman who dominated her husband and her own grown-up children and who, the patient felt, resented having to look after the twins and hated the irresponsible and drunken father while idealizing their perfect mother, who was constantly described as a "saint." Living in the household was an uncle who, so it happened, was also weak and ineffectual and a chronic drunkard, but towards whom Mrs. B was able to feel love, and who, in her fantasy life, played the role of her father.

Mrs. B's later choice of husband was, it soon appeared, based entirely on her relationship to her father image and her uncle. He too was dissolute, drunken, and had spent some time in a mental hospital. It seemed that if anyone was living in a field of stress, it was Mrs. B. Her twin sister, who had been very delicate and sickly as a child, had also married and had, just before my patient came to analysis, given birth to a boy. The sister had no overt sexual difficulties, but had suffered, since she was very small, with a bad stammer.

THE ANALYSIS OF HER VAGINISMUS

The analysis, which lasted in the first instance just over 2 years, progressed well. In particular, Mrs B was able to bring her main relations to her childhood figures directly into the treatment situa-tion. The first sign of this transferring of childhood relationships to the person of the analyst came in the form of an obstinate but intermittent tendency to silence, a silence that was due partly to a difficulty in thinking and partly to an inhibition of speech. It soon became clear that this paralleled, on a psychological level, the physical symptom of vaginismus. The similarity between the two was striking, and it seemed as if she suffered an involuntary spasm of a mental sphincter. With the analysis of the causes of this silence, we could understand the source of her inability to tolerate penetration, and as the silence disappeared in the course of the analysis, so there was an easing of her physical symptom. Thus, for example, it soon transpired that she wished me to attack her, to make her speak and to force my interpretations upon her. She was able to recall how her sexual fantasies in childhood had been rape fantasies, and the thought of being raped by the drunken uncle had been a very exciting one. With her symptom she nightly provoked her husband, who stood for her uncle and her father, to assault her. It turned out that although she had always meant to change to twin beds, she had shared a single bed with her husband from the beginning. If, in her analysis, when she was silent I was silent too, she would, after a while, berate me for my lack of cooperation.

GUILT AND SELF-PUNISHMENT

I do not propose to go into the many aspects of her psychopathology that revealed themselves during her analysis, but rather to summarize one or two of these very briefly. A central feature was her intensely masochistic character, and an inordinate "need for punishment." (On one occasion, when promoted at work, she had felt so guilty that she set herself on fire and spent several months in hospital.) All her relationships were colored by this tendency. Cramplike pain in the hands would occur in the analytic session whenever she felt guilty about feelings of violence towards me. When the pain occurred, she would put her hand under her body as if to hide it. When this was pointed out to her, she remembered an occasion as a small girl when she had hit her sister violently on the side of the head, causing her much pain. As the sister had then succumbed to a severe earache and had been in bed for several days, she had felt intensely guilty, and in restraining herself when moved to violence subsequently, she herself became the object of her own violence. The painful cramp was a muscular contraction in the hand that represented the forbidden wish to strike her sister or indeed any competitor. The pain of it served to satisfy her need for punishment.

We were able to trace her hostility towards her mother, her grandmother, and sister, and she could understand how, through feelings of guilt and a need for punishment, she made herself the object of her own aggressive wishes. With the discovery of her hostility, she was able to permit herself to be promoted at work and to manage more or less successfully without having to damage herself too much.

PENIS ENVY

Striking too, was her intense resentment of men, which existed side by side with her sexual attachment to them. She had always complained, in relation to many different things, that she "lacked something," and when she brought the information that she could not bear the sight of her husband's penis, and that she thought that analysts regarded themselves as superior people because they had something that others did not have, it was not difficult to see that she felt intensely bitter over her lack of a penis. It transpired that she had thought as a child that if she had not been a twin she would have been a boy, and that her younger twin sister was her broken-off penis. Her resentment of men for having this powerful organ was striking, and it soon became evident that with her symptom of vaginismus she regularly provoked and then emasculated her husband. Similarly in the analytic session, she would provoke me to ask her questions, and then would snub me. She felt, she said, that she got her revenge on men in this way. In relation to her silence, she would often say that there was something in her mind that blocked her thought, and this matched her fantasy that the broken-off stump of a penis remained in her vagina, and prevented successful penetration.

Following the analysis of this and much other material (for instance, she had the unconscious fantasy that through her vaginal spasm she could amputate the man's penis and also that she could protrude one of her own), she was able to leave her husband, who was in fact most disturbed and did not support her, and to take a lover with whom she had satisfactory intercourse. The backache turned out to be a result of the tensing of her body to reject either her husband's penis or my words in the session. It was striking to see in the early phases how she would arch her back whenever I began to speak. The analysis of her exhibitionistic fears (she was afraid of a strong wish to excite men by exhibiting her body) enabled her to take a new job demonstrating frozen food in a large department store.

Certainly her analysis was far from complete, but for various reasons it was expedient for both of us to stop at this point. A year later she wrote from her holiday that her improvement was maintained and that she was enjoying a happy sexual relationship.

COMMENT

A feature of the analytic work that related to the theme of this paper, and that is, I believe, of the utmost importance in the day-to-day handling of such patients is worth mentioning here. If Mrs. B had what she described as a "good" session, that is, one in which we made analytic progress and anxiety was relieved, then the following session would be marked by resistance; she would be unhappy, suffer pain, and would have difficulty in associating. I understood this to emanate from her very strict conscience—a conscience modeled on her perception of her grandmother—which made her suffer for our successful therapeutic work (which meant for her the attainment of forbidden sexual desires and a fulfillment of hostile competitive wishes towards the twin). I took this resistance as the expression of a "need for punishment" and a phenomenon similar to what has been described by psychoanalysts as a "negative therapeutic reaction."

Much of her silence and difficulty in association was meant to provoke me to anger, and being relatively inexperienced at the time, I occasionally betrayed my irritation with her either by my comments or by the tone of my voice. Whenever this happened, she would relax and the following session would be a "good" one; she would associate well and new material would emerge. This I understood at the time to be a result of having involuntarily satisfied her "need for punishment" and I proudly recorded in my notes that "it seems that there can be positive therapeutic reactions as well as negative ones." Later I understood more of this, and I shall presently take up this topic again.

THE ANALYSIS OF HER DEAFNESS

Four years later, Mrs. B wrote asking to see me, as she was extremely worried. It transpired that although her improvement had been maintained (she was now working full-time as an artist's model and was more or less satisfied with her sexual life), her husband, from whom she had remained separated, had been writing many letters to her in which he threatened suicide if she did not rejoin him. I agreed to see her, and did so for a year, once or twice weekly. The details of this further period of analytic work need not detain us here, except for one feature. In place of her vaginismus she was now mildly but noticeably deaf.

Her deafness had been diagnosed as "nerve deafness" at a London hospital, but it soon turned out that this new symptom derived from the same unconscious processes that led to her vaginal spasm. I was able to interpret that with her deafness, she resisted penetration, castrated both men and women, and lived out a fantasy that she retained a broken-off stump of a penis, in the form of the "blockage" in her ear. Certain fears and fantasies relating to the anus, which had emerged in the first part of her analysis, were also operative in relation to her deafness. In spite of working through all this material again, the deafness persisted. Clearly there was a further aspect to the whole problem that had not been analyzed. The answer came suddenly and rather unexpectedly. By being deaf, she could force me to shout at her as her grandmother had done when she was very small. It became clear that she was unconsciously recreating, in her relationship with me, an earlier relationship to the grandmother, who had been, in spite of her unkindness to and constant irritation with the patient, the most permanent and stable figure in Mrs. B's childhood.

"Stress" as Reassurance

We could now see that Mrs. B was defending against an intense separation anxiety by recreating, in the analytic session and out of it, a feeling of the physical presence of the grandmother, whose mode of contact with the child had been predominantly one of verbal criticism or of physical punishment. In the symptom of vaginismus she had, among many other things, provoked shouting and physical assault, in order to obtain the feeling that the grandmother was physically present. It seemed that pain and suffering was the price she paid for a bodily feeling of safety, for the reassurance that she would not undergo the miserable loneliness and separation that characterized her first year of life, and that she felt would be her lot if she showed any hostility at all.*

This aspect of my patient's material made it easier to understand her apparently paradoxical "negative" and "positive" therapeutic reactions and her catastrophic response to any situation that spelled success. Not only did she feel guilty about the consummation of forbidden incestuous and aggressive wishes when things went well, but she also experienced an intense feeling of loneliness and insecurity. Indeed, one may wonder to what extent she retained such a severe and punishing conscience as an attempt to preserve the feeling that her grandmother was present—that is, as a defense against the

---

*Her fear of separation was, of course, magnified by the projection of her own death wishes onto her grandmother.

threat of insecurity and loneliness. When success descended on her, she experienced a bewilderment and, as she put it, a feeling that she was in a "strange and unfamiliar situation." Her immediate response was to *recreate* or to *provoke* the familiar childhood situation of being a failure, and of being punished, in order to restore her early relationship to her grandmother which, in spite of its unpleasant and painful aspects, represented security to her. In her relationships to me in the analysis, she could experience relief (though no conscious pleasure) when I could be provoked to play grandmother's role; when she could reexperience, through hearing me raise my voice, the actual feeling that her grandmother was present.

Apart from the capacity to substitute one orifice for another, this patient is of interest in relation to current concepts of stress disorder. Certainly environmental stress *in the present* is an extremely important factor in the production of any illness, but the aspect I wish to emphasize here is that what can appear to be an environmental stress can really have been contrived by the patient to fulfill an unconscious need for that very sort of situation. The real source of Mrs. B's stress lay in her childhood fear of separation, a fear based on actual traumatic experiences. The external stress situation of adult life, in which she was attacked and nagged by her husband, her work, and by "fate" in general, was one she *needed*, and her symptoms provided an unconscious means through which she could provoke "stress" and the bodily security that these unpleasant situations represented.

In conclusion, I would venture to say that the moral of Mrs. B's story is this: A stressful situation need not always be what it appears to be. It may be performing a positive service to the patient, and if it is relieved, can in certain cases lead to a *worsening* of symptoms, the so-called negative therapeutic reaction.

3

The Concept of Superego

Joseph Sandler

The discussion of the superego concept that follows is the first major piece of conceptual research reported from the Index project. It arose as a direct consequence of the attempt to fit clinical material derived from child psychoanalysis into a theoretical classification. The discrepancies between what was expected on the basis of current psychoanalytic theory and what was found in practice led to a reformulation of the theory of the superego and to a revision of the basis upon which the superego material was classified and organized in the Index.

The publication of this paper in *The Psychoanalytic Study of the Child* in 1960 (Sandler, 1960*b*), together with Roy Schafer's paper on the superego (Schafer, 1960), which appeared side by side with the one reproduced here, marked a significant change in our understanding of the superego concept. The friendly, supporting, loving aspects of the superego received an emphasis that had been absent in the past. It has become clear over the years that the view that the superego is substantially more than a critical agency has profound clinical implications for the understanding of what is generally known as superego conflict.

The theory of psychoanalysis represents the common matrix within which the many different aspects of our work at The Hampstead Child-Therapy Clinic are conceived. We continually apply psychoanalytic theory as a frame of reference through which observations can be made and assessed, be it in diagnosis, therapy, education, or research. But this is far from being a one-way process, and we have learned from Freud the necessity to pause and to return, every now and then, to take stock of and to reexamine our theory in the light of experience, so that the understanding of our material can be more incisive and precise.

The work reported in this paper is in part the outcome of such a pause for taking stock, and it has been prompted by a specific and practical problem connected with the handling of analytic data that have accumulated over a number of years in therapists' regular reports and in the Index (see Appendix).

Whereas certain types of material are classified in great and fruitful detail in the Index, other types appear to have received a minimum of attention. A quite striking example of an understocked section of this sort is that relating to the superego. Now even the slightest acquaintance with the details of cases treated at the Clinic is sufficient to show that the role of the superego is implicitly, if not explicitly, appreciated, and it is necessary to ask why this has not been equally reflected in the Index, and why the tendency to veer away from the conceptualization of material in superego terms has occurred. Examination of the way in which cases have been indexed shows quite clearly that therapists have preferred to sort their clinical material in terms of object relationships, ego activities, and the transference, rather than in terms of the participation of the superego. It is partly the purpose of this study to investigate some of the reasons for this phenomenon, a phenomenon all the more surprising in view of the advantages that have accrued to psychoanalytic theory and practice as a result of the adoption of the structural point of view.

Once attention had been drawn to the problem, it was not difficult to see that two interrelated factors were operating in producing the tendency to formulate material in other-than-superego terms. The first is what I shall call the apparent "conceptual dissolution" of the superego, which can be regarded, in part at least, as a consequence of advances in the understanding of the superego's genetic roots. The second is the lack of theoretical precision that exists in the differentiation of superego content from ego content, and the confusion that still exists among psychoanalysts in regard to the mechanisms of superego formation. In the latter half of this paper, a provisional restatement of the superego concept will be put forward, a formulation that has followed directly from the difficulties experienced in indexing our observations, and that may provide a useful basis for a more systematic ordering of the relevant clinical material.*

---

*The difficulty that exists in integrating the superego concept into the psychoanalytic model does not appear to be only a Hampstead idiosyncrasy. Thus Rapaport, in his discussion of the conceptual model of psychoanalysis (1951a), mentions the superego very briefly, and then only to say that he leaves it undefined. Hartmann has traced, in an illuminating paper (1950), the development of the ego concept in Freud's work, but he explicitly puts the concept of superego to one side. In contrast, there are many papers that refer, either directly or indirectly or in passing, to the superego. But on the whole, the more theoretical these papers are, the more complicated and intricate they appear to be, in contrast to the relatively simple formulations of Freud (cf. Jones's paper on the superego, 1926).

THE APPARENT "CONCEPTUAL DISSOLUTION" OF
THE SUPEREGO*

Freud's View of the Superego (Ego Ideal)

Although it is possible to find, when looking back, germs of the superego concept in Freud's Project (see Freud, 1887–1902) and in *The Interpretation of Dreams* (1900), the notion of an ego ideal was first explicitly presented by Freud in his paper "On Narcissism" (1914). There he put forward the idea of an institution in the mind that watches the ego and that compares it with an ideal standard—an ideal that is derived from standards of behavior set by the parents.

Starting from the observation that libidinal impulses are repressed if they are in conflict with the subject's ethical ideas, he suggested that the formation of this ideal, against which the subject assesses himself, would be a necessary precondition for such repression. He speaks in this context of the self-respect of the ego. In the ideal image, the child embodies all the feelings of perfection that he felt himself to possess in his early childhood. If he can conform to it, he regains his early state of narcissistic perfection.

The conscience is formed as an institution in the mind that sees to it that the ego gains narcissistic gratification from the ego ideal, and that watches the real ego and constantly compares it with the ideal standard.

The main impetus to the formation of the ideal, Freud felt, stems from parental criticism, and this is later reinforced by further training and education. He points out that what has previously been spoken of as the dream censor is in fact the ego ideal. It is worth noting that he uses the same term to include both the ideal image and that organized part of the ego that constantly observes the ego and matches it up against the ideal standard.

In this paper, Freud discusses the role of the self-regarding attitude and of the vicissitudes of the libido in the development of the ego ideal. He saw the development of the ego as consisting in "a departure from primary narcissism" and this development "gives rise to a vigorous attempt to recover that state." He adds: "This departure is brought about by means of the displacement of libido on to an ego ideal imposed from without; and satisfaction is brought about from fulfilling this ideal."

In *Group Psychology and the Analysis of the Ego* (1921a), Freud expanded somewhat on his concept. He saw it as embodying "the sum

*The account of trends in the development of the superego concept given here is a selective one, influenced by a number of factors—not the least of which is the need to emphasize points that will be taken up later in this paper.

of all the limitations in which the ego has to acquiesce . . . ," and he noted that "all the interplay between the external object and the ego as a whole . . . may possibly be repeated upon this new scene of action within the ego." He emphasized again the positive rewarding aspect of the relationship between the ego and its ideal. When some thought or activity in the ego coincides with the standards of the ideal, there results a feeling of triumph and release—a return to the state of primary narcissistic union with the parents.

In joining a group, the subject may give up his ego ideal and substitute for it the group ideal as embodied in the leader. The leader becomes invested with all the individual's idealized qualities, and the fact that other members of the group are doing the same thing leads to a reinforcement of this process by an identification of the group members with one another. The ego in turn is experienced as an object to the ego ideal.

In the condition of mania, we find the extreme and pathological instance of the feeling of narcissistic union with the parents, in which ego and ego ideal are completely at one, and the subject can blithely disregard feelings of social responsibility. Conversely, the sense of guilt and feelings of inferiority represent an expression of tension between the ego and the ideal, finding its extreme expression in the abject misery of the melancholic.

Freud makes an explicit distinction between identification of the ego with an object (which results, for example, in the pleasure of being one of a group in such organizations as the army), and the embodiment of the ego ideal in an external person, in external authority (as in the Church).

Two years later, Freud presented the structural point of view in *The Ego and the Id* (1923a). The term "ego ideal" is replaced by "superego," but Freud did not imply by this change of term that he was dealing with two separate organizations. He saw the superego, as he had seen the ego ideal before, as constituting a modification of the ego. The superego—a structural precipitate within it—comes into existence at the time of the resolution of the Oedipus complex and, through its formation, becomes the main agent in bringing about a solution to the oedipal conflicts that occur so intensely during the phallic phase of instinctual development. He saw it as the vehicle of morality, reflecting the "higher nature" of man, and, as such, being a representative of the child's relation to his parents and to society. It exercises the function of self-judgment, and preserves throughout life the capacity to stand apart from the ego and to rule it. In the same way as the child had no choice but to obey his parents, so the ego later submits to the imperative demands of the superego. It exercises the "censorship of morals," and tension between ego and superego is manifest as a sense of guilt and worthlessness.

The superego is for the most part unconscious, and in analysis its critical functions can produce certain special forms of resistance. It can be hypermoral and even tyrannical toward the ego; but it is capable of modification to the extent that the standards and moral injunctions of other external authorities (such as teachers) may be absorbed into it.

Freud regarded the superego as being formed on the basis of identifications with the parents, such replacement of object cathexes by identification being an important part of character development, though superego identifications can be distinguished from those that enrich the ego. The decisive superego identifications take place as a consequence of the necessity to deal with both positive and negative Oedipus complexes. The parents are introjected after the fashion described in "Mourning and Melancholia" (1917a), and the child erects, in the superego, the same barrier to instinctual expression as existed outside in the shape of the parents. The superego represents, however, a definite structure within the ego, and it is more than the simple sum of the parental identifications—it is a consistent organization that stands apart from the other constituents of the ego. The more intense the Oedipus complex and the more rapidly it is repressed under the influence of external measures, the stricter becomes the superego.

Freud repeatedly stressed the fact that the superego is not only a product of parental identifications, but it functions also as a mode of expression of the most powerful id drives. By constructing the superego, the ego places itself in subjection to the id. Indeed, Freud says "the ego forms its superego out of the id," and it is the unhindered traffic between the id and the superego that accounts for its largely unconscious nature. Thus, the more a child controls his aggressive impulses toward another, the more tyrannical does his subsequent superego become. The dread of the superego persists from the earlier fear of castration, a fear that is reinforced, as we know, by the child's own aggressive impulses.

Thus the id finds a path through the ego in two ways: directly, to the extent to which its impulses are ego-syntonic; and indirectly, through the superego.

With every identification, Freud points out, there is a desexualization and at the same time an instinctual defusion. The libidinal cathexis no longer binds the destructive tendencies that now find expression in the severity and punitiveness of the superego. This defusion is particularly evident in melancholia.

The superego has also elements in it that represent *reactions* against the id. Thus it not only contains the precept "be like your father," but it also contains prohibitions—certain things are father's prerogatives.

In 1926 Freud published *Inhibitions, Symptoms and Anxiety*, in which he put forward his new theory of anxiety and stimulated the many subsequent developments in ego psychology. From this time he made no modification of the superego concept, though he recognized that it was by no means as clear and as uncomplicated as one might wish it to be. Nor did he feel the need to revise the theory of narcissism, which had played so important a role in the earliest delineations of the ego ideal.

Freud made subsequently, however, a number of statements that are relevant to our understanding of the superego. In *Inhibitions, Symptoms and Anxiety* itself, he refers to the many situations in which ego and superego are merged, and in which no distinction can be made between the two. He speaks of the ego acting "in obedience to the superego" (though in the *New Introductory Lectures* [1933] he spoke of repression being "the work of the superego," which it either carried out directly or "ordered" the ego to do). Freud saw the threat of the superego as being an extension of castration threat, which is in itself a development (by way of the danger of loss of object) from the earliest and primary danger, that of being helplessly overwhelmed by excitation. The little boy's penis has an immense narcissistic investment, and the threat to the penis becomes also a threat to his narcissism.

In the *New Introductory Lectures*, Freud refers, as he had done earlier, to the superego as a "function" in the ego, but adds that it is to a certain extent independent, pursuing its own ends. He reiterates the superego's role as a replacement of parental authority, as an inner agent that now dominates the ego by granting proofs of affection and by threats of punishment that in turn mean loss of love. He contrasts the harshness of the superego in many people with the kindness and gentleness of their real parents, and attributes this disproportion to the "transmutation of instincts" that occurs at the time of the resolution of the Oedipus complex.

In *The Future of an Illusion* (1927), Freud draws attention to the role of the superego in the perpetuation of culture, and much of what he has to say about the transmission of culture (in particular, the cultural illusions of religion) is pertinent to our understanding of the superego, which is, after all, the most effective agent of cultural transmission. He says, "Every individual is virtually an enemy of culture," and culture must protect man against his own hostile impulses. He goes on to say that the satisfaction provided by the attainment of a cultural ideal is essentially a narcissistic one.

In *Civilization and Its Discontents* (1930), Freud amplified the connection between the superego and the aggressive instinct. The child's dread of the parents, which had manifested itself as social anxiety, is, as he had previously described, felt as guilt once the parents have been replaced by conscience. But over and above this, the aggressiveness of the superego is reinforced every time the child renounces its own aggressive wishes on account of the demands of society. Indeed, frustration heightens the aggressiveness inherent in the child's ambivalence, and it is deflected into the superego, its strength now being seen to be a measure of the child's own hostility toward the prohibiting and restraining parent. Masochistic behavior can then be seen to be a function of the ego's erotic attachment to a sadistic superego.

In his first presentation of the concept of ego ideal (1914), Freud had stressed the importance of the libidinal, erotic aspects of the tie to the parents, especially the mother, in the formation of the ego ideal. Later, and most explicitly, in *Civilization and Its Discontents,* he emphasized the aggressive, sadistic side. Yet he did not fail to point out that the setting up of high ideals and standards is a function of the superego, as is also the punishment meted out to the ego by the conscience for failure to fulfill these ideals.

As late as 1938, in the *Outline of Psychoanalysis* (Freud, 1940), he reiterated his views on the superego, describing it as "a special agency in which . . . parental influence is prolonged." He added that "the details of the relation between the ego and the superego become completely intelligible if they are carried back to the child's attitude toward his parents"; and the parents' influence includes also the traditions of the larger group as well as the family.

Freud always related the development of the superego specifically to the resolution of oedipal conflict, and he saw its development as being the outcome of two factors: the long period of helplessness in the human infant, and the occurrence of the Oedipus complex.

The earliest relationship of the child to the mother is an anaclitic one—based, that is, on the mother's real capacity for gratifying the infant's instinctual needs. The father is dealt with, Freud suggests, through identification—not identification of the sort that leads to superego formation, but rather "a direct and immediate identification . . . [which] takes place earlier than any object cathexis."

This early state of affairs persists until intense phallic sexual wishes arise toward the mother. The father is now perceived (we are speaking of the little boy) as an obstacle to these sexual aims, and the child's feelings toward him become marked by ambivalence.

The cathexis of the mother as a sexual object must now be given up and it may be replaced either by identification with the mother, or by an intensified identification with the father. The latter identification endorses and consolidates the masculinity of the little boy and permits him an affectionate relation with the mother. The relative predominance of these identifications is also influenced by the negative Oedipus complex, and by the constitutional bisexuality of the child.

These identifications coincide with, and are an essential ingredient of, the oedipus complex. The father identification preserves the object relationship to the mother, and replaces the sexual relation to the father that belonged to the negative Oedipus complex. Similarly, the mother identification retains the object tie to the father, and replaces the normal phallic sexual relation to the mother. The child erects, in the superego, the same obstacle to instinctual expression as existed outside in the shape of the parents. The strength to do this was, as Freud puts it, "borrowed from the father" through the boy's prior identification with him.

Further Developments

Although Freud made a number of references to the complexity of the superego concept, there can be little doubt that the difficulties that he saw were for the most part peripheral rather than central to the concept. In tracing his references to the ego ideal and superego, particularly in the 15 years following *The Ego and the Id*, one cannot fail to be struck by the internal consistency of his formulations.

We know that the development of psychoanalysis has not taken place with equal speed in all directions; and following the publication of *The Ego and the Id*, the main advances in psychoanalysis have been concentrated on a few related fronts, and I should like to mention particularly ego psychology and child analysis.

The revision of the theory of anxiety in 1926 (in *Inhibitions, Symptoms and Anxiety*) with its insistence on the ego as the only seat of anxiety led, as Hartmann and Kris (1945) have shown, to far-reaching theoretical developments in the psychology of the ego. They say: "If we turn to the ego as the psychic system that controls perception, achieves solutions, and directs actions, we have to insist on distinctions that seemed irrelevant when Freud first formulated his genetic propositions." Anna Freud's *The Ego and the Mechanisms of Defence* (1936) deepened and systematized our knowledge of the ego's defenses and elaborated the concept of defenses to include the idea of defense against "pain" arising from the real world. Hartmann's *Ego Psychology and the Problem of Adaptation* (1939) introduced the concepts of the undifferentiated phase, conflict-free ego development, and primary and secondary autonomy. Ego functions such as reality testing, perception, memory, control of motility, and the synthetic function have all received increased attention, and the concept of neutralized energy has been introduced (Hartmann, Kris, & Lowenstein,

1949).* Attention has been paid to the development of ego apparatuses, particularly those concerned with thought and cognition (cf.
Rapaport, 1957), and psychoanalytic theory seems to be moving rapidly toward becoming a general psychology, and the findings of
academic laboratory psychologists are tending to be absorbed into
it.

Progress in ego psychology has highlighted certain areas that
are particularly relevant to our conception of the superego. Functions
of the superego have gradually been absorbed into our model of the
ego. This is a continuation of a tendency that was evident even in
Freud's own writings, for in 1914 and again in 1921 (Freud, 1921a)
he ascribed the function of reality testing to the ego ideal, only to
allocate it explicitly to the ego in 1923 (Freud, 1923a). The self-observing function of the superego has, however, not so readily been
yielded up to the ego (cf. Nunberg, 1932), and the question of structure versus function of the ego in relation to the superego itself has
not yet been satisfactorily investigated (Freud, on more than one
occasion, referred to the superego as a "function" of the ego).

Developments in ego psychology have also shown up a large
area of theory, fundamental to a consideration of the genesis of the
superego, that is still unclear. Although the concepts of identification,
introjection, and internalization are of the utmost clinical value, their
metapsychological status is at present complicated and often confused, even though numerous attempts have been made to disentangle them (e.g., Fenichel, 1926, 1945; Foulkes, 1937; Glover, 1949;
Greenson, 1954; Hendrick, 1951; Jacobson, 1953a; Knight, 1940). Freud
uses the term "identification" in a large number of different senses,
to include identification into the ego and into the superego, and he
speaks of an identification (with the father) that precedes object
relations. In addition, we must take into account the fact that some
identifications appear to be ego-dystonic (Greenson, 1954). Furthermore, identification as a defense is frequently not differentiated from
the defensive use of "introjection." This latter term is often also used
in the same sense as "incorporation" in relation to the processes of
inner enrichment, even though, strictly speaking, the term "incorporation" should be used only to refer to the oral instinctual activity
of physical "taking in," and "introjection" to the psychical counterpart of that activity (Glover, 1949; Greenson, 1954). One may also
ask whether introjection is wholly an instinctual activity, and to what
degree it represents an autonomous ego function, related, for example, to perceptual organization. The term "internalization" is used
by Hartmann (1939) to denote the set of processes whereby internal
regulation substitutes for external trial-and-error activity, but it is

*The list of postulated ego functions is continually growing, including even the func-
tion of consciousness (George Klein, 1959).

also often used synonymously with "incorporation," "introjection," and "identification."

To these problems we must add another that has arisen as a result of the growth of ego psychology. It seems to have become necessary to differentiate a part of the personality from the ego proper, a part nevertheless that is intimately associated with it; that is, the *self*. Consequent on a proposal of Hartmann's (1950), Edith Jacobson (1953a, 1954a, b, c) has put forward a concept of self-representation that has the same status within the ego as have object representations. It is then the self, the "endopsychic representation of our bodily and mental self in the system ego" (Hartmann), that receives the cathexis withdrawn from external objects and directed toward the ego. This concept, which appears to be not only of theoretical but of clinical value as well, has had a number of repercussions on the theory of narcissism and of masochism, and on our understanding of the processes of introjection, projection, and identification (which would then be seen to be a fusion of representations of object and self). It also affects our view of superego development, which Jacobson sees as the outcome of widespread reaction formations to the child's oedipal and narcissistic strivings, to sexual desires as well as aggressive impulses.

Certain authors have increased the conceptual differentiation between the libidinal (ego ideal) and the aggressive (superego "proper") aspects of the superego, to the extent of postulating, implicitly or explicitly, two separate structures. This tendency is evident in the work of a number of different authors. Piers and Singer, in their recent monograph on *Shame and Guilt* (1953), ascribe guilt to the tension between ego and superego, and shame to tension between ego and ego ideal. Nunberg (1932) speaks of two concepts, but goes on to say that it is difficult in practice to separate them sharply from each other.

Perhaps the most potent stimulus to further understanding of the superego concept has come from the experiences and insights of those engaged in child analysis. This is particularly true in relation to superego precursors and to the whole problem of the ontogenesis of the mature superego. Indeed, the genetic perspective may well prove, as Hartmann and Kris (1945) have suggested, the most illuminating and useful one from which to view this difficult concept from both its structural and functional aspects.

As long ago as 1926, Anna Freud, in a series of lectures to the Vienna Institute of Psychoanalysis (later published in *The Psycho-Analytical Treatment of Children*, 1946), put forward a number of considerations regarding the superego that represented an amplification of the description given by Freud in *The Ego and the Id*. She drew attention to the relative importance of the influence of the outer world, of the real parents in particular, in the mental life of the small child. Whereas in the mature superego the detachment from the parents and superego identification with them has led to a marked degree of independence, in the small child the detachment from the parents is far from complete. Although a superego does indeed exist, following the oedipal phase, its importance to the child is still correlated with the relationships actually obtaining between the child and its real parents. The child's control of its excretory activities, for example, although reflecting an inner prompting to cleanliness, is, in the early years largely dependent on the state of its relations to the real objects. If the object relationship to the mother is at all disturbed, a regression to soiling can easily take place. Even in latency, changes in the real object relationship can affect the established but immature superego of the child. This tie to the parents reveals itself in a double standard of morality—one for grown-ups and another for the child itself and for other children. This has important implications for analytic work with children, and Anna Freud went on to suggest that the analyst must take over the role of the child's ego ideal during the course of analysis. The modification of the child's superego was thus seen, because of the child's dependence on real objects, to be easier with the child than with adult patients.*

In 1927, in a symposium on child analysis held in London, Melanie Klein presented a vigorous attack on the technical and theoretical views that Anna Freud had expressed, and I want to describe her ideas insofar as they refer to the formation of the superego. Melanie Klein took the view that the superego of even the very young child closely resembles that of the adult, and is not greatly modified during the course of later development. This infantile superego can be of the highest degree of severity and, in this respect, can often stand in sharp distinction to the real parents; indeed, the objects introjected into the superego can on no account be identified with the real parents.

Melanie Klein expressed the view that the Oedipus complex occurs toward the end of the first year of life, following weaning, and that its early occurrence is associated with the beginnings of superego formation; a process that terminates with the onset of latency. The resulting superego is "at heart unalterable," and she distinguishes a true inner superego (as distinct from various other superegos set up by the child) that is not identical with that which Anna Freud described as still operative in the person of the real parents.

*Later Anna Freud (1946) pointed out that the guiding and educative functions could be left to educators and others from the child's environment, leaving the analyst free to concentrate on the analytic work proper.

Some years later, in a paper on "The Early Development of Conscience" (1933), Melanie Klein reiterated her view that there exists in the child a full superego of the utmost harshness and cruelty, before the resolution of the Oedipus complex. The fears of the external world that the small child displays are due to the fact that the child views the world fantastically under the influence of the superego. The child's first images are endowed with tremendous sadism, stemming from the death instinct, and in childhood fears, these terrifying images are reprojected. The early function of the superego is to arouse anxiety, but as its severity is reduced, during the phallic phase, by the positive side of the child's attachment to the mother, so anxiety is transformed into guilt. The sense of guilt arises from the child's feeling that in sadistically attacking its mother's body, it is attacking its father and brothers and sisters contained in her body. Social feeling develops from the urge to reconstruct and to repair the damage. It is of some interest, however, that Melanie Klein differentiates the conscience from the superego, the conscience being established only after the resolution of the phallic Oedipus complex.

In a paper "On the Development of Mental Functioning" (1958), Melanie Klein places the beginnings of the superego in the second quarter of the first year, and her account of its formation is as follows: The self-destructive (death instinct) impulses of the infant have to be projected outward as they would otherwise overwhelm him. Introjection, being largely in the service of the life instincts, serves to bind the death instincts, and these two sets of forces attach themselves to the mother's breast, which is then felt to be good or bad at different times. From this we get the primal "good" and "bad" objects, split from each other through the need to master persecutory anxiety. Melanie Klein relates the division into ego and superego to the polarity of the two sets of instincts. The internalized good object supports the ego, which is strengthened by an identification with it; a split-off portion of the death instinct, fused with a certain part of the life instincts, then becomes the basis of the superego. Because of the fusion with the life instincts, the superego acquires protective qualities as well as destructive ones. Melanie Klein points out now, however, that not all internalized objects are integrated into the superego, but they can be split off in a nonsuperego way and pushed into the deep unconscious. These nonsuperego objects are characterized by instinctual defusion, while it is the dominance of instinctual fusion in the supergo that allows the ego to accept it as the two institutions now share aspects of the same good object. As latency approaches, the organized part of the superego becomes more isolated from the unconscious, unorganized part.

These views of Melanie Klein, in spite of discrepancies that might be attributed to semantic differences, are very far removed from what we understand by ego psychology (Rapaport [1959] refers to them as an "id mythology"). Her assumption of an intricate psychic system elaborated soon after birth, capable of highly sophisticated fantasy activities; her equation of memory images, unconscious fantasies, introjections, and "internal objects"; her lack of distinction between affect and ideation; and so on—are all at variance with our meta-psychological thinking. Yet there can be little doubt that the controversial propositions of Melanie Klein regarding superego development have stimulated others to direct more attention to superego precursors in the preoedipal phases.

In addition to the earlier work on "precursors" of the superego, such as that of Aichhorn (1925), who was specially interested in the superego of delinquents, and Ferenczi (1925), who had described the way in which a child in the anal phase complies with the demands of the parents through the development of "sphincter morality," attention has been paid in recent years to forerunners of the superego. Thus Annie Reich (1954) has shown the existence of early "superego-type" identification that represent archaic elements in the supergo; and more recently David Beres, (1958), has reviewed the whole problem. The work of Spitz is particularly relevant (1945, 1946, 1950, 1957), and in a recent study (1958) he has discussed the development of superego "primordia" in the child's earliest years.

It is particularly the work of those engaged in direct observation of normal and disturbed children that has thrown light on early stages of superego formation, as the growth of the child's social sense and the appearance of an internal morality can be seen to have a close connection with the state of its object relationships in the first years of life; and disturbance in these relationships has been found to have a marked influence on later object relationships and on ego and superego development. Apart from the work on children separated from their parents carried out at the Hampstead Nurseries during the last war, the prevailing theoretical outlook at the Hampstead Clinic has been influenced by the studies of Ribble (1944), Fries (1946), and Ernst and Marianne Kris at the Child Study Center at Yale University (Marianne Kris, 1957). And to these may perhaps be added the unpublished recorded observations on superego precursors at the present Hampstead Nursery School.

Repercussions of Advances in Knowledge on the Superego Concept

We have seen that since Freud outlined his original views on the superego, a considerable amount of work, has been done on various aspects of this concept. What is striking about this work is, however, that it has been very largely analytic—analytic in the sense that superego elements have been put under the microscope, so to speak, and broken down into their structural, dynamic, economic, and genetic components; analytic, that is, in a sense opposite to synthetic. In the course of this process, much of what might be called superego territory has been yielded up to the ego. Other areas have been traced in greater details to their origins in the id, and still more has been connected with real experiences of the child in his early life. This process has gone on without any real regathering of the pieces into a coherent framework, so that some of the original power of the construct as a theoretical unity has been lost. The very process of examining the superego in detail in order to clarify it has blurred it to some extent, at any rate from the point of view of theoretical lucidity and simplicity. As we can regard the superego as being formed out of the interaction of id, ego, and the real world, so theoretical dissection of it, particularly dissection of its origins, has tended to some extent to diffuse it conceptually back into the ego, id, and the real world. In a sense the superego has thus lost some of its theoretical identity as a compact and coherent organization, as a thing-in-itself and an agency in the production of psychic conflict. In striking contrast, developments in ego psychology have served to enrich our view of the ego, for our examination of ego functions has not led us out of the ego (except perhaps to the notion of an undifferentiated state). ·

In the same way as increased theoretical interest in the superego has tended to complicate what was a relatively simple concept, so does a parallel process occur in relation to clinical psychoanalytic work. We aim in analysis to deal, in part at any rate, with the outcome of the oedipal conflict; yet it is the very resolution of the Oedipus complex that brings the superego into being. If we analyze superego conflict, we find that, in the course of the analysis, what we might call an apparent *conceptual dissolution* has taken place. The object relationships and conflicts that entered into superego formation have unfolded themselves onto the person of the analyst; the transformed id drives, which form so important a part of the superego, have been traced back to their origins in direct instinctual wishes and fantasies; and the introjective and identificatory processes that have contributed so much to superego genesis have been seen as defensive or adaptive ego mechanisms that were called into play during critical phases of oedipal and preoedipal developments. This process may cause us temporarily to lose sight of the superego as a coherent organization with properties of its own; and it seems clear that this apparent conceptual dissolution has been a potent factor in determining therapists' preferences in approaching their clinical material for purposes of indexing. In a sense, the Index has functioned rather like a microscope, and as in the examination of physical tissues, increasing magnification may cause grosser structures to disappear from sight—but this by no means implies that they cease to exist.

A VIEW OF THE SUPEREGO

The apparent "dissolution" of the superego concept, as a result of increased knowledge of its origins and as a consequence of the regressive processes that occur in the course of psychoanalytic work, by no means accounts for all the reluctance shown by therapists to conceptualize their clinical material in superego terms. The concept itself, even when used at a relatively low level of molecularity, is one that is indistinct, and it has become increasingly so with the absorption into our day-to-day thinking of advances in ego psychology. In particular, the distinction between identifications that enrich the ego, and those that can be regarded as leading to superego formation, is vague and ill defined. Similarly, the lack of clear differentiation between processes and internalization, introjection, and identification (Freud often used the terms "introjection" and "identification" synonymously) has led to further confusion, in spite of the efforts of a number of authors to clarify some of the issues involved.

Faced with the practical problem of devising a basis for classifying material in the superego section of the Index, it has been necessary to formulate our view of the superego and its development in such a way that both the tendency to "dissolution" and some of the theoretical problems that obscure its definition are overcome. Such a reformulation must of necessity fit well with theory and knowledge in other areas, but equally it must inevitably cut across a number of established ideas. The formulation presented here is a tentative and incomplete one, representing more an attempt at defining a theoretical framework rather than the presentation of a comprehensive statement.

A Framework for Viewing Superego Development

The development of the ego, from the earliest weeks of life onward, is marked by the construction, within the mind of the child, of organized frames of reference or schemata that subserve adaptation. These schemata or mental models revolve at first around experiences of need satisfaction, and no distinction is made by the child between sensations that arise from inside its own body and those that occur as a result of the activities of the mother. With development, these schemata gradually extend to include aspects of the external world other than those intimately associated with immediate need satisfaction. Essentially they enable the child to assess the properties of the outer world with increasing efficiency, and to predict the pleasurable or unpleasurable consequences of his behavior.

The term "internalization" has been used in regard to these processes, but as its current usage is such as to include processes of introjection and identification as well, it seems preferable to think in terms of an *organizing activity* to describe the construction of these inner models. The concept of an organizing activity seems a particularly appropriate one as the schemata of the child embrace not only data gained through sensory impressions arising from the outer world, but sense data (including affect data) arising from instinctual tensions as well. In addition, it will be necessary, as I hope to show later, to contrast organizing activities with those of introjection and identification, and to dissociate them from processes of "taking in" traditionally associated with oral instinctual aims. Indeed, organizing is primary to and must precede introjection and identification, in the sense in which these latter two processes will be used in this presentation. One can neither identify with nor introject aspects of another person unless one's ego has previously constructed some sort of mental model of that person. Organizing activity embraces those activities grouped by Piaget (1936, 1937) under the headings of "assimilation" and "accommodation," by Hartmann (1939) as "fitting together," the construction of "perceptual" and "effector" worlds (Üexküll's notion of *Umwelt* [1926] is relevant here), "differentiation" and "integration" (Werner, 1940), and is a reflection of the synthetic function of the ego.

Organizing activity begins to occur extremely early in life, from the moment when the child's experience of the present can be said to be modified by what has been experienced in the past; from the moment sensations begin to be transformed into percepts, however primitive these percepts may be; from the moment that differential cathexis of aspects of the child's world can be said to occur. Clearly, it is those experiences that are directly concerned with need satisfaction that are first registered and organized by the child, under the dominance of the pleasure principle, and the child's first models of the world (and the term "world" includes, of course, the child's own body) are extremely scanty, primitive, and self-centered. The child's inner world, Hartmann (1939) points out, arises as "a central regulating factor . . . interpolated between the receptors and the effectors."

Organizing activity is much more than the mere taking in of impressions from the outside, but is intimately connected with the development of all organized ego functions and secondary processes. It includes the construction of frames of reference, schemata, and all the techniques by which the child controls his perceptions (arising from the id or the outside world) and activities. It includes also the development of ego functions such as memory, thinking, imagination, and the capacity for purposive action, functions that in turn foster further organizing activity. Part of the child's inner world consists of models of his objects (or aspects of his objects) and of the self, models* that are composites and abstractions created† by the child out of its multiple experiences. The self-schema can also be classed as a type of object schema, cathected by instinctual energy as are the other object models of the child.

In the normal child, object relationships develop out of the child's first experiences of satisfaction and dissatisfaction, and their development is associated, in the inner world of the child, with the construction of a libidinally cathected mother schema or imago, although this is limited at first to qualities of experience associated by the child with need satisfaction. Initially these need-satisfying experiences are not differentiated from the self, but as time goes on, a distinct mother schema is organized. It consists, in essence, of a set of expectations relating to the mother's appearance and activities, and when the mother conforms to these expectations (which vary according to the state of instinctual tension within the child), the child experiences satisfaction. When the mother's behavior does not in fact correspond to the cathected internal mother imago, the child experiences frustration, unpleasure, and anger. Later the response of the child becomes more and more removed from the original gratifying situations, so that the presence of the mother, or even the knowledge of the mother's readiness to attend to the child, becomes a source of satisfaction it itself.

The internal imago of the mother is thus not a substitute for an object relationship, but is itself an indispensable part of the relationship. Without it no object relationship (in the psychological sense) exists. It is not in itself a source of real gratification to the child,

---

*The use of the term "schema" or "model" in this context by no means implies a static conception. The "models" are, in a sense, "working models," and include all the sequences of behavior on the part of the object which can be predicated by the child on the basis of its past experience.

†The term "introjection," which has been used to describe this process, is reserved in this paper for a very special sort of ego activity, a mechanism that is associated with unique and important changes in the disposition of instinctual energies.

although it may temporarily achieve a diminution of an instinctual tension through hallucination. The real source of gratification is the mother or any other object who can conform to the child's mother schema.

The child's inner world enables him to distinguish, localize, and interpret his sensory impressions; but it also functions to provide him with warning or guiding signals that regulate his behavior. Thus his developing body schema gives him a means of identifying sensations and experiences in his own body, and also assists him to coordinate his bodily activities, as, for example, in learning to walk. Similarly his mother and father schemata gradually enable him to recognize and interpret the activities of his parents, and at the same time allow him to predict what behavior will evoke their love and approval, and what their disapproval, and to control his behavior accordingly. I want to draw particular attention to these two functions of the child's inner world, the function of *representing* and the function of *guiding*, for they will ultimately be reflected in that specialized part of the inner world that later becomes the superego.

The growth of the inner world goes hand in hand with the partial abandonment of the pleasure principle in favor of the reality principle. The notion of "reality" in this context includes the reactions of the parents in the child's behavior, and no essential distinction can be made till relatively late in development between the "real world" as adults know it and the culturally determined or idiosyncratic commands, wishes, and precepts of the parents. There is as yet no distinction in kind between frustrations imposed by the parents and those that are a consequence of the resistance of other aspects of the "real world" to the demands of the child. Indeed, the child gains much of its knowledge of the properties of the real world, with consequent benefit to ego development, through parental interpretations of reality. It is largely through the agency of the parents that the reality principle replaces the pleasure principle.

Now we know that the needs of the child progress from the need for bodily satisfaction and comfort to a need to feel loved in a variety of other ways as well. With increasing discrimination between the self and other schemata, the child comes to realize that his early pleasurable, narcissistic state of union with the mother is threatened. He suffers a lowering of the level of libidinal cathexis of the self, with consequent narcissistic depletion, and, as Freud puts it (1914), he needs to restore the state of "a real happy love [which] corresponds to the primal condition in which object–libido and ego–libido [we would now say self-cathexis] cannot be "distinguished."

The child's many attempts to restore this original narcissistic state provide an enormous impetus to ego development. Freud (1914) says: "The development of the ego consists in a departure from primary narcissism and gives rise to a vigorous attempt to recover that state."*

The child has a number of techniques at its disposal for the restoration of this original state of well-being, and of these I want to consider only two that are relevant here:

1. *Obedience* to and compliance with the demands of the parents.
2. *Identification* with and imitation of the parents.

The term "identification," which refers both to a process and to the end product of that process, has been used by psychoanalysts in a variety of ways, and attempts to differentiate ego identifications from superego identifications have led to much confusion. In the present formulation, the term will be used only for identifications that modify the ego; so-called superego identifications will be seen as a combination of introjection on the one hand, and a corresponding "ego" identification on the other.

The observation of very young children has taught us that identifications with parents and others are an aspect of normal development, and that identification is by no means always a substitute for an object relationship, nor is it always used defensively. Transient identifications may later become a permanent feature of the child's personality, but the capacity to make temporary identifications remains after childhood, and is a particular feature of adolescence. We can define "identification" by saying that it represents a process of modifying the self-schema on the basis of a present or past perception of an object, and that such modification may be temporary or permanent, whole or partial, ego enriching or ego restrictive, depending on what is identified with and whether the need for such an identification is of short or long duration.

Whereas in primary identification the child fuses or confuses the rudimentary schema of the self with that of another person, so that

---

*The problem of what it means to "feel loved," or to "restore narcissistic cathexis," is one that has as yet been insufficiently explored. What the child is attempting to restore is an affective state of well-being that we can correlate, in terms of energy, with the level of narcissistic cathexis of the self. Initially this affective state, which normally forms a background to everyday experience, must be the state of bodily well-being that the infant experiences when his instinctual needs have been satisfied (as distinct from the pleasure in their satisfaction). This affective state later becomes localized in the self, and we see aspects of it in feelings of self-esteem as well as in normal background feelings of safety (Chapter 1). The maintenance of this *central affective state* is perhaps the most powerful motive for ego development, and we must regard the young child (and later the adult) as seeking well-being as well as pleasure; the two are by no means the same, and in analysis we can often observe a conflict between the two.

the distinction between self and not-self does not exist, in secondary identification the self-schema is modified so that it becomes *like* that of the object, and some of the libidinal cathexis of the object is transferred to the self. Secondary identification is a later acquisition of the child, and grows out of the more primitive mechanism, which remains, in a controlled way, within the ego as a constituent of the capacity for empathy. Primary identification also reappears as a feature of ego functioning in deteriorated schizophrenics, when the capacity for distinguishing between self and not-self has broken down. We might say that secondary identification represents an attempt to create the illusion of primary identification. Secondary identification is not very different from imitation in the small child, though conscious intent is more prominent in the latter. For present purposes we need not make a fundamental distinction between the two.

Identification is a means of feeling the same as the admired and idealized object, and therefore at one with it; and, as Freud has pointed out, it can exist side by side with object relationships. If we recall the joy with which the very young child imitates, consciously or unconsciously, a parent or an older sibling, we can see that identification represents an important technique whereby the child feels loved and obtains an inner state of well-being. We might say that the esteem in which the omnipotent and admired object is held is duplicated in the self and gives rise to self-esteem. The child feels at one with the object and close to it, and temporarily regains the feeling of happiness that he experienced during the earliest days of life. Identificatory behavior is further reinforced by the love, approval, and praise of the real object, and it is quite striking to observe the extent to which the education of the child progresses through the reward, not only of feeling omnipotent like the idealized parent, but also through the very positive signs of love and approval granted by parents and educators to the child. The sources of "feeling loved," and of self-esteem, are the real figures in the child's environment; and in these first years, identificatory behavior is directed by the child toward enhancing, via these real figures, his feeling of inner well-being.

Identification may also be used for the purposes of defense, particularly where the child is faced with a problem of resolving a conflict between its need for an object's love and its hostility to that object. In the familiar "identification with the aggressor" the child deals with his fear of a threatening person by identifying with his omnipotent, powerful, and terrifying qualities. It may also be called into play in an attempt to deal with a loss or a withdrawal from a loving object. In this latter case it is usually accompanied by an introjection of the object, a process that I shall discuss presently; but identification is not the same as introjection as it will be defined here, and the distinction between the two is, as we shall see, of supreme importance in understanding the formation of the superego.

The two techniques of restoring a feeling of being loved (of increasing the level of libidinal cathexis of the self) that I have mentioned, identification and obedience, make use of the two functions of the child's parental schemata that I have described earlier, the function of representing and the function of guiding respectively. But the mechanisms of identification and obedience by no means operate in isolation from each other. In many activities, the child obtains what amounts to a double gain through behaving in such a way as to identify with the parents and at the same time obey their wishes. Thus the toddler who seriously washes his hands after playing with dirt gains both from "doing what mother wants" and from "being like mother."

The Preautonomous Superego Schema

What develops in the ego of the child in the preoedipal years is an organization that reflects the idealized and desirable qualities of the parents on the one hand and that prompts the child to suitable object-related behavior on the other (behavior, that is, that will gain for the child a feeling of being loved). It contains approving and permissive as well as prohibiting and restraining features. It is not yet a structure (in the sense in which Freud used the term in *The Ego and the Id*), for the introjection of parental authority that will elevate it to autonomous superego status has not yet taken place. It is a preautonomous superego schema, a "plan" for the later superego. It is a sort of undergraduate superego that only works under the supervision of the parents, and is a differentiated part of the child's own "reality," influenced as is all the child's inner world by instinctual drives and fantasies. It has not yet gained a license for independent practice, so to speak, and it will only do so with the decisive introjections that go with the resolution of oedipal conflict. What might appear to be conflict between ego and "superego" in the preoedipal stages is based on the child's predictions, often distorted, of parental reaction.

We know that the child's view of his parents is objective only to a limited degree. His parental schemata will be colored by his fantasies, and in particular by the projection of unwanted qualities of his own onto them. The child may not be able to tolerate the aggressive and sadistic parts of his self, and transfers these features from one part of his inner world to another—from his model of his self to his model of his parents. In this sense, projection is the opposite of identification.

The warning signal of impending punishment or loss of love provided by the preautonomous superego schema does not yet deserve the name of guilt, though the affective state it produces in the ego may be identical with what we refer to as guilt later in the child's development.

I do not need to describe here the ways in which the child's conflict between his instinctual urges and his need to preserve his narcissism are intensified when the child enters the phallic stage. His positive and negative Oedipus complexes, the ambivalence inherent in them, the impossibility of really fulfilling his instinctual wishes, the fear of punishment and castration (which is correlated with a father image distorted by the projection of the child's own aggression)—all of these combine to create a situation of unbearable tension in the child. During the phallic phase, the superego schema is much elaborated and modified, although it will always bear the stamp of his pregenital relationships to his parents. This schema, not yet the superego, has the function of representing (albeit in a distorted way) the admired and feared qualities of the parents. But it also functions to indicate to the ego which piece of behavior will evoke the love and admiration of the parents, and which will cause their displeasure, with consequent lowering of the narcissistic level in the self.

We link the development of the superego proper with the resolution of the Oedipus complex. Freud regarded this development not only as the outcome of oedipal conflict, but also as the very means whereby the child effects a resolution of this conflict. The superego is formed, as Freud puts it, as a precipitate within the ego, and its formation is correlated with a partial and relative reduction of interest in and dependence on the real parents. The major source of self-esteem is no longer the real parents, but the superego. *Introjection* of the parents has taken place, and a structure has been formed that did not exist in this form before.

At this point it is necessary to indicate the meaning given to the term "introjection" in this context; for, after all, have not the functions that we call "superego" previously existed in the mind of the child in the shape of the parental schemata? What distinguishes the introject from the internal schema is precisely the capacity of the introject to substitute, in whole or in part, for the real object as a source of narcissistic gratification. This implies that the introject must somehow be developed out of the schema, crystallized and structuralized within the ego, so that it can be given the power to satisfy, and be felt by the ego to be a sufficient substitute for the objects. The construction of an introject is thus the sequel of a complete or partial dissolution of the relationship to the real object. Through introjection, the *relationship* to the object is maintained and perpetuated, but the real object is no longer so vital to the relationship. It follows that what is introjected is neither the personality nor the behavior of the parents, but their *authority*. (This view of introjection is therefore different from that of Ferenczi—who introduced the term—and that of Melanie Klein.)

With this elevation of the superego schema to autonomous status—with its structuralization, in the sense described by Freud in *The Ego and the Id* (1923*a*)—what was previously experienced as the threat of parental disapproval becomes guilt, though the affective experience is probably the same in both; and an essential component of this affective state is the drop in self-esteem. This differentiates guilt from anxiety, and links it with feelings of inferiority and inadequacy as well as with the affect that is experienced in pathological states of depression. An opposite and equally important affective state is also experienced by the ego, a state that occurs when the ego and superego are functioning together in a smooth and harmonious fashion; that is, when the feeling of being loved is restored by the approval of the superego. Perhaps this is best described as a state of mental comfort and well-being, of "eupathy." It is the counterpart of the affect experienced by the child when his parents show signs of approval and pleasure at his performance, when the earliest state of being at one with his mother is temporarily regained. It is related to the affective background of self-confidence and self-assurance, as well as to the pathological state of mania.

Freud has described the way in which both superego formation and identification are associated with a desexualization of the child's libidinal aims, and with an instinctual defusion. This defusion enables the child to retain his tender feelings toward his parents, and to divert his destructive urges into his now structuralized schema of parental attributes and behavior—that is, into his superego. The degree to which his hostile wishes cannot find expression through his ego will determine the degree of severity or even savagery of his superego. This may occur to such a degree that the superego may be a much-distorted representative of the real parents of childhood. In this way, as Freud has frequently pointed out, the superego is also a representative of the id, in close and constant touch with it.

There has been a strong tendency in psychoanalytic writings to overlook the very positive side of the child's relationship to his superego; a relation based on the fact that it can also be a splendid source of love and well-being. It functions to approve as well as to disapprove; and the relative understressing by psychoanalysts of the former may be due to the fact that they are primarily concerned as therapists, rather than as educators, with situations of conflict and inner disharmony.

It will be noticed that superego formation has been linked throughout with introjection, and has been separated conceptually from processes of identification. That the reinforcement of identifications with the parents is something that occurs concurrently with superego formation and progression into latency, is something that cannot be questioned. Freud himself did not always distinguish identification with the parents, particularly with the father, from their introjection and the consequent setting up of an internal authority that can act in opposition to the ego; but in view of recent developments, particularly the increasing theoretical importance of the concept of "self," such a distinction appears to be essential.

Identification is a technique whereby the self is modified so that it corresponds, to a greater or lesser extent, to an object as perceived by the ego. The model for the ego may be a real person, or an introject. Thus we have a state of affairs in which the ego can use its capacity for identification to obtain a libidinal gain through being at one either with another person who is idealized or feared (or both), or through feeling at one with the introject that contains a representation of the behavior, appearance, and attitudes of the parents. Thus we can replace the notion of superego identification with that of *identification with the introject*.* It changes and modifies the *content* of the self, but does not result in the formation of psychic structure. Where ego and superego work together harmoniously, the harmony may be achieved by such an identification on the part of the ego, and also by direct obedience to or compliance with superego precepts and demands. This harmonious working together does not represent a merging of the superego into the self (which we see in manic states and which is associated with primary identification), but a modification of the self on the basis of a model of the idealized qualities of the parents, or their demands and prohibitions, as embodied in the superego. Furthermore, if the child can both identify with and obey the introjected parents at one and the same time (as in the example I gave earlier of the child washing his hands "to be like mother" and "to please mother"), a double gain is effected.

We can also see, particularly in the course of an analysis, how guilt feelings may be dealt with by identification with the introject, and identification that shows itself through the adoption of a strict and moralizing attitude to another. The child who tells a doll or the

---

*Anna Freud has suggested that this is essentially similar to the mechanism of identification with the aggressor.

analyst not to be naughty deals with his feelings of guilt and gains a feeling of well-being by identifying with the critical aspects of his superego, projecting his self-imago onto another. In this extremely common mechanism there is also a double gain. We know that those who most vocally proclaim moral precepts are often those who feel most guilty about their own unconscious wish to do what they criticize in others.

That dependence on the superego is so long-lasting, and often results in more or less permanent changes in the ego, is a reflection of the child's dependence on his real parents as a source of narcissistic gain in the earliest years of life. But the superego is only supported by the ego as long as it functions, in its turn, to support the ego; and situations do exist in which the ego can and will totally disregard the standards and precepts of the superego, if it can gain a sufficient quantity of narcissistic support elsewhere. We see this impressive phenomenon in the striking changes in ideals, character, and morality that may result from the donning of a uniform and the feeling of identity with a group. If narcissistic support is available in sufficient quantity from an identification with the ideals of a group, or with the ideals of a leader, then the superego may be completely disregarded, and its functions taken over by the group ideals, precepts, and behavior. If these group ideals permit a direct gratification of instinctual wishes, then a complete character transformation may occur; and the extent to which the superego can be abandoned in this way is evident in the appalling atrocities committed by the Nazis before and during the last war. Changes in morality can sometimes be seen when a person becomes much loved by another; the superego is then not as necessary as before as a provider of love and as a source of well-being.

Many examples exist in ordinary life of the way in which group morality and group ideals may replace personal morality; these include religious conversion, and the gang formation and hero worship of adolescence. In psychotherapy or in analysis, the supporting role of the analyst, who may be invested with the authority of the parents, can permit the ego's dependence on its superego to be sufficiently reduced to enable forbidden and repressed material to be brought into consciousness and inner conflict worked through.

Similar phenomena occur when the feeling of well-being in the self can be obtained by means of drugs, and drug addiction can then replace what might be termed normal superego addiction. Indeed, the superego has been facetiously defined as that part of the mental apparatus that is soluble in alcohol.

Anna Freud has pointed out that the establishment of the superego does not entirely remove the child's dependence on the real parents and parental figures as a source of love, and when we speak of the latency child's "independence," we use a relative term. To some extent this reliance on others as a source of self-esteem persists throughout life, and we all know how the support and reassurance of a friend can mitigate unhappiness in oneself.

Lampl-de Groot, in two interesting papers (1936, 1947), has drawn attention to the importance for the child, and later for the adult, of maintaining a sufficient level of self-esteem, and to the ways in which threats to the self-esteem can give rise to disturbances of ego functioning. For the ego to operate well, it is necessary that one be in receipt of regular narcissistic supplies, and a study of the sources of an individual's self-esteem can enable much of his behavior, neurotic or otherwise, to be understood. Alfred Adler (1907) has taken one source of lowered self-esteem (organic inferiority) and embroidered it into a whole system. And although we reject Alder's highly oversimplified views, the techniques by which the ego can restore its self-esteem and the ways in which these techniques enter into character have been insufficiently studied.

In its dealings with its superego, the ego may involve other persons as well. It may do so when it has the need to force others to reinforce the superego through the provocation of approval, forgiveness, or punishment. In so-called superego projection (or externalization), we can observe an attempt by the ego to restore the existence of the original superego objects in the external world. In one sense, this is an attempt at regression, and it is particularly fostered by the analytic situation, where it appears in the form of a superego transference. The involvement of others in superego conflict also appears in moral masochism. (When the ego has a masochistic attitude to the superego, this is a reflection of an earlier masochistic tie to the parents.)

The problem of delinquent behavior has been studied by Aichhorn (1925) and other psychoanalysts, and it does seem that their findings, particularly in relation to the superego, can be integrated into the conceptual framework outlined in this paper. This applies in particular to the well-known distinction between those who are delinquent because of the introjection of a delinquent parental morality, those whose delinquency is a result of structural faults in the superego, and those neurotic delinquents who are hounded by an inordinate sense of guilt.

The tentative formulation of superego development given here leaves a number of crucial gaps unbridged. One of these gaps is in our knowledge of what the transfer of parental authority from the real parent to the superego schema in the process of introjection really implies. Nevertheless, the concept of superego, when approached from this point of view, has made it possible to categorize superego material in the Index (and therefore in our thoughts) in a more meaningful way. The basic ideas expressed here are to be found in Freud's paper "On Narcissism" (1914) and it is precisely the role of narcissism in the development and function of the superego that needs to be stressed. Threats to the narcissistic cathexis of the self exist from birth and stem from the interaction of the instinctual life of the child, in both its libidinal and aggressive aspects, with the demands and frustrations of the real world. The factors that ultimately determine the superego operate from the beginning, yet what we tend to call "superego precursors" are an integral part of the development of the ego itself; the superego as a structure comes into existence only with the resolution of the Oedipus complex. And although it is often the agent of pain and destruction, its existence appears to be brought about by the child's attempts to transform paradise lost into paradise regained.

Freud sums up the function of the superego, appropriately in the last chapter of his last book, *An Outline of Psychoanalysis* (1940), as follows. He says:

> The torments caused by the reproaches of conscience correspond precisely to a child's dread of losing his parents' love, a dread which has been replaced in him by the moral agency. On the other hand, if the ego has successfully resisted a temptation to do something that would be objectionable to the superego, it feels its self-respect raised and its pride increased, as though it had made some precious acquisition. In this way the superego continues to act the rôle of an external world toward the ego, although it has become part of the internal world. During the whole of a man's later life it represents the influence of his childhood, of the care and education given to him by his parents, of his dependence on them— of the childhood which is so greatly prolonged in human beings by a common family life. And in all of this what is operating is not only the personal qualities of these parents but also everything that produced a determining effect upon them themselves, the tastes and standards of the social class in which they live and the characteristics and traditions of the race from which they spring. (pp. 122–123)

APPLICATIONS TO CLINICAL MATERIAL

On the basis of the formulations presented here it has been found possible to devise a system of classification of superego-related material. This will form the basis of a later paper, which will include examples of clinical observations classified in the Index.

Because of the inevitable "dissolution" or regression of the superego in the course of treatment, it has been necessary to consider the child's relationships to authority without making, in the first instance, a distinction between inner and outer authority. These relationships can be categorized according, for example, to types of control—the ways in which the child gains or loses narcissistic supplies from his superego, its representatives, or other external persons. A large subsection deals with the responses of the ego in the face of the fear of or wish to please internal or external authority. This includes all the attempts made by the child to restore his narcissistic equilibrium as a result of conflict with authority. "Identification with the superego," and certain aspects of the construction of a system of ideals, fall into this subsection.

Parallel with this, it has been possible to classify statements by therapists relating to the nature and extent of structuralization (including stages of development) and to qualities and characteristics of the superego. (Both object and instinct sources have been categorized, together with special contents of behavior and fantasy that evoke tension with inner or outer authority. Special characteristics of the superego [e.g., severity or inconsistency] have also been indexed; and a number of further subsections deal with other aspects.)

It seems clear that the construction of a comprehensive framework for classifying clinical observations in the area of the superego as well as in other areas will inevitably have repercussions on the actual observations made by therapists; this, in turn, must lead to further theoretical reconsideration. In all of this, the formal process of indexing data assists the healthy interaction between practice and theory.

4

Psychology and Psychoanalysis

Joseph Sandler

The work on the superego reported in Chapter 3 led to a wider conceptualization—that of the *representational world*. The paper that forms
the present chapter, originally published in *The British Journal of Medical Psychology* (Sandler, 1962a) is included here because it provides
a useful bridge to the fuller exposition of the representational world
concept described in Chapter 5. The paper was given as an address
from the Chair to the Medical Section of the British Psychological Society, and its original form has been retained. The representational
world is introduced here by way of a consideration and extension of
the body image or body schema concept, while in the next chapter it
is approached rather differently, although there is a certain amount of
overlap between Chapters 4 and 5.

Psychology is usually defined as the study of behavior. This must
be a good definition, for a number of other disciplines have also laid
claim to it. It is, however, historically appropriate, because it represents the attempt of psychologists to wrest their field of study from
the hands of the speculative philosophers, and to establish it as a
field of scientific study in its own right. Apart from a few strict
behaviorists, psychologists are nowadays very much concerned with
such mental processes as thinking, imagery, and perception, and the
meaning of the word "behavior" has been extended to cover mental
events and personal experiences that cannot be directly observed by
anyone other than the subject himself, and even to completely unconscious mental processes. Nor is psychology exclusively concerned
with the study of *normal* behavior, and the mechanisms that cause
pathological mental disturbance appear to be well within the field
of study of the psychologist.

Psychologists make use of a large number of different theories
and you are all familiar with the various schools of psychology—the

Gestaltists, the Learning Theorists, the Psychostatisticians and so on. Each of the schools is concerned with its own psychological theory and although the various theories are often at variance with one another, there is no doubt that each has an influence on all the others. One of these schools of psychology is psychoanalysis. The word "psychoanalysis" means a number of different things—there are, as you are aware, a number of different "subschools" in psychoanalysis. It denotes a particular therapeutic method and also a theory of therapeutic technique. It is a theory of psychopathology. But above all, psychoanalysis has tended to become, in the last 2 or 3 decades, much more of a general psychology. Freud, it is true, based his psychoanalytic theory on the observations he made on his patients, but since such publications as *Two Principles of Mental Functioning* (Freud, 1911), and *Inhibitions, Symptoms and Anxiety* (Freud, 1926), psychoanalysis has moved increasingly in the direction of becoming a psychology of adaptation: adaptation, that is, to the demands of the instincts, of the real world, and of internalized morality. I need only refer you to the work of Hartmann (his *Ego Psychology and the Problem of Adaptation* [1939] was a turning point in modern psychoanalytic psychology), Kris, Loewenstein, Rapaport, and Erikson for the extent of this trend to become clear. Particular emphasis is now laid on adaptive mechanisms, and on the development of ego functions appropriate to adaptation. It is significant that psychoanalytic psychology, in its role as a general psychology, is no longer exclusively a psychology of conflict, and the important area of psychological functioning that is called the "conflict-free ego sphere" has been brought within the scope of psychoanalysis. It follows that the appropriate tools of investigation into psychoanalytic theory extend beyond the consulting room and include laboratory and statistical methods as well as the techniques appropriate to the investigation of social processes. There are, of course, psychoanalysts who still believe that the analytic situation and the transference are the only legitimate tools of psychoanalytic research and that progress in theory can only be made by illuminating more and more of the content of the unconscious.

There can be little doubt that psychoanalysts, whatever their approach or interests, make *psychological assumptions* in the course of their work, even if these assumptions are not always explicitly stated. In what follows I hope to illustrate the nature of some of these assumptions, and I shall do so by telling you of some work that has incidentally involved certain extensions of psychoanalytic theory in the process of exploring such assumptions.

The material that I want to present to you now has been drawn from the work of the number of research groups at the Hampstead

Child-Therapy Clinic. As you perhaps know, the Clinic is a training and research centre in child psychoanalysis, under the direction of Miss Anna Freud, and one of the research projects that has been in progress for some time is the exploration of the extent to which our present-day psychoanalytic theory can be applied to actual clinical observations made on children in analysis. The research work has taken the form of a large-scale cooperative attempt to categorize and to classify the psychoanalytic case material according to a comprehensive system of classification based on different aspects of psychoanalytic theory. The project was initiated by Mrs. Dorothy Burlingham and is known, for short, as the Index. The value of indexing as a scientific method in its own right, one that leads to refinement in the theoretical model used, has been described elsewhere, and so have some of the concrete results of the indexing procedure (see Appendix, as well as Chapters 3 and 5).

An integral part of the Index research has been the construction of a set of manuals of definitions of psychoanalytic concepts. These definitions can be used by those therapists and analysts who have to translate their actual psychoanalytical observations into theoretical terms. As a consequence of the work involved in preparing these manuals, it has emerged, rather to our surprise, that a number of accepted definitions, though meaningful in themselves, were inconsistent and mutually contradictory when brought together. Examples of these are the mechanisms of identification, introjection, internalization, and incorporation. Because these concepts do not, as they have been used in the past, fit nicely into one another, it was found to be extremely difficult to decide just when an item of recorded material showed the operation of one of these mechanisms and when another. Beginning with what appeared to be the relatively circumscribed task of tailoring concepts such as these, we were led into what proved to be an exciting theoretical excursion—one that seems to us to have forged clearer links between the clinical and psychological aspects of psychoanalysis. I am afraid that limitations of time prevent me from approaching this topic from the point of view of its historical development, and I shall have to ask you to take for granted the fact that the points that I intend to make have a history and do not represent the fruits of idle speculation. On the other hand, they are tentative and far from being in their final form. For the gaps in my presentation I must ask your tolerance, and I hope, as we go along, that some of the unspoken implications of these ideas for psychological theory will occur to you.

We can begin with the eminently respectable neurological concept of the body schema, or body image, first suggested many years ago by Henry Head. You may remember that Head put forward the

idea that the individual, during the course of his development, constructs an inner model or schema of his own body, based on the
integration of numerous bodily experiences, particularly of sensations that relate to the body's posture. The body schema, as it exists
in any point in development, profoundly affects the person's perception of any position, state, or condition of his body. As Head put
it:

> Every recognizable (postural) change enters into consciousness al-
> ready charged with its relation to something that has gone before,
> just as on a taximeter the distance is presented to us already
> transformed into shillings and pence. . . . By means of postural
> alterations in position we are always building up a postural model
> of ourselves which constantly changes. . . . The sensory cortex is
> the storehouse of past impressions. They may rise into conscious-
> ness as images, but more often, as in the case of spacial impres-
> sions, remain outside central consciousness. Here [that is, outside
> central consciousness] they form organized models of ourselves
> which may be called schemata. Such schemata modify the impres-
> sions produced by incoming sensory impulses in such a way that
> the final sensations of position or of locality rise into consciousness
> charged with a relation to something that has gone before. (Head,
> 1926).

Head was quite clear that the processes that go into the formation
of the body schema, as well as the schema itself, are predominately,
if not entirely, unconscious. This view continued to be held by Fred-
erick Bartlett (1931), who constructed a theory of remembering based
on the notion of schemata, and by Paul Schilder who linked the
concept of body schema (he referred to it as the body image) with
various clinical manifestations and with the theory of psychoanalysis
(Schilder, 1935).

Head was a neurologist, and therefore very much concerned
with the physical body. However, there is no reason why psychologists should not extend his valuable concept of body schema outside
the confines of the body. The conscious or unconscious feeling of
one's own identity, our knowledge of our own behavior and our
own possessions extend far beyond our somatic boundaries, and we
can postulate that on the basis of continuing experiences of the
interaction between ourselves and the rest of the world, we construct
an extended body schema that we can call the "self-schema." Everything that Head has said about the body schema can be extrapolated
to apply to the self-schema, if only we substitute such words as
"behavior" and "attitude" for posture. Thus the self-schema modifies
the impressions produced by incoming sensory impulses in such a
way that the final sensations relating to all of our behavior and

experience become charged, as Head put it, with a relation to something that has gone before.

There are many ways in which the self-schema is analogous to the body schema. The small child who enters nursery school for the first time may conduct himself very well, that is, in the ways expected of him, and may show an appropriate adaptation to his new circumstances for an hour or so. After this he may regress to more infantile behavior. We could say that the psychological posture, that is, the particular form of his self-schema at the time, was one that he was not very accustomed to, and could only sustain for a short while before fatigue set in and earlier, more usual and more comfortable postures reasserted themselves. We could say that he changed the position—"shape" might be a better word—of his self-schema, but could only maintain it for a limited time before psychological fatigue occurred.

The fact that even such material possessions as the clothing we habitually wear enter into our self-schema may be illustrated by the story of the traveling salesman in tsarist Russia who arrived late one night at a country inn and asked for a bed. He was told that the inn was full, but after much pleading the friendly landlord told him that he could sleep on the spare bed in a room occupied by a Russian general who was already asleep. He was warned that he would have to tiptoe into the room, undress in the dark, and would have to leave before dawn. The poor salesman accepted gratefully and, having paid his bill in advance, followed the landlord's instructions exactly. In the early hours he was woken by the landlord, dressed in the dark, and stole away to the local railway station. He arrived as dawn was breaking and entered the waiting room, where he caught sight of himself in the mirror, attired in the full regalia of a tsarist general. "My God," he exclaimed, "they woke the wrong man!"

We know, from many recent studies made by experimental psychologists and from clinical psychoanalytic observation that perception can take place without awareness, that is, without the quality of consciousness. I want to stress, as Head did for the body schema, that it is largely on the basis of such unconscious perception of our own experiences and behavior that we construct an increasingly complex and constantly changing internal representation of ourselves.

For a number of reasons, I want to use the term "self-representation" instead of self-schema. One of these is that later I shall introduce the concept of the "representational world" and the alternative of "schematic world" is rather misleading. The self representation is very different from some of the numerous other concepts of self that can be found in the literature. It does not correspond to any of the meanings of the Jungian Self, nor is it synonymous with the Freudian concept of ego, although Freud did on occasion use the term "ego" when he seemed to imply self-representation, as for instance in his paper "On Narcissism" (Freud, 1914). It is not one's *conscious* image or concept of self, for it contains numerous unconscious elements, and I hope to show that these unconscious elements of the self-representation play an important part in aspects of normal mental life and its pathological disturbances. It is a mental model that develops on the basis of sensory experience—and this includes the experience of our own behavior—and that acts as a frame of reference constantly modifying our conscious and unconscious experiences, as well as our behavior. Such a model of ourselves in our minds, constructed out of the whole history of all our experiences, is essential for any organized or adaptive behavior. The experiences upon which it is based include, of course, the sensations arising from our own emotional states. The affective component of our self-schema is extremely important, and we can normally distinguish between our own feelings and those of other persons.

Students of perception theory will no doubt have noticed that the self-representation is only one of a whole universe of schemata or representations that the developing child and later the adult creates and that enable incoming sensory information to be structured into meaningful percepts. Child psychologists know that the newborn infant does not possess the capacity to differentiate between "self" and "other"—he has to develop, over the months and years, a self-representation that will enable him to distinguish between "me" and "not me." We can assume that the newborn infant possesses a primitive sensorium registering little other than pleasure or pain, and it must take a relatively long time before he can build up schematic representations of himself and of objects in the outside world. We all tend to underestimate the rudimentary and unformed character of the infant's representational world, to fall into what William James called "the psychologist's fallacy" (James, 1890). We might equally call it the psychoanalyst's fallacy, for there is a tendency among many psychoanalysts, particularly in this country, to attribute a much higher degree of perceptual and cognitive organization to the small infant than can possibly exist. Our own representational worlds are those of adults, and it is all too easy to perceive the child's world in terms of our own. In 1890, James made the following remark, "The great snare of the psychologist is the confusion of his own standpoint with that of the mental fact about which he is making his report. I shall hereafter call this the 'psychologist's fallacy' par excellence." How valuable it would be for experimental psychologists to test out such *clinical* assumptions as, for example, that the child has a structured representation of the mother's breast at an extremely early age. We know so little of the child's perceptual maturation that the systematic investigation of perceptual development, at present a relatively unexplored field, would be invaluable. As I indicated earlier, psychoanalysts are constantly making psychological assumptions, and whatever light can be thrown on these assumptions, whether in the consulting room or the laboratory, must be of immense value.

The psychiatrists among us will be aware that disturbances of the self-representation, in particular of its affective aspects, enter into such normal and pathological states as depersonalization and derealization. They will know too that the organized self-representation is inhibited or has disintegrated in certain schizophrenic states, for a well-functioning self-representation is essential for the recognition of our body and self boundaries. Such a recognition is lost in a number of toxic and psychotic conditions, and you are all familiar with the rather bizarre phenomena that may result. Here again, a knowledge of the psychological factors involved in the construction of the self-representation can be of clinical value, for it is all too easy to attribute the peculiar behavior of certain schizophrenics to the same sort of psychopathological process that we are familiar with in neurotics. A simple disturbance in self boundaries, which need not be the outcome of conflict, can lead to such confusion that the schizophrenic may literally not know whether he is on his head or his heels.

Variations in the self-representation are constantly occurring in normal individuals, and the study of these variations can be, and indeed has been, approached by the methods of social and experimental psychology, and by the more clinical techniques of psychoanalysis. The self-representation can change its shape from moment to moment, and every clinician is aware of the vicissitudes of his patients' self-representation, which can assume a number of different forms during the course of an analytic session. The self-representation forms the basis for the self-images of daydreams, and we know what a variety of shapes and forms our own selves can take in our conscious fantasies.

From the concept of the self-representation, which is not very much removed from the body schema, it is not a difficult step to make the further extension to representations that correspond to all the nonself components of the child's world. As the child gradually creates a self-representation, so he builds up representations of others, in particular of his important love and hate objects. In the beginning, the representations that he constructs are those that are linked with need satisfaction, but he gradually creates schemata of many other things, activities, and relationships. He does all of this as a consequence of the successive experiences of his own internal needs and their interaction with his external environment. He gradually learns to distinguish between "inner" and "outer," a distinction that he cannot make in the earliest weeks and months of life, when the main differentiation between experiences must be based on whether they provide pleasure or pain. Incidentally, this is why I have avoided the use of the term "inner" or "internal" world for the representational world, for these terms as used, for instance, by Freud and Heinz Hartmann, refer to only a part of the child's representational world—that part that a child learns to localize as being inside himself.

Apart from Freud, perhaps the greatest contribution to our knowledge of the child's world has been made by Piaget. His work, which is fortunately attracting increasing attention among psychologists and psychoanalysts, has traced in some detail the development of representations and concepts in children of various ages. Unfortunately for us, he has not been concerned with the influence of unconscious needs, wishes, and conflicts on the world of the child. However, a number of workers have recently been devoting a great deal of attention to integrating psychoanalytic and Piagetian ideas.

So far I have done no more than pull together material that is known, in one form or another, by all of you. It is worth giving a good deal of thought however, to the psychological ramifications of the idea of the representational world. For example, we have to assume a developing representational world in the child in order to understand fully the development of his object relationships, but we also need to take it into account in order to explain the phenomena of perception, which involves a great deal of structuring of incoming sensory information in terms of the representations the child has built up in the past. The act of perception involves suppressing some items of information, adding extra intensity to others, and attributing meaning to what is finally perceived. You need not be reminded, I am sure, of the work of the Gestaltists in this connexion.

Thinking too, is an ego function that makes use of a specialized part of the representational world. This is a part that contains the mental shorthand of concepts and symbols, a shorthand that can be internally manipulated in processes of imagination and reasoning. Freud's theory of thinking was based on the notion that thinking is a sort of trial action, but there can be no trial actions without mental representations of those actions.

The notion of the representational world has elsewhere been compared to a stage set within a theatre (Chapter 5).

The characters on the stage represent the child's various objects, as well as the child himself. Needless to say, the child is usually the hero of the piece. The theatre, which contains the stage, would correspond to aspects of the Ego, and the various functions such as scene-shifting, raising or lowering the curtain, and all the machinery auxiliary to the actual stage production would correspond to those ego functions of which we are not normally aware. Whereas the characters on the stage correspond . . . to self and object representations, their particular form and expression at any one point in the play correspond to self and object images. (p. 63)

This quotation brings out, I hope, an important point. The representational world is by no means synonymous with the "ego" of psychoanalysis. It is one of the ego's functions to create the representational world, but there are many silent functions in the ego processes that are never sensed by the individual, and that correspond to all the silent physiological processes that go on in our bodies and do not attract our attention unless they become involved in pathology. We then become aware of them through their repercussions, that is, through our perceptions, through their influence on the representational world.

So far I have spoken of the representational world in rather static terms. However, it is far from being static. It changes from moment to moment under the influence of stimuli arising from the body, in particular from our instinctual drives, and also as a result of the impact of the external environment and as a consequence of our activities, thoughts, and fantasies. The change in our perceptions, from one instant to another, reflects changes in the representational world.

It may be well worth while pausing at this point to try to link these ideas with psychoanalytic theory, to see in what way they can be integrated with existing analytic concepts. There seems little doubt that these notions enable us to define a number of analytic concepts more precisely. For example, we can define "internalization," which is usually used to include identification, introjection, and incorporation, on the basis of the perceptual processes involved in the construction of the representational world. Quite simply, we can call internalization the process of representation formation. "Identification" falls into place as the modification of one's self-representation on the basis of a model of another person. The little boy who copies his father's behavior and mannerisms, either temporarily or permanently, is changing his self-representation so that it duplicates aspects of his father representation. This permits him to transfer to himself some of the feelings of admiration and love that he has for his father. It may also serve other functions. If he changes his self-representation so that it copies his father, he has then less need to preserve his father and may dispose of him, or deal with his loss, more effectively. The use of the concept of the representational world enables us to think rather more clearly about the ideas of the transfer of libidinal and aggressive cathexis, and such tricky problems as those of object love, and of primary and secondary narcissism.

Freud has pointed out, and this is something that is very apparent clinically, that if a child loves, without being loved in return, he suffers a narcissistic depletion. If, on the other hand, he is loved, his feeling of well-being rises. If we did not make use of such concepts as self and object *representation*, we would have to speak of the restoration of the child's libidinal level through a flow of libido from the mother to the child, a sort of ethereal communication. I, for one, am loath to accept such a formulation. Of course, on a descriptive level, which is the level on which Freud was speaking at the time, it is correct to say that if the mother loves the child, invests the child with libido, the child feels better; but it must be the child's own libido that is restored to his self-representation, not the mother's. From a psychological point of view, it makes a great deal of sense to speak of the child's feeling of well-being as located in his self-representation when a particular representational relationship exists between the self and mother representations in his representational world. We can then link the state of the child's libido with the particular relationship of the two images at the time—those of himself and of the loving parent.

Turning now to the important concept of "introjection," the use of the present model allows us to clear up some of the confusion that exists around it. The introjection of early childhood (Foulkes, 1937) can be defined in terms of the primitive development of such functions as the recording of memory traces, of attention, memory, and perception. It would then be synonymous with the earliest stages of internalization. The introjections that are characteristic of the resolution of the Oedipus complex, on the other hand, and that are related to the formation of the superego proper, can be formulated very differently. These latter introjections can be defined as occurring when the child acts in the absence of a parent figure as if the parent were really present. Rather than speak of the "taking in" of the parents, we would have to consider the changes that occur in the representational world that give the parent representations a status that they did not previously possess. Introjection does not necessarily involve a change in the self-representation and can be sharply distinguished from identification, which does involve such change.

"Incorporation," as the psychological counterpart of eating, would then be a change in the shape of the self-representation so that the taking in of an object, or part of an object, is represented. The incorporated father's penis, for example, would be the self-representation containing a penis representation inside it.

The process of "superego" formation, if considered in terms of the representational world, loses much of its psychological mystery. Similarly, the "ego ideal" can be seen in terms of an ideal self-representation or set of representations that the child constructs in his representational world, largely under the influence of his parents and educators. The self ideal would be the schema that the child creates, consciously or unconsciously, of the self-he-would-like-to-be, or the self-he-feels-he-ought-to-be.

What about mental conflict and the concept of defense? How does the notion of the representational world fit in? A wish is conceptualized in psychoanalysis as having two components. The first is the instinctual drive or need, and the second, the ideational content with which it has become associated. For example, a wish to exhibit oneself in the nude contains as its instinctual component the exhibitionistic part-instinct, and as its ideational part the image of oneself exhibiting to others. In the present context, the instinctual drive, which belongs to the id, will have its associated content within the representational world. Thus a wish, let us say, to smear with faeces would be sensed by the child as a temporary change in the constellation of his representational world, his self-representation assuming the shape of the child himself smearing. The object of the wish would appear in the representational world as an image of the object that the child wishes to smear. If this content is acceptable to the ego, as it often is in small children, it will find its way to consciousness as a conscious fantasy, and may find discharge in activity.

If, on the other hand, it arouses conflict and anxiety, it will remain in the unconscious part of the representational world, kept from consciousness or motility by the defensive activities of the ego. The pressure of the instinctual drives behind it will necessitate constant activity on the part of the ego to deal with it, but the significant point is that the unwanted wish must somehow be unconsciously or preconsciously sensed on the stage of the representational world for defensive activity to be initiated. If the unwanted images are simply blotted out (and, of course, such a blotting out involves the expenditure of energy) we have the process of "repression." Alternatively, the ego may act in such a way as to rearrange the contents of the representational world in such a way that a compromise is reached; or any one of a large number of other defensive steps may be taken. For example, a portion of the forbidden self-representation may be transferred to an object representation—a process that we know as "projection" or "externalization." The child will then not allow himself to smear nor even know that he wants to smear, but may react in a horrified way to similar activities undertaken by others. He may develop a "reaction formation" to his smearing wishes, in which case the conscious and unconscious parts of his representational world may be extremely different. He might build up a self-representation that is directly opposed to his unconscious self-image, and that is characterized by excessive cleanliness and obsessional character traits.

I have a patient in analysis whose self-representation is a highly denigrated one, arousing his disgust and shame. What he would unconsciously like to be does not fit at all with the image he has created as his ideal self. This patient habitually begins his analytic sessions by accusing his colleagues or myself of highly undesirable and loathsome activities, at the same time extolling his own virtues and achievements. His undesirable self representation is constantly forcing itself towards consciousness, and he defends against the arousal of disgust with himself by transferring parts of this unwanted self-image to the representations of others. At the same time, he defensively changes the shape of his self-image by changing the unwanted aspects of it into highly idealized characteristics, and provides himself with a feeling of well-being that he would not otherwise have. It is perhaps in the understanding of the ego's regulation of well-being and of self-esteem that the model that I have outlined here has had its most useful application. This is a topic that has been relatively neglected in psychoanalysis.

The unconscious parts of the self-representation can, of course, break through in slips or in dreams, and the mechanisms whereby the unconscious aspects of the representational world are transformed into acceptable manifest content are familiar to you all through Freud's *Interpretation of Dreams* (1900).

The notion of the representational world is, I believe, perfectly at one with the classical aspects of Freudian metapsychology and is by no means intended to replace any parts of it. It is an auxiliary way of looking at things, of pulling parts of the psychoanalytical model together. It is a point of view from which to examine data, in the same way as the structural and topographical theories of psychoanalysis are points of view from which observations can be examined and explained. It does, however, provide, I believe, a bridge between the structural and prestructural theories of Freud, for it seems possible that the tripartite division into conscious, preconscious, and unconscious systems can be integrated to a greater degree with the structural division of the mental apparatus into id, ego and super-ego, via the concept of the representational world. The construction of this world can be understood as a function of the developing ego. In so far as it is an organization, it is part of the ego, although it is constantly being influenced by the instinctual drives and by that specialized part of the ego that we call the superego. But at the same time, it can be well comprehended in topographical–dynamic formulations. Indeed, one of the most significant parts of it is the account it takes of the discrepancy that exists in both normal and disturbed persons between those parts of the representational world that enter into and are dealt with by the conscious, preconscious and unconscious systems. The ego on the other hand prevents unwanted unconscious representations from finding expression in consciousness and motility. We know that one of the things that has in the past distinguished psychoanalytic thinking from nonanalytic psychologies has been its insistence on the importance of an unconscious mental life. In this mental life, the representational world is all-important, and we can look forward eagerly to further psychological studies of the role of perception that occurs without awareness in preconscious and unconscious fantasy.

This is probably a good place to end my presentation, but before doing so I should like to digress a little on the subject of the difficulties that I encountered in writing the final paragraph. I do not think that these difficulties arose because the last word has not been said on the subject, but rather because of the inevitable personal involvement with the whole subject of giving an address from the Chair. When I was chosen chairman-elect last year, I was warned by a distinguished colleague that chairmen invariably speak about themselves, no matter how hard they try not to. Because of the magnitude of the temptation to speak about myself for nearly an hour to a captive audience, I determined to discourse on a purely scientific topic. All seemed to go well until the final paragraph, which emerged, in draft after draft, as flat and unconvincing. Finally, I was forced to the conclusion that I not only wanted to speak about myself, as I am doing at the moment, but that in fact I have been doing so the whole evening, although, I should like to believe, in a highly sublimated form. My own self-representation—in its professional aspects at least—was initially that of a psychologist. It was influenced by identifications with admired teachers (and you will remember that identification was defined as a change in the self-representation on the basis of a model of another person). Later I became a psychoanalyst, and made further professional identifications. Perhaps what I have really tied to show you this evening is that the resolution of conflicting identifications and their integration into an organized self-representation can be a stimulus to scientific creativity.

5

The Representational World

Joseph Sandler and Bernard Rosenblatt

The concept of the representational world, as distinct from the vaguer concept of "inner world," has played a central role in the line of thought developed in this collection of papers, culminating in the initial formulation of a "basic psychoanalytic model" (Chapters 15, 16, and 17). The representational world concept appeared first in 1962 in *The Psychoanalytic Study of the Child.* It provided a useful supplementary frame of reference to both the topographical and the structural theories of the mind and was in no way intended to replace these theories. The representational approach has proved particularly useful as a basis for the further theoretical and clinical understanding of object relationships and of mechanisms of internalization and externalization.

This chapter in based on material that has been selected from the work of three research groups (Superego, Fantasy, and Self-Esteem groups) of the Index. All this work is cooperative, a number of therapists and analysts being involved. The present account deals with a conceptual thread that has run through much of our research work, beginning with our work on the superego, and continuing into problems of self-esteem regulation and the function of fantasy.*

*The research groups are primarily discussion groups dealing with various theoretical issues in their relation to actual indexed clinical material, and the membership of the different groups overlaps considerably. One of the techniques used in the work of such groups is for one or more of the members to present, in rather dogmatic form, formulations as they stand at any one moment. These are then critically discussed by the other members. The paper shows the influence of this method, and it should be stressed that the theoretical propositions included in it are to some extent still tentative, and discussion of them is proceeding. Some of the terms used—for instance, "representation" and "representational world"—are provisional, and it is possible, in the light of correspondence with Mr. James Strachey, that these will be altered.

Essentially, this presentation is in the nature of a scaffolding, which raises in turn further interesting theoretical problems.

It has been noted (Chapter 3) that therapists, when indexing their cases, avoided conceptualizing their material in terms of the participation of the superego. A study of this phenomenon* showed that at least two factors were operating to produce it. The first was that what may have been internalized as the superego in a child patient often tended to be externalized as a transference relationship in the treatment situation. This led to an apparent "dissolution" of the superego. For example, if a child's superego had been largely influenced by the child's object relationship to his father, this might tend to reestablish itself as a relationship to the therapist in the course of treatment. The therapist might then be inclined to see the material produced by the child more clearly in terms of the externalized conflictual relationship rather than the internal structural one, and would index the material accordingly.

This observation has opened up a number of research problems. Do we see in this phenomenon a general tendency in all children (or adults, for that matter) to re-externalize internal conflicts, or, as seems more likely, is this tendency greater in some children than in others? If such differences exist, what determines them?

Apart from the so-called dissolution or regression of the superego in the analytic situation, it became clear to us that one of the difficulties that the therapists had in indexing their material in superego terms was the unclarities and contradictions that exist in psychoanalytic theory about such concepts as identification and introjection, the difference between "superego" and "ego" identifications, and so on.†

It was remarkable that as long as we did not have to categorize the actual analytic observations, we could set down definitions that appeared to be suitable and adequate. However, their relative lack of exactitude often emerged when we had to apply these definitions to the clinical observations; or, conversely, when we had to fit the clinical observations to the categories that we had defined in theoretical terms. At this point, we were forced to sit down and produce a theoretical construction that would be, at one and the same time, strictly psychoanalytic, and yet would prove serviceable enough to encompass our clinical observations. As a consequence of this, the Superego group produced a theoretical model that appeared to contain our material satisfactorily, and that we believe did no violence to Freud's statements on the ego ideal and superego. In this we

*A full discussion of the indexing problems leading to the formation of the Superego research group, and the findings and formulations that arose from the work of the group, may be found in Chapter 3.

†When the Superego group turned to the Ego research group for guidance, it was found that they had been encountering exactly the same difficulties.

found ourselves leaning particularly on the formulations in his paper "On Narcissism" (1914). We also felt that we had to take into account recent developments in psychoanalytic ego psychology and in the related theory of perception—a field of study that has become an increasingly important part of psychoanalytic psychology.

In all our considerations, we have made use of a notion that seems to us to be a central one in psychoanalysis, that of the child's subjective *world*, a world that is only gradually differentiated in the course of development as a consequence of processes of biological and psychological adaptation. As we have used it, this concept includes Freud's internal world (1940) and Hartmann's "inner world" (1939) (both *innere Welt* in the original German) and is related to the concepts of the child's world described by Piaget (1937) and Werner (1940) as well as to the work of Head (1926) and Schilder (1935) on the body schema or image.

In the last chapter of *An Outline of Psycho-Analysis* (1940), a chapter called "The Internal World," Freud differentiates between the *external* and *internal* worlds of the child. The child's objects are initially located in the external world, but by the age of about 5, an important change has taken place. "A portion of the external world has, at least partially, been given up as an object and instead, by means of identification, taken into the ego—that is, has become an integral part of the internal world. This new mental agency continues to carry on the functions which have hitherto been performed by the corresponding people in the external world. . . . " (In this account of superego formation, Freud did not find it necessary to differentiate between identification and introjection.)

Freud's use of the terms "internal" and "external" is meant to be purely descriptive. Before the formation of the superego proper, the child's objects exist in the external world, and with superego formation they acquire an autonomous existence in the mind of the child in the form of a new mental agency, and are thus, descriptively, internal.

However, if we take into account our knowledge that perception of objects in the external world cannot take place without the development, within the ego of the child, of an increasingly organized and complex set of representations of external reality, then we have to go further than a purely descriptive differentiation between "internal" and "external," and for our present theoretical purpose, we will have to approach the metapsychological problem of the child's "world" from a rather different point of view.

The representations that the child constructs enable him to perceive sensations arising from various sources, to organize, and structure them in a meaningful way. We know that perception is an *active* process (Chapter 1) by means of which the ego transforms raw sensory data into meaningful percepts. From this it follows that the child creates, within its perceptual or *representational* world, images and organizations of his internal as well as external environment. It is well known that the infant constantly confuses aspects of what we as *observers* would describe as "internal" and external" reality within its representational world.*

All this means that in order to know what is "outside," the child has to create a representation of that "outside" as part of his representational world, and this process is quite distinct from the internalization of aspects of the parents that accompanies the resolution of the Oedipus complex.

We know that in the course of development, the child creates stable images of objects existing in the external world. These images are located within the representational world of the child, but refer to what the child learns to experience as the "external" world. The process of superego formation, of transferring the authority and status of the love objects to the "inner" world, can only take place after the child has learned to perceive his objects, that is, after he has created stable object presentations in his representational world.

It is evident that if we take such a view, it is extremely difficult to talk of introjection or identification as simply "taking in" the parents. The parents must first be perceived in order later to be introjected† and in order to be perceived, they must have been built up within the representational world as object representations of one sort or another. In order to avoid confusion, it is necessary to relate the terms used here to those employed in Chapter 3.

From this it seemed to us that the notions of introjection and identification can be conceptualized in terms of changes of cathexis within the representational world. In order to do this, we have found it necessary to distinguish between the ego as a structure or organized set of functions on the one hand, and the representational world on the other. The construction of a representational world is one of the functions of the ego, which has, however, many additional functions—never sensed and thus never perceived consciously or unconsciously. A specialized part of the representational world con-

*The problem of consciousness is not discussed here. We take for granted the existence of unconscious perception, of unconscious representations. If a percept is to have the quality of consciousness, we may assume that it receives an additional cathexis (whether this is simply a hypercathexis or a special "attention" cathexis is a further problem).

†The term "introjection" is used here in a restricted sense to refer only to the processes of transfer of authority and status from objects in the "external" world to the superego in the "internal" world, as described by Freud in the *Outline*, referred to earlier in this chapter.

sists of symbols for things, activities, and relationships, and provides the furniture for the ego function of thinking.

The representational world contains more than object or thing representations. Sensations arising from the child's own body in its interaction with its environment result in the formation of a body representation (body schema), and the psychic representations of instinctual drives find form as need and affect representations.

At this point it is useful to introduce a distinction between representations and images. A "representation" can be considered to have a more or less enduring existence as an organization or schema that is constructed out of a multitude of impressions. A child experiences many "images" of his mother—mother feeding, mother talking, mother sitting down, mother standing up, mother preparing food, and so on and on the basis of these, gradually creates a mother representation that encompasses a whole range of mother images, all of which bear the label "mother."

The development of these representations has been studied in detail by Piaget, who has shown that an enduring representation (as distinct from image) cannot be said to be well established before about the 16th month of life. This would be "perceptual" object constancy as opposed to the "instinctual" object constancy of psychoanalysis. (Needless to say, these images are at first extremely rudimentary and are initially indistinguishable from experiences of need satisfaction.) Similarly we can distinguish a body representation that endures in time once maturity is reached, and that encompasses the whole range of experienced body states and activities, from a body image* that would be the temporary image of a particular body state or activity.

The notion of body representation can be extended to that of self-representation. Indeed, we can paraphrase Freud to say that the self-representation (one of the meanings of "ego" in Freud's writings) is first and foremost a body representation. The self-representation is, however, much more than a body representation. It includes all those aspects of the child's experience and activities that he later feels (consciously or unconsciously) to be his own. It has a status that parallels that of object representations, except that it refers to the child himself.†

---

*"Body image" in the sense in which it is used here is thus not the same as Schilder's use of the term. For Schilder, "body image" corresponds to Head's "body schema" and our "body representation."

†The ontogenetic development of representations of body and self from an undifferentiated sensorium is a fascinating study in itself, and much remains to be explored in this area. See Edith Jacobson's valuable contribution (1954).

The use of the term "self" by Spiegel (1959) appears to be identical with the present use of the term "self-representation."

By the "self-representation" we mean that organization that represents the person as he has consciously and unconsciously perceived himself, and that forms an integral part of the representational world. This self-organization is a perceptual and conceptual organization within the representational world. The construction of the representational world is a product of ego functions, and the self- and object representations are part of the representational world.

The representational world might be compared to a stage set within a theater. The characters on the stage represent the child's various objects, as well as the child himself. Needless to say, the child is usually the hero of the piece. The theater, which contains the stage, would correspond to aspects of the ego, and the various functions such as scene shifting, raising or lowering the curtain, and all the machinery auxiliary to the actual stage production would correspond to those ego functions of which we are not normally aware.

Whereas the characters on this stage correspond, in this model, to self- and object *representations,* their particular form and expression at any one point in the play correspond to self- and object *images.* (Although this distinction has not been fully maintained for the purposes of this paper, it is an important one.)

Clearly the delineation of discrete self- and object representations in the representational world can only come about gradually, with maturation and experience. We assume that initially the child's representational world contains only the crudest representations of pleasure and unpleasure, of need-satisfying experiences and activities, and it is only gradually that the infant learns to distinguish self from not-self, and self from object in his representational world. The gradual establishment of self-boundaries (at first body boundaries) is a part of normal development, and their absence at a time when we would expect them to have been established, or their disappearance once they have been established, would lead us to suspect a pathological affection of one or more important ego functions.

It is convenient at this juncture to introduce the idea of the "shape" of a self- or object representation or image to denote the particular form and character assumed by that representation or image in the representational world at any one moment. The notion of "shape" is particularly useful as a sort of shorthand, and we have made extensive use of it in simple diagrams in our discussions of the various changes that take place during the course of development and under the influence of various defensive activities of the ego in the child's representational world. The child who feels angry at one moment and the subject of attack at another shows a change in the shape of his self-representation—or, alternatively, his self-image (be it conscious or unconscious) has changed. Moreover, the shape of an unconscious self-representation may be different from that shape that is permitted access to consciousness or motility. Thus we could speak of a child who has an unconscious aggressive wish to attack on object as having a particular shape of his self-representation— the unconscious image of himself attacking the object—that is not ego-syntonic and that is only permitted to proceed to consciousness or motility once its shape has been changed by means of defensive activity on the part of the ego.

The self-representation can assume a wide variety of shapes and forms, depending on the pressures of the id, the requirements of the external world, and the demands and standards of the introjects. Some shapes of the self-representation would, as has been said, evoke conflicts within the ego if they were allowed discharge to motility or consciousness, and the defense mechanisms are directed against their emergence.

This refers, of course, to the expression of id impulses. It is perfectly consistent with psychoanalytic metapsychology to link the expression of an instinctual need with a shape of the self-representation, or for that matter, with the shape of an object representation. Needs soon become transformed into *wishes* of one sort or another in the course of development, and these wishes involve self- and object representations. Thus an unconscious wish, let us say, to exhibit one's body to another, involves the unconscious perception by the ego of an image of the object reacting in some way. These self- and object images must, it seems to us, be unconsciously appreciated by the ego and be dealt with in some way by it, for example, by repression (or some other form of defense) or by permitting an acceptable derivative to gain access to consciousness or motility. The distortion of the unconscious wish involves changes in the shape of the self- and object representations.

Other shapes of the self-representation are versions that would provide the child with the greatest narcissistic gain, and represent ideal selves for the child (as in the "superman" daydreams of latency). Clearly such ideal selves begin to be formed in pregenital times, and their exploration has thrown some light on a number of aspects of what has been broadly conceptualized as the ego ideal. More will be said of these ideal selves later.

It is important to delineate the relation between the representational world and the ego. It is a function of the ego to construct a representational world from the original undifferentiated sensorium of the infant. This goes hand in hand with ego development, for the building up of representations is a *sine qua non* for ego development, and is itself a prerequisite for progressive adaptation. In this the ego is and remains the active agency. The representational world is never an active agent—it is rather a set of indications that guides the ego to appropriate adaptive or defensive activity. It may be compared to a radar or television screen providing meaningful information upon which action can be based. The ego makes use of self-, object, or affect representations, and of the symbols derived from them, in its effort to maintain equilibrium. It can permit them in an undistorted way, or modify them according to its needs.

The representational world provides the material for the ego's perceptual structuring of sensory impulses, for imagination and fantasy, for direct and modified action, for language, symbols, and for trial action in thought.

Using the concept of the representational world, it has been possible to avoid certain theoretical difficulties that have been met with in the course of our work, and to define such mechanisms as identification and introjection in a relatively simple way. These definitions have been tested out in the course of indexing psychoanalytic case material, and have so far proved serviceable.

"Identification" becomes for us a modification of the self-representation on the basis of another (usually an object) representation as a model. Temporary identification and imitation would be a change in the shape of the self-image that would not show itself as an enduring change in the self-representation. More enduring identifications would be manifested as organized changes in the self-representation. The representation used as a model in identification may, of course, be largely based on fantasy.

While it is perfectly correct to say that identification is a modification of the ego, it would appear to be more specific and helpful to define it as a modification of the self-representation, a modification that can, nevertheless, result in far-reaching changes in the ego, for the representational world is intimately involved in the child's psychological experience and behavior.

Within the representational world of the child, identification with an object would be the coalescence or fusion of a self-representation and an object representation, or a change in the self-representation, so that the object representation is duplicated.

A child may also identify with an ideal self. In this case we would speak of "identification with the ideal." This is particularly important in superego formation. Thus, for example, a child may construct an "ideal self" based on parental example or precept before it is capable of changing the shape of the self to conform with the ideal. Then, perhaps at a much later date, circumstances (such as physical and psychological maturation) make it possible for the child to identify with the ideal (as in a child's later identification with the professional activities of a lost parent).

Identification that is the result of momentary *fusion* of self- and object representations is, under certain circumstances, a normal process, and the basis for such phenomena as empathy. Where such fusion is of longer duration, and self-boundaries are not intact, a psychotic process may be present.

Identification that is the outcome of *duplicating* the object representation is normally seen as part of the process of loosening the object tie; the object is then no longer as important as before, but still exists as an object representation apart from the self-representation. The boundaries of the self remain intact.

"Introjection," as we have defined it (we refer here to the introjections that normally accompany the resolution of the Oedipus complex, and that result in the formation of a structured superego), would be a completely different process. It can be regarded as the vesting of certain object representations with a special status, so that these are felt to have all the authority and power of the real parents. As Freud (1940) puts it: "This new mental agency continues to carry on the functions which have hitherto been performed by the corresponding people in the external world."

We know, however, that distortions in the object representation accompany the process of introjection. In particular, the child may transfer much of his own aggression to the parental representations, so that they can appear to him to be far more severe and punitive than his parents ever were in reality.

Introjection in this sense means that the child reacts, in the absence of the parents, as if they were present. It does not mean that the child copies the parents—this would be identification. It is as if the child says to himself, "I shall be what my parents wanted me to be, as if they were now here," rather than "I shall be like my parents." An example would be the child who obeys a parental injunction (in the absence of the parents) not to stay up late, even though the parents habitually do so themselves. If he identified with the parents, he would stay up late.

One could say, loosely, that the child identifies with the parents' demands. Probably, in introjection, there is always an accompanying identification with an *ideal self-representation* communicated to the child by the parents, or based on the child's distortions of the parents' wishes or reactions.

Identification can be observed to occur long before the onset of the oedipal phase, and continues, in one form or another, throughout life. Those identifications that have a special relation to the resolution of the Oedipus complex can be considered to differ from somewhat earlier identifications in their content rather than in their mechanism. The child who identifies with the moral attitudes and behavior of his parents may do so either as an identification with parental representations at the same time as introjection takes place, or may do so following introjection of his parental object representations (or aspects of these). In the latter case we may have the phenomenon of *identification with the introject*. This is an extremely common occurrence, seen particularly when the child has, in his turn, become a parent, and for the first time identifies with his (introjected) parental attitudes in his attitudes to his own children. Such identification with an introject probably plays an important part in a girl's normal transformation into a mother.

Identification with the introject can be seen in children's play. For example, it can be detected in the child who, feeling guilty (anticipating the disapproval of his supergo), turns on another child and criticizes him in exactly the same way as he feels criticized (or feels about to be criticized) by an introject. We all know those patients who bring their guilt feelings to an analytic session in the shape of self-righteous criticism of others.

On the basis of the theory of superego functioning that we constructed, it was possible in our Index work to attempt a classification of clinical observations that would resolve some of the difficulties we had previously met in indexing superego material. We did not now call upon therapists to distinguish between "ego" and "superego" identifications,* for in practice it is not possible to make any such distinction; nor did we ask them to decide in every case whether the superego conflict they saw was conflict with inner or outer authority, for the distinction between the two often fades when a patient externalizes an introject, re-creating an inner conflict in the transference.† What we did do was to devise a multiple approach under a number of different headings (Sandler et al., 1962).

One of these Index headings refers to statements that the therapist can make on the basis of his clinical material about the extent

---

*This theoretical differentiation, based in the main upon the observed differences between identifications made before the resolution of the Oedipus complex and those made as a consequence of it, represents an attempt to make a distinction between oedipal *introjections* and both preoedipal and oedipal *identifications*. If introjection and identification are distinguished as suggested earlier (Chapter 3), the need for separating these two types of "identification" disappears. Indeed, it is impossible in practice to make such a separation except on the often-arbitrary basis of the content of the identification.

†This has been referred to before as the apparent "dissolution" of the superego in the analytic situation. It is, of course, not confined to the analytic hour, for there are many people who have to keep their introjects more or less constantly externalized. It is often extremely difficult to decide in such cases whether introjection has in fact occurred or not, and the theoretical distinction between an internalized object relationship that is compulsively re-created and the externalization of an introject is one that needs further exploration.

of organization and structuralization of the superego, a second heading to its characteristics. This is followed by a section referring to its object and instinctual sources, and a section concerned with contents activating the superego system. It would not be appropriate to go into these here, but two further sections are perhaps of special interest. The first of these we have called the "Ego Response."

The ego has to deal with tension arising within itself in its desire to satisfy the instincts, to cope with reality, and to serve authority. It will use essentially the same techniques for dealing with inner authority as it has developed for coping with the real parents, and the way in which the ego attempts to resolve tension with inner or outer authority we have called the "ego response." Examination of our indexed material has shown us that there is an almost unlimited range of ego responses for coping with such tension with authority. These range from compliance and defiance to self-punishment of various sorts, to demands for approval and reassurance, to rationalization and concealment, and so on. Identification is one of the most important of the ego responses—the ego deals with tension with inner or outer authority by altering its self-representation to duplicate the object, and the child's feelings and behavior change accordingly.

Of special research interest for us has been the variety of methods used by the child for the reduction of tension with authority that involve the voluntary or involuntary cooperation of external persons. The Superego research group has prepared a tentative classification of those guilt-reducing techniques that involve the manipulation or provocation of others (for example, the ways in which others can be seduced into bearing responsibility for a forbidden act). This is particularly important in the study of delinquents.

A further part of the Superego section has been called "The Regulation of the Feeling of Well-Being." A central part of our theory of the superego is that the parental introjects serve not only to criticize and punish but also to encourage and support—as the parents do, although a gross difference may exist between the parent representations and introjects. We have taken the view that the ego creates and maintains the superego because the introjects in turn provide the child with positive libidinal and aggressive gains.

Reference has been made both to tension with authority and to guilt, and the terms have been used more or less synonymously. When we came to consider guilt feelings, it was found that these could arise from a number of *different* anxieties. We found, when confronted with index cards that related to tension between the ego on the one hand and authority on the other, that we had to ask questions such as these: Is the relationship between the child and parent or introject characterized by the expectation of loss or gain of affection from the object, or by the expectation of the loss or restoration of the object? Does the child anticipate the experiencing or avoidance of physical hurt or danger? Does it expect to lose or gain a penis or its equivalent? Does it expect retaliation in kind, or reward in kind, praise or condemnation? Does the child expect to be shamed or admired, to receive gifts or to suffer deprivations? And what is the degree of fantasy or historical reality in these expectations? It seems to be not enough, when we have to categorize our material, to use the broad categories of guilt feeling or castration anxiety.*

Linked with the problem of the regulation of well-being, and partly arising from our consideration of it in the Superego research group, has been the observation that the child directs much of his activity toward maintaining the narcissistic integrity of his self-representation. This involves us in the problem of the role and conceptual status of the ego ideal; in order to look at some of the problems that have arisen in this connection, the Self-Esteem research group was formed.

This group has been concerned with further exploring and elaborating our conceptualization of the representation world, with special reference to the development of a differentiated self-representation in the child, and to the methods that the child uses at different ages to maintain an optimal level of narcissistic cathexis of the self-representation. Our theoretical formulations have constantly been referred back to the indexed material.

The notion of the representational world as described earlier has made it easier to illustrate such concepts as primary and secondary narcissism. "Primary narcissism" would be the libidinal cathexis of the self-representation as it is formed from an initially undifferentiated sensory matrix. Even with the differentiation of objects in the representational world (which follows the differentiation of self-representation from "not-self"), object representations do not necessarily receive a libidinal cathexis except insofar as they serve a need-satisfying function.† When, however, the stage of object love is

---

*A number of interesting theoretical problems arise in this area. Is there, for instance, a general affective component in all these anxieties? How do the specific threats or rewards relate to various phases in the child's development? To what extent is there a fusion of all the different components, and so on?

†This does not exactly correspond to the formulations presented in Chapter 3 in which primary narcissism was regarded as existing before the differentiation of a self-representation. The present formulation is more consistent with Freud's statement that a phase of autoerotism precedes primary narcissism. The initial autoerotic phase can be considered to be one in which there is libidinal cathexis of pleasurable need-satisfying experiences only, before the existence of organized self- and object representations. The development of primary narcissism from autoerotism can be linked with the emergence of the self-representation.

reached, part of the libidinal cathexis of the self-representation is transferred to the object representation, and we get a differentiation of primary narcissism into (a) residual libidinal (narcissistic) cathexis of the self-representation, and (b) object cathexis.

If libidinal cathexis is withdrawn from an object representation and secondarily directed toward the self-representation, it would correspond to what we understand by *secondary narcissism*. It is clear that identification is one of the ego mechanisms that greatly facilitates the transposition of object cathexis into secondary narcissism.

In the same way as we can conceive of the libidinal cathexis of the growing child as being initially directed toward pleasurable experiences, so we can postulate an *aggressive* cathexis of unpleasurable experiences. Parallel with the development from the initial undifferentiated autoerotic phase through a stage of primary narcissism to object love and secondary narcissism, we can assume a corresponding development with regard to aggression.*

We can regard the transfer of aggressive cathexis from the object representation to the self-representation as being the counterpart of secondary narcissism, and being an important component of masochism.

One of the exercises undertaken by the Self-Esteem research group has been to examine a number of indexed cases from the point of view of constructing what might be called cathectic balance sheets. The narcissistic cathexis of the self-representation has to maintain minimum reserves, and a number of factors are always operating to reduce what might be called the child's narcissistic credit. Of course, owing to unfortunate occurrences in the early years, this narcissistic credit may have been low to start with, or there might, be something operating to cause a constant drain on the reserves.

Credit may be restored by a variety of measures, and these vary enormously from child to child. Some of the measures are, like the similar operations of the bank, short-term, while others may be long-term and manifest themselves as excellent adaptations and ego qualities, as symptoms or character traits of one sort or another, or as behavior problems and delinquencies. Such a narcissistic "balance sheet" is, as may be expected, a perfectly normal phenomenon, although healthy persons have substantial internal reserves and are not pathologically dependent on, for example, constant expressions

---

*This complicated subject will be dealt with elsewhere. It may be that the differentiation between impressions that receive a libidinal cathexis and those that are cathected with aggression is the vehicle for the differentiation of the self-representation from "not-self" and later from object representations. The first self-representation may be, as has often been suggested, a "pleasure self," everything unpleasant (and therefore cathected with aggression rather than libido) being relegated to the "not-self."

of approval from others. The study of the various techniques used by different people to regulate the level of narcissistic cathexis of the self-representation is fascinating and rewarding one, and reaches far into the domain of social psychology—into the study of the functions of the social group, of status symbols, and so on. We do not want to push the analogy of the bank balance too far, in spite of the temptation to draw a parallel between economic and psychic depressions.

Mention has been made of the notion of ideal self-images. It has become clear to us that the sources of these ideal selves are manifold, and that they represent more than mere copies of idealized parental figures in the representational world of the child. It may even be that they have been transmitted as ideals by parents who have never behaved in the ways concerned at all—much of what goes into the ideal self-image is second- or even thirdhand, and it is obviously of clinical importance whether the ideal that the child has gained from his parents is capable of realization or not.

The self-ideal is an ideal shape of the self-image that is capable of (conscious or unconscious) visualization by the child. It is a desired shape of the self—the "self-I-would-like-to-be," and when the child becomes capable of actually changing the shape of his self-representation to conform with one of the "ideal" shapes, we can speak of "identification with the ideal" having taken place.

In the course of looking at the various methods that children use to restore narcissistic cathexis, we have been struck by the enormous extent to which recourse is had to what we have called "compensation in fantasy." If we regard fantasy as the purposive manipulation in imagination of the representational world, it is easy to see how the narcissistic cathexis of the self-representation (the hero in such fantasies) is restored through the assumption in fantasy of one of the ideal shapes—that is, a self-image that will yield the greatest degree of narcissistic gratification and well-being.

Other techniques of narcissistic regulation are at present being explored by the Self-Esteem group, but the theoretical problems relating to the conceptualization of compensation in fantasy are of such interest that we have recently formed a Fantasy research group. This group is concerned not only with the metapsychology of fantasy, with special reference to the representational world, but also with the large task of providing a meaningful classification of the material contained in the fantasy section of the Index.*

---

*The need to classify this material has thrown up a number of further problems, and it appears that the Fantasy group will have to assume the functions of a play, dream, and drama group as well.

Indexed material relating to the employment of the various defense mechanisms and defensive measures are being examined from the point of view of the correlated changes in the representational world.

In this paper an attempt has been made to take up a single theme, namely, the possibilities for our psychoanalytic theory of the concept of the representational world. Although much of this must appear, as it has been presented here, as speculative and tentative, it should be stressed that it is not idle speculation. We have been guided throughout by our need to conceptualize and categorize the material recorded by therapists about their analytic cases according to psychoanalytic theory; and this theory is far from being a static one. The ultimate test of our theories must be their applicability to clinical observations, even though these observations must themselves inevitably be affected by the theoretical orientation of the observer. It seems that we have here a spiral of development, in which there is a progressive interaction of theory and observation. It is in this area of the testing out of theoretical ideas that the Index may be making one of its contributions to psychoanalysis.

6

Ego Ideal and Ideal Self

Joseph Sandler, Alex Holder, and Dale Meers

While the study of the superego (Chapter 3) was addressed to problems relating to the superego concept as it developed after the publication of Freud's *The Ego and the Id* (1923a), the related problems of ideal formation, usually linked with the concept of the "ego ideal" are focused on here. The work described here appeared in *The Psychoanalytic Study of the Child* in 1963 and was prompted by practical problems of classifying material relating to ideals in the Index. It had been found necessary to introduce the concept of "ideal self" as a working construct in order to allow more precision than was available with the "ego ideal" concept. It will be seen that the concept of ideal self—indeed, of a universe of ideal selves—fits well with the notion of the representational world (Chapters 4 and 5) because the "ideal self" is essentially a mental representation of an "ideal" state of the self.

This paper has been prompted by the need to resolve a number of practical problems that have arisen in the course of indexing psychoanalytic case material in the Hampstead Index. Faced with the need to classify observations relating to ideal formation in children, it has been found impossible to distinguish sharply between the operation of an "ego ideal" and the superego system, although a number of features that are commonly referred to as constituents of the ego ideal are not fully included within the concept of the superego. Accordingly, the model of superego functioning (Chapter 3 and Sandler *et al.*, 1962), and that of the representational world (Chapters 4 and 5), used as a theoretical basis for indexing superego material, have been extended in an attempt to take into account the different facets of the concept of the ego ideal as described at different times by Freud and in some of the subsequent psychoanalytic literature.

Briefly, the view has been taken that various elements of what might be referred to as the ego–ego ideal–superego system have to be considered both in isolation and in their interaction. In particular, we have found it valuable to distinguish the notion of the ideal self from that of the ideal object, and to consider our clinical material from the point of view of the factors determining the content of the ideal self at any given time.

The term "ego ideal," first introduced by Freud in 1914, has undergone a number of subtle changes in meaning during the course of the development of psychoanalytic metapsychology. Since the publication of *The Ego and the Id* (1923a), the predominant usage of the term has been as a synonym for the superego, although in relatively recent years, a number of attempts have been made to differentiate the ego ideal from the superego (e.g., Lampl-de Groot, 1962, Novy, 1955; Piers and Singer, 1953; A. Reich, 1954, 1960), to regard it either as a separate mental structure or as a descriptive term referring to some, but not all, of the functions of the superego. Most of the recent formulations have been concerned with the need to distinguish between the benevolent and critical aspects of the superego (cf. Schafer, 1960), or with the differences between the ontogenetic development of ideals on the one hand and the conscience on the other.

Much of the present ambiguity attached to the term (leading inevitably to a degree of theoretical confusion) derives from the different shades of meaning attached to it by Freud, and it is the purpose of this paper to examine some of these variations in meaning, beginning with Freud's own writings. At present "ego ideal" is an omnibus term, and it seems clear that a number of rather different concepts are subsumed under it. We cannot speak of the ego ideal without specifying the sense in which it is used. In order to attempt a theoretical clarification, the notion of the ego ideal will be examined in the final part of this paper from the point of view of previous Hampstead Index work on the superego and the representational world.

FREUD'S VIEWS ON THE EGO IDEAL

Freud introduced the term "ego ideal" in his paper "On Narcissism" (1914). He pointed out that impulses undergo repression if they come into conflict with the individual's cultural and ethical ideas. The person recognizes these ideals as a standard for himself and submits to their claims. "Repression . . . proceeds from the ego; we might say with greater precision that it proceeds from the self-respect of the ego" (p. 93). Freud goes on to say that such repression may occur before the objectionable ideas have entered consciousness. The individual "has set up an *ideal* in himself by which he measures his actual ego. . . . For the ego the formation of an ideal would be the conditioning factor of repression" (p. 93–94).

Freud saw here the development of the ideal as being in direct continuity with the original narcissistic state. "The subject's narcissism makes its appearance displaced on to this new ideal ego, which, like the infantile ego, finds itself possessed of every perfection that is of value. . . . What he projects before him as his ideal is the substitute for the lost narcissism of his childhood in which he was his own ideal" (p. 94).

Freud specifically distinguishes in this paper between the ego ideal and the "special psychical agency which performs the task of seeing that narcissistic satisfaction from the ego ideal is ensured and which, with this end in view, constantly watches the actual ego and measures it by that ideal" (p. 95). (In an editorial note to this paper, Strachey points out that the later concept of the superego evolved from a combination of this special agency and the ego ideal as described at this juncture.) Freud is quite clear here on the existence of a distinction between the "narcissistic ego ideal" and the "institution of conscience" which is basically "an embodiment, first of parental criticism, and subsequently of that of society" (p. 96). He also refers to the conscience as a "censoring agency."

In the *Introductory Lectures* (1916–17) Freud maintained the position he had taken in 1914. The ego ideal was seen as being created by man *for himself* "in the course of his development," and this is done "with the intention of re-establishing the self-satisfaction which was attached to primary infantile narcissism but which since then has suffered so many disturbances and mortifications." Distinguished from the ego ideal, we have the conscience. "We know the self-observing agency as the ego-censor, the conscience" (p. 429).

The next reference to the ego ideal comes in 1921 in *Group Psychology and the Analysis of the Ego,* where Freud then states that the melancholias show us "the ego divided, fallen apart into two pieces, one of which rages against the second . . . the piece which behaves so cruelly is not unknown to us. . . . It comprises the conscience, a critical agency within the ego, which even in normal times takes up a critical attitude towards the ego" (p. 109). However, Freud goes on to say:

> On previous occasions we have been driven to the hypothesis that some such agency develops in our ego which may cut itself off from the rest of the ego and come into conflict with it. We have called it the "ego ideal," and by way of functions we have ascribed to it self-observation, the moral conscience, the censorship of dreams,

and the chief influence in repression. We have said that it is the heir to the original narcissism in which the childish ego enjoyed self-sufficiency; it gradually gathers up from the influences of the environment the demands which that environment makes upon the ego and which the ego cannot always rise to; so that a man, when he cannot be satisfied with his ego itself, may nevertheless be able to find satisfaction in the ego ideal which has been differentiated out of the ego. (pp. 109–110).

In a comment on this passage, Freud refers to his papers "On Narcissism" (1914) and "Mourning and Melancholia" (1917a) for previous discussions of the "critical agency," and he gives the impression in the text (quoted above) of Group Psychology that the term "ego ideal" had been previously applied to the conscience. This is not in fact correct, for nowhere in "Mourning and Melancholia" does Freud refer to the ego ideal, and he specifically calls the "critical agency" the conscience. In "On Narcissism," moreover, the conscience was quite specifically distinguished from the ego ideal. It would appear that in Group Psychology, Freud now condensed his two former concepts into one, extending the term "ego ideal" to cover the agency of conscience as well as the ideal that the individual has set up for himself. Although, no doubt influenced by his earlier consideration of melancholia, the ego ideal is seen as critical and punitive; it is still linked with the formulations in the paper "On Narcissism." For example, we read: "It is even obvious, in many forms of love-choice, that the object serves as a substitute for some unattained ego ideal of our own. We love it on account of the perfections which we have striven to reach for our own ego, and which we should now like to procure in this roundabout way as a means of satisfying our narcissism" (1921a, p. 112–113).

Two years later, in The Ego and the Id (1923a) Freud proposed his structural theory. The ego ideal is now referred to as the superego, and Freud remarks that the considerations that led to the assumption of a differentiation within the ego have been stated in the paper "On Narcissism" and in Group Psychology. But, as Strachey points out in his introduction to The Ego and the Id, the distinction between the ideal itself and the agency concerned with its enforcement has been dropped. We can also detect a greater stress being laid by Freud on the critical and punitive aspects of what was now the superego.

Few other references to the ego ideal occur in Freud's writings. In "Remarks on the Theory and Practice of Dream-Interpretation" (1923b), written just prior to The Ego and the Id, Freud stated that "we should keep firmly to the fact that the separation of the ego from an observing, critical, punishing agency (an ego ideal) must be taken into account in the interpretation of dreams as well" (p. 121). Another, and rather significantly different use of the term came a decade later, in the *New Introductory Lectures* (1933), where Freud, for the first time since the introduction of the structural theory, seems to imply a distinction between the superego and the ego ideal. He states: "One more important function remains to be mentioned which we attribute to this super-ego. It is also the vehicle of the ego ideal by which the ego measures itself, which it emulates, and whose demand for ever greater perfection it strives to fulfil. There is no doubt that this ego ideal is the precipitate of the old picture of the parents, the expression of admiration for the perfection which the child then attributed to them" (pp. 64–65). It is worth noting that this formulation of the ego ideal is not identical with that given in "On Narcissism." In "The Economic Problem of Masochism," Freud (1924a) had spoken of the ego's "perception that it has not come up to the demands made by its ideal, the superego." (p. 167) In the same paper, he comments that "the super-ego, the substitute for the Oedipus complex, becomes a representative of the real external world as well and thus also becomes a model for the endeavours of the ego." It would appear that Freud here viewed the ego-ideal aspect of the superego in terms of the oedipal parents as *ideal figures* for the child. Thus the introjected parents who constitute the superego are regarded both as ideal models for the child and also as an internal self-observing and critical agency. This formulation would correspond to that given in "On Narcissism" only if we assumed that the ideal that the child "projects before him . . . the substitute for the lost narcissism of his childhood" (p. 94) is *identical* with the ideal parental figures that have been introjected as part of the process of resolving the Oedipus complex. However, the term "ideal" in Freud's later formulations is presented quite unambiguously as referring to the parents *as models,* while in the 1914 presentation, the term "ideal" is an ideal created by the child for himself, an ideal form of *himself,* representing a state that he strives to attain in an effort to regain the earliest condition of narcissistic perfection.*

We can conclude from the above discussion that Freud made use of the term "ego ideal" in a number of varying senses during the course of his writings from 1914 onward.

1. In "On Narcissism" (1914) and *Introductory Lectures* (1916–17) the term was used to refer to the individual's ideal for himself, constructed as a consequence of his efforts to regain infantile nar-

*This distinction is by no means merely an academic one. Attention has been drawn by various authors (e.g., Hartmann and Loewenstein, 1962; A. Reich, 1954) to the difference between idealization of the parents and early self-idealizations, but these authors stress the importance of the difference from the point of view of the genetic development of the ego ideal, whereas the view that we take is that the term "ego ideal" covers a number of aspects that should also be *functionally* differentiated at all ages.

cissism. It was here distinguished from the self-observing and critical agency, the conscience.

2. In *Group Psychology* (1921*a*) the term was used to cover the two ideas that had been distinguished in the earlier phase. It now included what had been referred to as the conscience.

3. In "Remarks on the Theory and Practice of Dream Interpretation" (1923*b*) the term was used in the same sense as the "superego," as a mental structure. In *The Ego and the Id* (1923*a*), the two terms are indeed used synonymously.

4. In the *New Introductory Lectures* (1933), the superego is referred to as the "vehicle of the ego ideal." This usage was foreshadowed in 1924 in "The Economic Problem of Masochism" in which Freud notes that "the ego reacts with feelings of anxiety . . . to the perception that it has not come up to the demands of its ideal, the superego" (p. 167). The use of the term "ideal" here refers to the ideal parents as embodied in the superego.*

LATER WORK ON THE EGO IDEAL

Freud did not in his later work conceive of the ego ideal as distinct from the superego. From 1923 he used the two terms synonymously, and where he spoke of the ego ideal in relation to the superego it was in the sense of the superego's function of maintaining and enforcing standards on the ego. In a very recent paper on the superego, Hartmann and Loewenstein (1962) uphold this view, and speak of the "ego-ideal aspect" of the superego, regarding preoedipal self and object idealizations as precursors of this aspect of the superego system. This formulation of Hartmann and Loewenstein is a consistent and legitimate one, but it carries with it the possible disadvantage that because Freud's early concept of ego ideal includes something other than his later concept of superego, a very wide spectrum of functions has to be subsumed under the term "superego," with the consequence that such statements as "conflict with the superego," or "tension between ego and superego" may be theoretically and clinically imprecise unless carefully qualified.† As

---

*Freud may have been making the unspoken assumption here that the ego's ideal standards for itself (the 1914 meaning of "ego ideal") are identical with the inner representation of the ideal parents.

†It was the existence of problems of his sort, arising in the course of indexing clinical material in the Hampstead Index, that prompted the formulations of the Superego Group of the Hampstead Clinic (Chapter 3) in which a distinction was made between the introjection of parental authority (resulting in the superego introjects) and various other ego mechanisms (such as identification).

Novey (1955) remarks: "The concept of the superego has been considerably hampered by its unwieldy nature. Because of this there has gradually crept into the psychoanalytic literature a splitting of this concept into a superego and an ego ideal."

It is worthwhile examining briefly some of the ways in which this "splitting of the concept" has been formulated.

Jones (1935) speaks of the topographical prolongation of the ego ideal into the unconscious, and equates the unconscious part of it with the superego. He goes on: "The love component, so evident with the more conscious ego ideal, is with the unconscious superego quite subordinate to fear and severity."

A differentiation between superego and ego ideal, based on the antithesis between the two types of instincts, was proposed by Nunberg (1932), who said: "When instinct gratification is renounced out of fear of losing the love object, this object is absorbed by the ego and cathected with the libido; it becomes a part of the ego. In contrast to the ideal ego, it is called ego ideal. Out of love for this ideal, man clings to it and submits to its demands. Whereas the ego submits to the superego out of punishment, it submits to the ego ideal out of love." He goes on to refer to the ego ideal as "an image of the loved objects in the ego," in contrast to the superego, which is "an image of the hated and feared objects." Nunberg relates this distinction to the shift in emphasis in Freud's writings from the libidinal to the more sadistic aspects of the ego ideal (superego), and comments that it is difficult in practice to separate these concepts sharply from each other.

Annie Reich (1954) distinguishes between the superego, "the later and more reality-syntonic structure," and the ego ideal, "the earlier, more narcissistic one." She sees the ego ideal as being based on "identifications with parental figures seen in a glorified light" while the superego represents the "identifications resulting from the breakdown of the oedipus complex." She further suggests that the "ego ideal expresses what one desires to be; the superego, what one ought to be" (p. 218).

In a more recent paper (1960), Annie Reich extended the idea of "primitive" and "archaic" ego ideals—primitive identifications with idealized infantile objects. She demonstrates the role of persistence of these early ego ideals in later pathology. What characterizes these early ego ideals is the feeling that the person is himself the admired, omnipotent, and idealized object. There is a magical fusion of self and object representations; he feels "as though he *were* his own ego ideal" (p. 226).

Edith Jacobson (1954c) regards the ego ideal "as part of the superego system, as a pilot and guide for the ego," but also sees its formation as a *precursor* to the establishment of the superego system proper. She refers to "processes [which] transform the magic images of the self and of the love objects into a unified ego ideal and, by internalization of the parental prohibitions and demands, establish superego identifications and self-critical superego functions" (p. 105). She adds: "This double face of the ego ideal, which is forged from ideal concepts of the self and from idealized features of the love objects, gratifies indeed the infantile longing of which we said that it is never fully relinquished: the desire to be one with the love object" (p. 107).

Piers and Singer (1953) relate the experiencing of shame to tension between ego and ego ideal, and guilt to the outcome of tension between ego and superego.* These authors consider it to be immaterial whether one wishes to regard the ego ideal merely as one particular aspect of the superego, or as a psychological formation entirely separate and independent from the latter. The superego sets *boundaries* for the ego, the ego ideal *goals*. Piers and Singer see the ego ideal as possessing four major attributes. It contains a core of narcissistic omnipotence. It represents the sum of the positive identifications with the parental images. It contains layers of later identifications, more subject to change than the earlier ones. Finally, it contains the goals of the drive to mastery (Bühler's *Funktionslust* [1918]).

Novey (1955) suggests that the term "ego ideal" should not be used as a synonym for the loving or punishing superego, as the superego is based on the resolution of oedipal conflicts. He says: "The concept of the ego ideal is of use to define that particular segment of introjected objects whose functional operation has to do with proposed standards of thoughts, feeling, and conduct acquired later than the Oedipal superego, but having its roots in the early pregenital narcissistic operations against anxiety. This operative unit seems to play a separate role in character formation and functioning. It is clearly related to the superego but has different origins and a different function from it" (p. 257). Novey regards the ego ideal as being rooted in primitive parental identifications, but in the mature individual, it is also dependent upon later significant persons. It is "a distinct psychic institution related to the ego and superego" (p. 259).

Recently Lampl-de Groot (1962) has proposed a clear differentiation between the ego ideal and the superego. The superego is considered to be equivalent to conscience, and is viewed as an essentially restricting and prohibiting agency. The ego ideal, on the contrary, has a different function, in that it is from early life a need-

*See also Devereux, 1950.

satisfying agency, and retains a degree of functional independence from the superego, although the two agencies normally work together harmoniously. The content of the ego ideal is "I am like my [omnipotent] parents," whereas the superego's content may be expressed as "I will live up to the demands of my parents" (p. 100).

Finally, Hartmann and Loewenstein (1962) link the ego-ideal aspect of the superego with positive aims, and contrast it with the moral restrictions and prohibitions that constitute another aspect. Although these are two sides to the superego, they are not always in harmony; yet in the developing normal individual they achieve a high degree of integration.

While the brief survey given above shows a number of alternative approaches to the problem of defining the ego ideal, there are certain common elements in all the approaches described. Perhaps the most striking is the recognition that Freud's later formulation of the ego ideal, in which it is equated with the structural superego, is insufficient to cover the phenomena to which the concept was earlier applied. In "On Narcissism," the ego ideal did not include the conscience, and its libidinal, rather than its aggressive, components were stressed. This situation has been dealt with by subsequent writers either by broadening the concept of the superego as presented in *The Ego and the Id*, or by retaining the latter concept and applying the term "ego ideal" to one or other elaboration of Freud's original ego-ideal concept.

There can be little doubt, on clinical and theoretical grounds, that some such step is necessary, and all the authors quoted earlier have made significant contributions in this area. However, it should be remembered that any new formulation of the ego ideal as distinct from the superego will not fully embrace all the meanings attributed to it by Freud at various times. Freud's 1914 ego ideal is different from his 1923 ego ideal, and even when the ego ideal is seen as an aspect of the superego system (e.g., Hartmann & Loewenstein, 1962) the resulting superego concept has had telescoped into it Freud's 1914 view of the ego ideal. In post-Freudian literature on the ego ideal, the term has been used either as a synonym for the structural superego or to refer to some development of the first formulations in "On Narcissism."

THE EGO AND THE SELF

Part of the difficulty that has been experienced by many authors in regard to the concept of the ego ideal has arisen from the fact that Freud used the same term to denote both the *ego* and the *self*. James

Strachey, in his editorial introductions to "On Narcissism" and *The Ego and the Id*, points out that the meaning that Freud attached to *das Ich* underwent a gradual modification. "At first," says Strachey, "he used the term without any great precision, as we might speak of 'the self' " (p. 71). Strachey also points out, in his introduction to the later paper, that it "seems possible to detect two main uses: one in which the term distinguishes a person's self as a whole . . . from other people, and the other in which it denotes a particular part of the mind characterized by special attributes and functions" (pp. 7–8). He adds: ". . . in some of his intervening works, particularly in connection with narcissism, the 'ego' seems to correspond rather to the 'self.' " In a footnote, Strachey remarks that in a few places in the *Standard Edition, das Ich* has been translated by "the self."

Hartmann (1956)* has suggested that, in the second decade of this century, the term "ego" as used by Freud became interchangeable with "one's own person" or the "self." He further remarks that this usage tends to obscure the fact that, particularly where the problem of narcissism is concerned, two quite different sets of propositions are involved. One refers to the functions and cathexes of the ego as a system (as distinct from the cathexes of different parts of the personality), the other to the opposition of the cathexis of one's own person to that of other persons (objects).

If we follow this formulation of Hartmann's, and distinguish between the ego and the self (self-representation and self-image), a distinction that is also maintained by others (e.g., Jacobson, 1954c; Spiegel, 1959), then we can consider the term "ego ideal" to carry the following set of meanings in Freud's writings:

1. The superego in the sense of that specialized set of ego functions that we call the "conscience";
2. Certain ego functions that were at one time considered to be functions of the superego (e.g., self-observing and defensive functions).
3. The ideal self-representation or ideal self-image.
4. Ideal parental introjects that serve as models for the self (the term "superego" has been used synonymously with "ego ideal" in this sense).

THE EGO IDEAL AND THE REPRESENTATIONAL WORLD

It would appear from the preceding discussion that the term "ego ideal" can embrace a selection of rather different, though related elements, and that no precise agreement exists on what particular combination of elements should be referred to as the ego ideal. Freud

*See also Hartmann, 1950 and Jacobson, 1954c.

and subsequent writers have all made use of the term to refer to various constellations within a larger system that includes functions and contents belonging to both the ego and the superego.

The lack of precise agreement in the literature has been reflected in the practical difficulties we have had in attempting to index clinical material derived from child analyses under the heading "ego ideal." In attempting to order our clinical observations on the conscious and unconscious ideals of children of different ages, we have been forced to the conclusion that these are for the most part so overdetermined that we could not differentiate an ego-ideal system or structure as functionally distinct from the ego and the superego. In Freud's later usage, the ego ideal is identical with the superego; and in his own writings and in those of other psychoanalysts, the concept has included, as we have previously shown, both ideal object and ideal self-representations. A child's ideal object may be embodied in one or other aspect of his superego introjects, or in the inner representation of some external person. It may also contain elements derived from reaction formations to unwanted impulses of his own. We can frequently detect elements of the child's own self-representation or elements of his ideal self externalized or projected onto the object. The ideal self may in turn gain its content from a variety of sources, and need not be a mirror image of the ideal object or introject.

In our clinical work, it is also necessary to take into account the fact that ideal self and object representations exist from early in life, well before the formation of the superego proper. A further difficulty in indexing has arisen from the fact that the content of the child's ideal self can vary from time to time, from one situation to another, although the ideals carried by the parental introjects remain relatively stable. It is well-known, for example, how a gang leader or teenage idols may replace the adolescent's parental introjects in determining the content of the ideal self (although parental ideals exert a profound and significant influence).

In our work with the analytic material of child patients in the Hampstead Index, we have found it convenient to view the superego in terms of what has been called the "representational world" of the child (See Hartmann, 1950; Jacobson, 1953a, 1954c).

A fuller account of the concept of the representational world will be found in Chapters 4 and 5. Briefly, it is the universe of representations,* of ideational and affective content, that the developing child constructs, on the basis of the sensory experiences arising from the drives and from the interaction between his own body and the outside world. At first it is extremely rudimentary, and the rep-

---

*The term "representation" covers, for the time being, both the organized and enduring "schema" (Chapter 4), which is always unconscious, and the various images (conscious and unconscious) that arise on the basis of the schema.

resentations that are constructed by the developing ego are linked with experiences of need satisfaction, but later the child creates representations of many other things, activities, feelings, and relationships. He differentiates a self-representation from object representations, and learns to distinguish between "inner" and "outer" experiences. As time goes on, certain representations (linked with unwanted instinctual wishes) are repressed, and remain unconscious, while other aspects are permitted access to consciousness and motility. A specialized part of the representational world consists of words and symbols and provides the furniture for the ego activity of thinking. The representational world is not at all synonymous with the ego, although it is one of the functions of the ego to create and organize the representational world.

Relevant to the present discussion is the idea of the *shape* of a *representation of self or object*—the particular form or character assumed by that representation at any given moment, determined by the pressures of the id, the requirements of the external world, and the standards and demands of the introjects. "Introjection" in this context is the elevation of the parental representations (or aspects of these) to special status. It occurs when the child acts in the absence of a parental authority figure as if the parent were actually present. It is the investment of object representations with an authority or status that they did not previously possess. The relationship of this type of introjection, associated with the resolution of the Oedipus complex, to superego formation has been discussed in detail elsewhere (Chapter 3). Introjection can take place without resulting in identification.

"Identification," as distinct from introjection, can be defined as the changing of the shape of one's self-representation on the basis of another representation as a model. Identification is not bound to introjection, and in its most primitive form represents fusion, in whole or in part, of self- and object representations. Later, it can take place as a conscious or unconscious copying of aspects of the "shape" of an object representation, and duplicating it in the self-representation, with the distinction between self- and object representations being maintained.

Identifications of one sort or another take place early in life, but the analysis of pregenital identifications forms an important part of analytic work with both children and adults. After the formation of the superego through the introjection of parental authority, there can occur identification with features of the introjects as well as with aspects of nonintrojected objects. The capacity to identify with objects (via object representations) continues through life, irrespective of whether these objects are persons in the subject's environment or introjects.

The self-representation is built up on the basis of the child's experiences of his own body through its interaction with the external world, and through identifications with his objects. (The object representation includes all the distortions through projection that the child has made during the course of his development.) One of the shapes that the self-representation can assume is one that we can call the "ideal self," that is, one which, at any moment, is a desired shape of the self—the "self-I-want-to-be." This is that shape of the self that, at that time, in those circumstances, and under the influence of the particular instinctual impulse of the moment, is the shape that would yield the greatest degree of well-being for the child. It is the shape that would provide the highest degree of narcissistic gratification and would minimize the quantity of aggressive discharge on the self.*

The ideal self at any moment is not necessarily simply that shape of the self that represents instinctual impulses as being fulfilled† but will be determined as well by the child's need to gain the love and approval of his parents or introjects, or to avoid their disapproval. In this sense the ideal self is at any moment a compromise formation, a compromise between the desired state of instinctual gratification and the need to win the love of, or to avoid punishment from, authority figures, internal or external. The ultimate criterion at any given time is an economic one. If the threat of punishment or of loss of love is greater than the libidinal or aggressive gains obtained through direct wish fulfillment, then the child will abandon his wish-fulfilling ideal in favor of one that is more acceptable to his objects, internal or external. It is clear, however, that in any given situation, there might be a conflict of choice between various shapes of the ideal self.

The special economic gain obtained through constructing the ideal self on the basis of *identification* deserves mention. If the parental injunction is "behave as I do," then the formation of an ideal self that is modeled on the object provides a double gain. In the first place, it represents compliance with the wishes of authority, and the child gains a feeling of being loved; in the second place, the child feels identified with his admired object and can love and admire himself as he does the object.

We are now in a position to distinguish between several types

*While this paper is primarily concerned with the elaboration of the concept of the ideal self, it is of some interest to note that in different situations the *ideal object*, the wished-for object, may also change. We can also speak of an "ideal relationship at any particular time, the "relationship-I-would-now-like-to-exist."

†From a genetic point of view, the earliest shape of the ideal self is probably a wish-fulfilling one exclusively. The consideration of the genetic development of the ideal self does not form part of this paper.

of ideals, all of which have been included by Freud and other writers in the concept of "ego ideal." The first we can refer to as the "ideal object," in which the child possesses an admired, idealized, and omnipotent object. The second represents those ideals that are held up to the child by his parents or introjects in the form of the ideal ("good," "well-behaved") child. This ideal, conveyed to the child by his parents, need not be identical with the ideals or behavior of the parents themselves. It represents the parents' ideal of a desirable and loved child, as perceived by the child. The child may be aware of these parental ideals, yet they need not have been integrated into the content of the child's self or ideal self. Whether they are or not depends on the child's ego development and on the economic loss or gain involved. Both these types of ideal appear to be included in the sense in which Freud spoke of the superego as the vehicle (*Träger*) of the ego ideal (1933).

Finally, we have the set of ideals that constitutes the content of the ideal self, and this is the sense in which Freud spoke of the ego ideal in his first formulation, in the paper "On Narcissism" (1914), and even in *Group Psychology* (1921a), although in the latter paper he had, in contrast to his 1914 formulation, included the "conscience" in the ego ideal.

Clearly the content of the ideal self on the one hand, and that of the ideal object or ideal child (as transmitted by the object) on the other, need not necessarily be the same, though they are often closely related. The child has a strong motive for identifying in his ideal self with the idealized features of his authority figure, whether real person or introject, for by identification, he can transfer some of the libidinal cathexis attached to the object to the ideal self. Object love is transformed into secondary narcissism, with resulting potential increase in well-being and self-esteem. By identifying in his ideal self with the "good" child image of his parents or introjects, he can feel loved and admired by them.

The ideal self is far more fluid and flexible than the ideals held up to the child by his introjects, although it will contain a solid core of identifications with the admired parents of his earliest years. In the well-adapted individual, the content of the ideal self will undergo continuous modification in the light of the person's experiences of reality. In states of regression, the content of the ideal self will approximate more closely to aspects of the idealized pregenital objects.

In normal development, parental ideals that have previously been taken over will be modified and displaced in a reality-syntonic fashion and will be integrated with the ideals taken over from other figures throughout life—such figures as friends, teachers, and colleagues; indeed, from any admired object. Ideals may also be derived from feared objects through a mechanism similar to "identification with the aggressor."

The sources of the content of the ideal self can be categorized as follows:

1. Identification with aspects of loved, admired, or feared objects. These objects may be introjects (after the formation of the superego proper), or may be at any time persons in the individual's environment.

2. Identification with the image of the "good" or "desirable" child as conveyed by the objects.

3. Identification with previous shapes of the individual's own self. By this is meant the construction of ideals based upon the wish to attain "ideal" states previously experienced in reality or in fantasy.*

To these sources we should perhaps add the influence of the individual's reality knowledge. The capacity to take reality into account in the construction of the ideal self of the moment is a most important one from the point of view of development and adaptation. Reality knowledge here includes knowledge of one's own potentialities and limitations as well as knowledge of the environment.

At any one moment and in any situation, the ideal self will be a resultant of the operation of all the factors mentioned. It will contain temporary and ad hoc elements to varying degree, but will also contain a more stable core, for the most part unconscious, based upon the ideals created in childhood. In particular, the ideals based on and maintained by the relationship to the introjects will play an important part in normal and pathological mental life. Conflict of choice between various shapes of the ideal self, especially between those derived at various stages of development, will also play a significant role in determining pathology.

When we have spoken in the preceding passages of the formation of the ideal self, we have been guilty of an oversimplification. The formation of the ideal self has been described as if, in fact, the individual is easily capable of changing the shape of his self-representation to conform to his ideal, but we know from clinical experience that this is often far from being the case. To the picture presented above, we have to apply the same modification as was made by Freud in the theory of dreams, when he amended his statement that the dream was a wish fulfillment, to the view that it was an *attempted* wish fulfillment. In the same way the construction

---

*The topic of regression in relation to the ideal self is relevant here, but will form the subject of another study (See Chapter 11).

of an ideal self, and the efforts to attain it, constitute an attempt to restore, sometimes in a most roundabout way, the primary narcissistic state of the earliest weeks of life. But the effort to attain the ideal self is not always successful. If the individual cannot change the shape of his self so as to identify it with his ideal self, then he will suffer the pangs of disappointment, and the affective states associated with lowered self-esteem. As Jacobson (1954c) has pointed out, self-esteem is a function of the discrepancy between the self-representation and the wishful concept of the self, which we refer to here as the ideal self. This is also the basic assumption made by Annie Reich in her paper on "Pathologic Forms of Self-Esteem Regulation" (1960), which covers and applies clinically a number of the ideas presented here.

The establishment of an ideal self within the representational world of the child provides him with a potential source of well-being. Some of the libido attached to the objects can now be transferred to the ideal and the child can become more independent of the love, praise, and encouragement of his objects, attempting to avoid disappointment and frustration by living up to his ideal self ("identification with the ideal self").*

We would stress that the system of ideal selves (like the representational world in general) has elements in all three of the systems *Unconscious, Preconscious,* and *Conscious.* As the child develops, the various shapes of his ideal self become modified and supplemented. Some aspects will be defended against, and may reappear in modified form. Regression to earlier forms of the ideal self may show itself in a number of clinically important states, and in the severest form of regression, we can see a state of magical omnipotence in which self, ideal self, and ideal object are fused into one.

Finally, a short comment on shame and guilt might be in place. A number of authors (e.g., Piers & Singer, 1953), have related shame to tension between the ego and the ego ideal, and guilt to tension between ego and superego. In the present frame of reference, it is

---

*It is of some interest that there are ways in which the ideal self can be "gained" other than by identification. In a form of "narcissistic object choice," parts of the ideal self are externalized (projected) onto an object, which then becomes the vehicle of desired aspects of the self (rather than "idealized parts of the self"). By forming a relationship with the object, the externalized parts of the ideal self are regained through a love that results in narcissistic gratification through a concealed union with the ideal self. Probably such a mechanism enters very frequently into object relationships, for we need only think of the way in which a woman may gain the penis, which forms part of her ideal self, through a love relationship with a man.

If the object that acts as a vehicle for the ideal self in reality differs markedly from the ideal, then what might be called an illusional or even delusional relationship ensues.

possible to suggest, more specifically, that the affect of shame arises when the individual perceives himself (or believes himself to have been perceived by others) as having failed to live up to ideal standards that he accepts, whereas guilt is experienced when his ideal self differs from what he feels to be dictated by his introjects. Shame might be related to "I cannot see myself as I want to see myself or as I want others to see me." Guilt, on the other hand, would be associated with "I do not really want to be what I feel I ought to be." This distinction is of clinical significance in relation to the formulation of appropriately worded interpretations and the aim to which they are directed.

7

The Metapsychology of Fantasy

Joseph Sandler and Humberto Nagera

In this detailed examination of the concept of fantasy (published in *The Psychoanalytic Study of the Child* in 1963) the reader will discern that the teasing out of the various aspects of the topographical model, especially in its dynamic aspects, provides a basis for some of the later "basic model" formulations (Chapter 17). Of particular relevance is the set of problems thrown up by the crucial distinction between the *system* Unconscious, and the *descriptive* notion of "unconscious." These problems had made the concept of unconscious fantasy extremely vague and difficult to comprehend.

In going through Freud's writings on the subject of fantasy it became clear that the topographical theory contained the seeds of its later difficulties even when it was introduced in *The Interpretation of Dreams* in 1900. The concept of the "second censorship," lying between the systems Preconscious and Conscious, introduced a fundamental contradiction into the concept of "the unconscious," a contradiction that led to endless difficulties and misconceptions in psychoanalytic thinking.

Some years ago, a number of analysts and child psychotherapists working on the Hampstead Index were faced with the need to create a workable classification of observed clinical material relating to the superego concept as it was developed by Freud and in subsequent psychoanalytic writings. This led to a formulation of the superego (Chapter 3) that stressed, among other things, its function as a source of well-being and self-esteem, and its general role in the regulation of narcissistic supplies. On the basis of these formulations and their interaction with actual clinical observations recorded in the Index, it became clear that one of the main mechanisms used by certain children to deal with lowered narcissistic cathexis of the self was the creation of daydreams in which the child could restore his diminished self-esteem through the creation of ideal and satisfying situations in which he played a central and often heroic role. (This applies, of course, to adults as well; cf. A. Reich, 1960.) The mechanism was provisionally called "compensation in fantasy," and it was a natural step to turn to the fantasy material recorded in the Index in order to explore it further. A small research group was set up in order to examine and elaborate the classification of our indexed fantasy material, so that fantasies of different types and fulfilling different functions could be differentiated.

Up to this point, the fantasies of the child patients had been classified for convenience according to their "manifest themes." In the Index Manual, regarding fantasies* the following instructions were provided for manifest themes:

> The text or content of conscious fantasies only are indexed under what the therapist judges to be the main theme. . . . The manifest theme card should contain (a) the content (text) of the fantasy; (b) the context in which the fantasy was understood and interpreted (i.e., the latent meaning).

For each card containing such fantasy material, a second card, listing the heading under which the latent theme was indexed, was also prepared.

An example of a "fantasy" card from the Index follows. It is quoted here merely as an illustration of the type of material recorded on the cards, and will thus be out of its fuller context.

Name: J.   Age: 10   Therapist: Miss S. Baker
FANTASIES: MANIFEST THEME: Vegetarianism
    LATENT THEME: Oral Incorporation of Father's Penis
J. said it was dangerous to eat meat because the animal inside might retaliate and start eating your inside. He expressed concern about the health of the therapist and the paternal grandmother (who are meat eaters). He then related a complicated fantasy that the dead animals might retaliate against the *relatives* of the meat eaters. He also worried because he had once been made to eat liver at his nursery school. He felt that this should not deserve retaliation because it was involuntary; he also said that it was all right to eat things which had been harmless when they were alive (Weekly Report: 2.12.60).
The therapist verbalized the secrecy surrounding father's relationship with K., and linked this with J.'s anxiety about K. (the father's girl friend) having meals at their home (known to be disapproved of by all the relatives), together with his fear of K.'s becoming

---

*Because of differences in American and British spelling, the Hampstead Index lists this under "Phantasy."

pregnant which he knew was similarly forbidden. The meals were
therefore dangerous, like eating wild animals who might retaliate
on the relatives, as in a public scandal father might lose his job
and therefore be unable to feed the children adequately (Weekly
Report: 9.12.60).

J. brought material linking his vegetarianism with his defenses
against the wish to take and eat the father's penis (Weekly Reports:
18.3.61, 25.3.61). When the therapist verbalized his wish to eat
meat, J. agreed but said it was difficult because he lived in a
vegetarian family; nevertheless he would not care whether his
father objected to his eating meat or not (Weekly Report: 31.3.61).
The direct material on the vegetarianism has come in relation to
J.'s masculine wish to eat meat in order to have a big penis, but
this was long preceded by J.'s fears of eating meat arising from
his feminine identification with the pregnant mother.

In addition to manifest and latent themes, the Fantasy section
of the Index contained a subsection with the general heading "Characteristics." The cards indexed here did not record the actual content
of the fantasies, but statements made by the therapists referring to
the frequency of fantasies in the child, the form in which the fantasies
were usually expressed, the functions of the child's fantasies, and
any other significant features relevant to fantasy production.

The existing system of classification into manifest and latent
themes was devised in order to bring together fantasy material of a
similar sort. Thus, investigators who were interested, for example,
in "rescue" fantasies, or in fantasies involving animals, could readily
find the appropriate material.

For a number of reasons, the existing system was found to be
not completely satisfactory. These reasons can be summarized as
follows:

1. The indexed material often referred not only to verbally expressed daydreams but also to other verbal communications of the
child—for example, observations, reported happenings (e.g., when
a child would recount a story that he had previously read), sexual
theories of one sort or another, as well as a certain amount of transference material relating to the child's speculations about the therapist. Under the existing system of classification practically any piece
of verbal communication could be indexed in the fantasy section if
the therapist indexing the case felt that it was appropriate.

2. In addition to this, material was permitted that was not expressed verbally, but communicated in the form of activities such as
dramatization and painting. This extended the permissible range of
manifest fantasy material to practically every derivative of the child's
unconscious mental life. In practice, however, such derivatives were
on the whole indexed elsewhere, for example, in the "Defense" and

"Treatment Situation and Technique" sections of the Index, unless the therapist wished to highlight the content of the child's material.

3. The fantasy, as recorded by the therapist, often contained a mixture of the patient's actual material and the therapist's psychoanalytic insight into the material. It was often impossible to extract the content of the child's communication from the reported data. Instead, in a certain number of cases, it was impossible to disentangle the child's material from the therapist's interpretations.

4. In the recorded fantasy material, no clear differentiation was made between the various elements that might enter into the manifest fantasy. The role of instinctual drives, unconscious wishes, affects, repressed memories, preconscious thoughts, and, in particular, of unconscious repressed earlier fantasies that enter into the formation of the manifest derivative could usually not be isolated from the material recorded on the card, and at times not from the more extensive weekly reports to which the cards referred.

5. The classification of latent themes in the fantasy material was not at all systematic, and employed such headings as "abortion," "bisexuality," "accidental conception," "doing and undoing," "masochism," "sacrifice of parents," "penis-feces equation," "guilt over soiling," and "treatment." Drives, content, pregenital fixations, affects, and defenses all found their place in the potentially endless list of latent fantasy themes.

6. A special difficulty seemed to be present in the indexing of childhood sexual theories. This difficulty had been apparent for some time, and the placing of this group in the fantasy section was provisional. Nevertheless, the question of whether a given sexual theory was a fantasy or not was frequently raised.

It will occasion no surprise when we say that this state of affairs gave rise to some misgivings over the use of the term "fantasy," and the research group set itself the task of formulating a more precise set of definitions so that the material contained in the Fantasy section could be ordered more suitably. As the term was used in practice, almost any derivative of the instinctual drives could qualify as a fantasy, or as pointing to a fantasy.

As a first step toward clarification, review of Freud's writings on the subject was undertaken, and this paper includes an attempt to summarize his views on the subject. This constitutes Part I of the chapter. Part II consists of a number of theoretical propositions put forward in an effort to extend Freud's views on fantasy. Finally, in Part III, a discussion of the varying uses of the term "fantasy" will be presented.

In order to make our task somewhat easier, and to minimize controversial issues as far as possible, we shall not be concerned here with the *dating* of fantasies, nor with their specific *content*.

I. FREUD'S VIEWS ON FANTASY

Freud had a great deal to say on the topic of fantasy, and his views on the subject show a progressive development from 1895 onward. As with many of his concepts, however, he had used the term in a number of different meanings on different occasions, and this necessitates a careful consideration of the full context wherever the term appears. He used the word "fantasy" to refer to conscious daydreams as well as to their unconscious analogues. At times "fantasy" was used more generally, to refer to all unconscious mental processes, as well as to unconscious thoughts. It was applied to normal as well as pathogenic phenomena, and served too to designate psychic reality in contrast to actual events. In addition, the content of psychotic delusions was referred to as fantasies. But in spite of minor inconsistencies in the use of the term, a clear and coherent theory of conscious and unconscious fantasy does emerge.*

It is worth noting that the theory of fantasy was developed very largely before the introduction of the structural theory (1923a), and its systematic formulation in structural terms was not attempted by Freud.

The metapsychology of fantasy was initially elaborated by Freud in connection with conscious daydreams, and we will begin our presentation by examining his statements relating to the metapsychology of daydreams. This will be followed by a description of the extensions that Freud found necessary in order to understand the nature and function of unconscious fantasy.

The Metapsychology of Daydreams

In *Studies on Hysteria*, (1893–95) Breuer and Freud put forward the view that the essential basis of hysteria is the existence of hypnoid states, and that daydreaming, which could be pathogenic if excessive, occurred in such a semihypnotic state.† The experiencing of a trauma during such a state of dissociation rendered the appropriate discharge of affect impossible, and a "pathogenic memory" could be implanted.

*A paper by David Beres (1962) considers some of the problems arising in connection with Freud's use of the concept of fantasy. We find ourselves largely in agreement with his views, and some of the formulations in this paper are extremely close to those expressed by Beres.

†This formulation appears to be a compromise between Breuer and Freud. Freud later abandoned Breuer's notion of the central role of hypnoid states in favor of a more dynamic conception of mental conflict, though he always attributed great importance to daydreams and the daydream state.

In referring to Anna O., the authors said: "She embellished her life in a manner which probably influenced her decisively in the direction of her illness, by indulging in systematic day-dreaming, which she described as her 'private theatre' " (p. 22). The authors later refer again to "harmful daydreaming."

Later Freud abandoned the view that an actual trauma, such as a sexual seduction, was the pathogenic agent in hysteria, and shifted the emphasis to the content and fate of the fantasies themselves.

The material that now follows has been ordered under a number of different headings, and a strict historical sequence will not be adhered to:

Fantasies as Distinct from Other Mental Processes

In *The Interpretation of Dreams* (1900), Freud said that daydreams are not normally confused with reality while they are taking place. However, later (1907) he pointed out that in delusions, fantasies have gained the upper hand, that is, have obtained *belief* and have acquired an influence on action. This quality of belief is also attached to hallucinations and to dreams (during daydreaming).

Fantasies have two sets of determinants. One is conscious and manifest to the subject. The other is unconscious and is revealed through analysis. The fantasy is the outcome of a struggle, and represents a compromise between these two sets of determinants.

Freud distinguishes between the fantasy on the one hand, and the instinct and wish on the other. The fantasy is a *wish-fulfilling* product of the imagination.

In "Two Principles" (1911), Freud referred to fantasy as a type of *thought*: "With the introduction of the reality principle one species of thought-activity was split off; it was kept free from reality-testing and remained subordinated to the pleasure principle alone. This activity is *phantasying*, which begins already in children's play, and later, continued as *day-dreaming*, abandons dependence on real objects" (p. 222). Freud's view that fantasying is a type of thinking is expressed in a number of other places (e.g., 1922). In 1921 he pointed out that daydreaming is freely wandering fantastic thinking as opposed to intentionally directed reflection, that is, nonfantasy thought (1921b).

Thoughts, which include fantasies, differ from dreams in that in the latter only the concrete subject matter of thought is visually represented, not the relation between the various elements, the specific characteristic of thought. Fantasy, therefore, is more than thinking in pictures, for it includes relations and hence is closely connected with verbal development.

We know, too, from *The Ego and the Id* (1923a) and subsequent writings, that mental content such as fantasies is not to be confused with aspects of the unconscious ego such as mechanisms of defense.

The Function of Fantasy

Fantasies are, for Freud, fulfillments of secret and repressed wishes and protect the ego from anxiety arising from undischarged instinctual tension. They may be compared to a dream in waking life, and the term "daydream" is thus appropriate. Because reality is on the whole unsatisfying, we develop a life of fantasy in which we make up for the insufficiencies of reality by the production of wish fulfillments. In 1897, in a letter to Fliess, Freud referred to fantasies as "defensive structures, sublimations and embellishments of the facts, [which] . . . at the same time serve the purpose of self-exoneration" (Freud, 1887–1902). In the case studies of Little Hans (1909b) and the Rat Man (1909c), he again speaks of defensive, self-justificatory fantasies. In his fantasies about his infancy, the individual tries to erase the memory of his autoerotic activities. Thus he may fantasy seductions and assaults in place of memories of such activities.

Fantasies may be a substitute for play. When play has to become secret it may be carried on in fantasy. The fantasy allows the repressed memories to become conscious in distorted form. In fantasies that accompany satisfaction, the sexual object is raised to a degree of perfection not readily found again in reality. The function of fantasy, says Freud as late as 1930, is to help make oneself independent of the external world by seeking satisfaction in internal psychic processes. It gives the ego time to modify external circumstances in order to attain instinctual discharge.

Thus the function of fantasy is to create a wish-fulfilling situation that allows a certain amount of instinctual discharge—a discharge that would not be permitted in the existing circumstances of external reality—and that also corrects and modifies that reality in the imagination.

In regard to the relation between fantasy and masturbatory activities (in the wider sense) Freud (1908a) points out that there was a time when the masturbatory act was compounded of two parts. One was the evocation of a fantasy, and the other some form of active self-gratificatory behavior. "Originally the action was a purely autoerotic procedure for the purpose of obtaining pleasure from some particular part of the body, which could be described as erotogenic. Later, this action became merged with a wishful idea from the sphere of object-love and served as a partial realization of the situation in which the phantasy culminated" (p. 161).

The Dating of Fantasy

Freud is quite explicit in linking the emergence of fantasy with the development of the reality principle. Before that, all mental functioning is pleasure-directed, whereas reality-directed thinking appears only with the reality principle. He made this point in "Two Principles of Mental Functioning" (1911) where he speaks of fantasying as a species of thought activity that splits off as the reality principle is introduced. In the *Introductory Lectures* (1916–17), Freud states the position very clearly. Out of external necessity the ego has to pursue the reality principle and renounces temporarily or permanently various of the objects and aims of its desire for pleasure. This is very hard to endure and cannot be accomplished without some kind of compensation. Consequently, a mental activity—fantasy—in which these relinquished sources of pleasure are permitted, has been evolved. Here they are free from the demands of reality and the reality principle. Longings are transformed into ideas of fulfillment. Dwelling upon a wish fulfillment in fantasy brings satisfaction, although the knowledge that it is not reality remains unobscured. Through fantasy, man can be alternately a pleasure-seeking animal and a reasonable being. Freud remarks that the realm of fantasy is like a reservation or nature park that has been reclaimed from the encroachments of the reality principle.

Later Freud brought this into line with the structural theory. In 1924 (Freud, 1924b), he speaks of a world of fantasy, a domain that has become separated from the external world at the time of the introduction of the reality principle. This domain has since been kept free from the exigencies of life. It is not inaccessible to the ego, but is only loosely attached to it. It is from this world of fantasy that the neurosis draws the material for its new wishful constructions, and it usually finds that material along the path of regression to a more satisfying real past. Again in 1930 Freud speaks of the intention to make oneself independent of the external world by seeking satisfaction in internal psychical processes. In turning to such internal processes, the connection with reality is further loosened; satisfaction is obtained from illusions, which are recognized as such, without the discrepancy between them and reality being allowed to interfere with enjoyment. The region from which these illusions arise is the life of the imagination. At the time when the development of the sense of reality emerged, this region, that is, the imagination, was expressly exempted from the demands of reality testing and was set apart from the purpose of fulfilling wishes that were difficult to carry out. The psychotic takes a further step and applies these delusions (fantasies) to reality.

There is thus no doubt that Freud links the emergence of fantasy as a distinct mental activity in the child with the development of a sense of reality. This specifically excludes such phenomena as the hallucinatory gratification of the infant from what Freud called fantasy. Since the sense of reality is one of the hallmarks of the ego, it seems to us clear that *fantasying* as Freud saw it could be considered an ego function, and he did not speak of fantasy as existing before the emergence of an ego capable of differentiating reality from other forms of experience.

The Component Parts of Fantasies

The relation between memories and fantasies is a subject with which Freud was concerned throughout his psychoanalytic writings. In 1897, in a letter to Fliess (Freud, 1887–1902), Freud defined fantasies as psychical facades constructed in order to bar the way to memories. At the same time, fantasies serve the purpose of modifying and purifying the memories. They are built up out of previous impressions, which are only subsequently employed; thus they combine past experiences, as well as things heard about past events.

In *The Interpretation of Dreams* (1900), Freud pointed out that daydreams share a large number of their properties with night dreams, and suggested that their investigation might, in fact, have served as the shortest and best approach to an understanding of night dreams. Like dreams, they are wish fulfillments; they are based to a great extent on infantile impressions; and they benefit by a certain degree of relaxation of censorship. The wish that is at work has rearranged the material and has formed it into a new whole. Daydreams stand in much the same relation to the childhood memories from which they are formed, says Freud, as do some of the baroque palaces of Rome to the ancient ruins whose pavements and columns have provided the material for the more recent structures.

In 1907 the relation of fantasies to memories is again discussed. Fantasies are seen as transformed and distorted derivatives of memories of youthful love, which have been prevented from making their way into consciousness in an unmodified form. They have an element of "today" about them. Freud refers to fantasies as the product of a compromise in the struggle between what is repressed and what is dominant in the present. As a result of this compromise, memories are turned into fantasies.

However, childhood memories themselves show the influence of the same struggle that results in daydreams. In "Leonardo" (1910b) Freud emphasized that childhood memories, unlike conscious memories of later life, are not fixed at the moment of being experienced, but are elicited only at a later age when childhood is already past.

In the process, they are altered and put into the service of later trends so that they usually cannot be sharply differentiated from fantasies.

In "Creative Writers and Day-Dreaming" (1908c), the driving force of the fantasy is considered to be an unsatisfied wish; and Freud points out that every single fantasy is the fulfillment of a wish, the correction of unsatisfying reality. The two main groups of wishes concerned are the ambitious and the erotic ones. In fantasies the actual link with the real object is diminished when the growing child stops playing, but this link is in fact retained in the fantasy.

In the same paper, Freud said that fantasies are not unalterable but accommodate themselves to the subject's new impressions of life and change with every change in his situation. They receive what might be called a "date stamp" from every new impression. Freud points out that the fantasy hovers between three moments in time: (1) some current impression that arouses one of the subject's major wishes; (2) it then harks back to a memory of an early experience (usually an infantile experience in which this wish was fulfilled); (3) the fantasy now creates a situation relating to the future that represents a fulfillment of the wish.

It follows from all this that the daydream, like the nocturnal dream, draws upon elements of recent and present experience as well as on past repressed memories. To this we must add the modification and elaboration of these memories in previous daydreams, now repressed. But the consideration of the role of repressed fantasies will be left to the section on unconscious fantasy, as will a short discussion of primal memories and fantasies, those attributed to phylogenetic inheritance.

Unconscious Fantasies

Thus far we have considered only Freud's statements relating to the metapsychology of conscious daydreams. But the notion of unconscious fantasies is a central one in psychoanalytic theory, and the elucidation of their nature and function presents a rather difficult task.

In *The Interpretation of Dreams* (1900), Freud points out that the frequent occurrence of conscious daytime fantasies brings the "structures," that is, the daydreams, to our knowledge; but just as there are fantasies of this kind, so too are there many unconscious ones that have to remain unconscious on account of their origin from repressed material.

At this juncture, we would like to call attention to a point that is of the utmost importance in Freud's writings on unconscious fantasy, one that we believe to have been the source of a great deal of confusion in the post-Freudian literature on this subject. It is simply this: When Freud spoke of unconscious fantasies, he meant *two quite distinct classes* of fantasy, and in his writings it is necessary to examine carefully the context in which his statements occur in order to determine which of the two classes he is describing. The first group comprises fantasies that arise predominantly from the repression of conscious and preconscious daydreams and that, as a consequence of the act of repression, enter the system Unconscious. There they are subject to the laws of functioning that characterize the system Unconscious (*Ucs.*), in short, to the primary processes. The second group contains fantasies that are formed in and remain in the system Preconscious (*Pcs.*); that is, they are subjected to modification and elaboration according to the secondary process. Yet both these groups of fantasies are not conscious, that is, *they are unconscious in a descriptive sense.* They do not have the attention cathexis of consciousness attached to them.

This poses a semantic problem. Should we refer to fantasies which belong to the system *Ucs.* as Unconscious fantasies and to all fantasies that do not have the property of consciousness as unconscious fantasies? Or should we rather reserve the term "unconscious fantasy" for all fantasies that reside in the system Unconscious, and call the remaining nonconscious fantasies "preconscious fantasies"? The latter suggestion may seem preferable to the former, but if we make this distinction, it should be borne in mind that Freud has stated quite clearly that the censorship can operate between the system Conscious (*Cs.*) and the system *Pcs.* as well as between the system *Ucs.* and the *Pcs.* He says: "The *Ucs.* is turned back on the frontier of the *Pcs.* by the censorship, but derivatives of the *Ucs.* can circumvent this censorship, achieve a high degree of organization and reach a certain intensity of cathexis in the *Pcs.* When, however, this intensity is exceeded and they try to force themselves into consciousness, they are recognized as derivatives of the *Ucs.* and are repressed afresh at the new frontier of censorship, between the *Pcs.* and the *Cs.* Thus the first of these censorships is exercised against the *Ucs.* itself, and the second against its *Pcs.* derivatives. . . . In psycho-analytic treatment the existence of the second censorship, located between the systems *Pcs.* and *Cs.*, is proved beyond question" (1915*b*, p. 193).

It follows that preconscious fantasies cannot be described as possessing the capacity for entry into consciousness without hindrance. Preconscious fantasies as well as those belonging to the *Ucs.*

can be subjected to repression, *and may perhaps never acquire the property of consciousness*. It was, of course, the existence of problems of this sort that provided some of the impetus for the creation of the structural theory.

We shall therefore ask the reader to keep in mind the fact that when Freud speaks of unconscious fantasies he may be referring to either one of these types of fantasy. Fortunately, it is not difficult to decide when he is speaking of one and when of the other type, and in what follows, we shall for the time being use the term "unconscious" fantasy to designate fantasies belonging to the system *Ucs.*, and shall make it clear whenever the term is to be used in reference to preconscious fantasy.

The Origin of Unconscious Fantasies

Clearly Freud considered one source, if not the major source, of unconscious fantasies to be conscious memories and daydreams that have been repressed. Thus in 1907, he remarks that repression acts upon feelings, but we can be aware of these only in their association with ideas; therefore if erotic feelings are repressed, the memories of the object of those feelings are forgotten.

In his classic paper on "Hysterical Phantasies" (1908a), Freud remarks that either unconscious fantasies have been formed in the *Ucs.*, or, as is more often the case, they were once-conscious fantasies, daydreams, and have since been purposely forgotten and have become unconscious through repression. Their contents may afterward either have remained the same or have undergone alteration, so that the present unconscious fantasies are derivatives of the once-conscious ones.

What of these unconscious alterations of fantasy content? In his paper on "Repression" (1915a), Freud indicates that repression does not hinder the instinctual representative—that is, the fantasy—from continuing to exist in the Unconscious, from organizing itself further, putting out derivatives, and establishing connections. He further says that the instinctual representative develops with less interference and more profusely if it is withdrawn by repression from conscious (and we must add preconscious) influence. It proliferates in the dark, as it were, and takes on extreme forms of expression that, when they are translated and presented, not only are bound to seem alien, but frighten by giving the picture of an extraordinary and dangerous strength of instinct. This deceptive strength of instinct is the result of an uninhibited development of fantasy and of the damming up consequent on frustrated satisfaction.

If we take into account Freud's remarks in the paper "The Un-conscious" (1915b), we can summarize the sources of unconscious fantasy that we have considered so far:

1. Repressed memories and daydreams;
2. Fantasies that have been subjected to elaboration in the system *Ucs.* according to primary-process laws;
3. Daydream derivatives of unconscious fantasies that have gained consciousness in a new form and that have again been repressed;
4. Derivatives of unconscious fantasies that have been elaborated in the system *Pcs.*, but that have been repressed into the *Ucs.* before they have reached consciousness.
5. To these we must add the possibility of the so-called primal fan-tasies, a subject that we will consider presently.

It is of some interest to note, as Freud pointed out in the *Intro-ductory Lectures* (1916–17), that daydreams can be tolerated in the *Pcs.* and *Cs.* as long as the amount of libido attached to them is below a certain quantitative level. If the amount of libido attached to the daydreams becomes too great, as occurs under conditions of frustration, the cathexis of the daydreams becomes so intense as to impel them toward realization; then conflict arises, the daydream fantasies are subjected to repression, and are exposed to the attrac-tion exerted from the side of the *Ucs.* The libido now travels back to the fixation points in the *Ucs.*, and a different outlet for the pent-up libido has to be found, for example, through art. If it is not found, symptoms may develop.

In "The Unconscious" (1915b), Freud mentions that object ca-thexes exist in the repressed fantasies in the *Ucs.*, and that it is these that are re-created in the transference.

A characteristic feature of unconscious fantasies, and one that is all-important for an understanding of unconscious mental func-tioning, is that unconscious fantasies possess *psychic reality* in contrast to material reality (Freud, 1916–17). Whereas conscious daydreams are known to be unreal, this knowledge does not apply to uncon-scious fantasies, which are treated as if they were, in fact, real events. Thus repressed memories and repressed daydreams have the same status in the *Ucs.*

We now turn briefly to the controversial problem of primal un-conscious fantasies, that is, fantasies that have never been conscious and that are phylogenetic or inherited.

The notion that fantasies may be inherited was put forward in the *Introductory Lectures* (1916–17) and in the "History of an Infantile Neurosis" (1918), written in 1914 and revised in 1918. Freud felt that it might be necessary to postulate such inherited fantasies in order to account for the universality of material relating to childhood seduction, to the phallic mother, to the witnessing of the primal scene, to the family romance, and to the threat of castration, even in the absence of relevant real experiences. However, he had himself considerable doubt as to the validity of the assumption of inherited memories, and drew attention to the fact that children may react subsequently in their fantasies to very early experiences that were not understood at the time. He put forward an alternative view in regard to the universal occurrence of primal-scene material in the analysis of neurotics. Based on the child's experience, for instance, of seeing animals copulate, a wish is constructed to see the parents in intercourse, and this wish gives rise to a fantasy that is later remembered. He remarked, however, that the whole problem of inherited fantasies was far from clear. We would like to add that in the ensuing 45 years it has become no clearer.

We return briefly to the question of fantasies belonging to the system *Ucs.* and those that show the influence of the system *Pcs.* The distinction between these two types of descriptively unconscious fantasy is vital because upon it hinges the possibility of successfully translating what Freud has had to say about fantasies into structural terms. It is quite clear that logical thinking of the sort that characterizes conscious thoughts can influence the form of unconscious fantasies. But the influence of organized and formal modes of thought can only be assumed to have occurred previously outside the system *Ucs.*, either in the construction of conscious daydreams, or in the formation of preconscious derivatives that do not succeed in reaching consciousness.

Freud (1911) made a statement that is crucial to this issue; he said: "In the realm of phantasy, repression remains all-powerful; it brings about the inhibition of ideas *in statu nascendi* before they can be noticed by consciousness, if their cathexis is likely to occasion a release of unpleasure" (p. 223). Again, in his introduction to Varendonck's book, *Day-Dreams* (1921b), he referred to the fact that even strictly directed thinking can occur without the cooperation of consciousness, that is to say, preconsciously.

The Role and Fate of Unconscious Fantasies

Unconscious fantasies, in particular repressed daydreams, play a major part in determining the form and content of later daydreams, which are now further derivatives, but they also occupy a crucial role in the formation of neurotic and certain psychotic symptoms, and in determining the content of dreams. Indeed they enter into all the derivatives of unconscious mental life that are permitted to find expression in consciousness or in motility.

It is convenient to deal with the material in this section under a number of different headings. Here the term "fantasy" will be used to denote unconscious fantasy in the system *Ucs.* unless otherwise specified.

FANTASIES AND PATHOLOGY

It will be remembered that Freud attributed importance to the state of daydreaming as a predisposing element in hysterical illness (Breuer & Freud, 1893–95). He further emphasized the importance of daydreams as the basis of hysterical symptoms (1887–1902).

The higher mental structures that constitute fantasies, when repressed together with the associated perverse impulses, give rise to the higher determination of the symptoms resulting from the memories and to new motives for clinging to the illness. He also pointed out that the defensive fictions of paranoia are fantasies that penetrate to the surface in a distorted form imposed by compromise.

In *The Interpretation of Dreams* (1900), Freud spoke of the hysterical woman's fantasy of seduction by a doctor as the emergence into reality of a fantasy. In the same work, he says that hysterical symptoms are attached in the first instance to fantasies, and that the forerunner of the hysterical attack is a repressed daydream fantasy. He also spoke of fantasies entering into phobias and other symptoms. In "Hysterical Phantasies" (1908*a*), Freud spoke of unconscious fantasies that express themselves in symptoms and attacks. In both paranoia and hysteria the unconscious fantasies may be the same. In paranoia they become conscious and acquire belief; in hysteria they become conscious through the devising of attacks and assaults. Behind these hysterical attacks lie conflicting fantasies, heterosexual and homosexual. In the paper "Hysterical Attacks" (1909*a*), he speaks more explicitly of the attack being the outcome of fantasies translated into the motor sphere, projected onto motility, and portrayed in pantomime. Indeed, much earlier (1887–1902, p. 278), he had already referred to hysterical vomiting as a consequence of a wish-fulfilling fantasy of having a baby together with the wish to cease to be attractive.

The relation of fantasies to delusions was discussed in 1907, and to obsessional symptoms in the paper on the Rat Man (1909*c*).

The neurosis draws its material from the world of fantasy for its new wishful constructions, and it usually finds that material along the path of regression to a more satisfying real past. In the psychosis the internal world is put in place of reality, while in neurosis, on the contrary, we find it attached to a piece of reality that has a symbolic meaning (1924*b*).

Both reality and fantasy play their part in the formation of a neurosis. If what is presented in reality is too close to what is most intensely longed for in daydreams, the neurotic flees from it. Conversely, daydream fantasies are indulged in most readily where there is no danger of seeing them realized (1905b).*

Finally, as in the dream, as we shall see presently, the relation between an unconscious fantasy and its expression as a symptom is similar to the relation that obtains between the latent dream thoughts and the manifest content of the dream.

We have spoken so far of the fate of unconscious fantasies as if these fantasies could lead a life of their own. This can be misleading unless we remember that the motive behind the fantasy is the instinctual drive with which it is cathected and that it has attempted to satisfy. Freud was quite clear on the point that the degree of resistance to an unconscious fantasy is a function of the degree to which it is invested with instinctual cathexis.

FANTASIES AND DREAMS

So far we have followed Freud in speaking of fantasies that exist in the system Unconscious, and that owe their origin in the main to the repression of previously experienced conscious daydreams. We know too, from Freud, that the conscious (and we may add, preconscious) daydream represents, like the nocturnal dream, an attempt at fabricating a wish-fulfilling or need-satisfying situation. An examination of the role of the various types of fantasy in the formation of the dream has made it evident that the unconscious fantasy, insofar as it exists in the system Ucs., functions not as a wish fulfillment as it did originally in the daydream *but as an unsatisfied wish* that has taken a particular form imposed upon it by the daydream when it was conscious. The wish-fulfilling daydream creation becomes transformed, when it is repressed, into a desire for the fantasied situation, a desire that increases in proportion to the instinctual drive with which it is cathected. This leads us to the conclusion, implicit in Freud's writings on unconscious fantasy, that the unconscious fantasy is fundamentally an elaborated and *unsatisfied* unconscious wish.

---

*This gives us some insight into a possible distinction between the processes that characterize normal and neurotic persons. The normal person may translate his fantasy into action under propitious circumstances, i.e., when he is offered the opportunity to gratify his wish-fulfilling daydream in external reality. The neurotic, on the other hand, may react to the same opportunity for gratification in reality by flight accompanied by repression of the previously tolerated fantasy.

Dreams are, for Freud, the royal road to the Unconscious, and repressed unconscious fantasies are clearly shown in the analysis of a nocturnal dream. There are some dreams that consist merely in the repetition of a preconscious or conscious daytime fantasy (1900). More often, however, the ready-made fantasy forms only a portion of the dream. The fantasy is treated in general like any other portion of the latent material, but it may often remain recognizable as an entity.

Different fantasies, like any other components of the dream thoughts, may be compressed and condensed, superimposed on one another, and so on. Freud points out that thus we can get the whole range from where they constitute the complete manifest content of the dream, to the case in which they are represented in the dream by one of their elements only or by a distant allusion. The fate of fantasies present in the dream thoughts is determined by the advantages that they offer in regard to the requirements of the censorship and secondary revision and by the possibilities for condensation. The less the fantasy derivative resembles the original mental content associated with the drive, the more likely it is to be brought to consciousness.

Maury's dream of being guillotined when a piece of wood struck his neck is explained by Freud as an unconscious fantasy that was utilized for the creation of an apparently long dream. The fantasy is then remembered as the dream. Freud uses this example to explain the apparent rapidity of mental processes in the dream. Furthermore, the labor of building up a façade (through secondary revision) for the dream is spared if a ready-made fantasy is available for use in the dream thoughts.

Symbolic representations in dreams are the expressions of certain unconscious fantasies, deriving probably from the sexual impulses, which find expression not only in dreams but also in hysterical phobias and other symptoms.

If is of interest that as late as 1925, Freud described the dream as a piece of fantasy working on behalf of the maintenance of sleep (1925c).

FANTASIES AND CREATIVITY

When fantasies receive an instinctual hypercathexis, the outcome need not necessarily be the formation of symptoms. In his paper "Creative Writers" (1908c), Freud refers to the way in which unconscious fantasies can find expression in stories. These are similar to daydreams, but creative productions also exist in which the writer is recognizable as the self. The artist represents his wishful fantasies as fulfilled; but they become a work of art only when they have undergone a transformation that modifies the offensive elements and conceals their personal origin (1913b). In the *Introductory Lectures* (1916–17), Freud points out that fantasy can find a way to reality through art. This explains why the artist has not far to go to become neurotic. In his work he expresses a stream of pleasure that temporarily adjusts things for him. Again in *Civilization and Its Discontents* (1930), Freud comments that at the head of all the satisfactions through fantasy stands the enjoyment of works of art.

As long ago as 1900, Freud suggested that what was new and essential in the creations of such men as Goethe came without premeditation and as an almost ready-made whole. In this Freud is presumably referring to the result of mental activity in the system *Pcs*.

In regard to the value of fantasy for reality adaptation, a subject that was later elaborated upon by Hartmann and others, Freud (1910a) pointed out that the successful man is one who succeeds in turning fantasies into reality. If this fails, he may withdraw into fantasy, the content of which is transformed into symptoms if he falls ill. Or he may find another path leading from fantasies to reality, for example, through artistic gifts. If he cannot find such a path, the libido, keeping to the source of the fantasies, will follow the path of regression, will revive infantile wishes, and end in neurosis. Neurosis takes the place of monasteries, said Freud, which used to be the refuge of all whom life disappointed.

OTHER DERIVATIVES OF FANTASY

Unconscious fantasies, as the ideational content of unsatisfied instinctual wishes, find a path to consciousness and motility in a multitude of ways. Only one of these is conscious daydreaming, and we have mentioned some of the others; but there are many more. Freud has shown, for example, how recalled memories screen repressed unconscious fantasies. Similarly, acting out and the reliving of object relationships in the transference have been described by Freud as being derivatives of repressed fantasies. Jokes and humor allow a discharge of forbidden instinctual wish fantasies; and so do the play, dramatizations, and artistic creations of our child patients. (In regard to play, it is of some interest that Freud's writings imply a distinction between two sorts of play. The first is the early play of childhood from which fantasies could be derived. Fantasies can, in one sense, be considered as internalized play. The second, or later type of play, is that in which unconscious wishes are expressed, in censored and symbolic form.)

Summary of Freud's Writings on Fantasy

1. Conscious fantasy, or daydreaming, is a reaction to frustrating external reality. It implies the creation of a wish-fulfilling situation in the imagination, and thereby brings about a temporary lessening of instinctual tension. Reality testing is discarded; the ego nevertheless remains aware that the imaginative construction is not reality, without this knowledge interfering with the gratification thus achieved.

Conscious fantasy differs from hallucinatory wish fulfillment in that the daydream is not normally confused with reality, whereas the hallucinatory gratification cannot be distinguished from reality.

2. Fantasies that are *descriptively* unconscious can be divided into two main classes: (i) those that are formed in the system *Pcs.*, and that parallel the formation of conscious daydreams, except that they do not possess the quality of consciousness; and (ii) those that are relegated by repression to the system *Ucs.* To the repressed daydreams in the system *Ucs.* we must add the proliferated derivatives of fantasies and memories that have been formed according to the laws of the primary process, as well as derivatives that have reached the systems *Pcs.* and *Cs.*, subjected to secondary-process elaboration, and then repressed. For the sake of completeness, we can add the hypothetical primal or inherited fantasies.

3. Once a conscious or preconscious fantasy has been repressed into the system *Ucs.*, it functions exactly like a *memory of instinctual satisfaction* and can provide the ideational content of the instinctual drives. Fantasies in the system *Ucs.*—perhaps we can say, unconscious fantasies proper—are *not* wish fulfillments, but are now the *ideational content of instinctual wishes*. They deserve the name of fantasy only inasmuch as they are *derived* from the content of conscious or preconscious fantasies. Fantasies belonging to the system *Ucs.* and those in the systems *Pcs.* and *Cs.* may be similar in their ideational content. They can be contrasted in the descriptive, dynamic, and topographical senses.

4. Unconscious fantasies can find expression in new conscious and preconscious daydreams; but they can also find expression and gratification in any one of a large number of other forms, none of which necessarily qualifies for the designation "fantasy."

II. SOME EXTENSIONS OF FREUD'S VIEWS ON FANTASY

1. As already mentioned, the term "unconscious fantasy" is capable of more than one interpretation in Freud's writings, and its unqualified use may lead to confusion. Freud himself did not always

specify the exact sense in which he used the term, although this could usually be elicited from the context in which the term occurred. Unconscious fantasy (in the *descriptive* sense, i.e., fantasy that is not conscious) includes fantasy in the system *Ucs.* as well as that in the system *Pcs.*, and there appears to be a clear theoretical distinction between the two types.

Fantasy in the Ucs. (the term "unconscious fantasy" is often used to denote only this type) was seen as dominated by primary- rather than secondary-process functioning. Moreover, this type of fantasy *does not constitute a wish fulfillment*; rather it provides the *ideational content of unsatisfied wishes*—a wished-for but not-attained experience. In the *Ucs.*, the fantasy functions like a *memory* of a real gratifying experience that, when cathected or recathected by the drives, provides the content of the wish in the *Ucs.*

Preconscious fantasy (descriptively, this is also a form of unconscious fantasy) can constitute an attempt at wish fulfillment in exactly the same way as conscious daydreams. (At times such fantasies may be repressed before they are permitted to reach awareness, their content being added to the content of the *Ucs.* [Freud, 1915b].)

In the system *Pcs.*, we can distinguish between (a) the preconscious fantasy as a wish fulfillment—the *Pcs.* fantasy proper; (b) the preconscious fantasy as the content of an unfulfilled preconscious wish. In this case the preconscious wish is a wish derivative of an unsatisfied wish in the *Ucs.* and will press toward some form of discharge. One of the forms in which it may obtain fulfillment is as a preconscious or conscious fantasy.

A clinical example may make this a little clearer. A patient, in the course of his associations, produces the daydream of being seduced by a certain actress. He is given the interpretation that this is the fulfillment of a wish to be seduced by the analyst. This interpretation is a reconstruction of a preconscious (but descriptively unconscious) wish that had been formed during the course of the analysis, and had then been warded off. As it came closer to consciousness, it was not permitted to proceed, and attained expression and satisfaction through a further derivative (the daydream brought in the material). The preconscious transference wish was itself, however, a derivative of a wish in the *Ucs.* to be seduced by the mother. This latter wish naturally met with more resistance than the preconscious transference wish derived from it. The content of the *Ucs.* wish (the *Ucs.* fantasy) was in its turn derived from a childhood fantasy, a wish-fulfilling oedipal daydream, created as the fulfillment of a wish to have active intercourse with the mother. This was subjected to repression at the time of the resolution of the Oedipus complex. With repression, the wish-fulfilling oedipal daydream was transformed into the content of an unsatisfied wish to be seduced by the mother, and strove for satisfaction under the pressure of the instinctual drives that it once satisfied in the childhood daydream, and with which it is now cathected.

This sequence can be summed up as follows:

1. Numerous precursors, leading to the
2. Oedipal wish to have intercourse with the mother.
3. This wish was satisfied through the (*Pcs.* or *Cs.*) daydream of being seduced by the mother.
4. The (*Pcs.* or *Cs.*) fantasy content was subjected to repression.
5. The fantasy content now became the content of a wish in the *Ucs.*
6. When activated in the transference, this unconscious wish was transformed into a preconscious wish to be seduced by the analyst.
7. This preconscious wish (probably) resulted in a preconscious fantasy of being seduced by the analyst.
8. As the preconscious fantasy was not acceptable, it was itself warded off, and the wish was finally fulfilled through the creation of a conscious daydream of seduction by an actress.

This example is, of course, a highly condensed and schematic one.

2. The ideas presented so far are incomplete in that Freud's statements on the subject were largely prestructural, and the difficulties that the structural theory was intended to solve are inherent in the presentation. Freud did not return to the subject of fantasy in any comprehensive way after the formulation of the structural theory (1923*a*), and a number of gaps remain to be filled in from the rest of his writings.

In some respects this task is not very difficult, as Freud made a number of additions to the theory of *dreams* in his later writings, and these can be extended to fantasies. In particular, he brought anxiety dreams and punishment dreams into line with the theory of wish fulfillment—dreams that were originally considered to be exceptions to the theory.*

It is well-known that anxiety fantasies and punishment fantasies exist that resemble anxiety and punishment dreams in their content. In the short statements that follow, the word "fantasy" has been added in brackets where "dream" occurs in Freud's description, and it can be seen that the definitions fit fantasies as well as dreams.

Anxiety fantasies: Freud pointed out that the censoring agency (the ego) may be caught unawares when the dream [fantasy] content is so outrageous that it had not been anticipated. Where such dreams

---

*The same holds true for the fantasies that parallel so-called counter-wish dreams (1900) and that show the fulfillment of masochistic trends.

[fantasies] affront the censorship, the ego experiences the affect of anxiety. Anxiety indicates the failure of the censorship to control or distort the dream [fantasy] contents (1917b, 1925a). In the *New Introductory Lectures* (1933), Freud modified his statement that the dream is a wish fulfillment to "the dream is an attempted wish fulfillment," and this must surely be true of fantasies as well.

Punishment fantasies: Freud says that "Punishment-dreams [fantasies], too, are fulfilments of wishes, though not of wishes of the instinctual impulses but of those of the critical, censoring and punishing agency in the mind" (1933, p. 27). In a footnote added to *The Interpretation of Dreams* (1900) in 1930, Freud refers to punishment dreams (and we may extrapolate this to fantasies). He says: "Since psycho-analysis has divided the personality into an ego and a super-ego . . . it has become easy to recognize in these punishment dreams fulfilments of the wishes of the super-ego" (p. 476).

3. With the transmutation of the system *Pcs.*–*Cs.* into the structural concept of the ego, the term "unconscious" came to be used more descriptively. This change brought with it a certain shift of emphasis. In the topographical view, the systems *Pcs.* and *Cs.* were conceived as being relatively superficially placed in the mental apparatus. The ego, however, was now seen as having areas that were deeply unconscious. These unconscious parts of the ego do not coincide with the repressed; they represent aspects of its structure, functions, and operations that, like the id and parts of the super-ego, are well removed from the "sense organ" of consciousness.

These considerations would imply that unconscious fantasies may be highly organized and structured, by virtue of the activities of the unconscious ego, and are capable of sharing the properties of the conscious daydream with the exception of the quality of consciousness.

However, before accepting this proposition, it is worth while examining its significance in relation to the various meanings that the term "fantasy" can assume in the present context. Particularly important is the differentiation between "fantasy" as representing a particular sensorimotor *content*, and "fantasy" as a mental *function* (fantasying); a distinction that is often lost or obscured in the discussion of this topic.

The Function of Fantasying

Freud saw this mental process as the effort to attain the fulfillment of an unsatisfied wish through the creation of an imagined wish-fulfilling situation, in which the wish was represented as being fulfilled (usually in a disguised form). Frustrating reality is known, but is temporarily put aside. This process, involving a knowledge of what is "real" and what is "unreal," can without difficulty be considered, from the structural point of view, as a *function* of the ego. It represents a technique whereby the ego temporarily avoids unpleasure or disappointment by holding reality in abeyance. Fantasying may represent the formation of a compromise between instinctual wishes and the demands of the superego, and, in general, lends itself well to defensive use.

As fantasying in this sense can be considered an ego function, it makes use of secondary (as well as primary) processes, and as an activity can reach a high degree of organization. It is a form of *thinking* that may be differentiated from reality-oriented thinking in that it involves a turning away from frustrating reality, although it may itself subserve adaptation (as in the creation of tentative fantasy solutions to problems, fantasies that may later be fulfilled by the manipulation of reality).

Fantasying involves a *fantasy work* that closely parallels the dream work, although the influence of secondary-process functioning is more evident in the former. The fantasy work of the ego will include much of what in dreaming constitutes secondary elaboration or revision. As in the process of dreaming, the fantasy work makes use of both repressed and nonrepressed mental contents (recent memories, percepts, the content of past fantasies and other derivatives, etc.), and will often make use of elements of reality knowledge in the elaboration of the fantasy. (This might be thought of as corresponding to the use of the day's residues in dream formation.)

The product of this process—the fantasy content—may be (descriptively) either conscious or unconscious.*

Fantasy Content

The products of the ego's *fantasying function* represent organized, structured, and often highly symbolic fantasies. Their form is imposed on them by the organization of the ego, and by its defensive requirements.

Fantasy content produced in this way may receive an attention cathexis and be perceived as a conscious daydream; it may remain

*It might be legitimate to add "preconscious" here, if one wished to designate unconscious content that is not repressed, but only temporarily latent; however, from a descriptive point of view, even temporarily latent contents are unconscious. Certainly degrees of consciousness or unconsciousness exist, and we do not have a satisfactory nomenclature for these.

outside consciousness, but be only temporarily latent, with the possibility of being brought into consciousness unchanged; or it may arouse an anxiety signal even after it has been formed, and be repressed. This repression would involve (i) the withdrawal of any attention cathexis that might have been directed toward it, or that was in the process of being directed toward it; and (ii) the construction of anticathexes directed against that fantasy content in that particular form. *Repression of fantasy content may therefore take place without the content ever having been conscious.*

The motives for such repression are numerous. We can include such factors as the heightening of the instinctual cathexis attached to the content, the increase in the dangerous quality of the fantasy content when reality tends to correspond to it, the tendency for the content to find expression in motility, and so on.

Once repressed, the fantasy content becomes potential wish content. It is added to the conglomerate of repressed contents that have, in a variety of different ways, become associated with the instinctual drive in question. Drive cathexis can then be displaced from one content to another, contents can be condensed, and so on; in short, they will be subject to the primary process. If drive cathexis is not withdrawn from a piece of repressed content, or if it is withdrawn and reapplied, it will be urged toward consciousness or motility, but can be permitted discharge only in the shape of a further derivative.

We come now to an important point. When in this way a fantasy becomes part of repressed id-cathected content* (a better formulation might be id representation), it takes its place alongside other repressed mental contents *that need not have originated in fantasies.* Such contents include memories of all sorts; nonfantasy imaginative contents such as reality-oriented thoughts; word representations (words as "things"), and indeed, sensorimotor images of every conceivable variety.† In general, any experience that leaves a memory trace can, with the recathexis of that trace by the id drives, constitute wish content. Moreover, if the path to direct discharge of this content via the ego is blocked, such content will possess "psychic reality," as

---

*The term "id-cathected content" though clumsy, is used here in place of "id-content," as there is some controversy over the consideration of repressed content (in the sense in which it is used here) as part of the id. Id-cathected content refers to mental representations that have become cathected by instinctual energies alone, as the result of the reactivation of memory traces. If this id-cathected content receives an ego cathexis as well as an id cathexis, it will be referred to as "ego-cathected" or as "ego-modified content."

†We do not propose to discuss the question of affective content, since this complicated subject deserves separate treatment. However, if the reader is willing to accept the notion of repressed affects, then they could be included here.

the labeling of content as "unreal" is an ego function. Any unconscious elaboration of these contents, *as far as the id is concerned*, will
follow the primary process.

At this point an apparent paradox emerges. There is clear evidence, particularly from the theory of dreams (1900) that the content
of a fantasy can retain a high degree of organization and coherence
even after the fantasy has been repressed. Yet the id, by definition, is
unorganized and incapable of organizing the mental content cathected by the instinctual drives (except via primary-process functioning). The capacity for secondary-process organization of content
belongs to the ego.

It seems necessary, therefore, to distinguish between the capacity of the ego *to organize* mental content (as it does in perception,
organized memory, reality-oriented thinking, as well as in fantasy),
and the *organized form* imposed on the mental content, an outcome
of the ego's work. *Once formed by the ego, fantasy content that becomes
id-cathected content (wish content) may retain all or part of the organized
qualities that have been imposed on it.* This is obviously also true for
repressed memories, for a memory derives from (conscious or unconscious) perception, an ego function that produces, in the percept,
highly organized mental content. (We speak here of the state of
affairs that exists after the ego has reached a fair degree of development, because unorganized impressions that are registered before
the beginnings of an ego, in the so-called undifferentiated state, must
be excepted, the organizing of mental content being by definition
one of the functions that we call "ego.")

4. In this presentation, the question of the dating of fantasy has
not been considered. It has been assumed throughout that the processes described occur in a child or adult in whom an ego capable of
differentiating the products of the imagination from real percepts
has developed. Before the operation of the reality principle, the infant
may be assumed to obtain partial and temporary gratification when
reality does not provide satisfaction through the process of *hallucinatory wish fulfillment*. By this is implied the perceiving (sensing would
perhaps be better) of the experiences previously associated with the
reduction of instinctual tension, as if these experiences were arising
anew from the sensory end of the primitive psychic apparatus. Hal-
ucinatory gratification, as described by Freud, is distinct from fantasy, which is an ego activity occurring when some degree of reality
testing and the capacity for *imagining* (as distinct from perceiving)
has developed. It is clear, however, that hallucinatory gratification
is a basic precursor of later fantasying. The difference between the
two reflects the difference between primary and secondary process.

III. ASPECTS OF THE USE OF THE TERM "FANTASY"

In this paper we have attempted to describe the concept of fantasy as we have understood it in Freud's work, and to integrate it to some extent into the structural theory. The impetus for this attempt has come from the need to classify and categorize fantasy material in the Hampstead Index, a project in which the structural point of view has been largely utilized.

The material presented here also constitutes an effort to make the task of communication easier, not only within a single analytic group, but between people of differing viewpoints. The terms "fantasy" and "unconscious fantasy" mean different things to different workers; yet in the course of scientific argument there often arise situations in which it is assumed that because the word used is the same, its meaning is constant.

Broadly speaking, there are two approaches to the notion of fantasy that can be discerned in psychoanalytic writings. The first is one that regards the content of all unconscious mental processes, even the most primitive content, as fantasy. This is the approach that is adopted by Melanie Klein and that was made explicit by Susan Isaacs in her well-known paper on fantasy (1948). There she states quite clearly (a) that fantasies are the primary content of unconscious mental processes; (b) that they are, in the first instance, the psychic representatives of the libidinal and destructive instincts, and early in development become elaborated into defenses as well as wish fulfillments and anxiety contents; (c) that the earliest fantasies are experienced in sensations—later they take the form of plastic images and dramatic representations. Isaacs makes it clear that she extended Freud's concept of fantasy and unconscious fantasy so as to give the term a wider meaning. The metapsychological implications of her view have been discussed by Glover (1945), and we will restrict ourselves to the comment that in her usage of the term "fantasy," the distinction between fantasying as an ego function and hallucinatory gratification is lost. In Kleinian usage, the term has become a synonym for the psychic representatives of the drives.

The second approach to fantasy regards fantasying as an ego function, and fantasy as only one type or source of conscious or unconscious mental content. This is the approach that is inherent in Freud's writings, which we have attempted to define and extend in this paper. It involves a narrower concept of fantasy than the first and is less simple; it involves a recognition, for example, of a double meaning of the term "unconscious fantasy," and of a distinction between content derived from fantasies on the one hand, and the

function or process of fantasying on the other. The distinction between fantasying as an ego function not present from birth and
hallucinatory wish fulfillment is an important one, although the latter
process can be regarded as a precursor of fantasying, a function
which is only gradually developed with maturation and experience.

We can assume that the laying down of memory traces of sensory
experiences associated with drive tension and discharge occurs from
very early in life, and that these memory traces, when recathected
by drive energies, can give rise to memory images that represent
instinctual gratification. Thus the infant who has experienced the
satisfaction of oral needs will, when he is hungry, temporarily hal-
lucinate the experiences that have been associated with relief of
hunger as well as the accompanying pleasure. This serves to provide
a partial and transitory satisfaction, which breaks down when the
drive tension increases. To the pleasurable and satisfying contents
associated with drive reduction can be added those associated with
unpleasure and even trauma that can reach hallucinatory intensity.

The hallucination of which we speak is not distinguishable from
a real sensory experience. It possesses psychic reality, for the ego
has not yet acquired the capacity to *disbelieve*, to invest psychic contents with the knowledge of their psychic unreality. We can assume
that the infant gradually begins to differentiate between hallucinatory
revival and fresh impressions, particularly as a result of those circumstances in which the hallucinated content does not receive a
reinforcement from the side of reality. Primary-process functioning
begins to be controlled by the secondary-process, the id by the developing ego. Hallucinatory wish fulfillment is given up, although
we can surmise that the child's perception of the outer world will
for a long time remain colored by gross apperceptive distortions.

With the progress of reality testing and the development of the
reality principle, a realm of trial perception and trial action becomes
established, and we can now speak of the ego's function of imagination, a function that can, as we know, create both conscious and
unconscious (the terms are used in their descriptive sense) fantasy
content. Imagination can operate side by side with perception, and
although the one function constantly influences the content produced
by the other, they are not identical. Thought, and in particular that
special form of thought that we refer to as fantasy, is now possible.
Fantasy is, for Freud, a wish-fulfilling product of the *imagination*,
quite different from hallucinatory wish fulfillment, for which "fantasying" would in any case appear to be too mild and weak a term.
The products of the latter process are perceptual rather than imaginative, and are at the start indistinguishable from sensations arising
from the real world.

Fantasying, then, can be regarded as an ego function, producing organized, wish-fulfilling, imaginative content, that may or may not become conscious. It involves a temporary laying aside of reality, although elements of reality can be utilized in the creation of the fantasy. Once formed by the ego, the fantasy content, which may show a high degree of organization and symbolization, can be repressed and subjected to primary-process functioning alone. Fantasy thinking differs from reality-oriented thinking precisely in the fact that the demands of reality are partially or wholly ignored. It does not aim at changing reality in order to obtain satisfaction; rather it involves the creation of an imagined alternative and satisfying state. It arises as a consequence of the frustrations inevitably imposed by reality, and although the ego remains aware that the imaginative construction is not reality, partial and immediate gratification is achieved.

There are, of course, many thoughts that occupy an intermediate position between fantasy and reality-oriented thoughts, and the two cases represent the extreme ends of a continuum. Moreover, fantasying, although it involves a turning away from immediate frustrating reality, can be utilized as an important aspect of scientific and artistic creativity. It should be added that these remarks on fantasying do not preclude the possibility that, in certain circumstances, reality can subsequently be changed so as to bring about a realization of the fantasy.

In our view, the following consideration would have to be taken into account in any consideration of fantasy.

1. As ideational contents (representations) may originate from a number of sources (early unorganized sensations, organized thoughts, percepts, memory images, fantasies, etc.), it would appear to be inappropriate to use the term "fantasying" for the primary-process elaboration of these into the content of instinctual wishes. It is only when the ego takes a hand in the organization of content into wish-fulfilling imaginative products, that we should speak of fantasy formation.

2. It would appear to be correct to speak of the content of the system Ucs. as unconscious fantasy only when that content has been derived from repressed fantasies. In using the term "unconscious fantasy" it should always be made clear whether the term is used to refer to those contents of the Ucs. that have been derived from fantasying, or in its broad descriptive sense.

3. We regard the process of fantasying as an ego function resulting in organized, wish-fulfilling, imaginative content that may or may not be consciously perceived. The fantasy may then be a derivative, a compromise constructed by the ego between that wish and

the demands of the superego. Reality knowledge may be partially or completely suspended in the formation of this derivative, or it may be utilized and influence the fantasy to a high degree. The fantasy content may be repressed soon after it has been created, or defended against in other ways.

4. The fantasy is only one of many derivatives that the ego can construct.

5. The possibility exists that some fantasies represent wish fulfillments, as when the wish in question arises neither from the id nor from the superego but from the ego itself.

It follows that we have a situation in which the ego may create a fantasy using, in distorted and censored form, id-cathected content that was derived, let us say, from a repressed memory. (Such a memory may, of course, have been distorted in its content by preconscious and unconscious wishes at the time when it constituted a percept.) On the other hand, id-cathected repressed fantasy content may find expression in such ego-modified derivatives as apperceptions, artistic creations, dramatic productions, free associations, delusions, and so on.

This can be expressed schematically in the following way:

Id-cathected content Derived from repressed:		Content of derivatives Expressed in:
Memory images		Perceptual images
Reality-oriented		(appercepts)
thoughts		Wishes
Dream images		Action
		Reality thinking
Fantasies	Repression	Dreams
Etc.	⟵	Play
(We include also		Free associations
primal memories)	Return of the	Screen memories
	⟶	Distorted recollections
	repressed	Manifest transference content
		Symptoms
		Delusions
		Scientific theories
		Hypnagogic phenomena
		Artistic and literary creations
		Daydream fantasies
		Etc.

In this scheme we distinguish between

1. *Id-cathected content*, subject to the primary process alone, which forms the content of instinctual wishes. This content consists of images arising from memory traces when these traces are recathected by the drives. Inasmuch as they possess only a drive cathexis, the ego function of judging whether they constitute real or imagined contents does not operate, and they possess "psychic reality."

2. *Ego-modified content*. Because repressed content is not permitted direct discharge, it can achieve this only through the formation of derivatives. We can assume that in order to circumvent the censorship, some degree of modification and organization of the id-cathected content must have occurred before the ego permits drive discharge. It can also be assumed that the content of the derivative has received, in addition to the drive cathexis that impels it toward discharge, ego cathexes of varying degree.

It can be argued that many of the derivatives listed above are very similar to fantasies, and deserve to be labeled as such. To do so would obscure, we believe, some of the essential character of the fantasy, and would lead to a generalization of the term that would then cover all derivatives and thus conceal the significant theoretical and important clinical distinctions.

It is certainly true that many nonfantasy derivatives occur simultaneously, or in close association, with wish-fulfilling fantasies; but others do not, being rather *alternatives* to fantasy. In the course of psychoanalytic treatment, we often interpret a derivative as being the outcome of an underlying fantasy. Even when this is not correct, the patient can bring material that appears to confirm this interpretation. What has happened is that, *through the interpretation*, we provide *alternative derivatives* (fantasies, thoughts, and wishes). This is one important step in the process of therapy, leading ultimately to further insight and the "making of the unconscious conscious."*

The importance of fantasies in mental life cannot be overestimated. In this study we have attempted to bring out something of the confusion that attends the use of the terms "fantasy" and "unconscious fantasy," and to offer a number of thoughts, based on Freud's work, that may lead to a clarification of the scientific and semantic problems involved. Although we have emphasized the distinction between the ego function of fantasying and other ego functions, and between fantasy content and other ideational content, we have hesitated to introduce any new terms, but there can be little

---

*Psychoanalytic therapy, particularly with children, can be understood in terms of the changes that occur in derivatives, and the substitution of new derivatives for old ones. A study based on this approach is in progress.

doubt that the "blanket" terms need to be supplemented in some way so that the different concepts subsumed under the terms can be more clearly differentiated.

The present project was begun to solve the practical problem of classifying "fantasies" in the Hampstead Index. As a consequence of the consideration expressed in this chapter, we have begun to devise a classification that is based on the differentiation of the various types of derivative, as well as on the dynamic meaning of the derivative content. From the point of view of the derivatives, fantasy is only one of many such derivatives, although repressed fantasies may dominate the content of derivatives other than fantasy. This classification shows a great deal of promise, for there is an indication that the delineation of the various derivatives will throw light on the differences in instinctual and ego development in different children. The door appears to be open for an investigation, through child analysis and observation, of the natural history of derivatives, and this may in turn lead to greater diagnostic and therapeutic precision.

8

Sexual Fantasies and Sexual Theories

Joseph Sandler

The paper from which this chapter has been derived was published in 1970, following its presentation on the occasion of the 20th anniversary of the founding of the Hampstead Clinic. It can be considered to be an extension of the work on the metapsychology of fantasy reported in Chapter 7. The first part of the original paper contained a detailed summary of that work (see Sandler, 1970). For obvious reasons it is unnecessary to reproduce that summary here, except to say that at the point at which it was pointed out that unconscious fantasies could be regarded as possessing *psychic reality* in contrast to *material reality*, the following footnote was added.

> This raises a problem of definition, because we may legitimately ask whether the loss of the knowledge of "unreality" attached to unconscious thoughts still enables us to call some of these thoughts fantasies. It would appear that unconscious fantasies, to the degree to which they possess psychic reality, might perhaps more appropriately be regarded as "unconscious delusions," although this in turn raises further problems of definition and other complications.

The question of the degree of psychic reality possessed by unconscious fantasies, especially those fantasies close to consciousness, is still unanswered. This problem is closely connected with the question of whether the unconscious fantasy can have an entirely wish-fulfilling function like the conscious daydream, or whether there has always to be an element of the unsatisfied wish contained in it.

Although we had satisfied ourselves in the Index that many of the problems surrounding the use of the term "fantasy" were related to the multiple meanings of the term, the problem of distinguishing between fantasies and theories, in particular between sexual fantasies and sexual theories, remains. In general usage, as well as in the psychoanalytic literature, the term "unconscious fantasy" is often used as a synonym for an "unconscious sexual theory," and the question arises whether it is possible and useful to distinguish between the two. Certainly, there are no clear-cut critera for distinguishing, in the material recorded in the Index, between what is a sexual fantasy and what is a sexual theory. Consider, for example, the following material derived from the analysis of a child of about 5 years of age at the time of indexing. The therapist treating the child recorded:

> Jenny quite evidently fantasied that she could achieve a fat tummy; that is, that she could become pregnant by dint of oral incorporation of food and water; and to this end she spent an inordinate amount of time compulsively consuming vast quantities of water which was often "poisonous filthy stuff" for adults, while the therapist as the baby was permitted strawberry-flavoured medicine. Water play would sometimes start as bathing the doll or cooking, but would quickly and effortlessly slide over to persistent and copious drinking during which Jenny appeared to exclude the therapist and barely to relate to her. . . .
> During this session the child drank water poured from a toy lavatory and told the therapist she was drinking wee-wee. When later mother told the therapist that Jenny had made a comment at home that earthworms eat their own wee-wee, it seemed that an important element of her fantasy was that impregnation could. occur through the drinking of urine.

We may ask: is this a fantasy or is it a theory? If it is a theory in a child of 5, what is its status if it appears in the material of an adult? It is then a fantasy?

We have seen that a conscious daydream fantasy can be regarded as a wish-fulfilling construct of the imagination that is known by the subject not to be real. It has a certain "stamp of unreality" attached to it. But this certainly does not apply to all the thoughts that the child may have, and children have many thoughts other than fantasies. The child may come to conclusions about himself and his world, which, when looked at with adult eyes, appear to be fantasies, but have the "stamp of reality" attached to them for the child.

Freud was quite clear on the point that the fantasy is a form of thinking, and it would seem that we have a continuum between reality-appropriate thoughts on the one hand, and purely imaginative constructions, known not to be real, on the other. Of course, a great many of the thoughts of the child occupy an intermediate position between the two ends of the continuum.

In line with the discussion in Chapter 7, it would appear that conscious, reality-oriented thoughts, if subsequently repressed, can later emerge in a distorted form, in one or other derivative of the Unconscious. We also know that it is highly likely that, just as we can have preconscious wish-fulfilling fantasying, so can we have preconscious reality-oriented thinking. Or, in structural terms, we can say that these processes occur in the unconscious ego.

If we return to the question of a distinction between fantasies and theories, a useful starting-off point might be the distinction that can be made in the adult between a theory and a daydream fantasy. The conscious fantasy has the hallmark of unreality, and is an imaginative production. The theory, on the other hand, is a belief about the real world that the child has created, upon which he acts, and that structures his further thinking, fantasying, and behavior. Of course, the theory may be developed on the basis of imaginative constructions, and be considered to be a derivative of instinctual wishes, but nevertheless it develops *as an explanation of reality* in contrast to the fantasy that is known to be a daydream. By starting at the conscious end, as it were, we can suggest a possible distinction between theories and fantasies. Fantasies would represent wish-fulfilling constructs of the imagination, but theories, although they may contain fantasy wish-fulfilling elements, will remain as assumptions and explanations about various aspects of the world, unless they are contradicted by reality testing. If they are contradicted, we would postulate that they do not disappear, but rather are put "out of use." In some way they can be considered to remain latent, but they can also remain operative in the construction of thoughts, ideas, and fantasies in the deeper layers of the ego (see the notion of "persistence of structures" put forward in Chapter 14). The *Oxford English Dictionary* considers a theory to be a "systematic conception or statement of principles." It is a conception or mental scheme of something to be done, or the method of doing it, and also a statement of the rules and principles involved. It would seem that theories can be considered to be mental *structures* belonging to the whole universe of perceptual, cognitive, and logical structures that are created in order to allow the child to interpret his experience of the universe in as reality-appropriate a way as possible. (That the use of such structures may be appropriate at one age, but inappropriate at another, is a separate question.) We know that careful perception will modify the child's theories,* but there is an interaction between theories and perception. What I am suggesting here is that the the-

---

*By the creation of further, superordinate structures, which generally also inhibit the use of the older ones.

ories represent an organized part of the whole set of thinking "structures" that enter into the child's conception of the way in which the world, including himself in that world, behaves, and that these structures affect not only his thinking but also memory and perception.

Before returning to the example with which this section began, it is appropriate to refer to Freud's paper (1908b) on the sexual theories of children. Freud refers to the point at which the child "comes to be occupied with the first, grand problem of life and asks himself the question: 'Where do babies come from?' " (p. 212). If the child is not too intimidated, he will ask his parents directly, but usually finds that this method fails. He is generally told something like "The stork brings the babies." Freud suggests that most children are dissatisfied with such an answer, but do not always openly admit their doubts. He goes on to speak of the "further researches" of the child, usually carried out under a "cloak of secrecy." The child develops "false theories which the state of his own sexuality imposes on him." The first of these theories, says Freud, starts out from the neglect of the differences between the sexes and consists "in *attributing to everyone, including females, the possession of a penis*, such as the boy knows from his own body" (p. 215). The boy's valuation of his penis falsifies his perception, but he comes to the conclusion that the girl's penis is too small, but when she gets bigger it will grow. Freud then speaks of the idea of a woman with a penis becoming "fixated" in certain individuals. Similar theories are constructed by little girls.

Freud also points out that the second of the sexual theories of the child is that which relates to birth. "If the baby grows in the mother's body and is then removed from it, this can only happen along the one possible pathway—the anal aperture. *The baby must be evacuated like a piece of excrement, like a stool.*" Later, further explanations are arrived at, for example, that the baby emerges from the naval, which opens up at birth. It follows that in both theories of birth it is *logical* that "the child should refuse to grant women the painful prerogative of giving birth to children" (p. 219).

The third theory referred to by Freud relates to the sadistic view of intercourse. However, it is sufficient at this point to emphasize that Freud spoke of children's sexual *theories*, that even though such theories might contain wish-fulfilling elements and be elaborated because of the pressure of particular drives, they are felt to be *real*, and that they are used, at first consciously, as explanations, assumptions, conclusions, and tenets that form the basis for the child's thinking about the subject matter involved. One can also add to Freud's description of the child's "researches" the important factor that *the logic of the young child differs enormously from that of the adult,* a subject that has been studied in detail by such cognitive psychologists as Piaget.

At this point it is worth making a further distinction that is relevant. In the first instance, a conscious daydream fantasy, or a conscious thought, is something *experienced* by the child. It is located in the experiential realm of the mental apparatus (Chapter 18). However, the conclusions arrived at by the child, whether influenced by instinctual wish elements or not, soon become "structuralized" in the nonexperiential realm. *What was originally a thought becomes an organized and automatic premise.* We can see this in ordinary everyday thinking about ordinary everyday things. The theory no longer enters into the *content* of the thought or fantasy, but becomes an assumption, of varying complexity, involved in the creation, in conscious or unconscious experience, of further thoughts and fantasies. The structuralized theory may be used at a later date to produce unconscious thought or fantasy content in the experiential realm, although such content may not be acceptable to consciousness or allowed by the ego to proceed toward conscious experience. Nevertheless, the theory remains, as all infantile theories remain, but the products of the unconscious ego (which makes use of these theories) are either rejected or distorted and disguised before being permitted to progress toward consciousness.

In the example quoted earlier, Jenny quite clearly had the theory that having a fat tummy was equivalent to pregnancy and that one becomes pregnant by oral incorporation of food and water. This theory colored her play, fantasies, and other derivatives, and we might expect that if she were to be in analysis as an adult, her productions would be similarly colored by her childhood theories, even though they might be much more heavily disguised.

In the construction of childhood theories, especially (but not exclusively) childhood sexual theories, we are dealing with perfectly reasonable conclusions reached by the child, using the facts at his disposal. We should take into account the fact that what is "reasonable" for a young child is not necessarily "reasonable" for an adult. The child who believes that babies are born through the anus is thinking rationally for a child of, say, 3 years of age, because he has had the experience that what appears to be a part of his body (his feces) can be separated from the body through defecation. Similarly, the child who believes in oral conception may have perfectly valid grounds at the time for believing in the reality of his theory. He may have been told that eating too much food makes one fat, that one should not eat the seeds of certain fruits (e.g., grapes) because the pips might stick in his tummy. He might also have been told that babies come from seeds, and that plants grow from seeds. He observes that when someone is to have a baby they grow fat, and so on. There are many reasons why the child may reach such conclusions. They may be perfectly reasonable at his age, but if produced as theories by an older child (or by an adult) would be dismissed by himself and others as being "unreasonable." And yet in the productions of older children and of adults, one sees the persistence of these earlier theories, in particular the earlier sexual theories. While a young child may consciously mention the thoughts arising on the basis of such beliefs, later such thoughts become unconscious or denied when the child knows them to be "silly," that is, when they are subjected to reality testing, they are rejected, but nevertheless persist (see Chapter 14).

Implicit in this is the assumption that primitive secondary-process functioning persists throughout life, although the products of such functioning can be dismissed before they reach consciousness. However, the thoughts may reappear in disguised form. It is very striking that in psychoanalytic thinking, we tend to contrast primary-process with secondary-process functioning, but do not usually consider the contrast between one level of secondary-process thinking and another.

I submit that the distinction between theories and fantasies is of clinical relevance. Indeed, we probably do make such a distinction, albeit implicitly, when we refer to unconscious fantasies. One type is the "here-and-now" fantasy: for example, a transference fantasy that may vary from one day to another. The second type, which we also tend to call "unconscious fantasies," comprises the persisting and enduring constructions that appear over and over again in the form of themes in the patient's material. The latter may well represent childhood theories that are still being invoked in the thinking that occurs in the unconscious ego. They include such theories as "all women have a penis; all fathers are castrating; anything aggressive is dangerous."

Although what has been put forward in this short account has been concerned with the well-known sexual theories of childhood, the conclusions must apply equally to all the other theories created by the developing child. The sexual theories of the child play (and have always played) an important part in psychoanalysis, but theories involving aggression, object relationships, noninstinctual factors, and the like are equally important, both in child development and in the psychoanalytic reconstruction of that development.

9

Trauma, Strain, and Development

Joseph Sandler

In 1964 the Psychoanalytic Research and Development Fund organized a small week-end meeting in New York on the topic of "psychic trauma." The discussants included Anna Freud, Sidney Furst, Phyllis Greenacre, Marianne Kris, Peter B. Neubauer, Leo Rangell, Albert J. Solnit, Robert Waelder, and myself. What follows is my contribution to the discussion, published in 1967 in *Psychic Trauma*, edited by Sidney Furst.

The work reported in this chapter shows that the occurrence of a "trauma," in any one of the variety of senses in which the term is used in clinical work, need not have a pathogenic effect. Moreover, there is a difference between the way in which the trauma concept is used clinically and the way in which it has usually been defined in psychoanalytic writings. As a consequence of the examination of indexed material, it has been possible to argue that the crucial factor in determining whether or not pathology will develop is the state of strain that may exist after a traumatic experience ("trauma" being defined in the usual metapsychological sense). This state of strain may also occur in the absence of a trauma.

The argument put forward here is relevant to the other work reported in this book in that it places emphasis on the subjective state of strain as the central factor in determining whether or not pathological development will ensue.

I

The concept of "trauma" is one that has been considered in some detail in the Index research groups, and the ideas put forward in this chapter represent in part the outcome of discussions that took place. The problem of classifying experiences or events as "traumatic" was taken up with reference to our clinical material on the one hand and the theoretical formulations of Freud and subsequent psychoanalytic writers on the other. Beginning with Freud's concept of trauma as expressed in *Inhibitions, Symptoms and Anxiety* (Freud, 1926), we embarked on the exercise of examining, in the large number of cases recorded in the Index, the relationship between the meta-psychological definition of trauma and the clinical usage of the term. Our procedure was to attempt to pinpoint those critical experiences in the lives of the child patients that could be labeled as "traumatic" in the broad sense of the term, and to assess them against the more precise theoretical definition. The results of this comparison are given in section II of this chapter, and it will be seen that a number of problems arise in relation to the integration of the metapsychological and clinical meanings of the term. This discrepancy, in a certain way inevitable, has a number of theoretical and clinical implications. Some of these will be considered later, with special reference to the assessment of childhood development.

II

Whatever changes may have occurred in the importance that Freud attributed to the role of the trauma in pathogenesis, his concept of trauma remained more or less unchanged over the long period of time covered by his writings. Thus in his "Preface and Footnotes to the Translation of Charcot's *Tuesday Lectures*" (1892–94), he says: "A trauma would have to be defined as an *accretion of excitation* in the nervous system, *which the latter has been unable to dispose of adequately by motor reaction*" (p. 137).*

In his *Introductory Lectures* (1916–17), he writes: "Indeed, the term 'traumatic' has no other sense than an economic one. We apply it to an experience which within a short period of time presents the mind with an increase of stimulus too powerful to be dealt with or worked off in the normal way, and this must result in permanent disturbances of the manner in which the energy operates" (p. 275).

In the *New Introductory Lectures* (1933), he reaffirms this view: "In all this it is a question of relative quantities. It is only the magnitude of the sum of excitation that turns an impression into a traumatic moment, paralyses the function of the pleasure principle and gives the situation of danger its significance" (p. 94).

It is clear that the economic view of trauma was consistently maintained by Freud. He saw it, as Strachey puts it in the editor's introduction to *Inhibitions, Symptoms and Anxiety* (Freud, 1926), as essentially "an experience of helplessness on the part of the ego in

*It is of some interest that in a manuscript sent to Breuer (Freud, 1892), he goes rather further than this. He suggests that "any impression which the nervous system has difficulty in disposing of by means of *associative thinking* or of motor reaction becomes a psychical trauma" (p. 154). (This formulation is placed in relation to the theory of constancy.)

the face of an accumulation of excitation, whether of external or of internal origin, which cannot be dealt with" (p. 81).

With this definition of trauma in mind we were able to draw a number of conclusions from the material of our indexed cases at Hampstead.

1. In a relatively small number of cases, sudden violent environmental disruption involving a high degree of shock, disorientation, and physical as well as psychological helplessness has been seen to have a profound effect on the child, and the subsequent development of the child's symptoms has an intimate relation to the undoubted traumatic experience. But even in these cases, we do not see a picture of a pure traumatic neurosis, but rather elements in the disturbance that can be traced to the operation of the trauma, in line with Freud's description of the "aetiological equation" (1895) and the "complemental series" (1916–17). We shall return to this topic later when we consider the trauma from the point of view of the concept of developmental disturbance.

2. We could confidently reaffirm Freud's view that we cannot assess a trauma in terms of the external situation alone, but that we have to consider in every case the internal situation of the child and the external situation *as experienced* by him. Thus a radical environmental upset may be in no way traumatic, and, at the opposite extreme, a trauma may be experienced in an external situation that appears to the observer to be perfectly ordinary, and indeed may even be one that the child has mastered in a satisfactory manner on previous occasions. (This frequently occurs, for instance, when the child is ill.)

It is probable that historical material provided by observers in the child's environment (e.g., the parents) inevitably colors the assessment of the nature and degree of traumatization that has taken place. When reconstruction of the child's psychopathology is based on analytic data, this tendency operates to a lesser degree, although other distorting factors may come into play.

3. It is apparent that the general clinical usage of the term "traumatic" is not always restricted to experiences that conform to Freud's definition of a trauma. Events may occur that have a definite influence on the child but do not necessarily at the time involve the passive experiencing of a state of helplessness. Yet because of the manifest association between the external event and the psychological change in the child, the event (or series of events) may be called traumatic, particularly if the change in the child is retrogressive rather than progressive. We believe this to be the most important area of misapplication of the concept of trauma.

4. In agreement with the findings of other investigators, we have found that an extended series of experiences, none of which may in

itself be traumatic, may combine to produce a traumatic effect. This was recognized by Breuer and Freud in *Studies on Hysteria*. Speaking of hysterical symptoms, they say: "It not infrequently happens that, instead of a single, major trauma, we find a number of partial traumas forming a *group* of provoking causes. These have only been able to exercise a traumatic effect by summation and they belong together insofar as they are in part components of a single story of suffering" (p. 6). Breuer and Freud go on to say: "There are other cases in which an apparently trivial circumstance combines with the actually operative event or occurs at a time of peculiar susceptibility to stimulation and in this way attains the dignity of a trauma which it would not otherwise have possessed but which thenceforward persists." (Breuer & Freud, 1893–95).

Freud, in writing on the case history of Fraulein Elisabeth von R. (1893–95), makes these comments on the groupings of traumas:

> Almost invariably when I have investigated the determinants of such conditions [hysterical symptoms] what I have come upon has not been a *single* traumatic cause but a group of similar ones. . . . In some of these instances it could be established that the symptom in question had already appeared for a short time after the first trauma and had then passed off, till it was brought on again and stabilized by a succeeding trauma. There is, however, in principle no difference between the symptom appearing in this temporary way after its first provoking cause and its being latent from the first. Indeed, in the great majority of instances we find that a first trauma has left no symptom behind, while a later trauma of the same kind produces a symptom, and yet that the latter could not have come into existence without the co-operation of the earlier provoking cause; nor can it be cleared up without taking all the provoking causes into account (p. 173).

Again, in "The Psychotherapy of Hysteria" (Breuer & Freud, 1893–95), Freud writes:

> We do not usually find a *single* hysterical symptom, but a number of them, partly independent of one another and partly linked together. We must not expect to meet with a *single* traumatic memory and a *single* pathogenic idea as its nucleus; we must be prepared for *sucessions* of *partial* traumas and *concatenations* of pathogenic trains of thought. A monosymptomatic traumatic hysteria is, as it were, an elementary organism, a unicellular creature, as compared with the complicated structure of such comparatively severe neuroses as we usually meet with (pp. 287–288).

It seems that Freud's use of the idea of *partial trauma* represents an early recognition of the fact that the accumulation of experiences that in themselves do not necessarily conform to the metapsychological definition of trauma may, in the summation, bring about an effect that is identical with what might have occurred as a result of a single traumatic episode.

5. In relation to this, Ernst Kris (1956) has drawn attention to the fact (amply confirmed by our cases in the Index) that in reconstructive work in analysis,

> we are not always, and only rarely with the desirable sharpness, able to distinguish between the effects of two kinds of traumatic situations; between the effects of a single experience, when reality powerfully and often suddenly impinges on the child's life—the shock trauma . . . —and the effect of long-lasting situations, which may cause traumatic effects by the accumulation of frustrating tensions—the strain trauma . . . (pp. 72–73).*

Kris goes on to describe the problem succinctly when he refers to a comment of Anna Freud (1951b) to the effect that the adult analytic patient may report as a single event an experience that may have been repeated many times in childhood. He then says,

> On the other hand, the single dramatic shock . . . appears usually not with sharp outline; the experience is overlaid with its aftermath, the guilt, terror and thrill elaborated in phantasies. . . . The problem is further complicated by the fact that the further course of life seems to determine which experience may gain significance as a traumatic one (p. 73).†

It is our experience that all these considerations apply to the reconstructive work in child analysis as much as to work with adults.

6. In a number of cases, we observed the occurrence of an apparently traumatic experience, followed by regression, but where the really disturbing experience for the child was the experience of the regression itself. This appeared to be particularly so where the regressive move involved the loss of control of excretory functions; the attendant guilt or shame appeared to have a more profound effect on the child than the original situation from which he had retreated (Schur, 1953).

7. It was further evident that in a substantial proportion of our cases the content of a traumatic episode of a particular sort (e.g., a seduction), while appearing on the surface to be something that

---

*Khan (1963) has dealt with this topic again from the point of view of his concept of "cumulative trauma."

†Following Anna Freud's and Kris's line of thought, it might be possible to speak in this connection of *screen traumas*—that is, memories of experiences that appear to have been of crucial traumatic significance in the life of the individual but that cover earlier and, from a psychopathological point of view, more significant traumatic experiences. The maintenance of a "screen trauma" may often have a defensive function, particularly where it involves the "shifting of guilt" (Sandler *et al*, 1962) for forbidden sexual or aggressive impulses.

accidentally "happened" to the child, was related in a highly specific way to the content of the child's fantasies immediately prior to the occurrence of the trauma. It would seem that children (and we know this to be true for adults) are able to exert a considerable degree of "choice" in their traumatic experiences; unconscious manipulation and provocation of external circumstances may enter into bringing the "trauma" about. This possibility was discussed by Abraham as early as 1907 in "The Experiencing of Sexual Traumas as a Form of Sexual Activity," and was later discussed by Frankl (1963) in relation to accident proneness.

8. Arising from the above point is the fact, also noted by Abraham (1907), that children who bring about or acquiesce in traumas repress the traumatic experiences and the associated sexual impulses because of the guilt associated with the breakthrough of their unconscious sexual wishes into reality. Such repression of experiences due to guilt is a common feature in the histories of our child patients, but what is important about this is that the motive for the repression stems not from the traumatic experience itself but from the fear of punishment reflected in internal feelings of guilt; and to feelings of guilt we may add the equally powerful feelings of shame or humiliation.

9. If we follow the metapsychological definition rather than the common clinical usages of the concept of trauma, it is almost axiomatic that every child experiences traumatic situations of one sort or another throughout development. We are thus faced with the problem of defining the criteria that distinguish those traumas that are "significant" for the child from those that are not. Furthermore, traumas may be significant either from the point of view of normal development or of pathogenesis. Every toddler, for example, will regularly experience states in which he is overwhelmed by excitation, and temporarily by helplessness. It is perhaps in the anal phase of development, when the ever-mobile and active child can elude the eye of even the most watchful mother, that such states of being overwhelmed can be witnessed most readily. But even before the appearance of such overt manifestations, the infant regularly experiences states of psychological helplessness. As Hoffer (1952) points out: "Such states are more characteristic for the undifferentiated state of the id–ego relationship than for any later stage of ego development. They may occur without the noisy concomitants of the traumatic event of birth or of later traumas suffered by the active child; they may be 'silent traumas' " (p. 38).*

---

*Greenacre (1952) has brought to our attention the importance of such early states, which may occur from a variety of causes, in determining the later predisposition to anxiety and the related vicissitudes of infantile narcissism.

Clearly it is not the experience of helplessness as such that is the important factor in normal or pathological development, but rather the *posttraumatic* condition of the child. The crucial question to be asked, it seems, is: Has the traumatic experience brought about a significant or observable effect on the child? And, indeed, we only consider traumas to be of importance in our analytic work if they have resulted in a significant change in, or impediment to, development in the child, or if it is thought they may do so in the future.

It could be argued at this point that it would be perfectly in accordance with Freud's views to restrict the notion of trauma to those instances in which the experience of being passively overwhelmed is not recovered from successfully. This may in fact have been in Freud's mind when he spoke of "an increase of stimulus too powerful to be dealt with or worked off in the normal way, and [that results] in permanent disturbances of the manner in which the energy operates" (1916–1917, p. 275).

We may, however, be stretching Freud's definition of trauma too far if we make our criterion for judging the occurrence of a trauma the ultimate outcome of the experience. The difficulties that result from this point of view are reinforced by our increasing recognition of the importance of *temporary regression* in normal development. We know that situations regularly occur in which the child experiences too great a demand on his ego—in which he is in fact overwhelmed by excitation of external or internal origin that he cannot discharge—and responds to this situation by partial or complete regression (Winnicott, 1958b). Do we have to wait for the outcome of such a perfectly normal regression, which may even produce transient symptoms, before labeling the experience that prompted it as traumatic?

10. The traumatic experience of being overwhelmed and helpless leads, under certain conditions, to the development of a danger situation, which may place a burden on the child's ego in that he is required to expend an increased amount of energy in the defensive process or restrict his ego in such a way as to avoid the danger. However, we have seen experiences occur that quality for admission as trauma in the strict sense of the definition but that are followed by a forward move, a progressive adaptation, and even an enrichment of the ego. Indeed, there is much to be said for the view that the process of ego development is normally stimulated by the regular occurrence of experiences that are, in the sense of Freud's definition, traumatic. They involve a temporary failure of mastery that may be an immediate impetus to progressive adaptation.

In many cases, the child's disturbance seemed to be intimately related to the occurrence of a specific trauma arising from a sudden change in the external environment. However, the child appeared

to cope with the traumatic situation in an active way, to master the
influx of excitation in an appropriate and adaptive fashion, but subsequently there was every indication that a new and intense danger
situation had in fact developed.

This observation is in line with the experiences of those who
have been concerned with the traumatic neuroses of wartime. Brenner (1953), in reviewing work on war neuroses in relation to Freud's
theory of anxiety, points out that none of the main writers on this
topic laid emphasis on an unmasterable influx of stimuli as a pathogenic factor. Brenner points out that, on the contrary, the literature
tends to support Freud's doubt as to whether objective danger could
on its own give rise to a neurosis.

11. A careful examination of those cases of neurotic disturbance
in children in which the traumatic factors were thought to play a
part in the genesis of the disturbance suggests that the operation of
the anxiety signal that *initiates* defensive measures on the part of the
ego can produce an effect on the child that may be indistinguishable
from the ego's response to a traumatic experience proper. The perception of a *danger situation*—that is, a situation that on the basis of
memory carries with it the *threat* of a traumatic overwhelming of the
ego—can function as if it were a traumatic experience in itself. This
usually happens in cases in which the child has elaborated a conscious or preconscious wish-fulfilling fantasy as an acceptable derivative of a dangerous wish. The fantasy is permitted as long as it has
what might be called the "hallmark of unreality." A perception by
the child that reality threatens to approximate the fantasy may cause
the fantasy content to be repressed or other defensive measures to
be initiated. Freud described this in his "Fragment of an Analysis of
a Case of Hysteria" (1905b) as follows: "Neurotics are dominated by
the opposition between reality and phantasy. If what they long for
the most intensely in their phantasies is presented to them in reality,
they none the less flee from it; and they abandon themselves to their
phantasies the most readily where they need no longer fear to see
them realised" (p. 110).

In the present context, I wish to emphasise the difficulty of
distinguishing in certain circumstances between the occurrence of a
traumatic situation in the strict sense of Freud's definition and the
occurrence of an anxiety signal that brings about defensive activity;*

*Weiss (1950) remarks: "In fact many traumatic experiences do not contain strong
sensory components at all, but consist only of the perception or the comprehension
of conditions which cannot be controlled and endured." Implicit in this comment is
an extension of Freud's definition of trauma to include the case in which the anxiety
signal associated with a *threat* produces a traumatic effect.

and the anxiety signal may arise equally from the perception of internal dangers as from external ones.

12. The indexed material of a number of cases suggests that what we have provisionally called a retrospective trauma has occurred. By this we mean that the perception of some particular situation evokes the *memory* of an earlier experience that under the present conditions becomes traumatic. A typical example of this is the traumatic reactivation of a primal-scene memory during the phallic–oedipal phase. The perception of the primal scene need not in itself have been traumatic, and it may have remained as a memory until a new link between it and the late sexual fantasies of the child occurs. The ego's sudden perception of such a link between present fantasy and the past memory may be a traumatic experience. Here the memory functions as a present perception.

The operation of retrospective trauma must present a further hazard to the accurate reconstruction of the child's infantile experiences by the analyst, for early memory can become a central component of unconscious strivings, although the actual perception that led to the memory did not create a danger situation at the time.

It is perhaps of some interest that the concept of retrospective trauma may be applicable in Freud's account of the pathology of the "Wolf Man" (1918). It was established that the boy's observation of the primal scene could have occurred at the age of 1½ years. Now although Freud assumed that the primal scene had an effect on the child's sexual life from the time of its perception, he explicitly states that "he understood it at the time of the dream when he was four years old, not at the time of observation." In referring to the sense of reality left behind by the Wolf Man's dream, Freud commented that "some part of the latent material of the dream is claiming in the dreamer's memory to possess the quality of reality, that is, that the dream relates to an occurrence that really took place and was not merely imagined" (p. 33). Although later in this paper, Freud discusses the possibility of the primal scene being a fantasy, the likelihood still remains of it being a fantasy elaboration of some real, but not necessarily traumatic, experience.

In the final section of the paper, Freud comments:

> It was at this point [the boy's 4th birthday] that the dream brought into deferred operation his observation of intercourse at the age of one and a half. . . . The activation of the picture, which, thanks to the advance in his intellectual development, he was now able to understand, operated not only like a fresh event, but like a new trauma, like an interference from outside analogous to the seduction (p. 109).

The importance of what we have called "restrospective trauma" is stressed by Freud some 20 years after the "Wolf Man" paper, in *Moses and Monotheism* (1939), in which he writes:

> It may, however, be less well known that the strongest compelling influence arises from impressions which impinge upon a child at a time when we would have to regard his psychical apparatus as not yet completely receptive. The fact itself cannot be doubted; but it is so puzzling that we may make it more comprehensible by comparing it with a photographic exposure which can be developed after any interval of time and transformed into a picture (p. 126).

III

The considerations listed in section II of this chapter point to the difficulties inherent in the clinical application of the concept of trauma. There are, of course, those cases that clearly exemplify a pathogenic effect of traumatic factors and in whose behavior the elements of a traumatic neurosis are clearly discernible. Such cases reveal—in their symptoms and in their analytic material—clear-cut indications of some overwhelming experience in reality that resulted in shock and disorganization of the ego at the time of its occurrence, and the bulk of the material that the patients bring to analysis leads in one way or another back to the traumatic episode. The memory of it has remained as a dangerous unassimilated drive-cathected experience that can only be dealt with by massive repression, or, if this fails, by attempts at mastery through repetition.

In contrast, we have all those cases of childhood disturbance in which complications and doubts arise in the clinical application of the concept. As we move away from the children in whom elements of the traumatic neurosis can be seen, so the notion of trauma becomes less clear in its application, and we are finally left with a clinical concept that is descriptive, top heavy, and imprecise. We come into territory where we are forced to speak of partial trauma, of strain traumas and cumulative traumas, of screen and retrospective traumas, of traumas fantasied and traumas provoked. We have to deal with the problem of differentiating unpleasant experiences in general from traumas in particular, and of differentiating response to the threat of trauma from reactions to the trauma itself; and we must distinguish between traumas reactivated and those experienced anew.

There are certain typical events or experiences that we usually refer to as "traumatic" in our analytic work. These include the death of a parent (or other love object) and experiences of hospitalisation that involve separation from the parents. We know that such painful events may leave their imprint on the child and that their influence is often discernible in the material that the child brings to analysis. These events may be truly traumatic in that they overwhelm the ego in their immediate impact, generating a state of psychic shock in the face of overwhelming excitation; or, where the ego is poorly developed and vulnerable, the accumulation of undischarged drive cathexes may swamp and overwhelm the weak ego. Yet it is our impression that in the vast majority of cases of the death of a parent, for example, a trauma in the strict sense of the definition does not occur.*

This holds true even if the child is in a phase of intense conflict due to his ambivalence towards the lost object, in which the event appears to him to be a fulfillment of hostile wishes of his own and, in consequence, has the implication for him that he is the agent that brought it about.

What we commonly see is a series of adaptive responses of the ego, responses that change as the reality of the situation is brought home to the child and his needs and conflicts intensify. Changes in the quality of the child's strivings due to drive regression operate at this point. We see the generation of a variety of accumulating tensions and affective states that gradually build up to what we can call, enlarging on Kris (1956), an increasing state of ego strain. Such strain can only be tolerated up to a certain point, and if the ego cannot adapt to it in time, so as to preserve its homeostatic equilibrium, a true *strain trauma* may result; the ego is disorganized, flooded, and overwhelmed. In the cases we are considering, however, the ego undertakes a series of maneuvers in order to accommodate itself in the state of strain, maneuvers that may be radical in nature and that may result in gross alterations in behavior or lead to the development of symptoms. Whether, in fact, the child can recover from this reaction, can reinstate himself on the path he was previously pursuing, will depend on a multitude of factors.

*It has been argued that a child who shows no immediate reaction to such an experience may indeed have experienced a trauma, but is using the mechanism of denial to temporarily cope with the traumatic experience. To my mind this argument is invalid, for if the child's denial *successfully* prevents his being overwhelmed, then by definition a trauma would not have occurred. However, it could (but need not) occur *at a later date* if the *memory* of the event results in the child's being overwhelmed with feelings with which he is unable to cope. Indeed, it may only be many years later (in the course of an analysis, for example) that the recall of the event may become traumatic in the strict sense of the definition. We could speak here of *traumatic recall* rather than the re-experiencing of trauma, in line with our comments on "retrospective trauma." Traumatic recall during analysis can, by virtue of the advantages offered by the analytic situation, result in an adaptive absorption of the repressed by the ego.

The child's response to a state of strain represents the development of a new organization that is progressively created in order to preserve the ego's feeling of safety (see Chapter 1) and *to avoid the experience of being traumatically overwhelmed*. The state of strain has anxiety as an essential component, anxiety that acts as a warning to the ego to take appropriate adaptive measures.

States of ego strain need not occur only in response to significant external events; they may be generated, for instance, by internal or internalized conflict alone, and the ego adjustment to states of strain not induced by environmental frustration may be as profound and as significant for the child as those that arise as a response to external events.

There is strong evidence that many children recover from truly traumatic experiences with little or no residual damage to their personalities. The degree of environmental support that the child receives is important here. What would seem to be crucial in deciding the outcome of a traumatic experience is not so much the traumatic experience itself as *the posttraumatic state of ego strain that it engenders and the child's adaptation to that state*, although there may be a specific correlation between the occurrence of a trauma and the ego's attempt to use massive repression to deal with the anxiety connected with the danger situation that has arisen as a consequence of the traumatic experience.

It should be emphasized that the drive regression that can occur as a response to the trauma or the state of strain (or both), and the anxieties that arise from it, may be important contributory factors in causing an increase in the level of strain.

There is a shift of emphasis implied in all this; from the point of view of pathogenesis, the traumatic experience as such becomes secondary to the state of strain and the ego's adaptation to it. This view is entirely in accord with the approach taken at the Hampstead Clinic to the assessment of the psychological disturbances of childhood. The assumption that underlies the whole of our work is that these disturbances are most appropriately assessed from the standpoint of the multitude of factors that influence and mould the ongoing development of the child. States of psychological health and normality in the child are considered to be states of normal ongoing development; and in assessing normality in this connection, we take into account the fact that states of strain regularly occur and that the child may show temporary regressions and transient symptoms as part of the flux of normal development. This viewpoint was put forward by Anna Freud in 1946 and more recently elaborated in her papers "Assessment of Childhood Disturbances" (1962) and "Regression as a Principle in Mental Development" (1963a). As Anna Freud put it, "neither symptomatology nor life tasks can be taken as reliable guides to the assessment of mental health or illness in children [and] we are left with the alternative idea that the capacity to develop progressively, or respectively the damage to that capacity, are the most significant factors in determining the child's mental future" (1962, p. 150). On the basis of this approach, Anna Freud put forward the idea of a developmental profile, an instrument that aims at providing a framework for the analyst's assessment of the case in metapsychological terms. Such an assessment leads to the placing of the child in one or other of the categories of developmental diagnosis that follow.*

1. The personality growth of the child is essentially healthy with the current behavior disturbances remaining within the wide range of "variations of normality."

2. The existent pathological formations (symptoms, etc.) are essentially transitory in nature and represent by-products of developmental strain.

3. There are on the side of the drives important fixation points and/or massive regressions to them that have an impoverishing effect on drive progression through involving the ego in conflict, initiating character disorders, or symptomatology of a neurotic nature.

4. For a variety of reasons, fixation and regression of drives is paralleled or accompanied by arrests and regressions of ego and superego development with crippling effects on personality growth and symptom formation of a borderline, delinquent, or psychotic nature.

5. There are primary organic deficiencies or earliest deprivations that distort development and structuralization and produce defective, retarded, and nontypical personalities.

6. There are destructive processes at work (of organic, toxic, or psychological, known or unknown origin) that have effected or are on the point of effecting a disruption of mental growth.

It is a *sine qua non* of the developmental approach that the child experiences recurring states of strain that have to be dealt with and mastered in one way or another. The child's total adaptation to each of these states affects the course of his later development.

IV

In this section, an outline will be given of the various factors that can contribute to the development of a state of strain and its final outcome.

---

*These are taken from the version of the profile in use at present at the Hampstead Clinic. The profile itself does not contain a "trauma" section, but section IV is entitled "Possibly Significant Environmental Experiences."

In general, we can depict the process schematically, as shown in Figure 9.1.

Among the external factors that operate to produce states of strain (whether preceded by trauma or not), we can mention the force of the external event or external frustration, its duration, and the swiftness of its occurrence. The internal factors that affect the development of strain are manifold. They include the predisposition to anxiety, the level of frustration tolerance (drive tolerance) and other ego thresholds, the preparedness of the ego for the perception of a specific external event, the sublimation potential of the child, the rigidity (inflexibility) and the range of defenses available and, linked with this, the amount of free cathexes available for binding. The level of self-esteem and its dependence on achievement and performance may be relevant.*

Apart from these factors, the degree of inner conflict (internal or internalized) is of the utmost significance. The drives in operation and the mental content cathected by them, as well as the degree of correspondence between the perception of external reality and the content of the child's memories, wishes, and fantasies, all play an important role. The extent to which phase dominance has been reached, the capacity for discharge, the backward pull of fixation points, the severity of the superego, and the child's relation to his objects and his introjects, are all factors that should be stressed. Finally, we can mention the influence of the ability to "turn passive into active," the

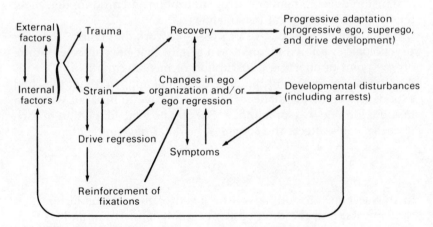

FIGURE 9.1 Factors that contribute to a state of strain and its consequences.

*It seems likely that both trauma and strain represent threats to self-esteem.

capacity for "working through," and, in general, the state of the progressive developmental forces as opposed to the regressive ones.

These factors are only a selection of those that determine the development of a state of strain and the child's response to it; many others, both general and specific, can be postulated.

10

Obsessional Manifestations in Children

Joseph Sandler and Walter G. Joffe

The study reported here was first presented at the International Psycho-Analytical Association Congress in 1965, and published in *The Psychoanalytic Study of the Child* in the same year (Sandler & Joffe, 1965a). On the basis of a clinical consideration of obsessional features in children, a number of theoretical conclusions are drawn, and it will be seen in later chapters that they converge with those made earlier. In particular, the concept of ego regression to functional fixation points is closely connected with the regulation of safety feeling, well-being, and function pleasure. Before the publication of this paper, ego regression was principally associated with organic brain lesions or with psychotic breakdown, but it could now be connected with neurotic disorders as well as with specific traits of character. Moreover, the consideration of perceptual and cognitive functions in this chapter links with the emphasis in previous and subsequent chapters on the role of perception in ego development.

This chapter can be regarded as introducing a train of thought that is further developed in Chapters 13, 14, and 16.

I

In surveying the psychoanalytic literature on the obsessive–compulsive disorders, one cannot fail to be impressed by the fact that there appears to be a continuing need to reexamine this topic. Yet, in spite of this, over the years little essential change has occurred in our views on obsessional phenomena. There is no doubt the Freud's ideas on the subject have stood the test of time and of clinical experience, and the fact that so many authors have arrived at formulations that are fundamentally identical with Freud's testifies to this; at the same time, their very need to explore and reexplore obsessional disturbances bears witness to a feeling that the subject is still far from being well understood.

In the present paper, we want to examine one or two facets of what is certainly a complicated subject, and we should like to begin by considering some of the manifestations of obsessive–compulsive disturbances as they occur in children. The study of cases referred for diagnosis to the Hampstead Child-Therapy Clinic, as well as those cases taken into analytic treatment, has made it clear to us that there are a number of different, but in some ways very similar, clinical pictures normally designated as obsessional, not all of which can be labeled "obsessional neurosis."

In considering these, we need to bear in mind the fact that the term "neurosis" must to some degree be qualified when it is applied to childhood disturbances. While it is true that, from a descriptive point of view, many of the symptom constellations that present themselves during the course of development resemble the more stable adult syndromes, they are not all necessarily carried on unchanged into adult life, and they often represent solutions that become modified during the course of development. The differences between adults and children in this respect have been discussed in some detail by Anna Freud (1965).

The true obsessional neurosis seen in children resembles its adult counterpart very closely. Its development follows what Anna Freud has called the "classical etiological formula" for neurosis in general:

> [There is] initial developmental progress to a comparatively high level of drive and ego development (i.e., for the child to the phallic-oedipal, for the adult to the genital level); an intolerable increase of anxiety or frustration on this position (for the child of castration anxiety within the oedipus complex); regression from the age-adequate drive position to pregenital fixation points; emergence of infantile pregenital sexual–aggressive impulses, wishes, and fantasies; anxiety and guilt with regard to these, mobilizing defensive reactions on the part of the ego under the influence of the superego; defense activity leading to compromise formations; resulting character disorders or neurotic symptoms which are determined in their details by the level of the fixation points to which regression has taken place, by the content of rejected impulses and fantasies, and by the choice of the particular defense mechanisms which are being used. (p. 150)

The obsessional neurosis is characterized by a drive regression to the anal–sadistic level, with heightened ambivalence. The drive impulses show the characteristic changes attributed to "drive defusion." On the side of the ego, we find an increase in magical thinking, with a heightened sexual and aggressive cathexis of thought. There is a prominent use of the defense mechanisms of displacement, reaction formation, isolation, and undoing, together with the excessive use of intellectualization and rationalization. Object relationships show regressive alterations, although residua of phallic–oedipal types of relationship may be discerned. Indeed, we hardly every see a complete and simple regression to the anal phase but rather see a regressive analization of oedipal relationships and conflicts, so that masturbation conflicts, for example, may be a dominant feature of the clinical picture.

The obsessional disturbance is marked by a tendency of the conflict to spread, with no stable compromise solution appearing as we see it in the classic hysterical symptom. There is a high degree of superego conflict, an the superego introjects show primitive features, with a reinforcement of their aggressive qualities. The form taken by the symptoms bears an intimate relationship to anal drive characteristics.

In a number of cases, an obsessional neurosis that develops in childhood continues into adult life, although there may be developmental fluctuations in the intensity of the disturbance. In other cases, obsessional neurotic symptoms may be transient, the regression to the anal–sadistic level being of a more temporary nature and representing a greater or lesser degree of developmental disturbance. These obsessional manifestations can occur both during childhood and adolescence, and range from an exaggeration of the type of normal ritual found in children's play, thoughts, fantasies, and general day-to-day activities, to gross symptoms that may, on the surface, appear to be indistinguishable from those of the more enduring obsessional neurosis.

A number of children show symptoms that resemble in form and content those of an obsessional neurosis, but that occur during the anal phase of development (Anna Freud, 1965). These are not, strictly speaking, neurotic in nature because they occur during the course of progressive development rather than as a consequence of regression. In these cases, the ego is relatively intact, and what we see are exaggerations of the normal modes of functioning characteristic of the anal phase. In other respects, development seems to be phase-adequate. The appearance of preoedipal obsessive–compulsive manifestations has been related to precocious ego development (Wulff, 1951), a factor which Freud (1909c, 1913a) considered to be of importance in creating the disposition to obsessional neurosis proper. We shall return to the question of precocious ego development later.

Obsessional manifestations in the borderline child often represent attempts on the part of the child's ego to deal with threats of annihilation or disintegration that are a consequence of the borderline pathology. The child's anxiety is not primarily derived from conflict, and the symptoms may take the form of what has been described as a "pseudo neurosis." They may constitute an attempt to achieve by magical means (by excessive controlling and ritualistic behavior) a degree of security and safety (Chapter 1).

Obsessive–compulsive symptoms have been seen to play the role of preventing or retarding personality disintegration in adult schizophrenics (Stengel, 1945). This has been confirmed in a comprehensive study by Ismond Rosen (1954), who examined the development of obsessional symptoms (occasionally going back to childhood) prior to the onset of a schizophrenic illness. Anna Freud (1965) also drew attention to the significance of obsessional manifestations in very young children as possible indicators of "splits and disharmonies within the structure, severe enough to lead later to a psychotic total disintegration of the personality" (p. 153).

We also see the development of behavior that resembles the compulsions and rituals of obsessional neurosis in a number of children who are neither borderline nor psychotic. Among these are children who have suffered severe traumatic experiences and who attempt to deal with the aftereffects of these by a form of "mastery through repetition" that may show itself in compulsive behavior. Obsessional manifestations can also be the outcome of the ego's struggle to control and to regulate phobic anxieties. Another group of children whose narcissism is constantly threatened (this includes many children with real deformities) resort to what appears to be obsessive–compulsive behavior in an attempt to regulate their self-esteem in a magical way.

In addition to all of these, obsessional character traits and symptoms occur in a wide variety of other contexts and associated with other clinical manifestations.

II

It is convenient to begin with a discussion of the nature of the regression that we know takes place in obsessional neurosis. Classically, this has been seen as a drive regression to the anal–sadistic phase, a regression that is facilitated by the existence of strong anal fixation points on the side of the libidinal and aggressive drives, and that occurs under the influence of intense oedipal conflict. Although much is known about fixation and regression when viewed from the side of the instinctual drives, the picture is not as clear when we come to examine the topic from the point of view of the changes that occur in the ego. These have for the most part been assumed to reflect drive regression, but it has been more or less taken for granted that it is not necessary to evoke the concept of ego regression to explain the phenomena that occur. This latter concept has on the whole been reserved for structural changes that occur in organic and psychotic pathologies.

In the development of the obsessional neurosis, as in all neuroses, we find a state of conflict in which the structure of the ego remains intact, the ideals held up by the superego introjects persist, and the defensive struggle is carried on against the drives and their derivatives at the drive-regressed level, with the resulting formation of neurotic symptoms. Changes in the severity of the superego are thought to be due more to economic changes consequent on the drive regression that to structural changes per se.

This view, correct as it is, does not help us a great deal to explain the ego changes that occur in obsessional neurosis. We know that different neurotic conditions are, to some extent, distinguished by differences in the defensive activities of the ego, defenses that appear in some way to have a special link with the fixation points on the side of the drives. Thus we assume that there is an association between drive regression to anal–sadistic fixation points on the one hand and such defense mechanisms as isolation, undoing, and reaction formation on the other; and that it is this association that results in typical obsessional symptoms. The changes that occur on the side of the drives and those that occur in the ego are by no means randomly related. Indeed, we would be extremely surprised to find, for instance, regression to predominantly passive–oral drive fixation points associated with the type of ego functioning and the defensive constellation that we find in obsessional neurosis. It is obvious that there is an intimate connection between the path of drive regression and the changes in function that we see on the side of the ego.

Although we can postulate a relationship of this sort between drives and ego, we know that a drive regression of exactly the same order as that which we see in obsessional neurosis need not necessarily lead to the development of obsessional symptoms. We can find, for example, the appearance of such symptoms as soiling in children. We also find nonobsessional anal–reactive characters as well as certain forms of homosexuality in adults. In the past, attempts have been made to explain these clinical differences on the basis of the relative strength of the sadistic components, the degree of instinctual defusion involved, and so on, but such notions seem to be rooted in a prestructural emphasis on drive transformation. Today the all-important role of the ego in determining the outcome of drive regression is obvious.

If we accept this statement, we are faced with the following problem: On the one hand, a change in the ego enters into determining the neurosis, and on the other hand, its structure remains essentially unaltered. This problem can be clarified to some extent by postulating a distinction between ego structure and ego function.* This distinction is related to one that we have made between structural and functional autonomy of the ego (Chapter 13). We now propose to make a further distinction between structural and functional regression of the ego, and to suggest that we see, in the obsessional neurosis, a disturbance that is the outcome not only of drive regression but also of functional regression of the ego. The latter shows itself in changes in the mode of ego functioning and in the evocation of specific defense mechanisms. The changes brought about by the functional regression of aspects of the ego may in turn secondarily interfere with other aspects of the ego.

We shall postulate a link between the evocation of specific defense mechanisms and functional regression of the ego, and this point deserves some amplification. Defenses in general can be taken to be special adaptations of normal ego functions, from which they do not essentially differ except in their application. For example, we can associate repression with the normal processes of clearing the perceptual field and separating present perception from memories of the past.† Denial is linked with a particular use of processes that are involved in normal concentration and attention. The defensive use of displacement can be seen to be a special application of a normal ego process that enters into such activities as symbol formation and sublimation; similar processes can be shown in all the mechanisms of defense.

It is likely that drive regression is always accompanied by some degree of functional regression in one or another area of the ego. When we come to examine the functional changes in the ego that accompany the development of obsessional disturbances, we shall see that they can be considered to be particular types of distortion or exaggeration of aspects of the ego's normal activities and functions; in particular those processes of control and mastery that are essential ingredients of secondary-process thinking. And we can add that this will occur only if the ego has specific characteristics and potentialities, that is, if it is a particular type of ego.

---

*The work of Hartmann (1964; Hartmann, Kris, & Loewenstein, 1964) on these and related topics is directly relevant to all the arguments in this paper.

†Freud has referred to this aspect of normal mental functioning in his gem of a paper "A Note upon the 'Mystic Writing-Pad' " (1925a). The existence of a relationship between the specific mechanisms of defense and particular ego functions has been suggested and discussed by Lampl-de Groot (1965).

Let us examine this a little further. The predisposition to a specific form of neurosis, determined as it is in part by particular drive fixation points, requires in addition that there be a correlated pattern of ego functioning that provides the appropriate matrix for the development of the specific pattern of defensive activity and the specific neurotic symptomatology. This is not to be equated with relatively macroscopic character traits, nor can we speak in general terms of intelligence and intellectual precocity in this connection. We would suggest that what is significant in the ego of the individual who may develop a particular neurotic symptomatology is (in addition to the specific drive fixation) his potentiality for using a particular type of defensive organization. This does not necessarily mean that he will have shown a disproportionate use of the defense mechanisms that we know to be characteristic of specific neuroses prior to the development of his disturbance. What he will have shown, however, is a particular mode of perceptual and cognitive functioning. In this we are suggesting that the particular type of defensive organization employed by the individual in situations of neurotic conflict is as crucial to the form of his illness as is fixation and regression on the side of the drives; and further, that *this defensive organization is latent and inherent in his particular mode or style of perception and cognition*.*

We may now legitimately look for those factors that enter into the development of the particular type and style of ego functioning that forms an integral part of the predisposition to obsessional neurosis. In this we make a distinction between character structure and style of ego functioning because we know that there is no direct correlation between the so-called anal character structure and obsessional neurosis. There is evidence (e.g., Sandler & Hazari, 1960) that patients who have, for example, a reactive anal character do not have a special tendency to develop an obsessional neurosis if they break down.

We have spoken of the notion of a functional regression of the ego that parallels drive regression. The question now arises whether processes occur in the ego that are the counterpart of instinctual drive fixation. We usually understand drive fixation in terms of quantities of drive cathexis that remain at particular points in psychosexual development, but it is clear that any explanation or description of drive fixation must include a consideration of the attraction of particular forms of drive discharge and the particular pleasure qualities associated with them. There seem to be good grounds for assuming that something similar may occur on the side of the ego functions.

---

*We shall make no attempt to review in this short chapter the extensive and pertinent literature on "cognitive style."

Ego functions can be viewed as the operation of the ego apparatuses of primary and secondary autonomy. But much more can be said about them. In Chapter 13, we take the view that the functioning of the ego apparatuses is accompanied by pleasurable experiences of a particular quality. We would say no more than that these experiences relate to what has been called "function-pleasure" (Bühler's *Funktionslust* [1918]), pleasure in mastery and "work-pleasure" (Hendrick, 1942, 1943). These (largely preconscious) pleasurable feeling tones accompany effective functioning of the ego, over and above any more sensual pleasures that may be generalized when the ego apparatuses operate in the service of direct drive discharge.

We suggested that in the course of normal development the ego apparatuses (whether apparatuses of primary or secondary autonomy) gradually show some of the characteristics of modes of instinctual drive discharge. The prototype of this is the way in which hand grasping gradually becomes a partial substitute for grasping with the mouth, and in the same way the eye also becomes a grasping organ. In this process the ego is able to bring about a reduction of the demand for work imposed on it by the oral drives, but the reduction in instinctual tension in hand and eye grasping is now accompanied by pleasures in functioning, mastery, and achievement, pleasures that are considerably less sensual, less somatically based, and of a lower intensity that the affective accompaniments of primitive instinctual discharge. We put forward the notion of "affective distancing" as a correlate of autonomous ego development; however, as a consequence of the genetic link between specific ego apparatuses and the drives that stimulate their development, the characteristics of the original somatic drive discharge are reflected in the functioning of these ego apparatuses, even though, from a maturational point of view, they may be apparatuses of primary autonomy in the sense of Hartmann's description (1950).

It follows from this that the ego apparatuses that develop during the oral phase will show something of the qualities of the passive and active oral aims that characterized the drives operating at that time. Equally, with the move of the child into the anal phase, the various aims of the anal component instincts leave their stamp on those ego apparatuses and functions that develop during the anal phase.

It seems very likely that the quality of the so-called "distanced" ego pleasures that arise at any developmental phase bears a relation to the qualities of the somatically based pleasures associated with the direct discharge of the dominant part instincts at that time. In this sense, the id is reinstated in the ego. The pleasure in the act of grasping, for instance, is probably in some way related to the much cruder and primitive pleasures that accompanied mouth activity. Similarly, the "ego pleasures" involved in much secondary-process thinking may have something in common with the pleasures derived from direct anal discharge.

Because of the pleasurable qualities associated with particular ego functions, we can assume that experiences that bring about drive fixation may also leave their mark on the ego in the form of a fixation to particular modes of ego functioning. If this view can be accepted, we are in a position to understand more of the nature of regression in general and that which occurs in obsessional neurosis in particular; and also to comment further on the question of the preconditions for the development of an obsessional neurosis.

The anal phase of development is characterized by vast strides forward on the part of the ego. The way in which ego functions develop and operate during this phase bears a close resemblance to the mode of functioning of the somatic apparatuses that subserve drive discharge in this phase. We see the development of a whole hierarchy of discharging, delaying, and controlling functions. Some of these relate to the control of feces, to their retention and expulsion, others to the control of motility and action, and still others to the control of internalized action in the form of thinking and fantasying. In the development of verbalization, speech, and thinking, we can discern the general characteristics of the phase in the way in which words and thoughts are formed and their expression controlled. Further, we can see the way in which words, actions, and thoughts have to be released at appropriate times and in appropriate circumstances. In the process of thinking and speaking, there is a delay in discharge, and inappropriate elements have to be held back. The child shows the beginnings of organized memory and voluntary recall.

In recent years, a number of psychoanalytically oriented psychologists have done important work on the interrelation between cognitive and perceptual controls, adaptation, mechanisms of defense, and the discharge of the instinctual drives (e.g., as reported by Gardner et al., 1959).

We have spoken of the hierarchy of id and ego functions that develops in the anal phase. This hierarchy of functions is associated with a hierarchy of feelings that show greater or less distance from the sensual feelings accompanying direct somatic drive discharge. Pleasure obtained through uncontrolled discharge may then be partially replaced by pleasures derived from delaying, postponing, and fashioning products in reality or in thought.

The essence of the view put forward at this point is that the functional characteristics of the ego in the anal phase bear a close resemblance to the mode of functioning of the somatic apparatuses that act in the service of anal drive discharge.

Of special interest in the present context is the development of those cognitive and perceptual processes that find expression, when they become exaggerated, in the defense mechanisms characteristic of obsessional neurosis. We have alluded to the "clearing of the perceptual screen," and the parallel between this and more directly instinctual anal activities needs no elaboration. But it is a form of discharge that makes use of maturationally predetermined apparatuses, and the pleasures associated with perceptual functioning are of a more highly refined and nonsensual form than the affective feeling accompaniments of more direct anal activities. The obsessional neurosis is characterized by a prominent use of such defenses as isolation, undoing, reaction formation, intellectualization, and rationalization, coupled with such features as omnipotence of thought and magical thinking. All of these can be considered to be an exaggeration of normal cognitive and perceptual processes, and, in particular, of cognitive and perceptual control. The particular ego processes that form the basis of the specific defenses we have mentioned are those that came into being or were extensively employed during the anal phase of development. If we think of the defense mechanism of isolation, for example, we can see it as a hypertrophy of the normal ego processes used by the ego to prevent the ideational content of thought from becoming too affect-laden for efficient secondary-process functioning. Undoing, in its turn, represents a caricature of the normal ego processes of trial thought and trial action.

We know that drive fixation points and regression to them may find expression through the ego in the form of character traits. These show classically the influence of both a particular component drive and the ego's defensive struggle against it. Thus, in the ego-syntonic traits that distinguish, for example, the anal–reactive character, we can discern disguised forms of anal–sadistic drive discharge as well as the operation 'of the mechanism of reaction formation. While it appears that character traits may reflect particular ways in which the ego mediates drive discharge, it may be that what has been referred to as cognitive and perceptual style is rather a reflection of fixation to the particular ego pleasures in functioning that we have discussed earlier.

The implication of all that we have said is that drive regression to the anal–sadistic phase is an essential ingredient in the genesis of an obsessional neurosis; but even with the addition of the particular character of the superego, of particular types of object relationships (involving a high degree of ambivalence), and with the increased sadism consequent on the drive regression, this is not enough.

We suggest that a particular type of ego organization is an essential component. This is not necessarily reflected in what we usually call traits of character; it is reflected rather in a particular style of the perceptual and cognitive functions of the ego, a style that indicates a functional fixation of the ego to the anal phase.

The precocious development of the ego that is so often thought to be an important feature in the development of obsessional neurosis can now be understood, more specifically, in terms of an early or developmentally premature "distancing" of the ego functions from the drives. This may show itself in a premature "intellectuality." We would suggest that fixations that occur at the anal phase of development need not influence drive and ego functions equally, and that a fixation of the sort that we have described in connection with ego functions need not be accompanied by a fixation of equal degree on the side of the drives, and vice versa. However, both drive fixation and functional fixation of the ego may occur at the anal–sadistic phase; and we would suggest that this is the case that obtains in the individual who is prone to develop an obsessional neurosis.

III

We can now return, very briefly, to the question of the applicability of the ideas that have been put forward to the clinical manifestations of obsessional phenomena. As far as the syndrome of obsessional neurosis proper is concerned, we may simply add to the classic formulation the notion that the ego changes that occur are attributable, in part at least, to a functional ego regression that accompanies the drive regression so prominent in this disturbance. The functional ego regression involves those ego functions that showed their most prominent development during the anal phase—particularly those functions that relate to cognition, perception, and to control in general. The functional ego regression brings into operation the defense mechanisms that are characteristic of the neurosis and that represent a natural development of the individual's particular style of ego functioning.

Those disturbances that occur in childhood during the anal phase itself need offer us no difficulty. Here we see an exacerbation of features of the normal developmental conflict, and we would suggest that in these children, a premature turning against direct instinctual drive discharge has taken place. We may assume that there has been a stronger-than-usual tendency for the replacement of direct drive gratification by pleasures in functioning, mastery, and control. On the other hand, perhaps even because of the premature affective distancing, the mode of functioning of the rapidly developing ego apparatuses is closer in form to the anal pattern of drive discharge. The modes of ego control, for instance, are probably patterned to a greater degree on the somatic sphincter-involved modes of discharge. All of this results in a tendency to use the particular methods of cognitive and perceptual control that we have discussed, and the emergence of the characteristic defense mechanisms is an inevitable consequence of this.

With progressive drive developments, this "anal" style of ego functioning may alter. This is probably what happens in the case of the transient obsessional phenomena that occur during the anal phase, but that disappear with its passing. However, drive progression may take place without substantial alteration in the "anal" style of ego functioning, and we have suggested that those individuals who have such a style possess, from the side of the ego, the propensity for the development of a later obsessional neurosis. This may be the case even though their anal phase of development was not necessarily characterized by the development of significant obsessional manifestations.

Finally, we come to those obsessional phenomena that do not emerge as a consequence of the classic obsessional psychopathology. These occur in many different circumstances and conditions, and range from the mildest and most transient to gross controlling mechanisms that constitute strenuous attempts to stave off threats of catastrophic disintegration. Their emergence is not primarily linked with drive regression to anal fixation points, but they indicate a functional regression to an "anal" mode of ego functioning. They are mobilized by the urgency of the need to control, and we would suggest that the likelihood of their appearance bears a relation to the degree to which an "anal" style of ego functioning has persisted.

11

Pain, Depression, and Individuation

Walter G. Joffe and Joseph Sandler

This chapter began its life with the publication of a relatively condensed paper entitled "Notes on Childhood Depression" and published in *The International Journal of Psycho-Analysis* (Sandler & Joffe, 1965*b*). There the view was put forward that depression in children could be regarded as a basic psychobiological response to a painful feeling state—an important extension of Edward Bibring's views on depression (1953). Pain was linked with a discrepancy between the present ("actual") state of the self as perceived by the child and an "ideal" wished-for state. The paper attacked the notion that depression is always linked with the actual loss of a love object, and subsumes this special cause of pain under the more general one.

What follows is a significantly expanded version of the original paper. It appeared in *The Psychoanalytic Study of the Child* in 1965.

I

The Depressive Reaction

In a previous study of depression in children (Sandler & Joffe, 1965*a*), based on material from the Hampstead Index, a picture that was called the "Depressive Reaction" was isolated. It was characterized by a mood that was variously described by therapists as "sadness," "unhappiness," or "depression." This mood had both mental and bodily components. The child looked unhappy, had little interest in his surroundings, and appeared withdrawn, bored or listless. He had a feeling of discontent with what was offered to him and showed little capacity for pleasure. He communicated a sense of feeling rejected or unloved, and showed a readiness to turn away from disappointing objects. He was not prepared to accept help or comfort readily, and if he did respond at all, his underlying disappointment and dissatisfaction would reemerge. He showed a tendency to regress to passive oral attitudes and behavior. Insomnia and various other sleep disturbances were noted, and autoerotic or repetitive self-comforting activities described. A general feature was that the therapist reported difficulty in making sustained contact with the child at this time.

The depressive reaction, which could be transitory or of long duration, intense or mild, occurred in different personality types and clinical conditions. It was seen at all stages of development and could be found in association with a variety of other symptoms. It was a reaction that, it seemed, can potentially occur in any child.

The clinical picture described as the depressive reaction consisted of a number of components, *having at its core a basic depressive affective response*. It was also associated with features that could be understood as representing attempts to deal with the existence of this affect *or to prevent its development*. It seemed that undischarged aggression played a significant role in its genesis, and derivatives of or defenses against aggressive manifestations were also part of the picture.

While the depressive reaction, as described in our earlier study, referred to a clinical constellation, the terms "depressive response" and "depressive reaction" will be used in a restricted sense in the present chapter, denoting the basic affective response that formed its core. This affect was thought to represent a fundamental psychobiological response that could be conceived of as being as basic as anxiety. It has its roots in a primary psychophysiological state that is an ultimate reaction to the experiencing of helplessness in the face of physical or psychological pain in one form or another. It occurs in babies who suffer from nutritional deficiency diseases and in infants who are deprived of adequate psychological stimulation (Provence & Lipton, 1962). The basic response was considered to be one that could occur at any time in the individual's life span. It ought not be confused with those forms of depressive illness that can be considered to be the consequence of further defensive and restitutive processes, and in which pathogenic introjections and identifications occur (Bibring, 1953; Jacobson, 1953a; Zetzel, 1960).

Depression, Pain, and Well-Being

The basic depressive response was regarded as representing a state of helplessness, hopelessness, and resignation in the face of mental pain.* It is not the only possible response to pain or to the anticipation

---

*There are different degrees of pain, and even qualities of pain. The relationship of pain to the spectrum of unpleasures, although touched on by Freud (1926, Addendum C), merits further investigation.

of pain, but a *particular* one, in which there is a feeling of being unable to restore a wished-for state, accompanied by an attitude that is essentially one of capitulation and retreat. The healthy response to the experiencing of pain is protest, "fight" rather than "flight." Many children who are called "unhappy" are not in fact manifesting a depressive response. They have not "capitulated," but rather show varying degrees of discontent and resentment, and their aggressive response to pain is much more directly manifest.

Biological separation of the young infant from his mother is one source of pain, as is separation in the somewhat older child in whom the mother image has been differentiated from the self-representation. The child's reaction to pain brought about by separation, as to pain brought about from any other cause in reality or in fantasy, may be that of the basic depressive response; on the other hand, it may not. Our nodal concept in this connection is not the factor of object loss per se, but rather the subjective state of pain and a depressive response to it.

Freud considered mental pain to be a phenomenon that paralleled physical pain. The painful place (in Freud's example [1926 Addendum C] the missing lost object) receives a hypercathexis of longing that mounts to an intolerable level. Although Freud conceived of this in the context of loss and mourning, his statements on the subject can be generalized in such a way that the loss of an object need not be seen as the only precondition for the experiencing of mental pain. When an object is lost and its representation receives a libidinal hypercathexis, this means that the cathected internal image of the object is not met by a corresponding perception arising from outer sources. Thus the painful hypercathexis can be taken as indicating a state of discrepancy between an existing state of the representational world (Chapter 5) and a wished-for, so-called ideal state. We would suggest that it is precisely such a discrepancy that reflects mental pain, and that, more specifically, it is a discrepancy between the actual state of the self on the one hand and an ideal state of well-being on the other.

The term "ideal state" needs some explanation. "Ideal" in this context refers to a state of well-being, a state that is fundamentally affective and that normally accompanies the harmonious and integrated functioning of all the biological and mental structures (Chapter 1). The striving toward the attainment of an ideal state is basic in human development and functioning. It represents the feeling component that is attributed to the state of primary narcissism (Freud, 1914). Much of the dynamics of ego functioning can be understood in terms of the ego's striving to maintain or attain a state of well-being, a state that even in the child who has been unhappy from birth exists as a biological goal. Freud put it: "The development of the ego consists in a departure from primary narcissism and gives rise to a vigorous attempt to recover that state." The ideal state of well-being is closely linked with feelings of safety and security. It is the polar opposite of feelings of pain, anxiety, or discomfort, and bears the same relation to these as the state of physical satiation and contentment in a small infant bears to the unpleasure of instinctual tension. The attainment of this state may follow or accompany successful drive discharge, but there are circumstances in which drive satisfaction does not lead to the development of well-being, but rather to the experiencing of its opposite, as in states of mental conflict.

In this there is a qualitative difference between the systems *id* and *ego*. The drives are characterized by states of tension and demands for discharge (and the body pleasures associated with such discharge) that change in the course of development. The dynamics of ego functioning appear to be much more related to the maintenance of affective states of well-being that do not change as grossly in the course of development (although the ideational content associated with the ideal state may change markedly). In what follows we shall use the term "ideal state" to refer to the affective state of well-being, and the term "ideal self" to denote the particular shape of the self-representation at any moment in the individual's life that is believed (consciously or unconsciously) to embody the ideal state. As the representational world of the child becomes increasingly structured, his system of self-representations includes images that reflect affective states of well-being. The "ideal self" derives its content not only from affect representations, but also contains ideational components that may originate from various sources.* These sources include memories of actual states of well-being previously experienced, or of fantastic and symbolic elaborations of such states. The elaborations in fantasy may subserve defensive functions, in which case we may get magical and omnipotent components in the ideal self. The specialized form of ideal that ensues when the child needs to aggrandize himself for the purpose of defense can be referred to as the "idealized self," but it should be borne in mind that idealization is only one possible source of the content of the ideal self. Similarly, where the ideal self is based on identification with an admired object, we can distinguish between qualities that the child attributes to the object because of its infantile perception of the object at the time, and those that are attributed to the object representation in fantasy (usually resulting from ambivalence conflicts).

*We have related the ideal state of well-being to the dynamics of ego functioning rather than to the gaining of pleasure associated with instinctual drive discharge.

The Role of the Object

We saw the role of the object as being that of a vehicle for the attainment of the ideal state of well-being. While this is perhaps obvious when object relationships are of the anaclitic, need-fulfilling (part-object) type, it is not so obvious when the state of object constancy has been reached. It could be argued that love for the object can be truly altruistic, that the object can be loved for and in itself. Yet we believe that this is never entirely true, and that the value that any object has is directly connected with its genetic and functional relation to the self. This would appear to be so even after the attainment of object constancy, when the object has developed "uniqueness" and has become an indispensable key to states of well-being. The subject was explored by Freud in his paper "On Narcissism" (1914), in which he traced the development of object love from primary narcissism. Object love, like the whole development of the ego, can be seen as a roundabout way of attempting to restore the ideal primary narcissistic state. The perception of the presence of the love object when its presence is expected is, moreover, a source of feelings of well-being and safety (Chapter 1). And this is true even when the object is fulfilling no drive-reducing role.* It is clear that if the presence of the object is a condition for a state of well-being in the self, then loss of the object signifies the loss of an aspect of the self, of a state of the self. One might say that for the representation of every love object there is a part of the self-representation that is complementary to it, that is, the part that *reflects the relation to the object*, and that constitutes the link between self and object. We can refer to this as the object-complementary aspect of the self-representation.

We have suggested that even if the highest level of object love has been reached, the object is ultimately the means whereby a desired state of the self may be attained, in fact or in fantasy. This does not imply any degree of undervaluation of the role of object relationships in development and in mental life in general; the object is, after a certain point in development has been passed, unique and

*The transition from anaclitic relationships to those characterized by object constancy reflects changes in the child's ego rather than in his drives. From the point of view of the id, objects are, in a sense, the means whereby the drives attain discharge. The relationship of the ego to objects, in the anaclitic phase, is determined by the requirements of drive discharge. The transition to the state of object constancy implies that the child's needs have become more complex, and now reflect not only the requirements of the drives, but also secondary needs related to the maintenance of states of safety and well-being. Object constancy, therefore, reflects not only the drive cathexes of the id, but, in addition, implies the existence of a secondary (ego) need for the *particular* object.

essential for the maintenance of well-being in the self. When a love object is lost, we not only have the loss of the object in its own right, but also the loss of the object-complementary aspect of the self and the affective state of well-being that is intimately bound up with it. In such a state of object loss, the affective value cathexis of the object is greatly increased, and attention is focused almost exclusively on the object because it is the key to the reattainment of the lost state of the self. This displacement is biologically conditioned because of the long period of dependence of the human infant on its biological object.* In the case of the toddler, the mere presence of the mother in the nursery may be sufficient for him to play happily, all but ignoring her presence. His state of well-being may be quite obvious from his contented play. If she leaves the room without his noticing her departure, he will go on playing happily until he notices her absence. His perception of this may precipitate a disruption of his well-being and a state of distress. All his attention and activity will be directed toward restoring her presence. What he feels is lost is the mother; what is actually lost is not only the mother but also the well-being implicit in the relationship.

II

The material in the previous section represents a summary, and to some extent an elaboration, of the views on pain and depression presented in a previous paper (Sandler & Joffe, 1965b). There we introduced briefly the application of the concept of individuation, a topic that will be taken up more fully in Part IV of this chapter. Individuation was related to normal development and referred to a process whereby the ego's striving to attain past ideal states was changed and new, ego-syntonic, and more reality-adapted ideals constructed. But before we proceed to a more detailed discussion of individuation and its relation to depression, it is appropriate to summarize and comment on the work of a number of authors in Great Britain whose contributions are relevant to the present topic.

Melanie Klein

Basic to Melanie Klein's theory of depression (1948) is the notion that the infant experiences a "depressive position" in the first half

---

*The infant has a biological object relationship to his mother from conception. This is quite different from the psychological object relationship that develops as the child gradually constructs a differentiated object representation from the initially inchoate mass of pleasure–pain sensations.

year of life. Before this, the child suffers multiple primordial anxieties from birth due to the conflict between the life and death instincts. In the first few months, when only part objects can be distinguished, the infant attempts to deal with his anxieties by splitting of the part object (breast) into "good" and "bad" parts, with a corresponding splitting of the ego into loving and hating parts. Projective and introjective processes are said to occur, that bring about, in favorable circumstances (when good experiences predominate over bad ones), a degree of integration and a capacity for love, stemming from the life instinct. In this period (the paranoid–schizoid position), the splitting of the object into good and bad parts can serve a valuable function in that the good object is preserved and the security of the ego enhanced (1957). These processes may follow a different course if, for various reasons, the "bad" experiences predominate over the "good." Persecutory anxieties may be more intense, confusion between self and object occurs, and defensive idealization indicates the strength of feelings of persecution. This is an unsatisfactory basis for the development of security.

The paranoid–schizoid position is normally followed by the depressive position in the second quarter of the first year. The child recognizes the mother as a whole object and begins to relate to it as such. Good and bad experiences are now felt to arise from the same object, and as a consequence the child experiences conflict based on ambivalence. The integration of the good and bad parts of the mother, as well as those parts that have been separated by splitting, is accompanied by a corresponding integration of the various aspects of the child's own ego. In contrast to the anxieties of the paranoid–schizoid position (in which the child feels that his ego is attacked by his own projected hostility), the main anxiety is now that the infant will destroy the object he loves and upon which he is dependent. The child is at the mercy of feelings of despair, guilt, and hopelessness when he feels that he has destroyed his external or internal mother. The conflict in the depressive position is thought by Melanie Klein to be mainly between the infant's destructive impulses and his love for, and wish to make reparation to, the object. If he can feel that reparation has been achieved, then this contributes to the "working through" of the depressive position. The infant begins to distinguish between himself and his objects, and to distinguish between fantasy and reality. The infant's belief in his own omnipotence becomes modified, and his relationship to reality becomes established. The ego is strengthened on this account, as well as by the further introjection of good objects into the ego. Concurrently the superego becomes more integrated, and with time resembles more the good parents than the persecuting ones.

Melanie Klein saw the depressive position as being a crucial and fundamental stage in the child's development. Much of the pathology seen later is thought to result from a failure to work through this "position," and a degree of success in its resolution may come only through repeated working over of the depressive position or through analysis. The depressive position implies a "pining" for the loved good object, and the ego may develop methods of defense, particularly manic defenses that are specifically directed against the pining for the lost object.

Hanna Segal (1973) comments as follows:

> The depressive position is never fully worked through. The anxieties pertaining to ambivalence and guilt, as well as situations of loss, which reawaken depressive experiences, are always with us. Good external objects in adult life always symbolize and contain aspects of the primary good object, internal and external, so that any loss in later life reawakens the anxiety of losing the good internal object and, with this anxiety, all the anxieties experienced originally in the depressive position. If the infant has been able to establish a good internal object relatively securely in the depressive position, situations of depressive anxiety will not lead to illness, but to a fruitful working through, leading to further enrichment and creativity (p. 80).

Melanie Klein makes little or no distinction between the dynamic, structural, economic, genetic, and adaptational points of view, and her theories represent a sort of condensation in concrete terms of all these approaches, allocated, moreover, to the very earliest months of life. In spite of this, her work has drawn clinical attention to certain aspects of the processes whereby the child and adult establish secure feelings of well-being and a stable state of the self that is relatively independent of the objects. These processes, as she sees them, involve the development of the ability to tolerate painful feelings of loss, a view that is consonant with our own. The link that she made between these processes and depression is important, although she viewed the child's experiences of pain and depression as identical with those that can be seen in later psychotic illnesses. We would approach the subject rather from the point of view of more basic and elemental instinctual and affective processes, and distinguish as Bibring (1953) and Zetzel (1960) have done, between depressive affect and depressive illness. However, insofar as what Melanie Klein has called "working through the depressive position" is related to the process of individuation, it reflects an important aspect of clinical psychoanalytic work with both children and adults. We would add that although Melanie Klein formulated successful working through of the depressive position in terms of the establishment of the primacy of the good object, it could be inferred that she is also referring to the establishment of a "good" state of the self, in spite of the fact that she considers the development of the self to be based primarily on object incorporation. It might follow, as a corollary of her views, that loss of a good object could also be seen as the loss of a good part of the self.

Winnicott

Winnicott's work is difficult to translate into metapsychological terms partly because of the richness of detail and the highly personal language he uses. His views are not identical with those of Melanie Klein, but he also conceives of the attainment of a state in early development in which the whole infant relates to the whole mother in an ambivalent way (1954). This phase is described as one of "concern for the object," and although Winnicott regards the term "depressive position" as a "thoroughly bad name for a normal process," he believes that no better one has been found. If all goes well with weaning, the depressive position should occur in the second half of the first year, but he suggests that it often takes much longer to be established, and some people never attain it. Winnicott regards the depressive position not as a phase but rather as an *achievement*, a position reached, and the earlier this occurs, the better the outlook for the child. The attainment of the depressive position signifies a development from the stage of ruthless demandingness to a state of concern for the object and, in particular, of concern about the effects of the infant's instinctual demands on the mother. The mother has been the object of "assault" during the phase of instinctual tension. During "quiet" phases, the mother is loved as the one who has been adapting to the infant. The coming together of these two functions in the mind of the child initiates the beginning of guilt feelings. This is an intrinsic personal source of the sense of guilt. Subsequent processes enrich the inner world, and ultimately the child builds up a store of "good" memories "so that the experience of the mother holding the situation becomes part of the self, becomes assimilated into the ego. In this way the actual mother becomes less and less necessary."

Winnicott suggests that if the individual has attained the depressive position, his reaction to loss is one of grief or sadness; if the depressive position has failed, if the processes in it go wrong, the child "wet-blankets" the whole inner world, functions at a low level of vitality, and the mood is one of depression. He points out that this type of failure and recovery differs from the manifestations of depressive illness seen in clinical psychiatry, is associated with depersonalization, hopelessness in respect to object relationships, and the special type of futility seen in the development of a false self (1956). These illnesses relate, he believes, to a developmental phase preceding the depressive position.

The depressive mood is distinguished from the anxieties associated with the depressive position. Winnicott details many of the defense mechanisms that are employed against depressive anxiety. The depressive mood is in itself seen as an overall control that is gradually lifted. This is a major defense through the relative inhibition of the instinct, so that all the consequences of instinctual experiences are correspondingly diminished. Other defenses include the negation of everything serious (the manic defense) and various forms of projection, introjection, and so on.

Winnicott's position in this connection is clarified to some extent in a paper (1964) in which he discusses the value of depression for individual development. He describes the way in which objects and the environment are differentiated from the self and the processes of integration that accompany this. A "good enough" environment is essential for the inborn maturation processes that underlie these developments to occur (Winnicott, 1958a).* When the child has developed a sense of identity, has gained a degree of ego strength, and can contain the stresses and strains that arise in his inner personal psychic reality, he becomes able to be depressed. Winnicott sees the depressed mood as evidence of the existence of a mental organization sufficiently strong to be able to control otherwise disrupting tensions, in particular those associated with hate. Crises that may arise later and that create a depressed mood are brought about by "a new experience of destructiveness and of destructive ideas that go with loving. The new experiences necessitate internal reassessment, and it is this reassessment which we see as depression." If the depression is free of "impurities," the individual will recover and may be "stronger, wiser and more stable" than before. The "impurities" of which Winnicott speaks are, for example, failures of ego organization, delusions of persecution, hypochondriacal tendencies, manic defenses, and so forth.

Winnicott concludes by remarking that depression belongs to psychopathology, and may range from being severe and crippling to a passing mood in a relatively healthy person. At the normal end of this continuum, depression "is a common, almost universal, phe-

---

*While Winnicott clearly states his views on the relation between environment and ego maturation, he does not formulate as explicitly his views on the dependence of maturation on drive stimulation.

nomenon [which] relates to mourning, to the capacity to feel guilt, and to the maturational process."

Balint

Balint's work over the past 30 years relates to the problem of individuation, although he approaches the subject mainly from the point of view of the changes that occur in the patient during the course of analysis. He has progressively refined his views over the period between his papers "Character Analysis and New Beginning" (1932) and "The Benign and Malignant Forms of Regression" (1963). In 1952, in a paper specifically relating his view of the new beginning to Melanie Klein's work, he formulated his ideas in a way that is particularly relevant to our present topic. He points out (1952) that, in favorable cases, the analytic patient relinquishes his accustomed and automatic forms of object relationship and makes tentative attempts to try out new ones. During the analysis he regresses to a pretraumatic, undefended state, begins anew to love and hate in a primitive way, and then develops mature and well-adapted ways of loving and hating.

Balint suggests that "the original and everlasting aim of all object relations is the primitive wish: *I must be loved* without any obligation on me and without any expectation of return from me. All 'adult' ways of object-relations, i.e. of loving and hating, are compromise formations between this original wish and the acceptance of an unkind, unpleasant, indifferent reality." It is this point that he believes is reached in the type of regression that he describes, and from which the "new beginnings" take their origin.

In the period preceding the new beginning, the patient's attitude is characterized by deep suspiciousness. "Everything, the most everyday happening, will inevitably be referred to the patient's own person." There are certain patients who can be successfully helped through this phase, which Balint links with Melanie Klein's paranoid position (although he does not accept her view that it constitutes the first phase of extrauterine existence). These patients then experience a state of depression (which has a differen' mechanism from the melancholic depressions discussed by Abraham and Freud). The essence of the depression is the feeling of being worthless and unlovable, and a belief that change for the better is impossible. There follows a hard and painful fight to give up "parts of ourselves as unlovable and unacceptable to our fellow men." During this struggle, these patients show dejection, loss of interest in the outside world, loss of the capacity to love, inhibition of activity, and a lowered self-esteem.

Balint points out that everyday adaptation to reality means the sacrifice of wishes that constitute part of the personality. Adaptation, together with mourning and all forms of depression, implies the acceptance of unpleasure. The narcissistic wound that results brings about responses that show both paranoid and depressive mechanisms. In the type of depression that is involved in the new beginning, the patient's aim is different from that which he has in other depressive states, in that it is now to enable the patient to be at one with himself.

"New beginning" thus implies, first, the abandonment of a paranoid attitude, and second, the acceptance of a certain amount of depression as "an inevitable condition of life." With this is coupled "the confidence that it is possible—nay certain—to emerge from this kind of depression as a better man."

Balint remarks later in his paper that real adaptations, which mean the acceptance of unpleasure, are possible only if depression can be faced without undue anxiety. Every line of development must pass through this focus.

Balint has always been an uncompromising opponent of the theory of primary narcissism. As a consequence, he has suggested that the wish "I want to be loved" is the final goal of all erotic striving (1937). This view is unacceptable to us, as it seems to be based on a confusion (which he shares with Melanie Klein) between the roles of the biological and psychological objects of the instinctual drives. Balint does, however, refer to the outcome of gratification as being a quiet, tranquil sense of well-being, and with this we would fully agree. We also found ourselves in agreement with his view that adaptation to reality always implies the acceptance of unpleasure and the relinquishing of certain valued parts of the personality, although we would formulate this in terms of acceptance of pain, the giving up of the striving toward infantile ideal states of the self, and all the sacrifices that have to be made in the renunciation of infantile modes of instinctual satisfaction.

Curiously enough, although Balint's "primary love" is conceptualized in terms of an object relationship existing from the beginning, many of his formulations are couched in terms that refer to states of the self; depression (not melancholia), for example, is related to "a deep, painful, narcissistic wound."

Balint (1959, 1963) modified his views on early development, and described a phase before that of the emergence of primary objects, one that he refers to as that of the undifferentiated environment." While Balint still insists on putting his thesis in terms of relationships (in this phase an interpenetrating relationship with primary substances), he is clearly concerned with the infant's feelings before objects have been differentiated in the psychological world of the child. He has also qualified (1963) his use of the term "regression," and has expressed the view that "new beginning" is not a true regression, or a repetition of a previous experience, but a new discovery, leading to a different, more satisfactory relationship to an important object. We would suggest that Balint has in fact described a process of individuation occurring as a special experience in the analytic situation.

Bowlby

For several decades, Bowlby has contributed substantially to the literature on separation and mourning (1954, 1958, 1960a, 1960b, 1960c, 1961a, 1961b, 1962). He has taken the view that the occurrence of separation anxiety (the fear of loss of the object) plays a crucial part in normal and pathological development, and although much of his work is not directly connected with our present topic, we shall comment briefly on those aspects that relate to individuation. It is important to note that the research strategy followed by Bowlby is to study the effects of object loss occurring at different ages and in different conditions; the depressive reaction is only one of many possible outcomes of object loss. Nor does Bowlby necessarily relate depression only to the specific event of object loss, and he does not attempt to construct a theory to account for all depressive reactions (Bowlby, 1965).

Taking into account observations made by Robertson (1953a, 1953b; Robertson & Bowlby, 1952), three phases in the child's reaction to gross separation (e.g., hospitalization) have been described. The initial phase of *protest* is one in which "the instinctual response systems binding the bereaved to the lost object remain focused on the object, because during this phase yearning and an angry effort to recover the lost object seem to be the rule" (Bowlby, 1962). We would see this as a phase of anger and discontent prompted by the changed state of the self arising, in this case, from the disappearance of the object. The child in this phase is certainly an unhappy child, reacting to pain with protest. We take the view that this particular type of response occurs frequently as a reaction to all states of mental pain, however determined.

The second phase is that of *despair*, described by Bowlby as follows (1960a): "The active physical movements diminish or come to an end, and he may cry monotonously or intermittently. He is withdrawn and inactive, makes no demand on the environment, and appears to be in a state of deep mourning." This would appear to correspond to the depressive affective response that we have described. However, Bowlby's interpretation of the child's behavior in this phase as "mourning" can, in our view, be questioned. He sees mourning as the set of psychological processes that are initiated by the loss of the love object, and that usually lead to relinquishment of the object. We find this definition too general and suggest that it is valuable to differentiate pain (whatever the cause) from the depressive response as such and from mourning. In the depressive response the yearning for the lost state is suppressed through a generalized inhibition of function without modification of the content of the ideal self. Mourning, in contrast, can be regarded as involving a continual facing of the painful situation, a gradual acceptance of the fact of the unattainability of the lost ideal state through a continual contrasting of the lost and wished-for state with present reality. This leads to a gradual recovery of hope through the creation of new ideals.

Bowlby's third phase is that of *detachment*. The child "no longer rejects the nurses, accepts their care and the food and the toys they bring, and may even smile and be sociable. When his mother visits, however, it can be seen that all is not well. . . . So far from greeting his mother he may seem hardly to know her; so far from clinging to her, he may remain remote and apathetic; instead of tears there is a listless turning away. He seems to have lost all interest in her" (1960a). We would suggest that the basic process in this phase is an attempt to restore a minimum level of well-being and feelings of safety. Whereas in the phase of despair we can discern a general inhibition of both id and ego functions, in the phase of detachment we can postulate a partial lifting of the generalized inhibition that is characteristic of the depressive response. This is made possible by a form of ego restriction, in particular a restriction of attention and a flattening of feelings. It shows itself in a devaluation of the unique affective importance of the mother or indeed of any object. The child settles, so to speak, for its actual state of the self. It is a type of resignation that can be seen as an attempt to do away with the awareness of the discrepancy between actual self and ideal self, and in this sense it is a form of adaptation that stands in contrast to processes of mourning.

Although Bowlby's three sequential phases may be an appropriate description of the reactions of children to gross separation experiences under unfavorable conditions, they do not necessarily occur as a response to painful states of the self in general. We can discern all the elements of Bowlby's phases as isolated responses to pain, or combined in a variety of different ways. Some children react with a state of unhappiness and discontent in which much hostility is evident. We can also see states of despair and responses of depression with or without a previous phase of "protest." And, of course, there exists the whole gamut of defensive operations directed either against the experiencing of pain or against the emergence of depressive affect. One particular defensive operation (among many) is "detachment," a reaction that is not an inherent response to a separation experience but rather one fostered by deficiencies in the supporting environment. We believe that "detachment" may occur even in situations where there is no actual separation, but rather chronically inadequate mothering.

The processes that Bowlby has studied relate to gross separation experiences, in which the attention of both child and observer is focused on the loss of the object. Starting from such observations as these, it would seem, on the face of it, to be understandable that so much emphasis has been placed on the state of object loss as such. Although Bowlby has elaborated what is essentially an object-oriented psychology, he does not believe, as Melanie Klein and Balint do, that psychological object relationships exist from the beginning. He says (1965):

> In an infant's behavioural equipment there is a built-in bias, genetically determined, that in the ordinary expectable environment leads to the development of object relations. The built-in bias is there from the first: the actual development of object relations takes time. The same is true of arms and legs. In the fertilised ovum there is a strong predisposition to develop arms and legs; but they take time actually to develop and, as the thalidomide story illustrates, they only do so if the chemical and physical environment is within certain limits.

Our own view in this connection is that psychological object relationships cannot start until a sufficient degree of perceptual differentiation has occurred, although when they have developed, they come to play an increasingly important role in the life of the child. They are crucial to the maintenance of well-being, which is, psychically and biologically, a state of the self. Object loss may bring about acute mental pain through creating a "wound" in the self. This view coincides with what Abraham and others have described as the "severe injury to infantile narcissism" that object loss entails. And although Bowlby has maintained (1960b) that such a statement misses the true significance of object loss, we take the view that it contains its essence.

III

Some Further Comments

Both Winnicott and Melanie Klein assume that the depressive re-action can occur only when a certain stage of development, char-acterized mainly by the capacity for "whole object" relationships and associated ambivalence toward the object, is reached. Both assume the depressive response to be a much more integrated one than the response characteristic of the preceding developmental stage.

The notion of a point in early development when a variety of highly complicated psychological changes take place almost simul-taneously (as embodied in the theory of the depressive position) is one that we do not find convincing. What Melanie Klein sees as a "position" seems to us to be an oversimplified condensation of a number of different facets of development that extend over varying lengths of time. These developmental processes include the emer-gence of social responses (as distinct from purely drive-satisfying behavior), the development of the capacity to recognize specific ob-jects, the capacity to visualize the object in its absence (and to dis-tinguish such visualization from perception), the development of ambivalence, the need to make reparation, the development of an internally structured superego, and so on.

Central to the theory of the depressive position is the role of aggression and ambivalence. While we would agree that conflict over ambivalence is an important source of pain, and therefore also a possible source of the depressive response, we consider it to be only one of a number of possible sources of pain, and the depressive response is by no means specifically and uniquely related to it.

Although Freud saw the painful state of longing in terms of the libidinal aspect of object relationships (1926), there is little doubt that the role of aggression is vitally important. As Freud put it in "In-stincts and their Vicissitudes" (1915c):

> It is noteworthy that in the use of the word "hate" no . . . intimate
> connection with sexual pleasure and the sexual function appears.
> The relation of *unpleasure* seems to be the sole decisive one. The
> ego hates, abhors and pursues with intent to destroy all objects
> which are a source of unpleasurable feeling for it. . . . Indeed, it
> may be asserted that the true prototypes of the relation of hate
> are derived not from sexual life, but from the ego's struggle to
> preserve and maintain itself (p. 138).

We can add that just as the child's love for the object has its counterpart in feelings of well-being in the self derived from the object relationship, so is there a state of the self that mirrors a *hostile* relationship to the object. If the object were only hated, loss of the object would tend to restore well-being, and the loss would be accompanied by relief because of the lessening of unpleasure in the self and the resulting approximation of the self to an ideal state. Here again, the feelings of unpleasure may be related by the child to the object representation that is felt to be the source of the existence of the undesired, painful state of the self.

If the object were only loved, regaining of the lost object would equally restore a sense of well-being. However, once the child has achieved a degree of object constancy, once so-called whole-object relationships have been established, no object is only hated or only loved. In simple ambivalence there is, on the one hand, the wish to maintain well-being in the self by ensuring the object's presence; on the other, there is a wish for it to disappear because it arouses feelings of unpleasure or pain in the self. This creates a state of conflict, and there are a variety of ways in which attempts may be made to deal with this conflict. There can be, for instance, the splitting of ambivalence, so that either the loved or hated aspect of the object is displaced onto another person who is treated accordingly; or one facet of the ambivalence may simply be denied or repressed. There can be identification with some attribute of the object. There are the various forms of externalization of an aspect of the self-representation (more commonly the aggressive aspect) as in projection ("I do not hate him, he hates me"); and, indeed, all the defense mechanisms can be called into play to deal with the conflict situation. The child may also attempt to control his environment by clinging or other methods of manipulating the object, but if his ambivalence is intense, no state of his environment will be felt to be satisfactory to him, that is, will be capable of producing feelings of well-being in the self.

It is self-evident that the situation of ambivalence that we have described is a painful one. The child cannot in reality approximate the actual state of his self to that of an ideal state, because the ideal object (which would only be loved and only love in return) and that would create a state of perfect contentment in the self does not exist in reality. It is here that the child so often turns to idealization and compensation in fantasy.

It seems obvious that pain is in itself not the depressive reaction. If the internal or external situation can be successfully defended against, the pain will lessen or disappear. If the child reacts to the experience of pain by an increase in his discontent, and, in particular, if he regresses to an oral demanding attitude, he becomes the typically unhappy and complaining child with whom we are all familiar. In such cases, one often sees an inner source of discontent, one that may have a long history in the development of the child, displaced onto the external environment, so that nothing really satisfies, nothing pleases. Children defend against the recognition of an inner source of pain, and find it more comfortable to blame an object for it.

This brings us to a further important point. If a state of pain is experienced in the self, then the actual self may become an object of the child's anger or even hate. It is an unsatisfactory self, and will be invested with aggressive cathexis. *The child may experience a state of ambivalence toward his own self.* This is quite distinct from the phenomenon of aggression directed toward the self on the basis of identification with an ambivalently loved object. Unless this is successfully dealt with by some externalizing mechanism, the child may become the victim of a circular process, in which ambivalence toward the self increases the degree of pain and discontent.

Important sources of pain are external authority figures (or the superego, once it has been established). Anger felt toward the object world (and the introjects) may be inhibited because of the fear of retaliation. Fear of punishment and guilt are themselves sources of pain; but, in addition, if the ego deals with these feelings by directing aggression against the self, then this too will result in pain. Aggression may be turned toward the self by a process of displacement from the object or via identification with the hated object.

The condensation of pain and depressive affect evident in the writings of Melanie Klein may perhaps have come about because of a tendency to confuse the depressive response with those feelings of misery and unhappiness that constitute a patient's inevitable response to successful analytic confrontation with the narcissistically painful state of his self. This unhappiness is not the same as the specific type of adaptation to pain that is the depressive response. The quality of the patient's response to the painful state will depend, to a very large degree, on the extent to which he is able to express and discharge the relevant hostile and aggressive feelings toward (what he regards as) the source of his pain.

The failure to distinguish between pain and depression lends itself to the elaboration of misleading and stereotyped links between the wide field of disturbance of narcissism and the specific affective response to depression. An individual may, for example, react to a painful discrepancy between the ideal self and his actual self by a response of angry resentment, or by overcompensation in fantasy, or by exhibitionistic behavior. This does not imply that he is either experiencing a depressive response or defending against one. What we can say, however, is that if he could, in some way, be prevented from using such defenses against the painful state in the self, and then reacted with a feeling of hopelessness and helplessness, he would become depressed. Thus, whereas Winnicott and Melanie Klein might see, for instance, phallic overassertiveness as a specific defense against depression, we would say that it can be more fruitfully considered to be, for example, a defense against a painful narcissistic wound. Only if the individual abandoned his existing adaptive and defensive measures, felt helpless and lost hope, would he then become depressed.

One of the effects of the development of the depressive reaction is a lowering of the level of drive activity and an inhibition of ego functions (Bibring, 1953). This is very much like a process of hibernation, or what Winnicott (1954) describes as "wet-blanketing." While it would appear that such a lowering of the level of mental functioning provides a breathing space that may, in certain cases, allow processes of recovery to occur, we do not believe that the experience of depression is a necessary precondition for recovery. It may, of course, ultimately prove to have been of value to the individual if he successfully recovers from it and if it does not become a habit. We deplore the tendency among some analysts to elevate depression to the status of a virtue without regard to the distinction between the mastery of pain in an adaptive way, the depressive response, and melancholia.

IV

Individuation

In a previous paper (Sandler & Joffe, 1965b) on this topic it was suggested that in the course of normal development the child constantly experiences discrepancies between actual and ideal states of the self. His progressive movement toward the appreciation of reality involves the relinquishing of previously experienced satisfactory states of the self. In the child's early years, these satisfactory states have been felt to be magical and omnipotent. We said: "This is a spur to adaptation, and the attractions offered by the child's new potentialities and experiences enable him to withdraw cathexis from the lost ideal states with the minimum of pain, cathexis which can be invested in new ideals created by processes of maturation and the move forward into a fresh developmental phase" (p. 94).

The picture of a smooth move forward conveyed by this statement is an optimal one, never occurring fully in reality. Conditions of frustration and suffering will bring about a turning toward the attainment of previous infantile ideals that can be reached in fact or in fantasy. This is probably the essence of the processes of temporary regression that we see in the course of normal development. The regression may in fact function as an attempt to stave off helplessness and its possible sequel, the depressive response. The overcoming of regression and the subsequent move forward must inevitably be linked with some degree of suffering, however small, and it follows that a process in some way analogous to processes of mourning must normally occur. The mourning is,* in this case, associated with the pain of giving up infantile ideal states of the self (but not necessarily with depression). This process is among those that have been referred to as individuation by Jung, Erich Fromm,† and Margaret Mahler. We shall adhere to the same term, meaning by it the gradual development of increasingly reality-adapted ideals for the child,‡ with the associated giving up of infantile aims and dependence on external objects for supplies of well-being.

This relates closely to the ideas expressed by Margaret Mahler (1952, 1957, 1958, 1961, 1963; Mahler & Furer, 1963). She has, over a number of years, elaborated her concepts of normal developmental

---

*The relation between mourning for a lost object and adaptation has been extensively discussed by Pollock (1961). His emphasis is, however, on adaptation to a changed external reality, while our own is related to adaptation to a loss of an ideal state of the self.

†The dictionary definition of the term "individuation" is the action or process of individuating, i.e., the process leading to individual existence, as distinct from that of the species. This usage dates at least from 1628. It also means the condition of being an individual, individuality, personal identity (1642). The biological meaning of the term is the sum of the processes on which the life of the individual depends (19th century). For Jung (1923), individuation "is the process of forming and specializing the individual nature—in particular, it is the development of the psychological individual as a differentiated being from the general, collective psychology. Individuation, therefore, is a *process of differentiation*, having for its goal the development of the individual personality." A discussion of the Jungian view has been presented by Fordham (1958).

Erich Fromm (1941) regards the process of individuation as the emergence of the individual from his original ties. He has discussed the process primarily in terms of the relation of the individual to society, pointing out that the individual pays the price of "growing isolation, insecurity . . . and a growing feeling of one's own powerlessness and insignificance as an individual." As this process occurs, it may result in anxiety and insecurity or in a new relationship with others if the child has been able to build up the necessary inner strength and productiveness. Fromm's view of this process is, in one sense, close to Jung's; but insofar as he deals with the growing individual's attempts to cope with pain through the development of new ideals, his view is related to ours. Tomkins (1963) has discussed the relation between what he refers to as "distress-anguish" and individuation, and has related many aspects of progressive development to the mastery of unpleasant affect.

‡Identification plays an important role in this connection.

phases in terms of *autism, symbiosis,* and *separation–individuation.* The separation–individuation phase is one in which the infant develops into a toddler, delimiting his own individual entity from the primal symbiotic mother–infant unit. It is in this phase that he separates the mental representation of his own self from that of the mother, and it occurs simultaneously with the consolidation and maturation of autonomous ego functions. The development of locomotion allows the child to separate from the mother, and he will then show pleasure in his new independence and mastery. He may, however, show anxiety at this separateness. Mahler emphasizes that such anxiety occurs even in the presence of the mother during the "separation–individuation" phase (in contrast to situations of traumatic separation of the type described by Bowlby). Mahler (1963) speaks of the "minimal threats of object loss which the maturationally predetermined ascendance of autonomous functioning by necessity entails." She makes a valuable point when she emphasizes that the development of autonomous functions itself constitutes a threat of some sort to the child. But whereas she sees the danger, however slight, in terms of threats of object loss, we would stress the painful necessity for the child to give up *ideal states of the self* previously experienced during the "symbiotic" phase. The mother representation is, of course, after a certain level of development has been reached, the prime perceptual key to states of well-being. In addition, the substitution of what might be called "pleasure in function," for libidinal gratifications through the object, is an important element in the formation of new, reality-adapted ideals for the child (Hendrick, 1942, 1943).

In addition to obtaining "pleasure in function" and "pleasure in mastery," the toddler attaches a "cathexis of value" or "value accent" (Hartmann, 1947) to his newly acquired achievements, and the alteration in his ideal self that ensues is one that enables him to achieve unity of actual self and ideal through his independent activities. The effective operation of this process minimizes the pain involved in the abandonment of previous mother-dependent ideal states of the self. Erikson (1946b) describes this: "To be 'one who can walk' becomes one of the many steps in child development which through the coincidence of physical mastery and cultural meaning, of functional pleasure and social recognition, contribute to a more realistic self-esteem."

It follows that individuation involves not only the giving up of the wish for past and inappropriate ideal states and the acquisition of new phase-specific reality-adapted ideals, but also the gradual attainment of pleasure in function and mastery (in addition to the gratification afforded by direct drive discharge).

In contrast to those who see such processes as occurring in a specific developmental phase, we consider individuation to be a line of development that continues throughout life. While it is true that failures in early development may later make individuation difficult, and conversely, that adequate early individuation lays the foundation for more successful individuation later in life, the growing individual is constantly confronted with situations that require further processes of individuation. Anna Freud (1963b) has described, in another context, certain developmental tasks that occur in the life of the child.* These situations confront the individual, we believe, with important individuation tasks and extend into adult life in such situations as university entrance, taking a job, engagement and marriage, parenthood, mid-life crises, menopause, bereavement, adaptation to retirement and old age, and so on. In each of these there is the necessity to relinquish not only earlier modes of drive satisfaction, but also previously satisfying or secure states of the self, in the service of adaptation. When individuation proceeds smoothly, the positive gains in well-being outweigh any pain that might accompany the loss of a previous source of satisfaction and states of the self.

The specific tasks and crisis situations that we have mentioned may exist as external sources of pain in their own right. The recognition of such situations forms a basis for the clinical approach of many practitioners in social and preventive psychiatry. However, it is common analytic experience that such tasks or demands are significant to the extent to which they are involved in the individual's unconscious inner conflicts.† What may appear as an external crisis may be predominantly an internal one, but we can distinguish between those situations that are created entirely by the repetition compulsion or by the need to externalize inner conflict and those that stimulate and intensify existing conflicts (either by disrupting the defensive organization or by reinforcing repressed infantile wishes or fantasies). Some individuals can deal with the painful state that arises only by attempting to reapply past solutions, while others may be able, under the pressure of the need to adapt to the new situation,

---

*For example, separation from the mother; birth of a sibling; illness and surgical intervention; hospitalization; entry into nursery school; school entry; the step from a triangular oedipal situation into a community of peers; the step from play to work; the arousal of new genital strivings in adolescence; the step from infantile objects within the family to new objects outside the family.

†The significance of external situations may be greater for the child before external conflict has been fully internalized. However, he constantly experiences internal developmental crises (e.g., the threats to security brought about by the realization of the failure of his omnipotence in the anal phase; by the need to reconcile himself to the unattainability of his oedipal objects, etc.).

to relinquish the tie to previous ideal selves in the process of individuation.*

The turning toward new, more reality-adapted ideals in the interest of pain avoidance does not necessitate a slavish acceptance of culturally determined norms. The important point here is that the new ideals, if individuation is successful, diminish by means of their conflict-reducing character the possibility of the individual's paralysis through intolerable feelings of ambivalence and envy. On the contrary, they permit progressive personality development to take place. We have stressed the construction of reality-syntonic ideals as an essential aspect of the process of individuation. It is clear, however, that these new ideals must have conflict-reducing properties. They may be regarded as ego-syntonic compromise formations, compounded of both external and internal reality.

Although we have spoken of the "giving up" of earlier ideals in individuation, what is given up is the pursuit of these infantile ideals by the ego in relatively unmodified form, through the establishment of appropriate countercathexes. These ideals are given up as unrealistic, although the fantasy content of previous ideals may show itself in the compromise formation that has become the new, reality-adapted ideal.

If we consider the relation of pain to depression and individuation, then a particular statement made by Melanie Klein is of some interest. In her paper "Mourning and its Relation to Manic–Depressive States" (1948), she remarks: "Any pain, caused by unhappy experiences, whatever their nature, has something in common with mourning. It reactivates the infantile depressive position; the encountering and overcoming of adversity of any kind entails mental work similar to mourning." This statement has something in common with what we have described as individuation; but we do not believe it necessary to evoke an infantile "depressive position" to explain adaptive responses to painful adversities. Nor do we consider that the loss entailed in "the encountering and overcoming of adversity of any kind" is always object loss, be it in the present or in the past, in reality or in fantasy, or of an internal or an external object. Further, we do not believe that we should take it as axiomatic that the "working through" involved in overcoming adversity is

---

*In this chapter we are dealing with the problem of individuation in fairly general terms. It is not our intention to discuss here the question of the role of the superego introjects and the whole problem of individuation from the infantile ideals that they sustain.

always accompanied by depressive affect, consciously or unconsciously.*

In this paper we have viewed the process of individuation predominantly from the side of the ego. Yet it represents, in a sense, a line of development that includes changes on the side of the drives, particularly as drive and ego development normally go hand in hand. What we have viewed as the state of well-being is genetically linked with the attained state of drive satisfaction (but not necessarily with the pleasures that arise during the course of drive discharge). During the course of development, the individual may retain ideal self-representations that reflect earlier states of instinctual satisfaction, even though the drives may have proceeded further along their developmental path. Normal individuation will therefore include the changes in the ideal self that are appropriate to drive progression.†

---

*It has been suggested that there is a possible link between our views and Melanie Klein's idea of the infant's need to make reparation. There may indeed be a common element in the notion of "restoring the wished-for state" and the process of reparation referred to by Melanie Klein in connection with the working through of the depressive position. In making this comparison we should bear in mind that there are two sides to the process of reparation as described by Melanie Klein. The first aspect relates to the *restoration* of a previous state, and the second to the need to *make amends* because of guilt about the effects of sadistic attacks on the love object. While the dictionary definition includes these alternative meanings of reparation (i.e., restoration and making amends), the two are not always the same. Insofar as Melanie Klein uses "reparation" in the sense of repair or restoration, we could find ourselves on common ground with her. But we do not believe that the motive for restoration is always to make amends for a sadistic attack on the object. In order to avoid misunderstanding, we would like to say at this point that we recognize that fantasies of sadistic attacks on the object can be an important source of pain (or the special form of pain that may be found in guilt) and that making amends to the object may be one form of dealing with such pain. However, what we refer to in our paper in this connection is a functional process in the ego whereby the ego attempts to maintain a state of maximal well-being. We have put forward the view that in painful states, whatever their cause, there is, of course, a loss of well-being, and that the ego may strive in many different ways to restore the ideal affective state. This may be attempted by defensive maneuvers of one sort or another, through attempts to re-create regressively past ideal situations, or through the progressive creation of new ideals (which we have called "individuation"). We do not subscribe to the view that it is always and only guilt about destruction of love objects that is the primary motive for restoration in the sense in which we use the word.

†The whole topic of the discrepancy between drive progression on the one hand and changes in content of the ideal self on the other requires much further study. For example, we have the very interesting situation in certain individuals in whom changes in the ideal self occur in advance of drive progression. Perhaps we can include in this broad group the case of the highly gifted person who has achieved an apparently successful adaptation through what might be termed *"pseudo-individuation,"* based on a massive magical identification with an idealized object.

Conclusion

We have defined mental pain, whatever its cause and extent, as reflecting a discrepancy between an actual state of the self and an ideal wished-for state. This can be based on the memory of a previous state of satisfaction or on fantasies that may have multiple determinants.

From the point of view of the drives, the normal response to pain is aggression, directed at whatever is considered to be the source of the pain. Projective, identificatory, and displacement processes enter here, in both normal and pathogenic development. Particularly after object constancy has been attained, the object representation comes to be an essential component of ideal states of well-being. Although clinically we may deal with states of object loss, we would stress again that what is lost in object loss is ultimately a state of the self for which the object is the vehicle. A failure to defend against pain, to discharge aggression adequately, or to reduce an intolerable "cathexis of longing" may be followed by a depressive response.

From the point of view of the ego, there are many possible responses to pain. Prominent among these is individuation, a process that involves "working through" in a manner analogous to mourning. It involves the adaptive abandoning of the pursuit of lost ideal states and their replacement by new ideals that are both ego and reality syntonic. Individuation occurs as a process throughout life, and in particular is associated with typical developmentally and culturally determined tasks and crises. It can fail for many reasons and such failure may be followed by maldevelopment or a depressive response.

The depressive response has previously been described in some detail. It represents a capitulation in the face of pain, a capitulation that involves a generalized inhibition of drive and ego functions. While this may blunt the pain and provide time for recovery, *it is not aimed at recovery*. It may be followed by individuation, but it may also be followed by other defensive measures that do not result in individuation; nor is depression an essential prerequisite for individuation.*

---

*We want to emphasize this point, for we believe that the association of depression with that individuation that occurs during the course of analysis is, to some extent, imposed by the analytic process itself. If a patient is confronted with a painful state that he has been defending against, and if all his further defensive attempts are aborted by interpretation, depression may follow as a natural consequence. Recovery from this depressive response may be associated with gradual working through and individuation with the help of the analysis. The occurrence of the depressive response *may indicate* that other defenses against pain are no longer effective. It is an aspect of

Theoretically, optimal individuation could be regarded as a relatively painless, depression-free process. In reality it is never seen without some degree of pain. In addition to this, there is often some degree of temporary regression to early ideal or idealized states, regression of the sort that is found in the course of normal development (Anna Freud, 1963a).

There are many factors that influence and determine the outcome of the individual's struggle to master pain and depression, and we should be wary of regarding any one specific cause, or a failure in any one developmental phase, as being the sole factor in determining the outcome of such a struggle. We can recognize, to mention but a few, the influence of constitutional factors (including the predisposition to use particular defenses, frustration and discharge thresholds, differences in the apparatuses of primary autonomy, and variations in drive endowment), the nature of the holding environment at various times in the person's life, the intensity of phase-specific anxieties, the influence of drive fixation points, and all the vicissitudes of superego formation.

---

correct analytic technique that it promotes conditions that facilitate progressive individuation. This is especially important in the case of those patients who cannot individuate without a measure of depression. The view expressed by Winnicott that depression contains a "built-in" therapy reflects a view that we do not share. We know that depressions tend to lift, particularly if, as Winnicott has put it, they are not contaminated by "impurities." We would correlate this, however, with the ego's recovery, and it does not imply that the painful state of affairs that prompted the depressive response has been resolved. In many instances the lifting of the depression is associated with nothing else but the bringing into play of more effective defenses, and the subsequent failure of these may be the reason that so many depressions tend to recur. The aspect of recurrence should always be considered when the aspect of remission is considered.

12

On Disorders of Narcissism

Walter G. Joffe and Joseph Sandler

When the papers reproduced in this chapter and in Chapter 13 were first published, they aroused some considerable disquiet because they contained a rejection of the energy-transformation theory that had been central to ego-psychological writings, especially those of Hartmann, Kris, and Loewenstein. The paper on disorders of narcissism (Joffe & Sandler, 1967a) linked narcissistic processes with feeling states rather than with energies, and was criticized on the basis that it did not leave room for the economic point of view. This criticism was based on the incorrect assumption that an economic viewpoint necessitated acceptance of the psychoanalytic energy theory.

An increasing amount of attention is being paid in psychoanalysis to the assessment and treatment of "disturbances of narcissism" in both children and adults. While originally the term "narcissistic disorder" was used by Freud (1923a) to refer to the psychoses, the term has nowadays come to be used in connection with a much wider field of clinical disturbances, a field that encompasses a variety of conditions reflecting major disturbances in attitudes towards the self and in the regulation of well-being and self-esteem. These disturbances, which include depressive reactions in children as well as adults, show in their pathology not only conflict over drive discharge but also substantial intrasystemic ego disturbance connected with the maintenance of self–object relationships and problems of self-regard and identity.

Thus while we may, for example, assess a child who has problems over exhibitionism from the point of view of neurotic conflict over the discharge of exhibitionistic drive impulses, we also include the consideration of the function of exhibitionism in connection with the maintenance by the child of a particular type of object relationship, and its function as a possible technique for gaining admiration and praise in order to do away with underlying feelings of unworthiness, inadequacy, or guilt. Thus, for example, it is well-known from psychoanalytic work with adults that actors may not only be attempting to sublimate their exhibitionistic impulses in their work. Acting to an audience can have an important function from the point of view of maintaining an "identity in action," an identification with some "ideal" self-image that may serve the function of defending against an underlying painful ego state, a state that can originate in many different ways.

Hartmann (1950) has pointed out that it is essential to distinguish clearly between ego, self, and personality if we are to examine problems of narcissism within a structural framework. He proposed that narcissism be defined not as the libidinal cathexis of the ego but of the self-representation; in this sense, narcissism could be contrasted with the libidinal cathexis of an object representation (object cathexis). Hartmann's formulation retained Freud's (1914) view that narcissistic libidinal cathexis can be transformed into object cathexis and vice versa. A higher degree of narcissistic (i.e., self) cathexis was seen to imply a lower level of object cathexis, and similarly, an overinvestment of the object representation with libido meant that the amount of narcissistic investment must be correspondingly low.

That there is an assumption of a fixed quantity of libido contained in Freud's original formulation is borne out by the following remark in the "On Narcissism" paper (1914): "We see also, broadly speaking, an antithesis between ego-libido [we would now say libidinal cathexis of the self] and object-libido. The more of the one is employed, the more the other becomes depleted" (p. 76).

When we come to apply the concept of libido distribution to clinical material, we find that certain difficulties arise. For example, a child may have intense feelings of inferiority, appear to be very insecure, and show marked dependence on the attitude of his objects for his well-being. From this, one might be tempted to infer that the level of his narcissistic cathexis of his self-representation is low. However, the same child may show a high degree of self-interest and self-preoccupation in one form or another. He may, for example, indulge in many daydreams in which he figures as the hero, he may be concerned about his physical health, and so on. The constant attention that he pays to his objects may be predominantly in relation to the use he makes of them to gratify his need for admiration, support, or praise. Indeed, he may present the features of what is often referred to as a "narcissistic character," and we might accordingly be inclined to assess him, from this point of view, as having a high degree of narcissistic cathexis. We have here an immediate problem if we attempt to encompass these phenomena in terms of the distribution of libidinal cathexis between the child's self and object representations.

The opposite case raises similar problems. We may see a child who appears to be extremely secure, who maintains a basically constant state of well-being in spite of adverse environmental conditions. We might confidently say that he has an adequate and sufficient degree of narcissistic self-cathexis. We might be surprised at any suggestion that such a child's narcissism was depleted. Yet it is usually precisely such children who are capable of more mature types of object relationship, who show consideration, love, and concern for their objects, and who would have accordingly to be assessed as the possessors of a high degree of object cathexis.

We take such clinical states for granted, but if we are to apply metapsychological formulations to the clinical material meticulously, it seems clear that a simple statement of the distribution of libidinal cathexis between self and object representations is at best insufficient for our purposes, even if we allow for the assumption of differences in quantity of libido in different children. We are all, of course, in dealing with the sort of clinical material that we have attempted to subsume under the heading of "disturbances of narcissism," compelled to use what are in fact highly sophisticated qualitative descriptions that are not adequately encompassed by drive-energic formulations. While it is true that dynamic, structural, genetic, developmental, and adaptational considerations are usually taken into account, it is worthwhile exploring the extent to which the concept of energy distribution can remain useful if we extend our theoretical framework.

The first thought that comes to mind is that a distinction between primary and secondary narcissistic cathexis of the self might be of value. We could say, for instance, that if there is a low degree of residual primary narcissism and the quantity of secondary narcissism is high, then this would fit the picture of the insecure and dependent child who may nevertheless be referred to as "narcissistic." However, it must be evident that if such a formulation is to be satisfactorily applied, then additional *qualitative* assumptions are necessary. The inadequacy of a description in terms of a distinction between primary and secondary narcissism in this context becomes clear if we remember that we are dealing with the addition and subtraction of quantities of libido. Once secondary narcissistic cathexis is added to primary narcissism we cannot, *from the point of view of quantity alone,* differentiate between them. To do so would be as difficult as ascertaining, from the total amount of money in a bank account, how much was derived from capital and how much from income.

What we have said does not mean that there are no differences between the *states* that we call primary and secondary narcissism; of course there are, but they have always been described in terms that are not simply statements relating to energy distribution. Existing psychoanalytic theory certainly does make allowances for qualitative distinctions, and we shall touch on some of these later. For the time being, however, we shall be concerned with rigorously pursuing the "energy-distribution" aspects of narcissism in order to "test the limits" of its application.

It seems possible to make a step forward in the application of the libido distribution concept if we take into account the fact that different aspects of the self-representation—different self-images—can be regarded as being cathected by different quantities of libido. We can conveniently speak in this connection of different *shapes* of the self-representation (Chapter 5), and say that the child might invest a high degree of libidinal cathexis in that "shape" that is "ideal" self, and a low amount in that image that is his perception or apperception of the actual state of his self at any time. The same considerations would apply to different images of the object, and we can differentiate between, "ideal" and "actual" object representations, the first being assumed to receive a greater quantity of libidinal investment than the second. We are now in a position to apply such a model to the hypothetical cases that were cited earlier. We might say, for example, that the first child has a low degree of libidinal cathexis of his "actual" self-representation, but a high investment in his ideal. Similarly, the representation of his "actual" object might have a low object cathexis, and that of the ideal object may be substantially invested with libido.

Although this may seem at first sight to be a considerable step forward in the application of the energy-distribution concept, the increasing importance in our metapsychology of aggression and of aggressive cathexis must lead us to give it an equal place alongside libido in our consideration of narcissism. Edith Jacobson (1954c) has demonstrated very convincingly that the discussion of primary and secondary narcissism must, if it is to be profitable, be considered along with primary and secondary masochism. Primary masochism may be regarded as the very early cathexis of the self with aggression, and secondary masochism the turning of aggressive cathexis from object representations to the self-representation.

If we expand our scheme to include aggression, we would have to take into account that each and every representation of self or object may receive quantities of libidinal and aggressive cathexis. The system of self and object representations must also include ideal selves and ideal objects as well as "actual" self and objects. But this is not all. Kaplan and Whitman (1965) have drawn attention to the role of so-called negative ideals that represent the "introjected negative standards of the parents and of the culture" (p. 183). The "negative ideal" represents the "self-I-do-not-want-to-be." These negative ideals have clearly to be taken into account, but if we do so in relation to quantities of libido and aggression, we may then find ourselves in a position of such complexity in regard to clinical assessment that it would take a mathematician to disentangle us. And even with all this refinement, we cannot be at all certain that we have encompassed more than a small part of the relevant aspects of our clinical material in an adequate theoretical fashion.

It must be abundantly clear by now that concepts that are auxiliary to those of energy distribution must be called upon if we are to account for the state of an individual's "narcissism" in a meaningful way. What we propose to do now is to examine the way in which such auxiliary concepts have been used, either implicitly or explicitly, in the work of various authors. We may begin with Freud who, although he defined narcissism in terms of libidinal investment in 1914, stated at that time that narcissism was the libidinal complement to the egoism of the instinct of self-preservation (page 74). His descriptions in this connection always involved statements referring to attitudes of what later came to be called the ego as we now understand it. Thus he made statements such as the following: "The libido that has been withdrawn from the external world has been directed to the ego and thus gives rise to *an attitude* which may be called narcissism" (p. 75, our italics).

Throughout his writings, even after the abandonment of the theory of ego instincts, Freud used such terms as "self-regard," "self-love," and "narcissistic libido" interchangeably.

Edith Jacobson, in her valuable paper on "The Self and the Object World" (1954c), elaborated the intimate connection between the psychoeconomic processes of narcissism and masochism on the one hand and affective experience on the other. On this basis she goes on to make such statements as: "he is apt to undergo experiences of realistic physical and of mental hurt accompanied by feelings of inferiority which clearly manifest an increasing cathexis of the self-representation with aggression turned away from the love objects" (p. 92). "The rising cathexis of the [whole self] manifests itself in general feelings of increased self-confidence" (p. 94).

In speaking of people who relate well to the object world, she says: "The wide and rich affective scale, the manifold and subtle feeling shades, the warm and vivid emotional qualities . . . point to the predominance of object-libido and the variety of its fusions with more or less neutralized energy" (pp. 96–97).

Jacobson introduced a great many sophisticated ideas into her consideration of narcissism and object love, and she demonstrated unequivocally both in her 1954 paper and in her recent book (*The Self and the Object World*, 1964) that any attempt to link such concepts as affects, values, self-esteem, and self-devaluation with quantities of energy must indeed be extremely complicated.

Fenichel had, in 1945, made use of the concepts of narcissistic *needs* and narcissistic *supplies* without deeming it necessary to define these in terms of quantities of energic cathexis. Thus he says:

"The full capacity for love not only changes the relations toward other persons but also the relation towards one's own ego. The contrast between object-love and self-love again is a relative one: in primary narcissism there is self-love, *instead* of object-love; in secondary narcissism there is a need for self-love (self-esteem) which overshadows the object-love. With the capacity for object-love another, higher, post-narcissistic type of self-respect becomes available." (p. 85)

As early as 1928, Rado had remarked that frustration during the oral phase lowers feelings of security and the self-esteem of the infantile ego. Bibring took this a step further in 1953 when he equated lowered self-esteem with the ego state of depression.

Fenichel equated self-esteem with self-love, and also defined it as the expression of closeness to infantile omnipotent feelings (1945). Jacobson's formulation was that self-esteem was "expressive of the discrepancy or harmony between the self-representations and the wishful concepts of the self" (1954c, p. 123).

Lampl-de Groot (1936, 1947) drew attention to the importance of maintaining a sufficient level of self-esteem, both for the child and for the adult, and illustrated the way in which threats to self-esteem affect ego functioning.

Annie Reich, in her paper on "Pathologic Forms of Self-Esteem Regulation" (1960) applied Jacobson's definition of self-esteem and demonstrated its usefulness in the understanding of certain types of narcissistic disorder. Her clinical formulations are couched in terms that refer to ego states—ego attitudes and defensive formations.

With all these formulations, we find ourselves, with the authors quoted, unequivocally in the sphere of feeling states of the ego. It would seem that a full understanding of narcissism and its disorders must take into account all that we have learned in psychoanalytic theory—and much that we have not yet learned—about feeling states and their modes of regulation. It is striking that when we come to describe clinical states in which the relationship between self and object is important, we tend to phrase our formulations in terms of feelings and attitudes. When, however, we speak of love or hate of an object, or love or hate of the self, and go on to characterize this clinical state metapsychologically in terms of energy distribution, we are certainly in danger of obscuring and blunting both our clinical and theoretical formulations.

Freud was, of course, well aware of this problem, and he attempted to deal with the clinical manifestations of differences between, for example, crude sensuality and tenderness, by postulating a process of aim inhibition of the instinctual drive. Later writers, particularly Hartmann, Kris, Loewenstein, and Jacobson, have also been aware of the difficulties involved and have dealt with it by extending Freud's theory of sublimated or desexualized libido to the aggressive drives as well (Hartmann, Kris, & Loewenstein, 1949), postulating degrees of neutralization of drive energies in addition to a primary neutral energy.

In all these approaches there is either the implicit or explicit assumption that feeling states mirror, either functionally or genetically, the cathectic distribution of the various energies.

Consider, for example, the following quotation from Edith Jacobson (1954c):

> Hence disturbances of self-esteem may originate from many sources and represent a very complex pathology: on the one hand, a pathology of the ego ideal and of the self-critical ego and superego functions; on the other hand a pathology of the ego functions and of the self-representations. Increase or decrease of libidinous or aggressive discharge, inhibitions or stimulation of ego functions, libidinous impoverishment or enrichment of the self caused by external or internal factors, from somatic, psychosomatic, or psychological sources, *may induce or enhance the libidinous or aggressive cathexis of the self-representations and lead to fluctuations of self-esteem."* (pp. 123–4, our italics).

However, Jacobson has herself pointed out that there are difficulties in the way of linking affects entirely to drive concepts (1953b), and it seems likely that the difficulties remain even if we bring neutralized energy into the picture (see Chapter 13).

We would like to offer, in this paper, an alternative approach to the problem of "disturbances of narcissism," an approach based on the view that Freud's formulations of the pleasure principle really referred to *two* aspects of the organism's functioning, namely the regulation of energic homeostasis on the one hand, and the various experiences that accompanied this regulation on the other. That there is an intimate link between these two aspects in early infancy is indisputable, but this should not obscure the difference between feelings and instinctual drives. Max Schur has treated this topic in some considerable detail in a recent monograph (1966).

From the point of view of the simple biological animal, the principle of energic homeostasis may be useful and adequate. However, from the moment the infant becomes a psychological being, from the moment it begins to construct a representational world as the mediator of adaptation, much of its functioning is regulated by feeling states of one sort or another. The demands of the drives, and the reduction of these demands, have a major influence on feeling states, but they are not the only influence. Feeling states are produced and influenced by stimuli arising from sources other than the drives, for example, from the external environment; and it is an oversimplification to assume that the vicissitudes of the development of affects are a direct reflection of the vicissitudes of the drives.

In addition to his condensation of the energic and experiential aspects of the pleasure principle, Freud did not distinguish pleasure accompanying drive discharge from the state of satisfaction, of well-being, that follows it. The double meaning of the term "gratification" was pointed out over 30 years ago by Waelder (1933) when he spoke of the "fatal equivocation resident in the word 'gratification' (*Befriedigung*)." Waelder, Bühler, Hendrick, Hartmann, and others have also drawn attention to the existence of "function pleasure" and its role in mental activity, and it is difficult to see how this type of feeling experience can be encompassed by a simple pleasure principle.

It must be self-evident that the feeling experiences of even the very young infant include not only feelings of pleasure and unpleasure but also feelings of well-being associated with the somatic states that follow instinctual gratification. While it is true that well-being may be the feeling state that accompanies drive quiescence in the neonate, it is by no means certain that it is equally a reflection of drive quiescence in the older child or adult. While we may link pleasure, unpleasure, and well-being with the state of the instinctual drives in the very young infant, there is evidence that the newborn infant is able to distinguish feelings of pain from the unpleasure associated with unsatisfied instinctual urges. Thus, for example, it has been demonstrated (Lind, 1965) that the newborn infant produces a different cry when it is hurt than when it is hungry, and we can perhaps infer that its subjective experience is also different in the two conditions. As the child develops, so its organization of affective experiences becomes increasingly complex and more removed from its actual bodily state.

It is obvious that a formulation such as that of the pleasure principle (and its descendant, the reality principle) cannot alone do justice to the processes whereby these experiential states (we include here both conscious and unconscious experience) are brought about and regulated. For example, it is evident from clinical work with both children and adults that the need to preserve well-being and safety may take precedence over the wish to gain sensual pleasure. The striving for sexual pleasure is, as we all know, readily sacrificed in the interest of preserving feelings of safety. Any attempt to explain all of this as a reflection of the disposition of drive energies within the whole mental apparatus is obviously bound to be unsatisfactory. Feelings, we have suggested, do not only reflect fluctuations in the drives, although genetically there may be a close (but still far from complete) connection.

Freud drew attention to the function of the affect of anxiety as a signal that initiates special forms of adaptive activity (1926), and we believe that there is a strong argument in favor of the idea that all adaptive activity, defensive or otherwise, is instigated and regulated by the ego's conscious and unconscious scanning and perception of changes in its feeling states. We can assume that, from the very beginning of life, the development of the individual is influenced not only by the search for pleasurable experiences and the avoidance of unpleasurable ones. The striving to attain states that embody feelings of well-being and safety (Chapter 1) are, we suggest, of cardinal importance.

The implication of all this discussion is that we take the view that the states that are important in any consideration of narcissism are not only determined by the state of the drives nor can they be more than partially understood in terms of the hypothetical distribution of energic cathexes. We would suggest that the clinical understanding of narcissism and its disorders should be explicitly oriented towards a conceptualization in terms of a metapsychology of affects, attitudes, values, and the ideational contents associated with these, from the standpoint of both present function and genetic development.

It seems to us that it is possible to approach narcissism and its disorders from the view point of deviations from an ideal state of well-being, in which emphasis is placed on affective and ideational aspects rather than on drive energies, however transformed, modified, or neutralized these may be. And in order to avoid any possible misunderstanding on this point, we wish to make it perfectly clear that we regard the most potent factors in maintaining or disrupting the ideal state to be the instinctual drives, and that the ideational and affective content of what we refer to as the ideal state (or indeed, any other affective state of the ego) are profoundly affected by the sensori-motor components of instinctual wishes.

During the course of development, affective experiences become increasingly integrated with ideational content, and aspects of both self and object representations become linked with affective qualities, often of the most complicated sort. In his connection, the notion of an *affective cathexis* of a representation becomes meaningful and valuable; and affective cathexes can range from the most primitive feelings of pleasure and unpleasure to the subtle complexities of love and hate.

In Chapter 11 we pointed out that the term 'ideal' in this context refers to an affective state of well-being. This was seen as the feeling component linked with primary narcissism, and it was considered that many of the dynamics of ego functioning could be understood in relation to the ego's motivation to preserve the dynamic homeostasis associated with the maintenance of a state of well-being. A connection was made with the concept of the representational world (Chapter 5), and it was emphasized that the developing child's system of self and object representations includes both images and affective states.

It follows from this that the state of psychological well-being can be said to exist when there is a substantial correspondence between the mental representation of the actual state of the self and an ideal "shape" of the self. This formulation is, of course, similar to Jacobson's (1954c), although her view is presented in terms of self-esteem. It seems to us that the basic form of unpleasure in disturbances of narcissism is an affective experience of mental pain (Sandler & Joffe, 1965b). Mental pain, in the sense in which we are using the term, reflects a substantial discrepancy between the mental representation of the actual self of the moment and an ideal shape of the self. Lack of self-esteem, feelings of inferiority and unworthiness, shame and guilt, all represent particular higher-order derivatives of the basic affect of pain. These higher-order derivatives are determined and influenced by the manifold and complex elements that enter into the formation of the ideal self (Chapter 6).

At this point we are in a position to make a step towards the definition of narcissistic disorder. We would regard its central feature to be the existence of an overt or latent state of pain that has constantly to be dealt with by the ego; and the defensive and adaptive maneuvers that are responses to it can assume pathological proportions. The developmental causes of the state of pain may be many and varied, and the major part of the individual's activities may be directed towards coping with it or preventing its occurrence. These activities may take various forms; the so-called seeking of narcissistic supplies, overcompensation in fantasy, identification with idealized and omnipotent figures, pathologically exaggerated forms of narcissistic object choice, the compulsive pseudosexuality characteristic of

nymphomania, many aspects of homosexual activity and other perversions, and the like. Various forms of self-punishment may be
seen, particularly when superego factors predominate in causing
pain. Self-damaging and self-denigrating activities may be sexualized
and reinforced by masochistic trends.

If the individual's adaptive and defensive maneuvers fail, and
he is left helpless and hopeless in the face of the (conscious or
unconscious) state of pain, he may then develop a depressive reaction—this view places the depressions in the wide realm of narcissistic disorders (see Chapter 11).

Important in all of this is the role played by the particular *values*
attached to various representations of the self, and the genesis and
pathology of these values. We have suggested elsewhere that enduring and constant attitudes to objects differ from more primitive
need-satisfying ones by virtue of the object representations being
invested not only with drive-related pleasure and unpleasure cathexis, but also with an enduring affective ego cathexis of *value* (cf.
Hartmann, 1938, 1947, and Chapter 13). By "value" in this connection
we do not refer specifically to moral value, but the term is used
rather in the sense of feeling qualities that may be positive or negative, relatively simple or extremely complicated. It is these affective
values, sign-values so to speak, that give all representations their
particular significance to the ego. Thus in studying the narcissistic
disorders, we are involved in questions of attitudes to the self that
are intimately bound up with the enduring affective value cathexes
attached to self and object representations. Thus the self-representation can be invested with an enduring affective value cathexis of
love or hate in the same way as object representations can be; like
objects, the self may be ambivalently loved and hated. And these
value cathexes can be attached to all the extensions of self and object
that the various activities of the individual may come to represent.

13

On Sublimation

Joseph Sandler and Walter G. Joffe

The discussion of sublimation in this chapter raises many general issues, particularly in regard to the theory of energy transformation, which has been a central aspect of psychoanalytic metapsychology for many years. It now seems clear that the idea of neutralization of mental energy, while it may have been useful in the past, is now not only limited but also imposes limitations on the further development of psychoanalytic psychology.

The paper that constitutes this chapter was presented at the Fall Meetings of The American Psychoanalytic Association in 1964. It was read at a session chaired by Joan Fleming, who permitted the heated discussion to exceed the alloted time by more than an hour. Rudolf Loewenstein was emphatically critical and warned us that we were treading a dangerous path. On the other hand, Heinz Hartmann was positive and supportive and commented that the formulation of the idea of sublimation as a transformation (in particular, neutralization) of energy "was the best that could be done at the time." The paper appeared in *The Journal of the American Psychoanalytic Association* in 1966.

Introducing the panel discussion on sublimation at the Midwinter Meeting,* Hartmann pointed out that despite "the broad and general use made by analysts of the concept of sublimation and despite many attempts to free it from its ambiguities, there is no doubt that a certain amount of discontent with some of its facets is rather common among us." The formulations of Hartmann and Kris, and the contributions of the other panel discussants did much to advance the

---

*The panel on sublimation at the Midwinter Meeting of the American Psychoanalytic Association was held in December 1954, and the proceedings were reported by Arlow (1955). The presentations of Hartmann and Kris were both published in 1955.

theory of sublimation. The concept of neutralization has brought us to a new level of understanding; but, as always with any major contribution to theory, the new insights have generated further problems and questions to be answered.

In our work on the classification of analytic material derived from the analysis of children at the Hampstead Clinic, we have found that the practical problem of indexing sublimations faced us with certain challenging and stimulating issues. In order to discuss these, the Sublimation Research Group was set up as part of the Index project, and this paper is a description of some of the tentative formulations and speculations that emerged. The procedure we followed was essentially the same as that adopted in a number of previous Index studies of psychoanalytic concepts. Clinical material that could in any way qualify for the designation "sublimation" according to a broad list of criteria culled from the work of Freud and subsequent authors was examined in order to establish a basis for distinguishing sublimation from related phenomena. With these criteria in mind, a large number of children's activities were examined, including both those that were intimately related to direct drive discharge and those more remote from it. We included in this the intensive study of the relevant changes occurring in individual children during the course of treatment.

From the beginning of our project, we had very much in mind what Hartmann (1955) has called "the genetic fallacy in psychoanalysis." The lack of clear distinction between the genetic precursors of a function and the function itself has led to confusion in many areas; conversely, the distinction between the two is, as Hartmann has shown, inherent in the structural point of view. In the study of sublimation in children, the maintenance of this important distinction is particularly difficult because of the complex interaction in the growing child between processes of sublimation and processes of ego development as such; and the situation is not made easier for us by the fact, as both Hartmann (1955) and Kris (1955) have demonstrated, that the establishment of sublimations in the more mature individual is very similar to the changes in mode of drive discharge occurring during the course of the normal development of ego functions and apparatuses. To start with, we should like to introduce our discussion of sublimation by a brief examination of the concept of energy transformation, and then to proceed to discuss some of the problems involved in defining sublimation.

In *Inhibitions, Symptoms and Anxiety* (1926), Freud rejected his previous view that libido could be directly transformed into anxiety, and suggested that this was in part due to the fact that "analysis was still a long way from distinguishing between processes in the

ego and processes in the id." Our thesis in this paper will be that
Freud's amendment of the libido-transformation theory in connection
with the theory of anxiety can be generalized to all drive–ego relationships, both from the genetic and functional points of view. Further, the ideas that we have tried to develop can, we believe, be
profitably applied to an understanding of the difficult concept of
sublimation.

In 1905 Freud had defined the "aim" of an instinctual impulse
as "obtaining satisfaction by means of an appropriate stimulation of
the erotic zone," (1905a) and he consistently defined sublimation
thereafter in terms of the change in the aim of the instinctual drive.
It seems clear, therefore, that the change of aim (and also the change
of object) involved in sublimation is a change in the mode of discharge of the drive and, we would add, involves an inevitable alteration in the feeling accompaniments of drive discharge. Freud
(1915c) conceptualized the *pressure* of an instinct as "the amount of
force or the measure of the demand for work which it represents"
(p. 122). We can add that drive discharge can be seen, by implication,
as a reduction of this demand for work. The demand for work is
accompanied by feelings of tension and its reduction by feelings of
accompanying pleasure and subsequent satisfaction.

If we look at this from a structural viewpoint, it could be said
that sublimation would be achieved if the ego can find a way of
bringing about a reduction in the "demand for work" imposed on
it by the drive, a means of drive discharge that does not involve the
experiencing of the type of gross pleasure originally associated with
it. However, with his revised view of instincts in *Beyond the Pleasure
Principle* (1920), and with the formal presentation of the structural
theory in 1923, Freud extended his ideas on sublimation (1923a). It
now included the notion of the desexualization of sexual energies.
Freud saw object libido as having sexual aims, and contrasted it with
narcissistic libido, which arises out of it and which does not have
such aims. He said:

> The transformation of object-libido into narcissistic libido which
> thus takes place obviously implies an abandonment of sexual aims,
> a desexualization—a kind of sublimation, therefore. Indeed, the
> question arises, and deserves careful consideration, whether this
> is not the universal road to sublimation, whether all sublimation
> does not take place through the mediation of the ego, which begins
> by changing sexual object-libido into narcissistic libido and then
> perhaps goes on to give it another aim. (p. 30)

Sublimation still remained for Freud the stripping of the sexual
aims from the instinctual drive. There is no reason to believe that in

his new formulations he had gone back on the view that an instinct obtained its quality only from its sources and its aims. In a passage added to the *Three Essays* (1905*a*) in 1915, he had said:

> The simplest and likeliest assumption as to the nature of instincts would seem to be that in itself an instinct is *without quality* [our italics], and, so far as mental life is concerned, is only to be regarded as a measure of the demand made upon the mind for work. What distinguishes the instincts from one another, and endows them with specific qualities, is their relation to their somatic sources and to their aims. (p. 168)

Thus, although Freud, in his later formulations, saw desexualization (which he equated with sublimation in 1923*a*) as a qualitative change in the energy itself, we would suggest that an alternative formulation is possible without doing violence to Freud's views. This is that desexualization involves the *freeing* of that aspect of a drive that is in itself without quality from its association with particular forms of discharge and from the feelings associated with them. And in this we should distinguish between the drive as a "demand for work" and the energies that are employed in the functioning of the somatic and psychic discharge apparatuses.*

Hartmann, Kris, and Loewenstein (1949) extended Freud's concept of desexualization to include the aggressive drives and made use of the term "neutralization" to cover this extension. For Hartmann, "neutralization" is synonymous with "sublimation,"† and in his writings on this subject he quite specifically considers the process of neutralization to be one of energy transformation. This is, however, not, in our view, the same as the removal of a qualitative component of the drive. The various instinctual *drives* can be differentiated from one another by their sources, by their modes of discharge (this includes aim and object), by the quality of the affect associated with the particular drive tension, and by the affective experience that accompanies drive discharge. The additional components that give a particular drive its character are, on the whole, determined by the apparatus or apparatuses that mediate their discharge, that is, the apparatuses that bring about a reduction in drive tension, in the "demand for work," that is the essential characteristic of the drive.

The apparatuses employed in primitive instinctual discharge are closely linked with body tensions and stimulation. Drive discharge

---

*These energies are probably "without quality" (Hartmann, 1955; Jacobson, 1964; Schur, 1960).

†Kris (1955) preferred to reserve the term "sublimation" for displacement of goal and to distinguish it from "neutralization" in the sense in which Hartmann used it.

is accompanied by qualities of pleasure specific to these apparatuses. To the extent to which the whole organism is involved in the drive–tension experience, so will the affective elements allied to it be of a general diffuse quality. If only specific apparatuses are involved, the affects will be specific and localized. In the case of aggressive discharge, we do not get specific erotic sensations accompanying tension and its discharge, but we get a more diffuse quality of tension and of discharge pleasure.

Let us consider for a moment the oft-quoted example of the small infant sucking at the breast. The drive tension that initiates reflex searching for the nipple and sucking produces a fairly widespread affective tension with, however, a specific concentration in the oral zone. The reflex activities involved in a satisfactory feeding situation bring about a diffuse affective change, general unpleasure being replaced eventually by a feeling of postprandial satisfaction. Stimulation of the lips during feeding produces a highly pleasurable sensual experience located in the buccal area. But this is not all. The activity of the apparatuses involved in feeding must also bring about a nonerotic work pleasure (Hendrick, 1943) or function pleasure (Bühler's *Funktionslust*). The affects associated with drive discharge would therefore appear to be relatively complex. It also seems likely that the reflex searching and finding of the nipple provide feelings of nonerotic pleasure and gratification that are the precursors of later pleasure in mastery.

We would suggest that if we are to speak in terms of energy, we should speak only of one type of qualityless energy providing the *power* for all the diverse activities involved in the simple act of sucking. If, on the other hand, we speak of drives, there must be many, of different qualities, operating simultaneously or in sequence, giving impetus to or setting one another in motion even in a primitive activity such as sucking at the breast. The drives whose discharge produces a pleasure of a nonerotic sort form the basis for later ego development—Glover's term of "ego nuclei" is perhaps appropriate here. The apparatuses that subserve these drives, which operate to bring about their discharge, are the apparatuses of primary autonomy present at birth or destined to appear during the course of maturation under conditions of adequate stimulation. If the mode of discharge of the instinctual drives alters during the course of development and the primitive sensual accompaniments of drive reduction are replaced by others that have different, nonsensual and nonorgastic qualities, then we have the phenomenon that Hartmann and his collaborators have conceptualized as "neutralization." There is thus a close relationship obtaining between drive and apparatus. What we normally understand by the sexual and aggressive instinctual drives are com-

plex phenomena involving a whole spectrum of discharge characteristics and associated tensions and pleasures.

The remarks that we have made in relation to the apparatuses
of primary autonomy apply to the apparatuses of secondary autonomy as well. The construction of these apparatuses is perhaps best
demonstrated by the development of hand and eye skills in the
young infant. Hoffer, in an illuminating paper (1949), has shown
that the hand, intimately associated with the gaining of satisfaction
through mouth stimulation in the infant, gradually acquires the further function of grasping the spoon or food in the feeding process.
He said: "The hands . . . now function more independently of the
oral zone and are more under the influence of the eyes, playing the
part of an intermediary between eyes and mouth. They have developed from instruments serving as a means for discharging tension
into tools which control the outer world. They have at this stage
become a most active extension of the growing ego" (p. 53).

In a study of the ego development of blind children at the
Hampstead Clinic, Anne-Marie Sandler (1963) has extended Hoffer's
observation to include the normal function of sight. She remarks:

> Vision plays a corresponding and complementary role in this move
> forward. As with the hand, the eye becomes a searching and
> grasping organ in the service of the mouth. Even before the infant
> has any facility in grasping with his hand, he grasps . . . with eyes
> alone. This intrinsic property of vision is of paramount importance
> in initiating progressive ego development of the sighted child and
> his turning to the outside world. . . .
>
> One might say that as the hands and eyes slowly become
> independent of the mouth, they become masters in their own right,
> whereas they had previously functioned as servants. The hands
> and eyes have now taken over both the libidinal and aggressive
> attributes of the oral drive . . . [and] hand and eye functions attain
> a relative autonomy as part of the growing ego. Exploration and
> mastery of the world partially replace and become independent of
> sucking and biting, and yield, as any observer can testify, a pleas-
> ure of their own. . . . *The child's center of interest becomes partially
> removed from his own body and his aims no longer consist exclusively of
> zonal stimulation.* (italics added; pp. 350–351)

The development of the blind child is in sharp contrast to this.

> In his effort to make sense of the world around him the blind baby
> will be forced to stay close to bodily cues. He will, for example,
> tend to bring everything he can grasp to his mouth for a much
> longer period than his sighted counterpart. For the blind baby,
> sucking, biting, and sniffing will supplement his tactile and kin-
> aesthetic experiences, and all his activities will therefore be wedded
> to immediate somatic sensations. . . . The blind child's lack of sight

makes the transition from mouth grasping to hand grasping more difficult, and because of this the development of hand autonomy . . . will proceed to a lesser degree than in the sighted child. The hand is forced to remain subservient to direct body gratification, to remain linked with modes of satisfaction characteristic of the first phase. Thus the most meaningful avenue of exploration . . . remains dangerously close to direct bodily gratification and discharge. The absence of vision, which is the prime neutralizing agent in that it interposes a distance between the perception of the object and zonal stimulation, has hindered the hand in becoming an autonomous agent of the growing ego, and the pleasure of the blind child remains far more directly sensual than that of the sighted child. (pp. 354–355)

If we extend the process that has been described as occurring in normal, sighted children, we can postulate that the action skills that the child develops become partially transformed into mental skills. Freud has shown us that thought is internalized action, but this is only possible when apparatuses subserving such functions as imagination and visualization mature and develop. The child, instead of grasping with the hand or eye, now grasps with his mind. Just as erotic mouth pleasure gave way to the dominance of nonerotic function pleasure in hand and eye activity, so does pleasure in mental function become established.

What we have been describing is a process of increasing the "distance" from the original sensual affects accompanying somatic stimulation and discharge. In the clinical manifestations of resexualization and reaggressivization, this distance decreases. The mental discharge characteristics and accompanying pleasures become tinged, to greater or lesser degree, with somatic discharge characteristics and accompanying discharge pleasures. There seems to be good evidence that there is always at least a weak and subliminal link with body sensations during even the highest forms of mental activity.* This is a fascinating and as yet relatively unexplored field of investigation.

In regressive sexualization or aggressivization, the link with primitive discharge excitement and pleasure is reinforced. This may be an old link that is strengthened, or a new one that now appears for the first time. What we have here is a theory of displacement and affect change, rather than one of energy transformation.

The loss of distance that we have described leads to a degree of loss of what could be termed the "functional autonomy" of the apparatus. *Structural* autonomy is never, in the ordinary course of events, lost. Once a skill has been acquired, once an ego apparatus

---

*It seems clear that the modes of discharge that reduce the "demand for work" imposed by the drive must remain anchored to some degree to somatic apparatuses.

has been created, it can lose its structural autonomy only by virtue
of pathological ego-destructive processes such as occur in some psychoses and in organic brain conditions. There may, of course, be a
certain amount of atrophy through disuse. Loss of *functional* autonomy, on the other hand, involves the regressive contamination of
the function or apparatus with primitive drive-discharge characteristics.

The fact that the functioning of the ego apparatuses yields pleasurable feelings means that we have a whole hierarchy of affective
feeling tones within the ego, associated with the hierarchy of ego
functions and apparatuses. These range from crudely sensual experiences to feelings of safety and well-being and the more subtle
feelings that Hartmann has called "positive value accents." Without
being able to take this subject up in detail here, we would like to
offer for consideration the idea that the component that differentiates
constant object relationships from need-satisfying ones is a contribution of the ego, an additional affective ego value cathexis that we
could describe in such terms as "nonsensual love," "esteem for the
object," and so on. This is not the same as the aim-inhibited instinctual components.

We have suggested that there is a hierarchy of positive feelings
that the ego is capable of experiencing. Similarly we could postulate
a hierarchy of "unpleasures" of all gradations. If we take the view
that the ego funtions to maintain a positive feeling of well-being in
the self, then the experiencing of any degree of unpleasure will set
in motion the adaptive and defensive functioning of the ego apparatuses. This homeostatic view enables us to consider the dynamics
of independent ego functioning in the light of motive forces associated with the various ego apparatuses that have as their aim the
avoidance of unpleasure and the preservation of well-being. We can
thus contain a theory of ego motivation within a structural framework. These motive forces can be seen as "demands for work" (similar to that imposed by the drives) on the ego apparatuses. This
"demand for work" is again quite different from the energy that
"powers" the apparatus.

If there is a high degree of functional autonomy in the ego, we
get the freedom of action that Hartmann and Kris have conceptualized in terms of a high availability of neutralized energy. Fluctuations
in the degree of functional autonomy correspond to what has been
called "the degree of ego flux."

The theoretical preamble bears directly on the problem of the
definition and usage of the term "sublimation." If the development
of the ego is seen in terms of a theory of energy transformation,
then the term "sublimation" might be appropriate to describe some

of the processes through which the ego functions, apparatuses, skills—
in short, all the instruments of the ego—are built up. If, however,
we adopt the point of view that we have outlined in this paper, then
we can say that the achievement of the displacement of aim that
Freud consistently took to be characteristic of sublimation can act
rather as a *stimulus* to the development of the ego instruments.

   An example may serve to illustrate some of these points. A child
may learn to ride a bicycle, an activity that, once the skill has been
developed, becomes structurally autonomous. We could, for the purposes of our argument, say that he has developed a bicycle-riding
function and a bicycle-riding ego "apparatus." This function and
apparatus may then be used by him to discharge aggressive and
exhibitionistic impulses that have formerly been expressed in a more
direct anxiety-evoking form. The bicycle-riding skill can be used for
exhibitionistic purposes, but we need not call the skill itself a sublimation. Moreover, we do not have here a *change of function* from
bicycle riding to sublimation. The bicycle-riding ability enables the
child to ride a bicycle; riding a bicycle may, in its turn, be used for
the attainment of sublimation. We should add, of course, that the
satisfactions afforded by the achievement of the sublimation may
have acted as a tremendous spur to the acquisition and development
of the autonomous ego apparatus and functions, in the same way
as the activity of weight lifting acts as a stimulus to muscular development. If our cyclist goes on to become a circus performer, with
a hypertrophy of bicycle-riding skill, then this skill may have developed under the pressure of his urge to exhibit, but, as we have
suggested, we need not postulate that his sexual drive provided the
energy for the bicycle-riding function, although it may have mobilized it.

   It would seem that we need not consider ego functions, apparatuses, and skills to be sublimations, nor need we see sublimation
as an ego function in the sense in which the term "ego function" is
normally used. It is an end product, an achievement. It is synonymous neither with the activities that bring it about nor with those
that it stimulates. The position is quite different when we come to
consider the capacity for sublimation (Hartmann, 1955) or sublimation potential (A. Freud, 1962). When we come to assess this potential
for sublimation, we have to take many aspects of the ego's capacities
and its overall functioning into account. We can assess the ego's
sublimation potential by such factors as frustration tolerance, the
resistance to regressive loss of functional autonomy, the capacity for
obtaining substitute gratifications, inborn talents, the capacity for
postponement and delay of discharge. Probably the most important
is the degree to which function pleasures can be substituted for

instinctual ones. All of these factors can probably be assessed to some degree very early in the child's development, but they constitute no more than preconditions for the attainment of sublimation.

Thus far we have spoken of sublimation as having occurred when instinctual drive tensions are discharged with an alteration in the discharge characteristics of the drive. This does not mean that the drive is itself altered but rather than anxiety-arousing directly instinctual discharge patterns are replaced by alternative modes of expression and discharge. These may involve the symbolic and compromise gratification of the unconscious wishes, but, above all, they imply a change in the type of pleasure and satisfaction that accompany drive discharge. But, as we hope to show presently, a further element is necessary before we can speak of sublimation.

From the side of the superego, the changed mode of expression of the drives may bring about a reduction of guilt and other forms of tension with the superego introjects. From the viewpoint of the ego itself, sublimation provides a means of avoiding or reducing areas of conflict and anxiety. It can also operate as a stimulus to the further development of ego functions and apparatuses.

What we have said so far relates to the role of sublimation in regard to the discharge of instinctual drives. This aspect of mental functioning has always been the one that has been the *sine qua non* of all definitions of sublimation. However, examination of our clinical material has shown us that there is another important aspect that has to be taken into account, one that we believe to be essential for a definition of this concept.

We should like to introduce this aspect of our thinking by quoting from a report in a local newspaper that appeared at an opportune moment during the work of the Sublimation Group at the Hampstead Clinic.

> The secret of the man who followed the fire engines was told yesterday when a messenger from London Museum arrived at his bedside at ——— Hospital, London. White-haired Mr. Fred B., 81, has been in hospital for the last four months. And tucked away in his locker have been 13 large volumes, telling of every big London fire since 1890.
> "I've always been interested in fires and fire fighting," he told our reporter. "As a lad of 10 I used to follow the fire wagons through the streets. For 70 years I've collected press cuttings, photographs and pictures of London fires and written them up in my books."
> At the hospital to take the books to the museum—where they will be copied and put in the library as a valuable work of reference—was the museum's special messenger.
> He put the books into a bag and then stayed to hear Mr. B.'s

stories of the day the Crystal Palace was burnt to the ground and the great fire at Madame Tussaud's.

Mr. B. was never a fireman; he worked as a lavatory attendant for 40 years. But during that time he was busy watching and writing about fires.

His other hobby was drawing. "I have hundreds of drawings at home," he said. "Many of them are of fires and firemen but I drew other things as well. The biggest thing I've ever done is a fire frieze."

Mr. B.'s hand-written manuscript was discovered by a hospital visitor. One volume was sent to the museum and the curator wrote back saying that he would like the complete work for the library as it was one of the most comprehensive studies of the fire-brigade in existence.

"This is a wonderful day for me," said Mr. B., as he handed over the books. "I feel very proud."

This report can illustrate many things; but what it indicates, above all, is that we have here an account of someone employed in a relatively unskilled capacity, performing tasks that are, one way or another, close to direct drive discharge. He developed an interest that resulted in the production of a comprehensive and valuable historical document. Of interest in this connection is the fact that no special skill was required. If, as a child of 10, Mr. B had only followed his hobby for a short while, and had then abandoned it, it could surely not have been said that he had developed a conflict-solving sublimation of urethral drives, even though we could assume that the skills involved would have retained their autonomy for many years. However, 70 years of sustained effort and interest probably entitle us to designate Mr. B's hobby as a sublimation.

It seems evident that the capacity of an activity to bring about drive discharge in the way in which it has been described is not sufficient for us to label it as a sublimation. We are all familiar with children who develop interest in one activity after another, investing each with enthusiasm, but readily abandoning each one, even though it appears to constitute a suitable vehicle for sublimation.

The example of Mr. B highlights, we believe, a crucial element in sublimation, namely the role of the relationship to the activity as such, over and above its function as a vehicle of drive discharge. We were impressed by the parallel that exists between different types of object relationship on the one hand and relationships to activities and their products on the other. We may profitably explore this parallel a little further by reference to a comparison between anaclitic object relationships and the more "constant" forms that normally exist in the mature individual.

The anaclitic, need-fulfilling, or so-called part-object relationship is based on the urgency and immediacy of the child's needs and drives. It fluctuates and is intermittent, and the object is valued solely on the basis of its capacity to provide gratification. It is clear that this type of relationship can exist in regard to ego activities and the products of these activities as well. A child may use an activity for purposes of drive discharge (albeit with modification of the discharge characteristics of the drive), and, having achieved a reduction in drive tension, lose interest in the activity until such time as drive pressures mount once more. The activity and its products have no interest or value for him in the drive-quiescent phase, and he may subsequently turn to alternative activities for drive discharge. He has not invested the activity with what we might call an enduring affective attachment cathexis, value cathexis or love cathexis that persists independently of need satisfaction.

We may contrast this with the type of mature object relationship that characterizes successful marriage. The wife, for example, serves as the means for obtaining sexual satisfaction. She is the object of the sexual drive and is the vehicle for the reduction of sexual drive tension. But, over and above this, she is valued, loved, cared for, and treated with all the consideration that an object may receive. Indeed, any characteristic of an object relationship (e.g., ambivalence, possessiveness, etc.) can be found in the relationship that an individual has to his activities, to the products of these activities, and to the material things that he employs in carrying them out.

The investigation of clinical material, particularly that of children of latency age or older, suggests that the cathexis of an activity may not only parallel object cathexis, but that the activity can also function as a permanent or temporary replacement of an object. We are familiar with this process when it occurs in the form of identification, a process that involves attributes of the object being duplicated in the self-representation, with the result that object love is transformed into secondary narcissism. Love for the object becomes love for the self. The transfer of cathexis from object representations to activity representations must surely play an important part in the lives of those individuals who are, so to speak, "married to their work."

There is no doubt that this is a complicated area. The activity itself probably always represents an extension of the self, receiving value cathexis either by an extension of self cathexis or by transfer of object cathexis. The physical tools employed in the activity and the products of the activity may equally be extensions of the self-representation, but as often as not they become extensions of or substitutes for the object. We do not propose to pursue this problem in detail here, except to say that it would seem that when we come to consider an activity used for purposes of sublimation, we should also consider the degree to which it is invested with narcissistic cathexis, with object cathexis, or, as more commonly occurs, with a mixture of the two. We have suggested that the activity itself may be treated as part of the self, and the products of the activity, or the tools used, as a substitute for the object. In the whole performance, a love relationship may be created or reproduced. Thus in the content of sublimations, as in the content of fantasies, we find symbols that refer not only to instinctual wishes, but also to other aspects of the self and objects or to compromises between these.

It should perhaps be added that an activity that is used for purposes of sublimation may provide an excellent source of narcissistic supplies for the child. This has been conceptualized in terms of attaining an ideal state of the self. The sources of the child's ideal self may be manifold (Chapter 6) and include not only those derived from the introjects but also those that have been taken over from the individual's cultural and social environment.

The following excerpts from case material recorded on index cards headed "Ego: Sublimation" illustrates these points.

Catherine
Age at beginning of treatment 3 years 9 months.
Indexed at 5 years 5 months.

Catherine seems to have a high capacity for sublimation. In her role playing during sessions she showed an extraordinary virtuosity in her ability to portray adult roles which went beyond mimicry and identification to artistic expressiveness. She had at her disposal a vast range of accurately remembered adult vocabulary, turns of phrase, and many well-observed details of behavior. She seemed to try to make her acting as realistic as possible for the sheer pleasure in artistic recreation, as well as for pleasure in her growing mastery of the environment through understanding. At four, telephone sequences in her dramatizations were included because she enjoyed playing telephone, and just the facts necessary for the plot were conveyed. At five, the mother-on-the-phone sequences grew into set pieces of painstaking and exquisite verisimilitude, which she seemed to enjoy just for the pleasure in artistic reaction of observed reality (though behind it lay the identification with an ideal fantasy mother who would have a telephone and friends, and who would assist her daughter's social life). But Catherine's most striking achievement was her portrayal of adult character by an economy of means—a few telling words in a certain tone. Here she was at her best in portraying attitudes she had accurately observed in her mother—the insincere enthusiasm, the mood of strained tolerance and willed kindness, or her way of deliberately underplaying Catherine's distress with an assumed casualness—which Catherine would contrast with portraits of genuine tenderness and affection.

Catherine's acting ability can thus be seen to serve the purpose of sublimating her need to keep a watchful empathic rapport with the depressed mother of her oral phase, and of her need to use identification in the face of the chronic threat of object loss. In her role playing she preserves, via identification, both the depressed and the idealized mother. It is interesting that her portrayals of men and other children, while imaginative, remain fragmentary and unconvincing; only her portrayals of mothers have an uncanny truthfulness.

Gertrude
Age at beginning of treatment 11 years 11 months.
Indexed at 13 years 4 months.

At the beginning of treatment Gertrude's sublimating activities appeared very limited, restricted to her proficiency in and enjoyment of Hebrew, which was thought to be related to the fact that this is her father's interest, and that she had a male teacher whom she liked and who liked her. She had to give up lessons in order to come to treatment, but retained her interest in this subject.

In the course of treatment she became good at and enjoyed Domestic Science at school, coming top in her exams. Her mother had always encouraged cooking as an activity for her, but Gertrude had wanted help from her mother, and seemed unable to proceed with this activity on her own.

The development of this activity for purposes of sublimation appeared to be based on her own wish to be given and to give tasty foods. (Although she had an early difficulty in taking food, she had also wanted to feed herself very early, and was permitted this.) In the treatment she had expressed envy of the luxuries she imagined the therapist enjoyed on holiday. She also showed her wish to have these by pretending to order large quantities of groceries for her parents' golden wedding; and suggested that the therapist, as a mother, should also order large quantities for her daughter's wedding. Following interpretation of her envy of her mother's cleverness and her feeling of being no good herself, she was able to do rather better in her schoolwork. Her particular interest in Domestic Science was related to this, to her interest in food, and also to the fact that her mother encouraged and "allowed" her to be successful in this subject; she could also identify with her mother in this. Gertrude's lack of actual oral gratification was of interest, in that she could not eat the non-Kosher food she prepared at school. Although she regretted this, her interest remained in the techniques of cooking, in recipes, etc.

Diana
Age at beginning of treatment 8 years and 6 months.
Age at time of indexing 11 years 6 months.

Diana possesses a considerable artistic talent; her drawing, painting, and modeling show a highly creative capacity, and even apparently useless odds and ends of materials can be turned into
something attractive in her hands. When engaged in any of these
activities, she will work with concentration, perseverance, and
patience for hours on end, completely absorbed in her work. Her
capacity for and pleasure in these activities is rarely disturbed by
external events or by the state of her own feelings. In treatment
there were only a few occasions when, as a result of particularly
unwelcome interpretations, she stopped drawing and retreated
into highly obsessional and uncreative pattern making. Difficulties
in the actual execution of her task are usually overcome; e.g., she
would patiently mend fragile clay models whenever they broke,
rarely giving up and throwing them away. On one occasion she
found that a collection of plasticine horses had been squashed and
broken by things she had put on top of them in her locker. It was
an extremely difficult task to sort out and reassemble the pieces
of about fifteen horses, but Diana persevered until she had succeeded.

Though she derives great pleasure and satisfaction from the
activities themselves, at the beginning of treatment her attitude to
the products of these activities paralleled her attitude to herself.
She could not accept praise for her drawings or models, as she
could not accept it for herself, but always had to respond by
denigrating them as no good, messy, etc. In spite of this need to
devalue her products she liked nevertheless to have her models
and drawings on show at home, and it seems probable that she
could admire and enjoy her own products as long as no one else
commented on them. It seemed that her need to denigrate them
and herself was an aspect of her need to placate those objects
toward whom she felt compelled to deny her competitive wishes,
rather than being evidence of her true feelings about her artistic
capacities and products.

Diana enjoyed and cared for her artistic activities for their own
sake, even though she also used them for other purposes. She
turned to them as an escape from other unpleasurable situations,
principally (1) *Unsatisfying object relationships:* Diana expected and
typically recreated situations of rejection in her object relationships.
Being solitary pursuits her artistic activities required no help from
objects, and thus served her defensive independence, as well as
giving her the pleasure and satisfaction she failed to obtain from
object relationships. (2) *Intolerable affects:* Diana had to defend strongly
against her affects, and would avoid situations that aroused them
by turning instead to her painting and modeling, since she could

readily become absorbed in these activities and so could completely forget distressing events or feelings. (3) *The experience of failure:* For various reasons Diana could not tolerate doing badly in any activity, or even being in a situation where she needed to be taught or helped. Her artistic endowments enabled her to do well without help or teaching in drawing, painting, and modeling, and she therefore preferred these to other activities.

Diana's artistic activities were not subject to the ego inhibition which restricted her in many other areas. Though at the beginning of treatment her choice of subjects was strongly influenced by her psychopathology, when she entered treatment she drew and modeled almost nothing but horses, a result of her unresolved penis envy, among other things. These drawings and models were graceful, fluid, and full of life. By contrast, her rare drawings of people were stiff, lifeless, and poorly executed. This restriction on the range of content of her productions was mainly a result of her unsatisfactory object relationships. As her difficulties in this area were analyzed her drawings of people improved and gained something of the liveliness and grace of her animal drawings. There was altogether a great widening in scope of the content of her pictures and models as treatment proceeded. The analysis of her feelings about herself, which improved her self-esteem, made it possible for her to accept praise for her products and to admit overtly to her own pleasure in them. The satisfactions Diana gained from her activities became increasingly removed from and independent of the situations which originally prompted her special interest in and use of her artistic skills.

These examples illustrate, we believe, the value of differentiating between an activity or skill on the one hand, and the use of the skill for purposes of sublimation on the other. The skill or activity does not in itself constitute a sublimation, but rather *it can be used for purposes of sublimation.* If it is so used we may discern that it can provide a reduction in the demand for work imposed by the instinctual drive in a form which is much more "distanced" than the primitive mode of drive discharge, which is accompanied by feelings of pleasure removed from crude instinctual pleasures. In addition, the activity itself receives a "value cathexis" of the sort that distinguishes object relationships beyond the level of simple need satisfaction.

SUMMARY

We were concerned at the start of the project reported in this chapter with the establishment of greater precision in the definition of sublimation. The energy-transformation theory of sublimation was rejected as being inadequate, and it was suggested that in order to clarify the relation of sublimation to the instinctual drives and to the ego, we should differentiate between the following:

1. The drive tensions, sexual or aggressive, that are reduced by means of the ego apparatuses. Drive tension is the "demand for work" imposed on these apparatuses.

2. The primary sexual or aggressive affects that accompany somatic excitation and discharge.

3. The energies that power the discharge apparatuses. This is not regarded as transformed drive energy but seen as the neutral energy that is, from the beginning, available to all apparatuses, including somatic apparatuses and those of primary and secondary autonomy.

4. The nonsensual affects that accompany function and that exist from the beginning, side by side with sensual or aggressive affects.

5. The affect cathexes, which we have referred to as love cathexis or value cathexis, invested in the mental representation of objects, the self, and activities.

We have suggested that the development of an ego activity or a skill does not in itself constitute a sublimation; rather, *it can be used for purposes of sublimation*. Sublimation is seen to be an end result, an outcome of the operation of a number of factors. Involved in this achievement is the employment of skills and activities for the purpose of bringing about drive reduction in modified form, so that the drives acquire a new type of satisfaction. However, this may be fulfilled without our being able to talk of sublimation. It would seem necessary that the achievement, and the means whereby it is accomplished, not only subserve indirect drive discharge, but also be invested with a constant value cathexis of the sort that characterizes object constancy.

14

The Tendency to Persistence in Psychological Function and Development

Joseph Sandler and Walter G. Joffe

The paper contained in this chapter was presented at the Fall Meetings of The American Psychoanalytic Association in 1965, and published in *The Bulletin of the Menninger Clinic* (Sandler & Joffe, 1967b). It is a particularly significant one for the whole line of thought developed in this volume. The view that no psychological "structure" is ever lost is emphasized, and the idea that later structures also function to inhibit the use of earlier ones leads to a revised conception of regression, which can now be looked at as a "disinhibition" rather than a "going back."

The theoretical view presented here ties in well with that given in Chapter 10, in which the concept of functional fixation on the side of the ego is proposed and discussed.

The assumption that the past persists in the present has been a cornerstone of our psychoanalytic thinking from the very beginning. Freud's emphasis on the genetic point of view and on genetic reconstructions in analysis led him, from the material of adult cases, to postulate a sequence of characteristic developmental phases, each leaving its mark on those that succeed it. The existence of these phases, described and identified in terms that have been derived from genetic reconstructions, has been amply confirmed by the observations of child psychoanalysts. These observations, together with the introduction into psychoanalytic theory of concepts such as the conflict-free sphere of the ego, primary and secondary autonomy (Hartmann, 1939), and neutralization (Hartmann, Kris, & Loewenstein, 1949) have made us more aware of the complexities of development and have led us to view it increasingly from the point of view of the interaction between id, ego, superego, and reality.

Anna Freud has summarized (1963*b*) the present position with regard to the phases of childhood development. She says:

> In our psychoanalytic theory such developmental sequences are laid down so far as certain circumscribed parts of the child's personality are concerned. With regard to the development of the sexual drive, for example, we possess the sequence of libidinal phases . . . which, in spite of considerable overlapping, correspond roughly with specific ages. With regard to the aggressive drive we are already less precise and are usually content to correlate specific aggressive expressions with specific libidinal phases. . . . On the side of the ego, the analytically known stages and levels of the sense of reality, in the chronology of defense activity and in the growth of moral sense, lay down a norm. (pp. 245–246)

In order to balance any artificiality in looking at development from the point of view of separate psychic institutions, Anna Freud has proposed (1963*b*) an extension of our developmental framework by means of developmental lines in which various aspects of the personality come together in certain well-defined and age-related sequences. While we can normally expect a certain degree of correspondence between the various developmental lines, there can be a variable degree of discrepancy between them.

The application of the concept of developmental lines has enabled us to overcome the potential one-sidedness inherent in viewing development in terms of one or another of the various psychic institutions. It seems clear that the psychoanalytic understanding of multiple processes of interaction in progressive development has gradually been substantially increased; and over the past 2 or 3 decades, our knowledge of the individual's interaction with reality has been integrated into the theory of development. However, if we consider the phenomenon of regression, we find that a clear and indeed major distinction is usually maintained between regressive processes in the id and those in the ego. Here again, we may turn to Anna Freud for a statement of the present position (1965):

> In our work as analysts we have become so familiar with this constant interplay between drive fixations and regressions that we have to guard against the almost automatic mistake to view the regressive processes on the side of ego and superego in corresponding terms. While the former are determined above all by the stubborn adhesion of the drives to all objects and positions which have ever yielded satisfaction, characteristics of this kind play no part in ego regression, which is based on different principles and follows different rules. (p. 98)

In regard to ego regression, she remarks:

> There is one distinguishing characteristic of ego regression to be
> noted, irrespective of the various causative factors. In contrast to
> drive regression, the retrograde moves on the ego scale do not
> lead back to previously established positions, since no fixation
> points exist. Instead, they retrace the way, step by step, along the
> line which had been pursued during the forward course. This is
> borne out by the clinical finding that in ego regression it is invar-
> iably the most recent achievement which is lost first. (pp. 103–
> 104)

While there can be little doubt that the laws of regression differ
in regard to instinctual drive discharge characteristics on the one
hand and those controlling and organizing functions that we associate with the ego on the other, we are still left with certain difficulties
and complexities in the theory of regression. How far, for example,
can we allocate the loss of bowel control and a reversion to soiling,
to regression in the ego or to regression of the id? How do we explain
the changes in ego functioning that we find in the development of
an obsessional neurosis on the basis of drive regression alone? Does
not regression to earlier forms of object relationships involve changes
in the ego as well as in the id? And so on.

Freud had in fact pointed out in *Inhibitions, Symptoms and Anxiety*
(1926) that the theoretical distinction between ego and id, although
useful for certain purposes, should not be too rigidly maintained.
The ego, he suggested, is at times "identical with the id, and is
merely a specially differentiated part of it" (p. 97). The idea of a
degree of functional continuity between ego and id has also been
elaborated by subsequent workers.

The present paper represents an approach to problems of id–
ego interaction from the point of view of the distinction between
structure and function. Both drive and ego regression will be discussed in the light of this distinction. The notion of a "tendency to
persistence" will be put forward, embodying the idea that primitive
modes of functioning tend to persist actively in the present in the
form of "trials" that are normally inhibited. This tendency is seen
as basic to all forms of regression, which is not regarded as a simple
"going back" or "revival," but as a process of release and disinhibition of past modes of functioning.

In two recent papers (Sandler & Joffe, 1965a, 1966), we have
suggested that some of the complexities inherent in the theory of
regression may profitably be approached from the point of view of
the distinction between structure and function. This distinction is
one that has been explored by a number of authors in recent years,
and it is one that extends across the whole sphere of mental func-

tioning. Although Freud focused the concept of structure in 1923 on what Merton Gill (1963) has called the "macrostructures" of id, ego, and superego, he had used the concept in a far more general sense many years earlier. Thus in *The Interpretation of Dreams* (1900), he had spoken of a structure in referring to what he called a "mental grouping" (p. 610), and it has become increasingly apparent in recent years that there is both a need and a place for a broader and more general concept of structure than that used by Freud in 1923. Hartmann, in referring to the automatized defense apparatus, said in 1939: "Such an apparatus may, as a relatively independent structure, come to serve other functions" (p. 26), introducing here his important concept of "change of function," a concept that is the basis for much of the discussion that follows in this paper.

Rapaport has used the concept of structure very extensively to include also cognitive structures that are "both those quasi-permanent means which cognitive processes use and do not have to create *de novo* each time and those quasi-permanent organizations of such means that are the framework for the individual's cognitive processes" (p. 157). The most common of such cognitive structures are, Rapaport points out, the structures of memory (Bruner et al., 1957).

Gill has considered the distinction between structure and function in some detail in his recent monograph (1963). He remarks (p. 136) that "it seems warranted to postulate that all mental mechanisms conform to a possible definition of a psychic structure—a form of functioning which is not created *ad hoc* but which is permanently at the disposal of the psychic process." He distinguishes between the agency and the function carried out by that agency.

Holt (1965) has also spoken of the persistence of structures. In referring to a perceptual structure, he suggests that it can be seen as "a program for processing a combination of internal and environmental information to yield a perceptual result." However, whereas Holt has taken the view that these programs (i.e., structures) can be "rewritten" (this is perhaps in line with Rapaport's idea of *quasi-permanent* structures), we have put forward the suggestion in a previous paper (Sandler & Joffe, 1966) that structures are in the normal course of events never lost, but rather that new and auxiliary structures of increasing complexity are created, the newer structures becoming superimposed on the old in the course of development. The more complex emergent organization must not only provide an effective means for discharge and control, but must also include systems of inhibition directed against the utilization of the older structures. In Holt's terms we might say that programs are not exactly rewritten, but rather that the older programs are constantly being modified by a process of superimposition. And in order for the resultant program (i.e., structure) to be used effectively, it must include aspects that relate to the inhibition of earlier forms (See also Joffe & Sandler, 1967a).

David Beres (1965) has drawn attention to some of the ambiguities that exist in past and present uses of the concepts of structure and function. In the light of his comments, we should note that in the present context we are making use of the concepts of function and structure to contrast activities and processes on the one hand with patterns of organization, schemata, agencies, apparatuses, and mechanisms on the other. On the basis of this distinction, it is possible to say that once a degree of structural organization has been achieved, it is never lost (except under the influence of organic changes in the brain), whereas mode of functioning can vary within very great limits.

Perhaps we can be allowed to illustrate the distinction between function and structure by reference to the story* of the Irishman who had been brought before the Justices on a charge of illicitly distilling whisky. In spite of his plea of "Not Guilty," the presiding magistrate announced that he must inevitably be found guilty for he had been discovered in possession of the apparatus for distilling whisky, and the possession of an illegal still was sufficient evidence to justify a conviction. When asked whether he would like to say anything before sentence was passed, Paddy remarked with some heat, "Yes, I would like you to take into account the additional crimes of incest, sodomy, bestiality and rape." "May the Lord spare us, did you really commit these terrible crimes?" exclaimed the magistrate. "No your honor," said Paddy, "but I was in possession of the apparatus!"

If we now return to the question of structural development, we can perhaps elaborate our thoughts a little further. We know that in the course of development, structural changes occur. These correspond, of course, to changes in the organization of functions that are allocated to various phases of development. We have suggested that we see a superimposition of one modifying structure upon another, with a degree of progressive integration, the find or most recent showing the influence of previous structural organizations (or even retaining parts of these) and including, as an essential component, a whole hierarchy of inhibiting structures. This is in line with Rapaport's description of the ego as an "emergent organization," the final organizational gestalt being more than the simple sum of its parts.

Changes in the ego's functioning, such as those that we see in

---

*Another version of the same story has been given by Freud in his paper "The Expert Opinion in the Halsmann Case" (1931).

neurotic regressions, do not necessarily involve changes in the structure of the ego. What we see is rather the reemployment of previous structures that have been inhibited in the course of development. This is what we referred to as loss of *functional autonomy* in our paper on sublimation (1966, Chapter 13 in this book). In contrast to the loss of functional autonomy, we suggested that *structural autonomy* is only lost in the course of certain, psychotic and organic pathology. Following up the concept of functional autonomy, we have spoken of the concept of functional regression of the ego (1965a). We might also speak in this context of a fixation of the ego, meaning by this both the undue persistence of the influence of earlier organized modes of functioning on the later organizations, and the special tendency to the reemployment of earlier structures under the influence of internal or external stress. The effects of fixation of the ego shows itself in what has been called the "style" of ego functioning, the pattern of organization that influences perceptual and cognitive controls as well as the choice of particular defenses (Gardner *et al.*, 1959; Holzman, 1962; Klein, 1958).

We are now in a position to examine further the distinction between drive regression and functional ego regression. While functional ego regression may be influenced by drive regression and vice versa, the two processes are by no means perfectly correlated, and we can perhaps understand the differences between various psychopathological states in terms of the predominance of one form of regression over the other. However, in all instances there is an interrelationship and interaction between the two forms of regression reflecting the interaction that exists between drive and control in every phase of development. Indeed, although we have differentiated between functional ego regression and drive regression—a distinction that we believe is of substantial clinical relevance—both are in fact forms of functional regression; the former a functional regression of the ego and the latter of the id. The structures and apparatuses of the id, like the structures of the ego, remain with us for life, even though, as the story of Paddy exemplifies, they may not always be fully employed.

In Chapter 10, in a discussion of the genesis of the obsessional neurosis, we attempted to account for the fact that drive regression to the anal–sadistic phase is not always associated with the development of an obsessional neurosis; nor are the economic and other factors usually mentioned sufficient to account for the particular form of the disturbance. We put forward, as a solution, the hypothesis that the changes that occur in obsessional neurosis can be related both to drive regression and a co-existent functional regression of the ego. The specific nature of this ego regression was thought to be predetermined by the particular style of perceptual and cognitive functioning that the individual had developed, a style that was strongly influenced by the vicissitudes of ego development during the anal phase. The defenses characteristic of the obsessional neurosis were seen as hypertrophied forms of those ego controls that assume importance in that phase. As Lampl-de Groot (1957) has remarked, "We [can] view the neurotic defense mechanisms as pathologically exaggerated or distorted regulation and adaptation mechanisms, which in themselves belong to normal development" (p. 117).

We have spoken earlier of inhibitory structures, i.e., organizations of inhibitory processes. By "inhibition" we refer here to some form of internal action that checks discharge along a particular pathway. This inhibition should not be considered to be a static process— it has often been described, for example, in terms of the erection of dams that prevent discharge. We see it rather as a dynamic process, an internal checking action that follows a partial or trail discharge, a trial that may eventually come to be limited to a "signal" discharge, or a "sample" discharge. This is perfectly in accord with Freud's description of the role of inhibition in secondary process functioning given in *The Interpretation of Dreams* (1900, pp. 598–609). Although the trial action may be limited to a "sample" action, it is nevertheless a covert internal action that is rapidly inhibited after it has been, in some way, evaluated by the unconscious ego. We can postulate that any overt discharge (whether in action, perception, imagination, or thought) is preceded by processes of trial and inhibition. These may occur extremely quickly, and certainly outside conscious awareness, so that only the briefest moment of time may be involved. We shall presently put forward the argument that, even in this brief moment of time, trial forms of discharge are scanned and tentatively sampled by the ego. Unsatisfactory ones are normally rejected or inhibited, and suitable ones permitted some form of overt discharge in consciousness or motility.

We should like to give an example that illustrates this process from our own experience. Both the authors were born in South Africa and received their early education there. Now the word used by all South Africans for a threepenny piece (a coin worth about 4¢) is a "tickey." This word is unknown in England, where the word "threepence" is used. Obviously the use of the word "tickey" had to be given up when we came to England, but we have both independently become aware that our first reaction to the symbol for threepence (3d.) is the vocalization "tickey," which had been suppressed and had become, descriptively speaking, unconscious. The use of "threepence" had appeared to us to be automatic; in fact what had happened was that the "trial" action of saying "tickey" was regularly inhibited and "threepence" substituted. Now we had both noted that under the influence of certain stresses the word "tickey" slipped out in conversation, and this could perhaps be designated as a form of regression. This sort of phenomenon has probably been noted by all who learn and habitually use a new language. The general point we want to emphasize here is that what we see is not a "going back" but rather a lifting of a dynamic inhibition that has to be normally imposed over and over again in the present.

Another example relating to language is perhaps worth mentioning. When an experimental laboratory situation is created in which the subject is prevented from hearing himself speak (through feeding in a so-called white noise through earphones), his monitoring of his own speech is interfered with, and a variety of phenomena occur. Thus if the subject had spoken with a foreign accent in his childhood, this may reappear. What we are suggesting is that the old accent persists as a form of "trial discharge" that is ordinarily and regularly inhibited, an inhibition that is temporarily put out of action by interfering with the process of auditory feedback.

Phenomena such as these come under the heading of what Werner (1956, 1957) has called "microgenesis" and have been investigated by the so-called laboratory genetic experiments. Microgenesis has been described as follows (Flavell & Draguns, 1957):

> The term "microgenesis," first coined by Werner (1956) as an approximate translation of the German word *Aktualgenese,* will refer here to the sequence of events which are assumed to occur in the temporal period between the presentation of a stimulus and the formation of a single, relatively stabilized cognitive response (percept or thought) to this stimulus. More specifically, the term will refer primarily to the prestages of extremely *brief* cognitive acts, e.g. the processes involved in immediately perceiving a simple visual and auditory stimulus, conceptually generating a word association, etc.

It is no great step to apply the concept of microgenesis to all mental and behavioral responses, and to all forms of stimuli, including those representations that are stimulated and revived under the pressure of the drives. However, most of the experimental work that has been done relates to perceptual and cognitive reactions to external stimuli presented in the laboratory.

Much of the early work on perceptual microgenesis was performed in the 10 or 15 years before the war by the Gestaltist F. Sander and his colleagues (1927) who proceeded on the basis that if the formation of clear and complete percepts could be blocked by presenting stimuli for very short periods of time, the normal precursors to complete perception could be elicited. The details of the work of Sander and his colleagues need not concern us here, except to say that the steps in the microdevelopment of perception in the "here-and-now" appear to follow the steps that had occurred in the ontogenetic development of perception. We see what might be called a "microgenetic recapitulation" of ontogenetic development.

Schilder (1920, 1942) has also formulated and elaborated what is essentially a microgenetic theory of thought formation. He suggested that in schizophrenia we see the emergence of early types of cognitive formation that intrude into consciousness and overt expression as though they were finished thoughts. It seems plausible to assume that in this condition, normal inhibiting structures fail to operate effectively.

Werner's own experiments were introduced in a study of microgenesis and aphasia (1956), in which he showed the existence of a parallel between the normal microgenesis of perception and the disorders of perception and cognition that are discernible in aphasic patients. He discussed aphasic symptoms in terms of "microgenetic derailment," and the parallel between this and processes of functional regression is a topic well worth investigating.*

Ivo Köhler, working in Innsbruck, has recently extended Stratton's experiments with reversing spectacles, and has shown extremely convincingly that the steps in learning to perceive and control a visually distorted world follow the normal developmental steps in percept formation. For example, there is an early sensorimotor stage of spatial orientation followed by a stage in which objects are distinguished in terms of "things of action." The subjects first learn to move about without error, and then to perceive things that they *use*. These "things of action" fall into place perceptually at a time when pictures on the wall remain reversed (Köhler, 1951, 1953, 1964; Wer-

---

*It is of some considerable interest that Freud's concept of regression probably stems directly from his own pre-psychoanalytic work on aphasia (1891), in which he adopted Hughlings Jackson's doctrine of "dissolution" (a term coined by Herbert Spencer in 1857 to denote the opposite of "evolution") in aphasic and other conditions (e.g., epilepsy). Freud wrote "all these [aphasic] modes of reaction represent instances of functional retiogression (dis-involution) of a highly organized apparatus, and therefore correspond to earlier states of its functional development. This means that under all circumstances an arrangement of associations which, having been acquired later, belongs to a higher level of functioning, will be lost, while an earlier and simpler one will be preserved" (page 87).

It is also of interest that the distinction between structure and function that we have explored in this paper was central to Freud's theory of aphasia. Thus in disturbances of understanding what is read, Freud writes: "Reading with understanding . . . is a function which is independent of the act of reading itself" (page 75), and he consistently distinguishes the "speech apparatus" from the functions of reading and speaking.

ner & Wapner, 1955). Such "genetic experiments" carried out by psychologists in Germany and the United States offer us a most promising technique for the experimental investigation of processes of progression, fixation, and regression.

If we apply the point of view described here to the mechanisms of defense, we can conceive, for example, of *repression* as an ongoing dynamic process, one that is not really sufficiently described in terms of the withdrawal of attention cathexis and the application of anti-cathexis. We can regard the repressed instinctual drive impulse as taking the form of a sensorimotor representation that is repeatedly impelled toward full discharge under the pressure of the drive. The process of repression includes then a rapid unconscious recognition by the ego of the emergent representation, a recognition that is then followed by the application of a counterforce that restricts the representation from proceeding further. It is as if the ego can, quite outside consciousness, scan the field of emergent id-propelled representations and, perhaps on the basis of warning signals of anxiety, direct an inhibitory counterforce against them, so that the instinctual drive is either prevented from obtaining discharge or has to find discharge via sensorimotor representations that are more acceptable. The ego is continually performing acts of judgment, influenced not only by the content of the drive representation, but by all the information, past and present, available to it. We can assume that the ego scans and organizes the data presented to its internally oriented sense organ in much the same way as it scans, selects, and organizes the information arising from other senses.

The ego is repeatedly being faced with what are essentially problem-solving tasks in which the problem to be solved is that of effecting a resolution from moment to moment of the frequently conflicting demands of reality and of the various psychic institutions. If existing organizations are adequate to cope with the immediate adaptation task, then the processes of trial action and inhibition proceed rapidly and smoothly, so much so that we can speak in this connection of what Hartmann has called "automatization."* When the existing organization is not able to cope efficiently and adequately with the problem at hand, there will be a tendency to test, in internal trial form, solutions that have previously been effective *and to integrate them into a new organization that is appropriate to the task.* Even if this reorganization takes only a brief moment of time, a form of temporary

---

*It would be ludicrous to maintain that every one of all former solutions is experienced in "trial" form; we are referring here to a *tendency* for such solutions to persist, and it is obvious that a great many shortcuts must inevitably occur, so that a whole body of previous solutions may come to be represented by a single signal.

regression in the service of the ego (to use Kris's term) will have occurred. It is tempting to expand this notion in the content of the many contributions that have been made on the subject of creativity, but we will confine ourselves here to calling attention to the existence of individual differences in the capacity for such temporary creative regression (cf. the work of George Klein and others), and to re-marking that, in the creative moment, regression and progression go hand in hand.*

If, for some reason, higher level and progressively adaptive or-ganizations cannot be created, we may see the emergence of a so-lution that is dominated by a genetically older structure (i.e., orga-nization); and in this case we can speak of regression proper, in the sense with which we are clinically so familiar. If this regression affects mainly the controlling, delaying, and inhibiting aspects of discharge, we have functional ego regression; if it affects the pathways of drive discharge we can speak of drive regression. The particular fixation points that determine the nature and extent of the particular func-tional regression can be regarded, in the sense of the views discussed here, as being inherent in the *style* of the organism's functioning. We use "style" in this context to relate to both overt and inhibited modes of functioning. This is a topic that needs fuller elaboration of the sort that is impossible to present here.

All of this can be conceptualized in terms of a tendency to *persistence*. The essential point is that in every psychological "event" or in every attempt at problem solving (we include in this the finding, at any moment, of an appropriate form of drive discharge, the ap-propriate negotiation of environmental tasks, as well as the functions of cognition, perception, etc.), the attained resolution is preceded by a rapid recapitulatory exploration of previous solutions established in the course of the individual's ontogenetic development. The con-cept of persistence also implies that the organization of previous situations that we have conceptualized as "structures" persists even though new structures of increasing complexity are continually being formed.

We should like to conclude with a consideration of one or two implications and applications of the notion of persistence.

We are all familiar with the processes that we refer to as "iden-tification" and "projection." Identification (we refer here to second-ary identification), as a number of authors now see it, involves a change in the self-representation on the model of an object repre-sentation; and projection the attribution to an object representation of some aspect of the self-representation. These processes can occur

*A subject studied in detail by Duncker (1945).

after the boundaries between self and object representations have been created; before that, we have the state referred to by Freud as "primary identification," "adualism" by Piaget, and "primary identity" by others. A better term to designate this early state might be "primary confusion" (Sandler, 1960b).

If we apply the idea of persistence to processes of identification and projection in the older child or adult, we can postulate that there will always be a momentary persistence of the primary state of confusion, however fleeting, whenever an object is perceived or its representation recalled. What happens then is that the boundaries between self and object *become imposed* by a definite act of inhibiting and of boundary setting. It is as if the ego says "This is I and that is he." This is a very different idea from that of a static ego boundary or self-boundary that remains once it has been created. What develops is the inhibition of the state of primary confusion and the ego function of *disidentifying*, a mental act of distinguishing between self and object that has to be repeated over and over again; and the function of disidentifying makes use of structures that we can call boundaries.

The persistence of this genetically earlier primary confusion in normal experience is evident when we think of the way in which we move and tense our bodies when we watch ice skaters, or see a Western. We must all surely have had the experience of righting ourselves when we see someone slip or stumble. In these everyday experiences, there is a persistence of the primary confusion between self and object; and this may more readily occur in states of relaxation or of intense concentration in which the bringing into play of boundary setting may temporarily be suspended or delayed. Herbert Spencer referred to something like this when he spoke of "primitive passive sympathy." McDougall, in commenting on the phenomenon, pointed out that "the fundamental and primitive form of sympathy is exactly what the word implies, a suffering with the experiencing of any form of emotion when and because we observe in other persons or creatures the expression of that feeling or emotion." The persistence of this genetically early state in the microgenesis of perception and thought must surely provide the basis for feelings of empathy, for aesthetic appreciation, for forms of transference and countertransference in analysis (here we can see one aspect of the value of the reclining position of the patient and the free-floating attention of the analyst). And in connection with what we call secondary identification and projection, we would suggest that the bridge to these processes is the persisting momentary state of primary confusion or primary identification that occurs before the process of "sorting out" or "disidentifying" occurs. One result of this "sorting out" may be that aspects of the object representation are incorporated into the self-representation and vice versa.

What we have called "persistence" is an essential part of normal mental functioning, and it has direct relevance to the changes that occur as a consequence of successful psychoanalytic treatment. These can be related to changes in function and to processes of reorganization. Even with the resolution of a neurotic conflict, the undoing of regression, the disappearance of symptoms, and the emergence of new and progressively adaptive modes of behavior, the previous solutions inherent in neurotic organization persist, but their functioning is restricted to "trials" or "samples" of the type we have described. The maintenance of the newer modes of functioning must therefore depend on the capacity to continually inhibit and to restrict the neurotic solution to a "trial" form. This raises many interesting questions in regard to the therapeutic process in general, to problems of establishing criteria for the termination of analysis, to the differences between child and adult analysis, and to a whole host of allied problems.

15

Adaptation, Affects, and the Representational World

Walter G. Joffe and Joseph Sandler

This chapter pulls together many of the ideas that were formulated or foreshadowed in previous chapters. It was first published in *The International Journal of Psycho-Analysis* in 1968 and leans heavily on the discussion of the "safety principle" in Chapter 1, on the work on the superego (Chapter 3), and on the proposals regarding the representational world (Chapters 4 and 5). It goes on to integrate these earlier theoretical ideas with those put forward in the chapters on the ego ideal and the ideal self (Chapter 6), on depression and individuation (Chapter 11), and on the tendency to persistence.

The discussion that follows is particularly useful because it provides a basis for a further step, that is, the crystallization of the "basic model" concepts in Chapter 16.

I

In the first phase of Freud's psychoanalytic thinking* he elaborated a model of pathogenesis based on adaptation to an external traumatic event or to the memory traces of such an event. The early model of the neuroses can be defined in terms of pathogenic adaptation to the after-effects of a particular reality event or to experiences deriving from the real world. The model of hysteria at this time was that its manifestations were an outcome of affect generated by an external traumatic experience occurring while the subject was in a hypnoid state of diminished consciousness. The affectively charged memories were warded off as incompatible with consciousness and the hysterical symptoms emerged at a later time as symbolic representations of the repressed memories. Cure was through catharsis of the affect.

---

*For a detailed description of the phases in the development of Freud's theories, see Rapaport (1953, 1959) and Hartmann (1956).

Central to this predrive phase of Freud's theory was the role of affect as a response to any sort of stimulation. Although "affect" had for him a number of different meanings during this phase, it was mainly equated with a sum of excitation that was displaceable and sought discharge. It is of interest that Freud saw the dissociation of the affectively charged memories of the trauma as an active process rather than as a reflection of weakness of the mind, the view of dissociation held by his French psychiatric teachers. Active dissociation (seen as one of the forms of defense) could thus be regarded as a form of adaptation to internal processes set in train by external reality.

A central idea in this phase was that affect pressed for discharge in some form or another, and this, of course, can be related to the principle of constancy, a principle that was consistently reflected in Freud's theoretical views throughout his scientific life.

The decisive event of discovering that hysterics were suffering from fantasies rather than from memories of traumatic experiences (Freud, 1887–1902, letter to Fliess, September 21, 1897) led to the beginning of the second phase of psychoanalysis in which the major theoretical emphasis was on formulations relating to unconscious wishes, a phase that lasted through to the early 1920s. During this time, Freud developed the concept of a defensive apparatus whose main task was ultimately to protect consciousness from conflict aroused by alien drive-invested memories and fantasies. Whereas previously, quantities of affect were regarded as the energic forces in themselves, affect now assumed a role as an indicator of a quantity of drive energy or as a measure of the demand for work made by the drive, that is, of the pressure of the drive. Inherent in this theory was the view that the affect measured the extent to which the drive was dammed up, and that drive energy could itself be transformed into affect. This is the first theory of anxiety, in which anxiety is seen as transformed libido.

In this phase of Freud's thinking, adaptation to external reality was not his major concern, although certain formulations were made relating to the development of secondary process functioning, to that part of the system *Pcs.* (which was to become the ego in the structural theory), and to the development of the reality principle out of the pleasure principle. Although Freud was considering aspects of adaptation to reality, the reality principle was seen mainly as a modified pleasure principle, a roundabout way of gaining that state of energic equilibrium that was an inherent aspect of the pleasure principle. Another way of putting this homeostatic principle is to be found in Freud's remark in the "On Narcissism" paper (1914) in which he suggested that the development of the ego could be seen as a consequence of disturbances of the state of primary narcissism and represented a roundabout way of attempting to regain that original state. There his conception of narcissism can be seen not only in terms of distribution of libidinal energy and energic equilibrium but also in terms of maintaining the feeling state that existed in the child during the earliest period of its life.

Towards the end of the second decade of the century, for reasons that have been described in detail by Hartmann (1956) and Rapaport (1959), Freud's attention concentrated once more on that part of the mental apparatus that was concerned with defence. It now became apparent that this part of the apparatus was not solely concerned with defenses against the instinctual drives or their representatives and derivatives, but was also concerned with adaptation to the demands of the conscience on the one hand and reality on the other. Although there was this shift of emphasis in the latter part of the second phase, affect remained drive-linked throughout, and the consideration of its role in regard to adaptation did not undergo any substantial development.

In *The Ego and the Id* (1923a) and in *Inhibitions, Symptoms and Anxiety* (1926), the third phase was introduced. Here the ego is defined as a coherent organization of mental processes organized primarily around the perceptual system, but including the defensive structures as well. In addition to being able to transform instinctual energies for its own purposes, the ego was thought to possess neutral energies of its own. It was no longer seen as totally subservient to the drives, but could automatically instigate defensive activities via the anxiety signal. There is here a change in the role attributed to affect, but one that was only partially made explicit, as his main considerations related to the specific affect of anxiety. The view that affect arises within the ego as a response to a stimulus represented a fundamental change in his theoretical conception (the second theory of anxiety). It can be generalized within a far more extensive model of mental functioning. The second theory of anxiety saw the affective anxiety signal as being prompted by the threat of danger from any source. Affect was therefore partially removed from its total link with the drives and by implication given an important role as a mediator of adaptation. The part played by the ego is clearly seen as that of negotiating adaptation, adaptation conjointly to id, superego, and reality. The feeling component of affect* is unambiguously

---

*Freud was fully aware of the problems that existed in connection with the biological bases of affective experiences. He partially dealt with these by reference to "affective symbols" that represented situations of danger (1926, p. 94). We would nowadays speak of feelings as "affect-representations," and distinguish, as Freud did, between the feeling (representational) aspect of affect and the physiological processes that may be functionally or genetically linked with it. In the second theory of anxiety the feeling representation is given particular emphasis, especially in its role as a signal.

located in the ego, and although Freud dealt for the most part with the unpleasurable feelings of anxiety and pain, the change of view inherent in the new theory of anxiety in 1926 is of general application to the whole theory of adaptation.

II

Many authors have made significant contributions to the theory of adaptation since Freud. The extension of the concept of defence to include defence against external dangers connected the defence concept now more intimately with adaptation in general, leading to the increasingly accepted view that the mechanisms of defense are special applications of more general adaptive techniques. In general, the functioning of the ego as the main instrument of adaptation has been given increasing importance in recent years. As Hoffer put it (1955):

> From the year 1920 onwards the concept of defense had to be widened beyond that developed from the field of psychopathology. The concept of the ego and the understanding of the varieties of mechanisms which it uses in mediating between inner sources of tension, i.e. the instinctual drives and outer reality, has come to occupy a place in psychoanalytic thinking of equal importance with that of the theory of instinctual drives.

Hartmann (1939) has placed special emphasis on the innate development of the ego apparatuses of primary autonomy and the innate origins of what was to become, during the course of the child's development, the conflict-free sphere of the ego. In addition, structures that may be born of conflict may achieve relative autonomy by means of a change of function. These become structures or apparatuses of secondary autonomy. Thus secondary process thinking can, unless it is drawn into conflict again, operate relatively freely and independently of the drives.

While it is not possible here to go into the many relevant contributions to the understanding of ego functioning made by such workers as Hartmann and his collaborators, Hoffer, Erikson, Jacobson, and many others, we would like to touch briefly on Rapaport's work on the concept of autonomy (1951b, 1958), for we believe that the concept of autonomy is central to the whole problem of adaptation. Rapaport extended the autonomy concept from autonomy from the instinctual drives, to include as well the notion of autonomy from the environment. As he put it, the degree to which the individual's ego can function autonomously is a reflection of independence from the drives, freedom from "slavery" to the drives; but it also reflects the capacity to function independently of the environment. Environmental demands need not, to the extent that autonomy exists, evoke automatic, stereotyped, and immediate responses; the relatively autonomous individual is equally not a slave to his environment. To Rapaport's description of autonomy from the drives and from the environment we can add the notion of autonomy from the superego introjects, a consideration that is of substantial theoretical as well as of clinical importance. We will touch on this point again later in this paper. An obvious conclusion from all of this is that a high degree of autonomy from the drives, the superego, and from the environment indicates a relatively greater range of choices in adaptive responses in problem solving and in decision making, and in the development of the means of obtaining pleasure, gratification, and well being.

It should be clear by now that our concept of adaptation is more than that of adaptation to the external world, but includes adaptation to inner forces and inner states, as well as to the demands or promptings of external reality. It is perhaps unfortunate that the way in which the term "adaptation" is generally employed is to denote reality relationships this has certainly influenced a number of psychoanalytic writers on the topic, and even Hartmann, in his classical work on adaptation (1939), placed emphasis on adaptation in relation to the tasks of reality mastery, although he took the ego's role as a mediator between drives and reality fully into account. Our own emphasis is different from this, and it will become apparent in what follows that we regard adaptation to reality as a (biologically predisposed) consequence of a more general principle of regulation and control.

Before going further, it is appropriate to stress what we regard as a fundamental theoretical distinction between the apparatuses, structures, functions, and mechanisms that subserve adaptation on the one hand, and the experiential criteria that lead to the utilization of these apparatuses, structures, functions and mechanisms on the other.

In Freud's view, the ultimate criterion or regulating principle was the pleasure principle, a homeostatic principle of constancy that, as Schur has pointed out so well in his book (1966), embodies both energic and feeling aspects. It is indeed a compound of more than one regulatory principle, and it is apparent that Freud in fact included several principles of regulation under the single heading of pleasure principle. Schur remarks that it is necessary to distinguish between the pleasure and unpleasure regulatory principles and the *affective* experiences of pleasure and unpleasure. However, Schur does not consider the regulation of *experience* a primary regulating principle, and in this regard it will be seen that our own emphasis is different from his.* In what follows, the idea is put forward that the ultimate guiding or regulatory principle in adaptation from a psychological point of view relates to feeling states of one form or another and that to equate these with energic equilibrium and with drive equilibrium in particular may be misleading or incorrect. We prefer here to use the term "feeling states" rather than "affect" because of the broadness of the concept of affect, which includes both feelings and bodily changes. This is a great source of confusion unless one differentiates the different aspects of what is meant by affect, as a number of authors have recently done. We are also by no means convinced that changes in feeling states always mirror somatic affective changes, although feelings must be connected with processes occurring in the central nervous system.

III

In this section we would like to describe the development of a line of thought that has led to our present views on adaptation. The starting point for this development was a paper "The Background of Safety" (Chapter 1) that in turn took as its point of departure Freud's theory of trauma and anxiety as described in *Inhibitions, Symptoms and Anxiety* in 1926. Starting from the consideration in particular of the act of perception as a very positive process rather than a passive experience, the view was put forward that the act of perception is an act of sensory integration that prevents the ego from being overwhelmed by unorganized sense data. The successful performance of such an act of integration is accompanied by a definite feeling of safety, a sort of ego tone, a background feeling state. This feeling state is fully described in Chapter 1.

In the same paper, some of the steps taken by the ego to deal with any reduction in the background tone of safety feeling were described, and the conclusion was drawn that there could be seen in all of this the workings of what might be called a "safety principle":

> This would simply reflect the fact that the ego makes every effort
> to maintain a minimum level of safety feeling, of . . . ego tone,
> through the development and control of integrative processes within
> the ego, foremost among these being perception.

---

*We can assume that, in the earliest, so-called undifferentiated phase of development, the regulation of the infant's biological homeostasis, constantly disturbed by the drives, is mirrored in the infant's feeling states. However, we would suggest that as the ego develops as an active controlling and facilitating agency, its prime regulating principle is intimately connected with its conscious or unconscious perception of its feeling states.

It was pointed out that any experience of anxiety or disorganization lowers the level of safety feeling and that we may see the
development of types of activity that at first sight seem to be inappropriate and unadaptive, but in fact *are* adaptive in that they are
aimed at restoring some minimum level of safety feeling. Included
in this are, for example, some of the stereotyped and bizarre forms
of behavior shown by psychotics—but it is also to be seen in the
child's need for familiar objects in his environment, or in certain
forms of normal or neurotic regression. It was also pointed out that
this is not the same as the investment of objects for the purpose of
obtaining instinctual gratification.

In a paper "The Concept of Superego" (Chapter 3), Freud's
writings on the ego ideal and the superego were reviewed, and it
was noted that Freud had started his formulations regarding the *ego
ideal* in his "On Narcissism" paper (1914) by observing that libidinal
(i.e., drive) impulses are repressed if they are in conflict with the
child's ideal for himself, and that the ideal image embodies all the
feelings of perfection that the child felt himself to possess in his early
childhood. Following a review of the literature, a view of the superego was put forward in that paper that leaned heavily on the
framework of the inner world as elaborated by Piaget and by such
analytic authors as Hartmann and Jacobson. The internal schemata
constructed by the child were taken to relate not only to data gained
by sensory impressions but also to internal sense data (and what
was referred to at the time as "affect data" as well). What is known
to the child as "reality" is only a specially differentiated part of his
inner world.

At this time, the classical formulations were still being followed
in the use of the term "narcissistic cathexis" to refer to both an
energic investment and a feeling state, and a model of superego
functioning was elaborated based on the assumption that the child
transfers authority to superego introjects in order to preserve a feeling of safety—but at that time, the distinction between energies and
feelings had not been clarified, and the confusion was evident in the
equivalence implied in such terms as "safety," "well-being," self-
esteem, "feelings of being loved" and the maintenance of a sufficient
level of narcissistic self-cathexis. However, in that paper, some of
the unease about the confusion between energy and feeling was
again evident.

In that paper, the development of the superego system was
related to conflict between the child's instinctual strivings on the one
hand and the need to preserve his well-being on the other. What
was the fear of parental disapproval becomes guilt, and an essential
component of the feeling state of guilt was seen as the drop in self-

esteem or well-being. However, the converse is also true, and the comment was made that an opposite and equally important affective state of well-being is experienced when ego and superego work harmoniously together.

Implicit in these formulations is the concept that superego formation comes about as a consequence of processes of adaptation, and that the regulating principle, the ultimate psychological determinant, is the control of the feeling state of safety and well-being. This is not only a developmental cause for superego formation but also implies that it has an adaptive function *in the present*.

In 1962, in two papers (Chapters 4 and 5), the concept of what was called the representational world was elaborated. These papers extended, elaborated, and made more explicit the concept of the internal world, bringing it into line with structural (and also to some extent with topographical) concepts. Here the concept of the *shape* of self and object representation was introduced, as described: in Chapter 5.

In a paper on "The Ego Ideal and the Ideal Self" (Chapter 6), the concept of ego ideal was dissected into its components, one of which was described as the "ideal shape of the self." This represented the "wished-for" shape of the self at any particular time and in any particular set of circumstances. In tracing some of the sources of the ideal shape of the self, it was linked with the requirements of the superego introjects, the conscious or unconscious requirements communicated by the real parents or other important figures in the present, and the demands arising from the instinctual drives. The ideal self at any moment was defined as that shape of the self that would yield the greatest degree of well-being. At the same time it was regarded as the shape that would provide the highest degree of narcissistic gratification. Following Jacobson (1954c), Bibring (1953), and Annie Reich (1960), the degree of discrepancy (or lack of it) between representations of self and ideal self measured the self-esteem of the individual. It should be noted that here again, the concepts of narcissism, self-esteem, and well-being were used interchangeably.

A crucial development in this line of thought was reflected in two papers on childhood depression (Sandler & Joffe, 1965b and Chapter 11), and developed in two further papers (Joffe & Sandler, 1967b and Chapter 12). The "ideal state" was considered to be fundamentally a feeling state of well-being that normally accompanied harmonious and integrated *psychobiological* functioning. The striving to attain or maintain such a feeling state is seen as basic in human development and functioning, and an understanding of its regulation is essential to the understanding of the dynamics of ego functioning. Extending and including the "safety" concept formulated earlier, the feeling of well-being was regarded as the polar opposite of pain (*Schmerz*); pain was seen to be a fundamental component of all forms of unpleasure, including that of instinctual tension and anxiety. From early in development, the "ideal state" becomes increasingly linked with ideational content derived from perception, memory, and fantasy. The feeling state of well-being becomes embodied in what has been referred to as "ideal shapes of the self," and discrepancy between the actual shape of the self at any moment and the corresponding or appropriate ideal self is (consciously or unconsciously) experienced as pain.*

Although thus far we have spoken of the discrepancy between actual and ideal states of the self-representation as being linked with feelings that have a painful component, it should be remembered that from early in the infant's development, the self-representation is closely linked with various forms of object representation; we cannot consider any shape of the self-representation in isolation. It would probably be more correct to consider (after a certain stage of development has been reached) the actual and ideal shapes of the self-representation in terms of self–object representations; for all psychological object relationships are, in representational terms, self–object relationships. In more general terms we can refer to representational discrepancy as being linked with feelings of pain or unpleasure, and lack of representational discrepancy (i.e., states of representational congruity) being associated with feelings of well-being and safety.†

From the point of view of the ego's functioning, we are now in a position to say that the prime motivators are conscious or unconscious feeling states; and that these are, in turn, associated with various forms of representational congruity or discrepancy. *The aim of all ego functioning is to reduce conscious or unconscious representational discrepancy and through this to attain or maintain a basic feeling state of well-being.* From this point of view we can say that the ego seeks to maintain a feeling homeostasis, and this is not to be confused with the notion of energic homeostais. This question has been discussed in some detail in Chapter 12.

---

*The thresholds for experiencing and for tolerating painful feeling states varies in different individuals and at different times in the same individual.

†In this formulation, two lines have converged. The first is that which has developed from the initial formulation of the safety principle and the second from the studies on the ego ideal and the ideal self (Chapter 6). In regard to the former line of thought, what was originally formulated in terms of perceptual functioning has been generalized and extended to a primary psychological principle. In regard to the latter, what was originally seen in relation to superego processes is now seen as an integral part of the dynamics of total ego functioning.

The developmental aspects in all of this are important, and have been considered in Chapter 11.

In the course of the child's everyday life he develops and creates various shapes of the ideal self that are appropriate to his home, to his school, to his groups of friends, and so forth. These ideal shapes of the self may vary quite considerably from one set of circumstances to another, and tendencies, wishes, or impulses that may be permitted in one situation may create a painful internal state in another. The content of the "ideal" states may be derived from present reality, or from past experience—we include here the set of ideals that are related to the parental introjects once the superego has been established, and that we know can often be a source of intense pain when the child feels that he does not conform (or wish to conform) to his superego ideals.

While internal conflict is a major source of painful states, reality factors also play a part. Every child is constantly being faced with situations that create discrepancies between actual and ideal states of the self, but some children experience these discrepancies to a far greater degree than others when they are exposed to special external circumstances.

It is clear that the progressive movement towards adequate appreciation of, and adaptation to, reality must involve the relinquishing of ideals that are no longer appropriate to present reality—reality-dystonic ideal shapes of the self, so to speak. We have made use of the term "individuation" to describe the gradual development of increasingly reality-adapted ideals in the growing child, together with the giving up of infantile ideals and dependence on external objects for supplies of well-being. This does not mean that we regard individuation as synonymous with development, but rather as an important adaptational aspect of it. However, previous ideal shapes of the self are not always readily abandoned, and will often show their influence in the content of new ideals. If the child is not able to make the necessary progressive modifications in the shape of his ideal self, he may well turn towards ideal states that have been satisfactory in the past, and that he can attain in reality or in fantasy. This is an important aspect of the regressive processes that we can observe in the course of normal and pathological development, and that subserve purposes of adaptation.

Individuation is essentially an outcome of processes in the ego, and successful individuation is a fundamental component in the child's development towards psychological maturity. It is in part determined by drive progression, and the correlated establishment in the representational world of what can be called "phase-adequate ideal states" appropriate to the new development level. A further factor influencing individuation is the well-being that results from social recognition and approval—a factor that continues to operate when superego introjection has taken place and the child is able to obtain so-called "narcissistic supplies" from internal as well as external sources (Chapter 3). A third, and extremely important factor in individuation, is the effect on the child of the maturation, development, and consolidation of autonomous (primary and secondary) ego functions. The attractions offered by the child's new potentialities and experiences enable him to relinquish his attachment to previous ideal states, and to strive towards attaining the well-being offered by new ideals created by processes of maturation and by the move forward into a fresh developmental phase. "Pleasure in function" and "mastery pleasure" play an important part here, as well as the pleasure from direct drive discharge and the affective gains that can ensue from the capacity to identify with admired objects (especially parents and older siblings). The child attaches a "feeling cathexis of value" to his newly acquired achievements, and the alteration in his ideal self enables him to achieve a unity of actual and ideal self through independent activities.

We consider individuation to be a line of development that continues throughout life, and while failures in early development may make later individuation difficult (and similarly, early failures in individuation may later affect various lines of development), the growing individual is constantly confronted with situations (particularly crisis situations and developmental transitions) which require further processes of individuation. These situations give rise to mental pain, and individuation appears to be the most adaptive response to such pain. The capacity for progressive individuation varies in different individuals; the capacity for "distancing" (Chapter 11) and the capacity to dis-invest object representations and to invest feelings in activities and interests appear to be important factors.

While, from the point of view of the ego, individuation is the most adaptive response to pain, from the side of the drives, the normal response to pain is aggression directed at whatever is considered to be the source of the pain. However, if the child does not go on to individuate, he may remain as a miserable, unhappy, unsettled, and discontented child who shows a chronic feeling of resentment towards himself or towards those whom he feels are responsible for his lack of satisfaction.

In these formulations, there is a qualitative difference between the systems id and ego. The demands of the drives (which can be regarded as stimuli arising from an internal source) give rise to feeling states within the ego, states that include a particular feeling quality of pain or unpleasure. Reduction in drive tension (so-called drive discharge) is accompanied by pleasurable feeling states and is normally followed by a positive feeling state of well-being. The control that the ego can exert on the instinctual drives is instigated and regulated by the ego's awareness of changes in its representational world. Ideational content is always linked, however tenuous this may on occasion be, with feelings of one sort or another, and ultimately it is always the feeling state, existing in the present or anticipated, that is the criterion upon which the ego bases its adaptive maneuvers.

In speaking of the adaptive and progressive process of individuation, we have referred to the "giving up" of earlier ideals and ideal self–object relationships, and although we qualified this by saying that earlier ideals are not always readily abandoned and show their influence in later ideals, a further qualification or modification of this statement is necessary. In a paper on the concept of persistence (Chapter 14), we put forward the view that structures (and this includes the structures of the representational world) are not lost in the course of development. This would imply that the content of earlier shapes of the self or of self–object relationships can be seen as adaptive solutions that are never lost.

> The essential point is that in every psychological "event" or in every attempt at problem solving (we include in this the finding, at any moment, of an appropriate form of drive discharge, the appropriate negotiation of environmental tasks, as well as the functions of cognition, perception, etc.) the attained resolution is preceded by a rapid recapitulatory exploration of previous solutions established in the course of the individual's ontogenetic development. The concept of persistence also implies that the organization of previous solutions . . . persists even though new structures of increasing complexity are increasingly being formed. (Chapter 14)

It is possible to regard the mental apparatus as having developed as a superordinate control system responsible for the very characteristics of behavior that such writers as Hartmann and Rapaport, as well as Holt (1965) have described as ego autonomy. The regulatory basis of the psychological control system, as distinct from the anatomical–physiological one are, in our view, based on the maintenance of a dynamic feeling homeostasis.* Feelings within the ego, including variations in the basic feeling of well-being, are not deter-

---

*It is perhaps of interest that the experiential phenomena reported, for example, on experiments on stimulus deprivation and isolation can be understood in terms of the ego's adaptation to a lower feeling of safety or security that is only in turn consequent on the reduction of sensory input. It is a feeling deprivation rather than a stimulus deprivation. There is a lowering of the background safety level due to the absence of sensory input.

mined solely by stimuli arising from the instinctual drives nor by stimuli from the external world, although it is true that an imbalance of one or another source will affect feeling states. Changes in feeling states are, as we see it, the *impetus* to the development of psychological structure. Earlier in this paper, we spoke of the distinction between the criteria for development and adaptation on the one hand and the structures and functions involved. Changes in the feeling state and in the representations associated with these changes provide the impetus for the development of psychological structures and represents the ultimate basis for the ego's regulatory activities.

We mentioned ego autonomy earlier as being closely related to adaptation, and this can be seen to have a close relation to internal conscious or unconscious feeling states. Ego autonomy can be regarded as the individual's freedom to explore and to find new solutions without suffering intolerable disruption of the internal feeling state of well-being or safety. In a sense, the degree of autonomy is a reflection of the range of ways and means that the person has been able to find during the course of his development to maintain his basic feelings of well-being and safety in the face of superimposed disruption of his feeling state *arising from any source*, from the drives, from the superego, or from the external world. Of particular relevance is the degree to which the individual can explore different solutions in the trial actions that constitute thought, while still maintaining a minimum level of well-being and then to base appropriate action on the basis of this exploration in thought and in imagination. Moreover, a high degree of ego autonomy would imply a capacity to divorce the maintenance of the basic feeling tone from stereotyped and automatic responses to either drive or reality demands.

There are many directions in which this conception can be explored and expanded. One of these relates to the question of autonomy from the standards and ideals of the superego introject. Another relates to the degree of freedom that the individual can attain from infantile ideals. Changes in the ego's basic feeling state may be gross or may be restricted to signals (as in the anxiety signal, or other painful signals, or signals of well-being, or of sensual or other pleasures). Implicit in this is the notion that even the most refined and abstract intellectual representations have feeling signals attached to them. We would reiterate that the apparatuses that the ego constructs during the course of its maturation and development are prompted in their development ultimately by the need to control feelings and that their principle role is to widen the tolerable range of conscious or unconscious experiences without unduly disrupting the basic feeling tone of safety, well-being, or security.

In conclusion we would note that the model, presented here is an intrapsychic one. As such, it provides a basis for uniting a general theory of adaptation with a fully psychoanalytic point of view. Indeed, its essence is that psychoanalytic psychology is a psychology of adaptation to changes in feeling states, and that any particular aspect of the theory of adaptation (e.g., adaptation to the demands of the drives, or to the external environment) can be encompassed within the framework of the wider model.

16

Toward a Basic Psychoanalytic Model

Joseph Sandler and Walter G. Joffe

The paper on which this chapter is based was presented in 1969 to the Congress of the International Psycho-Analytical Association, and published in *The International Journal of Psycho-Analysis* (Sandler and Joffe, 1969).

In the course of examining the relation of a number of psychoanalytic concepts to observed clinical material, it has become evident (and is clearly shown in many of the previous chapters) that there is an inherent ambiguity and unclarity in many of these concepts. This led to the pursuing of a number of studies aimed at reaching greater precision in conceptualization. It was evident that a number of conceptual changes were necessary, and attempts were made to make appropriate adjustments and reformulations in the particular areas under study. Although a by-product of these discrete studies was the emergence of the model proposed in this paper, the creation of such a model was not the original aim. Only the Hampstead Index studies will be quoted in this chapter even though we are fully aware that they represent only a fraction of the work undertaken by many psychoanalysts in recent years in the direction of theoretical clarification. However, we refer to them for two main reasons. The first is that they represent the work that led to this paper; the second is that they illustrate some of the problems that arise as secondary effects of attempts at clarification and reformulation.

Two studies of the concept of the superego (Chapter 3 and Sandler *et al.*, 1962) led to a distinction between "identification" and "introjection" in terms of the content and structure of self and object representations, and an attempt was made to conceive of the superego as a *system*, and to couch these formulations in psychologically as well as clinically meaningful terms. These studies led to the formulation of the concept of the "representational world" (Chapters 4 and 5) elaborating ideas put forward by Hartmann and others, and drawing on relevant findings in the field of perception made by nonpsychoanalytical psychologists such as Piaget. In the following year, a study of the concept of the "ego ideal" suggested that much of the confusion that surrounds this concept comes from the fact that Freud used the term in different senses at different points in his theoretical development (Chapter 6). It was implicitly suggested that the concept of "ego ideal" was too vague to be useful, and that a more precisely formulated concept of "ideal self" or "ideal self-representation" be used instead.

In the same year, a study of the concept of fantasy (Chapter 7) showed that an enormous amount of confusion existed in relation to the use of the term "unconscious fantasy." It was necessary to distinguish between the process of *fantasying* and the products of this process. These included conscious fantasies (daydreams), preconscious (but descriptively unconscious) fantasies, and fantasies that had once been wish fulfillments but that were now repressed or otherwise defended against.

A number of further studies followed. An examination of the concept of "trauma," presented at a symposium in 1964 (Chapter 9), showed that the wide clinical usages of the term did not fit the classical definition of trauma given by Freud, and it was suggested that we should think, both clinically and theoretically, not so much in terms of "trauma" as originally defined but rather in terms of states of *ego strain* that might, or might not, be posttraumatic.

In a paper on sublimation presented in 1964 (Chapter 13), it was argued that it is imprecise to speak of "sublimations," but that we should rather consider that any activity could be used *for purposes of sublimation*. In the course of this chapter, we distinguished between "structural" and "functional autonomy" and emphasized the role of "feeling states," "feeling cathexis," and "value cathexis." The notion of a multidimensional "distancing" was introduced as being of greater theoretical use than that of the transformation of energy "neutralization." The notion of instinctual drive as "energy" was rejected in favor of a particular formulation of Freud's, that is, that the instinctual drive can be considered to be a repeated stimulus—a "demand for work."

A study of obsessional manifestations in children (Chapter 10) led to the conclusion that the concept of drive regression was insufficient to account for the development of an obsessional neurosis, and the concepts of "functional regression of the ego" and of "ego fixation" were introduced. The employment of the particular defense mechanisms that characterize an obsessional neurosis was related to the particular cognitive and perceptual style of the individual. Here again, we turned to the findings of psychologists working in the fields of cognition and perception.

Two papers on depression in children (Sandler & Joffe, 1965b and Chapter 11) embodied the conclusion that the term "depression" was used very imprecisely, and that it is necessary to distinguish between states of unhappiness and misery (pain) and the "depressive affective response." Pain was linked to a state of discrepancy between the *actual* and *ideal* self-representations, and the depressive response was seen as a type of affective adaptation arising in particular circumstances to the experiencing of helplessness in the face of pain. The concept of "pain," as used in this context, was further elaborated in another paper (Joffe & Sandler, 1967b), in which it was seen as the common ingredient in all forms of unpleasure, including anxiety.

A consideration of the concept of narcissism presented in 1965 (Chapter 12) led to the conclusion that the concept of narcissism as the "libidinal cathexis of the ego" or even as the "libidinal cathexis of the self or of the self-representation"was untenable from the point of view of a psychoanalytic psychology, as was the concept of a fixed quantity of libido distributed between self and object (or self and object representations). We suggested that a psychology of feelings and values would have to be invoked in order to account adequately for the observable variations in what is usually called "narcissism," and that the relation of such feelings and values to the instinctual drives is not a simple and straightforward one.

An investigation into the concept of "transference" (Chapter 18) resulted in a dissection of several components of transference, and to the conclusion that the dimensions of what was usually referred to clinically as "transference" were identical with those of object relations in general. It was suggested that the clinical concept of transference broke from the point of view of a general psychoanalytic psychology.

Four theoretical papers emerged towards the end of this period. One, on the concept of "persistence" presented in 1965 (Chapter 14), grew out of a number of considerations relating to the concepts of "psychic structure" and "regression," and led to the formulation that no structure, once formed, was ever lost, but that its employment may be inhibited during the course of development. Regression was seen as a consequence of a form of "disinhibition." A further paper on the concept of autonomy (Sandler & Joffe, 1967a) discussed the relation of autonomy to the feeling components of the basic regulatory principles, and adumbrated some of the propositions put forward in a paper on the psychology of adaptation (Chapter 15). In this paper, we provide a basis for a general theory of adaptation within the theoretical framework of a psychoanalytic psychology. Finally, an earlier version of the model was applied to learning theory in order to show that it is possible to construct a psychoanalytic learning theory that could generate hypotheses capable of being tested experimentally (Chapter 17).

Current psychoanalytic terminology is, by and large, that used by Freud. Freud's language bears the imprint of the physiology, neurology, psychiatry, and the classical education of his age. It is colored by its use in the therapeutic procedure, hence the richness of metaphors. Freud was not concerned with semantics. The correct use of a term had little meaning to him; it was the context that mattered. One might say that such insouciance is the hallmark of genius; it undoubtedly is its prerogative. When a generation or two of scientists arrogate such a prerogative the lack of concern for semantics may well lead to confusion. . . .

Even more urgent is the *systematic* clarification. Throughout fifty years, psychoanalytic hypotheses have frequently been revised and reformulated. Rarely, however, have all previous findings been integrated with new insight. In 1926, in *Inhibition Symptoms and Anxiety*, Freud reformulated a considerable set of his previous hypotheses. I am convinced that this reformulation reaches further than was realized at the time of publication, possibly by Freud himself. At present, hypotheses in psychoanalysis are formulated in various terminologies according to the various stages of development of psychoanalysis in which they were suggested.

Ernst Kris (1947)

The disagreements between the model makers dwarf all their agreements—except one: that model making is necessary.

David Rapaport (1951*a*)

I

In this chapter we intend to present a tentative outline of what we have called a "basic psychoanalytic model." Before doing so, however, a number of points need to be made by way of introduction.

It is natural to conceive of any new theoretical formulation as being in competition with older ones. This is a view that we reject completely, although we ourselves have subscribed to it in the past. A theory or concept may be useful for one set of purposes but not for another, and the coexistence of concepts such as the "Unconscious" and the "Id" in our present psychoanalytic thinking bears testimony to the fact that each must be useful in different circumstances. Freud himself constantly reverted to prestructural theoretical concepts after 1923. This phenomenon exists in sciences other than psychoanalysis. Kaplan, writing on methodology in relation to the behavioral sciences, puts it as follows (1964):

Since Kant, we have come to recognize every concept as a rule of judging or acting, a prescription for organizing the materials of experience so as to be able to go on about our business. Everything depends, of course, what our business is. . . . A concept as a rule of judging or acting is plainly subject to determination by the context in which the judgment is to be made or the action taken.

The model to be presented in the second part of this chapter does not aim to replace any existing part of psychoanalytic theory. It is a model that has emerged as a consequence of having attempted to clarify a number of psychoanalytic concepts, and represents a crystallization of what might be called a "frame of reference" against which existing concepts can be examined. Some of the possible advantages of such a frame of reference are:

1. It can represent some sort of unifying scheme that may allow links between different psychoanalytic concepts or models to be made (e.g., between the topographic and structural theories).

2. It may allow the relation between normal and pathological processes to be seen more clearly.

3. It may permit of a greater degree of bridge building between psychoanalysis and adjacent disciplines.

4. It may permit an approach to the teaching of psychoanalytic ideas at present couched in an esoteric scientific language and difficult for the scientists in other fields to grasp.

5. By its interaction with psychoanalytic concepts and theories at different levels, it may stimulate new formulations and further development.

It should be emphasized that what follows is not a general all-purpose psychoanalytic theory capable of application in every corner of the field. We would reiterate that it is a *frame of reference*, an attempt at an organized basic model, standing in the same relation to the body of psychoanalytic theory as does biochemistry or physiology to clinical medicine.

We should like to add that some aspect of practically every facet of what follows is to be found in one place or another in Freud's work and in the writings of others far too numerous to quote. It is in the organization of the relationships between these facets that we hope to have made a contribution.

II

Psychic Adaptation

Psychoanalytic psychology can be regarded as a psychology of adaptation. While this is not a new idea, it has not been consistently applied. We would stress that this is an "intrapsychic" view and that adaptation to the external world is only one aspect of adaptation in the sense in which it is used here. Other aspects of adaptation have also to be included—to inner drives and wishes, as well as to those internal standards that have arisen during the course of development and that we normally refer to as "superego." This is in line with Freud's statement that the ego "serves three masters and does what it can to bring their claims and demands into harmony with one another" (1933). However, we would now specify that it is not only a part of the apparatus—the ego—that has to "adapt" but that the apparatus as a whole is involved.*

Some of the implications of this view of "psychic adaptation" are:

1. The development of the psychic apparatus can be seen as the consequence of the whole series of adaptive processes that have occurred since birth. While development includes maturational aspects, maturational changes in themselves bring about the need for further adaptation by the psychic apparatus. The developmental and genetic points of view are thus subordinate to that of psychic adaptation.

2. In moment-to-moment functioning, the psychic apparatus can be regarded as adapting in the "best" possible way to all the demands being made on it. In this sense it has a "problem-solving" function. The "best" solution at any given time is based on experiential criteria—experiential regulatory principles—that will be discussed further below. From this point of view a neurotic or psychotic state can be considered to be the "best" solution that the apparatus can find in the given circumstances and with the resources at its disposal. Obviously developmental as well as current factors are involved.

3. We have previously suggested (Chapter 15) that the apparatus responds to only one ultimate "master" that determines the course of psychic adaptation to only one basic regulatory principle. This is its own awareness of (and the consequent "demand for work" imposed by) changes in the conscious or unconscious feeling state. Adaptation to reality (and the "reality principle") can be regarded as a normal but secondary consequence of the operation of the primary regulatory principle.

4. The point of view of psychic adaptation can be regarded as being superordinate to all the other psychological (or metapsychological) points of view.

*While it is extremely valuable, and indeed necessary, to conceptualize certain aspects of the psychic apparatus as "id," "ego," and "superego," these "macrostructures" (Gill, 1963) are higher level concepts referring to different aspects of the functioning of a total apparatus.

The Experiential and Nonexperiential Realms

A great deal of confusion has arisen in psychoanalytic theory because of a failure to take into account a fundamental distinction between two very different areas, and we would propose that a sharp distinction be made between what we would like to call (for want of better terms) the "experiential" and the "nonexperiential" realms.

The realm of subjective experience (in German *Erlebnis* but not *Erfahrung*) refers to the experience of the phenomenal content of wishes, impulses, memories, fantasies, sensations, percepts, feelings, and the like. All we "know," we know only through such subjective phenomenal representations, which may vary widely in content, quality, and intensity.

Having said this, we would add immediately that experiential content of any sort, including feelings, *can be either conscious or unconscious*. Implicit in this is the view that the individual may "know" his own experiential content outside consciousness, that ideas can be experienced and feelings felt outside conscious awareness; and that he does not know that he unconsciously "knows." All this makes necessary the conceptualization of the existence of what we can call a representational "field" or "screen" upon which content can appear and be assessed. And, we would stress again, this content may or may not possess the quality of consciousness.

In sharp contrast is the "nonexperiential realm." This is the realm of forces and energies; of mechanisms and apparatuses; of organized structures, both biological and psychological; of sense organs and means of discharge. The nonexperiential realm is intrinsically unknowable, except insofar as it can become known through the creation or occurrence of a phenomenal event in the realm of subjective experience. From this point of view *the whole of the mental apparatus* is in the nonexperiential realm, capable of becoming known to us (only to a limited extent) via subjective experiences of one sort or another.*

It follows that the dimension or antithesis of consciousness–unconsciousness should only be applied to the realm of experience and not to the nonexperiential realm. This extends a remark of Freud's

---

*This is, of course, as true of the "real" world as well. We can only "know" phenomenal events, even though we may refer these to "extreme reality." When we speak of our ability to control the external world, or ourselves, we are essentially referring to the controlling of experience. In this context we are reminded of Kant's distinction between *noumena* ("things-in-themselves") and *phenomena*.

in regard to instincts (1915*b*) to the whole of the nonexperiential realm:

> I am in fact of the opinion that the antithesis of conscious and unconscious is not applicable to instincts. An instinct can never become the object of consciousness—only the idea that represents the instinct can. Even in the unconscious, moreover, an instinct cannot be represented otherwise than by an idea. If the instinct did not attach itself to an idea or manifest itself as an effective state, we could know nothing about it. (p. 177)

The more stable components of the nonexperiential realm can be considered to be "structures" in the sense in which they have been defined by Rapaport (1957), that is, as organizations that are permanent or have a relatively slow rate of change. The concept of structure is a very broad one, and applies not only to the basic inborn biological structures (e.g., the organs that subserve primitive instinctual discharge) but also includes all the psychological structures that are created during the course of development as a consequence of adaptation (in the sense in which it is used in the present paper). Thus, for example, perceptual structures range from the biologically given sense organs to the psychological structures that play a part in organizing raw sensory data into formed percepts. Again, the structural aspects of memory include memory traces as well as the formal psychological organization of memory and the structures used in remembering. Included here are all the organized patterns of drive discharge and control (at different levels of psychosexual development).

There is an intimate relation between the experiential and the nonexperiential realms. The construction of a new percept, for example, involves the utilization of older structures and the creation of a new one. Thus new structures are continually being created. Structures become modified and may be controlled by the psychic apparatus itself via (conscious or unconscious) experiential representations. Apart from the maturational influences, the mental apparatus develops only through conscious or unconscious awareness of changes in experiential content and related attempts to control that content. Thus the elements in the nonexperiential realm are employed, mobilized, and changed—all outside the realm of experience—although changes in the nonexperiential realm are mediated by experience and their employment or modification provides, in turn, new experiential data.

Thus, for example, we can diminish a number of aspects of what

we usually call "fantasy." There is the organized function of fantasying (Chapter 7) that falls wholly within the nonexperiential realm.
The image and feelings that are the products of fantasying fall within
the realm of experience (conscious or unconscious), and the memory
traces of the fantasy in turn belong to the nonexperiential realm,
although they can later give rise to a revived memory image in the
realm of experience. Similarly, affects can be regarded as falling
within both realms, that which is experienced being the "feeling"
component of the affect.*

It is important to note that experience itself is not an active
agent. It is a *guide* to the mental apparatus. Thus if an unconscious
wish is defended against, the apparatus has reacted on the basis of
experiential signals and makes use of mechanisms or structures in
the nonexperiential realm to bring about appropriate changes in experiential content as it approaches consciousness or as consciousness
is directed towards it. Similarly, the (largely conscious but to some
extent unconscious) experiential representation of the external world
guides the apparatus to make appropriate adjustments to external
reality—adjustments which in turn generate changes in the realm
of experience.

If we learn to perform a particular voluntary intentional act (like
reaching to pick up an object) we are not dealing with a simple and
purely motor act. Motor activity and sensation are intimately connected. From the initiation of the action we experience a constant
feedback of proprioceptive and other information that acts to guide
the particular action. The two-way traffic between the employment
of structures in the nonexperiential realm on the one hand and the
realm of experience on the other is very rapid and of the highest
importance. Further, motor activity accompanies such exercises as
imagining oneself performing some activity, and this covert motor
activity is related to the overt activity that would constitute the action
if it were really performed. We all know how we change our posture
when watching others move—a phenomenon which shows itself
most dramatically when we watch ice-skating or a Western at the
cinema. The point which we wish to make here is that psychological
structures have both a sensory and motor aspect, and that subjective
experiences are highly correlated with particular forms of action, even
though these actions may be restricted to covert trial actions. Thus
one cannot speak of a mental image or experience without taking

---

*In our clinical work it is often the somatic aspects of an affect that indicate the feeling
state of the patient to us.

into account the actions or trial actions which accompany it and which are an intrinsic part of it.*

In the assessment of the contents of the experiential field, a process of rapid *scanning* of the field by the apparatus is involved, and we can make use of the concept of a "scanning function" that operates to guide the apparatus to some sort of action. Such action includes the organization of experience arising from stimuli from the outside world as well as experience prompted by drive stimuli. This scanning function is the internal sense organ of the apparatus. It is part of the nonexperiential realm, but a major part of its function is to scan the material of the experiential realm *before it reaches consciousness.*

The Basic Regulatory Principle

From the point of view we have taken, it is clear that the "pleasure principle" has at least two main aspects. One refers to the notion of energic changes or to changes in the rate and pattern of stimuli arising from internal drive sources, and to dynamic energic homeostasis. Such changes would fall into the nonexperiential realm. In the realm of experience, we have the aspect of changes in feeling state that accompany states of drive tension and discharge, changes that can be broadly subsumed under the headings of pleasure and unpleasure. In the very young infant there is a close correlation between these two aspects of the pleasure principle, a correlation that has major survival value for the individual. The regulation of feelings aroused by drive stimuli and those that accompany drive-reducing activities normally succeeds in bringing about the regulation of the drives themselves. However, feelings reflect more than the state of the drives and gradually become attached to the ideational content reflecting the self and the outer world. Stimuli from the outer world affect the feeling state increasingly as development progresses,

*It follows that when we speak of a wish, we are not only speaking of the mental image of a desired state of affairs. A wish may carry with it a picture of what is desired, but also implies an impulse to act in a particular way, although this impulse may be inhibited before it reaches the threshold of overt activity. An exhibitionistic wish may, for example, be an impulse to expose oneself sexually—this action is usually restrained. One could say that in such a wish the ideo-motor structures relating to self-representations and object representations, as well as those connected with the wish-fulfilling activities, are involved. A wish, therefore, implies a subjective representation of an action being propelled towards discharge and all that this involves. The force behind the wish can be conceptualized as the pressure or urgency that accompanies and propels the representation towards consciousness or motility. If the gratification of the wish provides a basic instinctual satisfaction (e.g., of a sexual or aggressive sort), then we speak of an instinctual wish.

although the instinctual drives always remain the main sources of disruption of the individual's feeling state.

In addition, a gradual differentiation of feelings occurs with development. Perhaps even from the beginning, there must be a difference between the sensual pleasures that accompany drive discharge and the feelings of satisfaction that follow such discharge. There is also possibly a subjective distinction from early on between the unpleasure of instinctual tension and pain (*Schmerz*) arising from other sources. Postdischarge satisfaction can be conceptualized as well-being, and we can regard this as a positive feeling state rather than being a mere absence of feeling. Feelings become differentiated during development, often becoming remote from primitive drive-related experiences, and are increasingly linked with ideational content.

As feelings differentiate, one type of feeling comes to play a major role in the regulation of experience; indeed, to such a degree that its maintenance above a minimum level (when it falls or threatens to fall below that level) becomes the dominant criterion in determining the activity of the psychic apparatus. This is the feeling of *safety* that can be regarded as being generated by smooth and integrated functioning of the apparatus as a whole (including its drive-discharge aspects). The gaining of pleasure will, as the suffering of our neurotic patients testifies, be sacrificed in the interests of maintaining or attaining a minimum level of safety feeling.

Any experience of anxiety or feeling of disorganization lowers the level of safety feeling, and, indeed, we may see the development of types of activity that at first sight seem to be inappropriate and unadaptive, but that are in fact adaptive in that they are aimed at restoring some minimum level of safety feeling. Included in this are, for example, some of the stereotyped and bizarre forms of behavior shown by psychotics, who attempt in this way to control their activities in order to obtain a higher degree of what we may call perceptual security. They have to create a stable perceptual situation by hiding in a corner, clutching a doll, or repeating a ritual, and must avoid activity that would lead to disorganized activity or the experience of loss of safety feeling.

The need to maintain a feeling of safety (which is quite different from pleasure in direct instinctual gratification, though it may or may not accompany it) is of enormous importance in adaptation in general. An activity that leads to pleasure may be inhibited if it lowers the level of safety feeling. The feeling of anxiety, when it acts as a signal to the apparatus, must be accompanied by a drop in the level of safety feeling. Different individuals will vary in the degree to which drive impulses or external factors affect their safety feeling level, and the whole history of the individual enters into determining this (as probably also do constitutional factors).*

The view of adaptation taken here implies that the experiences are constantly being aroused that disrupt the person's basic feeling state, and that the aim, function, or purpose of adaptation is to maintain a basic stability of the central feeling state. Of course the individual will allow his immediate impulses to proceed if these lead to pleasure, but only if at the same time they do not radically lower the safety level, or lead to unpleasure or threatened unpleasure. If, as the impulse proceeds, there is a signal of danger, then his psychic apparatus is activated to apply the appropriate psychological structures in order to change the content of the realm of experience into a form that is safer, even if it means giving up direct instinctual gratifications. Thus, whatever he becomes conscious of, or what he finally actually does, is related to this regulatory criterion. The structures that he uses may be the ordinary perceptual or cognitive structures aimed at the avoidance of perceptual or cognitive "dissonance," or they may be the employment of defense mechanisms in such degree that neurotic or even psychotic disturbances ensue (as in the massive use of projection in paranoid illness).

Köhler (1964) and others have shown that it is "things of action" that are first organized in the child's perceptual world. We can take this further by suggesting that the whole development of knowledge of the "world" is created through the link between the ideo-motor experiential representations and feeling states. Even the highest form of symbolic representation is only meaningful, and indeed is only created, through its direct or indirect link with feelings. In this sense there is no such thing as a purely cognitive or intellectual process. A successful mathematical manipulation is associated with feelings of "rightness," and these in turn have links with feelings of safety, of "good" feelings, of mastery and of "function pleasure" (Bühler, 1918).

---

*The clinical and technical implications of the need to maintain safety at an adequate level are of the greatest importance. This need enters into many aspects of the "repetition compulsion," into aspects of the negative therapeutic reaction (as distinct from guilt and masochistic gratifications), into many of the phenomena of masochism itself (where pain is suffered because it raises the safety level, quite apart from the sexual pleasure in suffering). It can become an aspect of "secondary gain," and indeed may contribute to the perpetuation of symptoms once the original conflict has been resolved. Just as "ego functions" and "apparatuses" can be considered as attaining "secondary autonomy" (Hartmann, 1939), so we can speak of the secondary autonomy of some symptoms. Where techniques other than psychoanalysis are effective, one of the causes may be that they affect symptoms that have gained autonomy and provide alternative safety-giving solutions and techniques (e.g., in "behavior therapy").

The apparatus is thus continually engaging in processes of problem solving, and in all of this, its basic problems relate to the regulation of feelings. In this context we can speak of an "economics of feeling states"; the solution that is acceptable to the apparatus is one that represents the best possible compromise at any one time (and with the particular resources of the individual) between the various "good" and "bad" feelings that it may experience or anticipate. It is clear that to speak of "signal anxiety" is not enough. We have to include signals of anticipated sensual gratification, safety, pain, and possibly others. An economic point of view is thus essential to this model, but it is insufficient at this level of conceptualization to put it in terms of the distribution of quantities of energy. The relation between the more macroscopic quantitative viewpoint to the microeconomics of feelings will, of course, require further exploration.

The "reality principle" falls into place here (in line with Freud's view of it as an extension of the pleasure principle). It represents the taking into account of reality (as it is known or anticipated by the individual). To ignore it usually arouses a signal of anxiety or some other unpleasurable feeling; to take it into account usually provides an anticipated pleasure *or a feeling of safety*, or both. Thus present and future reality are only taken into account on a "here-and-now" feeling basis. If, for one reason or another, it is more economical for the individual not to take reality into account—for example, if being aware of reality increases the sum total of unpleasant or threatening feelings and *lowers* the feeling of safety to an intolerable degree, he may adapt by finding a "pathological" solution of one sort or another.

Schematic Representation of the Basic Model

Figure 16.1 shows the distinction between the nonexperiential realm and the realm of experience. It can be regarded as a sort of cross-section of the schema shown in Figure 16.2, and both show some of the essentials of the basic model as it can now be formulated.

Drive stimuli, arising from the inside, arouse instinctual wishes, the content of which is based on the experiences of situations and activities that have previously been associated with the reduction of instinctual tension and with the attainment of the appropriate gratifiation. "External" stimuli also arouse sensorimotor representations that are impelled towards discharge. It should be noted, however, that these "external" stimuli are not truly external, as they create an effect through the arousal of internal impulses within the nervous

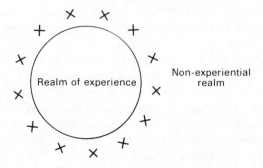

FIGURE 16.1. Experiential and nonexperiential realms

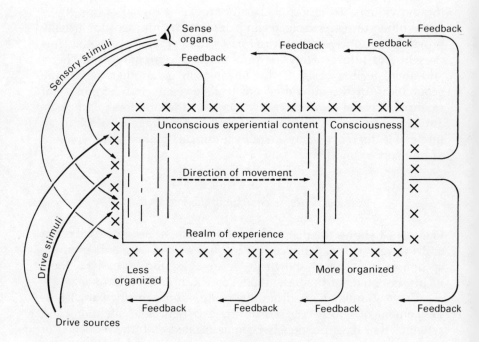

FIGURE 16.2. Schematic representation of the proposed basic psychoanalytic model of the mental apparatus. X=structures in the general sense; they range from biological structures to psychological controlling and facilitating structures, and exist in all parts of the apparatus; vertical lines: unconscious and conscious ideomotor representations; it is only experiential content that can become conscious.

TOWARD A BASIC PSYCHOANALYTIC MODEL

system. Indeed, from a psychological point of view, all the stimuli that the psychologist locates outside the organism only *appear* to be the essential stimuli to which responses may be linked. All external stimuli act by arousing, in one way or another, internal signals that are the internal representations of the external world. If an external situation is to acquire meaning and significance, its internal conscious or unconscious perceptual representation must acquire that meaning.

Changes in the external world and the instinctual drives arouse associated sensorimotor representations that are (see left-hand side of Fig. 16.2) fragmentary and chaotic, being linked by primary process functioning. Their experiential aspects are scanned, processed, modified, checked, organized, and "censored" before they are allowed to reach consciousness or motor discharge. There is an interesting parallel between the processes involved in organizing crude sensations and their associated memories into a final percept on the one hand, and the processes whereby the revival of infantile memories by drive stimuli are modified along their path to consciousness (as, for example, during dreaming).

Thus, from the point of view of psychoanalytical psychology, stimuli both from the external world and from the inner drives arouse internal changes that evoke sensorimotor representations that have an experiential as well as a structural aspect. These representations are based on those that have previously been associated with the gaining of pleasure or with the avoidance of one or other form of unpleasure. The revival of such representations immediately presents a problem to the individual—are they to be allowed discharge, to flower into full action or into conscious awareness, or not? And this applies as much to normal processes of perception as to the revival of past memories under the influence of the drives.

The distinction between the perception of reality and the hallucinatory revival of the memories of past experiences by the drives is a learned one; and this process of learning involves the development of psychological controlling structures based, of course, on appropriate biological ones. The sum total of these controlling structures is what we often refer to as the "ego."

An essential part of the processing referred to above is the translation of input and primitive mental content into something that is reasonable or logical—that "makes sense" and resolves conflict. A primitive wish, or the content associated with it, may be fully inhibited (repressed) or may be absorbed into a thought or action that seems reasonable, logical, and nonthreatening, and that can then be allowed to proceed to discharge in consciousness or in action. We would emphasize that the ultimate criterion in determining what is permitted to proceed and what is not, is based on feelings (very largely in the form of feeling signals as development proceeds).

We can postulate a tendency for continuous movement of experiential content from left to right in the schematic model shown in Figure 16.2. On the left, primitive mental content is aroused as a response to inner stimuli (and "outer" stimuli must be treated as inner in this context). There will be a tendency for such primitive content to be propelled towards consciousness or action (via the appropriate and correlated structures), that is, to move to the right of the diagram. During the course of this movement, the aroused content may be acted upon, turned back, deflected, modified, integrated, or processed in various ways (all this activity taking place in the nonexperiential realm, but prompted and instigated by what appears in the realm of experience, and effecting changes in the realm of experience).

Persistence of Structures

It is essential to make a further point that is vital to the model proposed here. No structure, once treated, is ever lost (although it may be affected by normal processes of decay). Structures are continually being modified on the basis of experience, but this modification comes about through the superimposition of further structures (which may retain substantial parts of the older ones). An essential component of these further structures is that they contain elements that are employed to inhibit the use of those structures that have been superseded. This is discussed in Chapter 14.

The implication here is that we would make use of past modes of discharge and adaptive solutions were it not for the fact that, on balance, these are less comfortable than present ones. When a point is reached (in terms of the economics of feeling states) when a higher order adaptive solution is *less* comfortable, it will readily be abandoned in favor of a more primitive one. This has immediate application to the consideration of the changes that take place during and after psychoanalytic treatment and to such phenomena as the reappearance of symptoms (which have been restricted to "trial" form as a consequence of therapy) when later states of strain occur. Psychoanalytic therapy never undoes the structures that underlie conflict, symptoms, and the like; it only provides alternative solutions that are then utilized (and experienced) in preference to the older ones.

III

In this concluding section we shall use the basic model as a frame of reference in order to examine, briefly and by way of demonstration, its applicability to a few familiar psychoanalytic concepts.

Structural Concepts

The id can be conceived of as lying in both experiential and nonexperiential realms. The instinctual forces and stimuli belong to the latter, as do the structures that they activate and that would, if their activity were permitted to proceed unhindered, reduce feelings of tension and yield primitive instinctual pleasures. In the experiential realm, the subjective ideational and feeling experiences associated with the process of direct drive discharge are aroused (towards the left of Fig. 16.2), and represent the "seething cauldron" of feelings and wishes. These experiential representations give rise to warning signals, and inhibiting structures are called into play, in turn modifying the content of experience. Thus the id represents, as Rapaport has put it, *"peremptory* aspects of behavior". In contrast, the ego refers to aspects related to *delay* (Rapaport, 1959, p. 5). Thus id and ego are aspects of the total apparatus.

The "superego" is a concept relating to a special aspect of the functioning of the apparatus. It consists of those structures that have evolved during the course of progressive adaptations that present guiding standards to the individual and are made use of to the degree to which they provide positive feelings of gratification, well-being, and safety by creating an unconscious illusion of the presence and love of authority figures. In return for this, the individual accepts all sorts of restrictions on his wishes and behavior. If he disregards them, he experiences special forms of anxiety (e.g., guilt, see Chapter 3). Thus the "superego introjects" are organizations within the nonexperiential realm. They give rise to special subjective representations (ideals, "self-I-ought-to-be," etc.), that act as guides or goals in the realm of conscious or unconscious experience. In essence, the superego is a system that provides warning, threatening, but also in some way reassuring feeling signals of a particular sort and has an ongoing function in the "here-and-now." We believe that the adaptational point of view of superego development and functioning allows us further insight into those situations in which superego changes are said to occur (e.g., in psychoanalytic therapy, group situations, etc.), and into the relation between the concepts of superego and ego ideal (Chapter 6).

Topographical Concepts

The basic model as presented here can be seen to encompass the topographical model, that has both experiential (content) as well as nonexperiential (energies, laws of functioning, mental apparatus, etc.) aspects, and the "direction of movement," which is part of our basic model, differs in no essential way from the topographical point of view put forward by Freud. One difference in the present model is the location of the sense organs as "deep" rather than peripheral to the mental apparatus, that is, they have been removed from their original direct relation to consciousness.*

Mental Conflict

At a more macroscopic level, it is *convenient* to see the psychic apparatus as divided into separate structures and to conceive of *intersystemic* as well as *intrasystemic* conflict. At the more microscopic level of theorizing to which the present model is related, conflict can be seen in different terms.† What would be described as a conflict between id and superego in the structural model is regarded here as a dynamic sequence of events that involves the total apparatus. The instinctual impulse causes processes to occur in the nonexperiential realm that move in the direction of primitive instinctual discharge. This is reflected in the realm of experience in the manner described earlier. A whole variety of experiential contents linked with drive tension and gratification appear, involving at their center both self and object representations, as well as a representation of the instinctual aim. As these intensify and move forward, they in turn arouse unpleasant feelings that would be overwhelming if they were to develop unchecked. These unpleasant feelings relate to the anticipation of the consequences of overt instinctual activity, that is, to the dread of annihilation, disintegration, punishment, castration, loss of love, lowered self-esteem, feelings associated with loss or destruction of the object, and the like. The unconscious awareness of these feelings prompts immediate action on the part of the apparatus to inhibit the movement towards drive discharge ("repression," the application of "countercathexis," etc.). A whole sequence of to-and-fro movements occurs, with previous solutions being repeated in trial form, until one is found or constructed that represents a satisfactory compromise solution so that feelings of drive tension are reduced and the basic feeling state maintained within tolerable limits. This represents the "best" solution that the apparatus can produce through multiple trial-and-error processes—"best" as previously described in terms of the economics of feeling states. Normally such "problem-solving" activity goes on smoothly and extremely rapidly,

*A view supported by recent work on subliminal perception and "perceptual defense."

†The view of conflict presented here is similar to that which has been formulated in great detail (but in rather different terms) by Rangell (1963a, 1963b) and the reader is referred to his writings on this topic.

and progressive development in terms of new (and therefore newly structured) solutions can take place. At this level of conceptualization, normal conflict is not distinguished from neurotic conflict, though progressively adaptive *solutions* may be distinguished from pathological ones. The essence of conflict is the arousal of unpleasant feelings, and the apparatus will *always* find a solution that leads to the control of the feeling content of experience. What we describe as a "pathological" solution usually involves the heightened use of particular mechanisms of defense, the revival and utilization of more primitive solutions, the construction of "symptoms," and so on.*

Object Relations

We have left this important but extremely complicated area as we intend to discuss it at length elsewhere, and will make only a few comments.

The primitive sensorium of the infant is dominated by chaotic and intense feeling experiences that become increasingly linked with other sensory contents as development proceeds. The development of perception and of the distinction between self and non-self, and between self and objects, can be seen as a consequence of the child's need to control and to regulate feelings (which are affected both by the drives and by objects in the outer world). Inasmuch as the child's objects play a vital role in this regulation, their representation becomes bound up with feeling associations of a most intense and varied sort. We could say that as a consequence, self and object representations receive an increasing abundance of *feeling cathexes* as development proceeds. The feelings involved may be crude and primitive, but may also later be of the most refined and asensual sort (we can speak here of *value cathexes*). We should also add that, in addition to feelings derived from instinctual tension and discharge, those derived from postdischarge gratification (well-being) and feelings of safety and of "function pleasure" are also significant.

We can conceive of object relations as always being self–object relations. They are reflected experientially as wishes toward the object, attitudes towards and expectations from the object, mutual interaction between self and object, and in all the feelings and values attached to these representations.† This experiential content is, of course, a reflection of underlying structural links and organizations

---

*Some solutions may cause pain in consciousness, yet still represent the best that the apparatus can achieve. In terms of the economics of feelings it "settles for a loss."

†The problems involved in the theory of narcissism fall more into place when looked at from the point of view of the vicissitudes of the feeling and value cathexes attached to self and object representations (Chapter 12).

in the nonexperiential realm, involving a connection both with instinctual stimuli and with the impact of the external world.*

It is both theoretically and clinically important that from the point of view of psychic adaptation there is no such thing as an unselfish or altruistic love or concern for an object. The ultimate criterion in determining whether or not a particular object relation is maintained or striven for is its effect on the central feeling state of the individual.

The psychoanalytic developmental psychology of object relations is at present in a confused and unsystematic state, and we believe that an approach from the viewpoint described here might be of value in attempting some sort of systematic clarification.

*So-called internal objects can be understood in a variety of ways in this model. The "internal object" can be the organization of the representation of a past or present object in the nonexperiential realm; it can be the experiential representation of the object closely tied to the content of instinctual wishes; it can be an object created in the fantasy life of the individual, in which defensive processes play a major part; etc.

17

Psychoanalytic Psychology and Learning Theory

Joseph Sandler and Walter G. Joffe

This chapter represents an effort to construct a learning theory within the framework of psychoanalytic psychology. The formulations contained in it are a direct extension of the work contained in the previous chapters in this volume. The need to integrate the theoretical conceptions that had previously emerged in order to provide a learning theory (based on the concept of structure formation and the notion of reinforcement through changes in feeling states) also led, not long afterwards, to the construction of the psychoanalytic "basic model" described in Chapter 16. While the learning theory contained in this chapter can be regarded as being, in one sense, a preliminary version of that "basic model," it is best presented after Chapter 16. Areas of overlap with Chapter 16 have been omitted.

This material was first given at a Ciba Foundation symposium published in 1968 as *The Role of Learning in Psychotherapy*.

Since the beginnings of psychoanalysis, certain basic and stable concepts have been the cornerstones of psychoanalytic theory. Such concepts include, for example, the notions of unconscious mental functioning and of instinctual drives and impulses. But psychoanalytic concepts have never been fully organized into a coherent and integrated theoretical model, and the various concepts in current use can only be fully understood if they are considered from a frame of reference that includes a historical dimension. This is largely because advances in psychoanalytic theory have tended to take place along specific fronts, and because there has always been a state of affairs in which older concepts have existed alongside new ones. Perhaps the major attempt to formulate an explicit and coherent model was the introduction of the structural theory (Freud, 1923*a*), but important revisions of psychoanalytic theory, such as that of the theory of anxiety (Freud, 1926), have left us with further problems of conceptual integration that have not as yet been faced.

This chapter is an attempt to sketch an approach to psychoanalytic theory that has evolved during the past 10 years as an outcome of a specific method of research into the conceptual problems of psychoanalysis. The method used (Appendix) has been one in which theoretical concepts are tested against recorded clinical material in a systematic way. The procedure has shown up many of the problems in regard to definitions in psychoanalytic theory, and has led to the creation of altered and at times new definitions within a revised theoretical framework. We have found more and more that the findings and formulations of psychologists who are not psychoanalysts have had to be brought into the psychoanalytic model— for example, the studies of Jean Piaget and other psychologists working in the fields of cognition, perception, memory, and the like. Thus, for example, the conceptualization of an object relationship as the investment of a love object with libido has altered to a concept in which the notion of inner object representation (as opposed to the "real" external object) is given prime importance. The idea of an investment of an object with energy has had to be replaced with the idea of feelings attached to the internal object representation (Chapter 12). Indeed, the whole area of the development of the inner (or representational) world has come to play an increasingly important part in psychoanalytic theory, particularly in regard to children; and this not only from the emotional but also from the cognitive point of view.

There has been a general move in recent years to turn psychoanalysis into a theory that is not only a psychology of abnormal mental functioning, but which embraces a normal general psychology. This has been achieved partly by removing some of the links of psychoanalysis with treatment. The development of psychoanalytic theory has been strongly influenced in the past by its association with psychoanalytic therapy, and a model that is aimed primarily at meeting the needs of psychoanalytic practice may be substantially different from that created by the wish to construct a general psychology. The latter demands the building of conceptual bridges to other disciplines, and this presentation is addressed primarily to the possibilities of building a bridge between psychoanalysis and learning theory.

Many problems are involved in such an attempt. The levels of detail at which phenomena are being studied may vary; learning theories tend to emphasize external stimulus and overt response while psychoanalytic theory places stress on the inner, subjective world of the individual; and so on. But it is gratifying that certain learning theorists have shifted emphasis from external stimuli and observable behavior and have utilized concepts that are aimed at encompassing intrapersonal phenomena. There is an increasing realization that the stimulus–response model is inadequate, and mediating concepts are now being used—for example, in relating studies of perception and problem solving to learning theories. Such mediating concepts range from Hull's "habit strength" to such concepts as strategies, schemata, and programs.

Parallel changes are taking place in psychoanalytic theory. Influences from other fields include that of Piaget's work; computer models are being drawn upon; and experimental findings by psychoanalysts in the laboratory are having repercussions on basic psychoanalytic theory.

Some recent formulations will now be presented very briefly. We assume that our readers have a knowledge of the essentials of psychoanalytic theory—although it is unfortunate that what most people know of this theory may have been wholly derived from earlier formulations made at a time when psychoanalysis was investigating the derivatives of unconscious instinctual wishes as expressed in the material brought by patients in psychoanalytic sessions.

SOME RECENT ASPECTS OF PSYCHOANALYTIC THEORY

Psychoanalysis as a Psychology of Adaptation

By this we do not mean simply adaptation to the external world, but would emphasize that adaptation should be regarded as applying, on the one hand, to the external situation (as it is perceived by the individual) and on the other, to inner promptings (wishes, needs, impulses, and so on) that may arise spontaneously or may be triggered by external situations. We should also include the concept of adaptation to those internal standards that have arisen during the course of development—standards that may be quite at odds with present-day reality, and that we subsume under the concept of the superego (Chapter 3).

The Psychoanalytic Concept of the Representational World

Apart from the conceptualization of the psychic apparatus into id, ego, and superego, we have to formulate more clearly the psychoanalytic concept of the inner world. We have done this by putting forward the concept of the representational world (Chapters 4 and 5). This can be regarded as the whole complex of mental representations of inner wishes, feelings, memories, percepts, and symbols. One specialized part of the representational world is that which contains the representations of what is external to the individual; another refers to the representation of the person himself (his self-representation); and other areas relate to images with various symbolic meanings. The representations of words and mathematical symbols are prime examples of this last, and form a substantial part of the representational content of normal thinking. Further, the *representation* of what is outside is never an exact reflection of what we assume to be *actually* outside the person concerned. His perceptions are structured and colored by what has gone before and by his own (conscious or unconscious) wishes and desires.

Essential to the representational world are the many organized schemata that the individual constructs during the course of his development and that form the background frame of reference to all current processes of perception, imagining, remembering, feeling, and thinking. The representational world in all the different aspects of its organization is constantly influenced by stimuli arising both from within and without the individual, and new schemata are constantly being created as new perceptual and conceptual solutions are being found. These schemata form the basis for future attempts at adaptation (in the sense in which we have used the term) and problem solving, although they may in turn be modified by experience.

The Fundamental Distinction Between Structure and Experience

We can now make a distinction that is implicit in the whole body of psychoanalytic theory, and that is a crucial basis for what follows: the distinction between "structure" and "experience." The concept of structure refers not only to the basic inborn biological structures, but also to all the secondary psychological structures that are created during the course of development through interaction between the individual and the outside world. The concept of structure, as used here, is broad, including not only the schemata that relate to the person's inner world but also everything that is usually subsumed by the terms "mechanism," "apparatus," and so on. Thus perceptual structures will range from the biological, such as the sense organs, to the secondary psychological, which organize sensory input into formed percepts. Again, the structural aspects of memory include the so-called memory traces as well as the formal psychological organization of memories. The body schema can in this sense also be considered to be a structure—a frame of reference that informs us about our posture, provides the background frame of reference for purposive acts, and so on. In this context, a "strategy" would also be a structure and, indeed, any learned link between sets of experiences or activities would imply the existence of some sort of structural connection between them. Structures are essentially unknowable and exist outside consciousness. They can only become known to us indirectly through the formation of an ideational representation—in which case what we know is not the structure itself but its mental representation. In general, a structure can be defined as a relatively permanent organization or an organization with a relatively slow rate of change.

Unfortunately the English term "experience" has more than one meaning. In this paper we do not refer to so-called life experience, that is, past training and learning and the like, but rather to the content of purely subjective experience—the experiencing of the content of sensation, perception, memory, and so on.* Thus a memory has both structural and experiental aspects, and the two should be sharply distinguished. Similarly, in regard to the body image, we can distinguish between the subjective experience of our body at any one time, and the body schema that is the structural basis that lies behind, mediates, and gives form to the subjective experience.

When we speak of a wish, we are not only speaking of the mental image of a desired state of affairs. A wish may carry with it a picture of what is desired, but also implies an impulse to act in a particular way, although this impulse may be inhibited before it reaches the threshold of overt activity. An exhibitionistic wish may, as has been said, be an impulse to expose onself sexually—this action is usually restrained. One could say that in such a wish, the ideomotor structures relating to self-representations and object representations, as well as those connected with the wish-fulfilling activities, are involved. A wish, therefore, implies a subjective representation of an action being propelled toward discharge and all that this involves. The force behind the wish can be conceptualized as the pressure or urgency that accompanies and propels the representation towards consciousness or motility. If the gratification of the wish provides a basic instinctual satisfaction (for example, of a sexual or aggressive sort), then we speak of an instinctual wish.

---

*In German there are different words for these two aspects of experience. In this chapter we refer to *Erlebnis* rather than *Erfahrung*.

THE BASIC PSYCHOANALYTIC MODEL

In Chapter 16 we discussed the way in which motor activity provides a feedback of proprioceptive and other information that can act to guide the particular action. The link between motor activity and perception was emphasized, in order to point to the fact that psychological structures have both a sensory and a motor aspect, and that subjective experience is highly correlated with forms of action, although these may be restricted to covert actions.

The essentials of the basic model have been given in Chapter 16. Stimuli and information arising both as a result of changes in the external world and from the instinctual drives arouse associated sensorimotor representations that are fragmentary and chaotic, being linked together only by processes of simple association (referred to by psychoanalysts as the "primary process"). Before being allowed to reach consciousness or motor discharge, they are processed, modified, checked, organized, and censored. There is an interesting parallel between the processes involved in organizing crude sensations and their associated memories into a final percept on the one hand, and the processes whereby the revival of infantile memories by drive stimuli are modified along their path to consciousness (as, for example, during dreaming).

Thus, from the point of view of psychoanalytic psychology, stimuli both from the external world and from the inner drives arouse internal signals that evoke sensorimotor representations. These representations are those that have previously been associated with the gaining of pleasure or with the avoidance of some form of unpleasure (for example subjective drive tension, anxiety, pain). The revival of these representations immediately presents a problem to the individual—are they to be allowed discharge, to flower into full action or into conscious experience, or not? And this applies as much to normal processes of perception as to the revival of past memories under the influence of the drives. "It seems that the central feature of the perceptual process is that it attempts to organize and structure the incoming data from the sense organs. In this way the ego deals with incoming stimulation in exactly the same way as it modifies latent dream thoughts and transforms them into manifest content. There is a 'perception work' corresponding to the 'dream work.' Indeed, this need not surprise us if we consider that the distinction between the various sources of excitation, between drive excitation and excitation from the real world, is only painstakingly built up in the infant over months and years." (Chapter 1).

Thus the distinction between the perception of reality and the hallucinatory revival of the memories of past experiences by the drives is a learned one; and this process of learning involves the development of psychological controlling structures based, of course, on appropriate inborn biological ones. The sum total of these controlling structures is what psychoanalysts usually refer to as "the ego".

An essential part of this processing is the translation of input and primitive mental content into something that is reasonable or logical—that "makes sense." A primitive wish or the content associated with it may be fully inhibited (repressed) or may be absorbed into a thought or action that seems reasonable, logical, and non-threatening, and that can then be allowed to proceed to discharge in consciousness or in action.

A distinction has been made between *structures* (which include the biological and psychological apparatuses, defense mechanisms, memory traces, schemata, and so on) and *experiential content*, which embraces both ideational and "feeling" elements.*

Primitive mental content is aroused as a response to inner stimuli (and outer stimuli must be treated as inner in this context), and there will be a tendency for such primitive content to be propelled towards consciousness or action. During the course of this movement, the aroused content may be acted upon, turned back, deflected, modified, or processed in various ways. (See figure 2 in Chapter 16.)

THE SAFETY PRINCIPLE

It is clear today that Freud's pleasure principle is an amalgam of several different regulatory principles. It covers the seeking of sensual pleasure and the avoidance of unpleasure as well as being a principle of energic homeostasis. Some 10 years ago, it was proposed that a further regulatory principle had to be invoked in order to account for certain forms of abnormal behavior. This was referred to as the "safety principle" (Chapter 1), and it also has direct relevance to theories of learning.

In the same chapter some of the steps taken by the ego to deal with any reduction in the background tone of safety feeling were described, and the conclusion was drawn that there could be seen in all of this the workings of what might be called a safety principle. "This would simply reflect the fact that the ego makes every effort to maintain a minimum level of safety feelings . . . through the development and control of integrative processes within the ego, foremost among these being perception."

---

*The term "feeling" is used here instead of "affect," for the term "affect" often embraces both bodily and feeling aspects. The distinction between the two is important in the present context.

The need to maintain a feeling state of safety (which is quite different from pleasure in direct instinctual gratification) is of enormous importance in learning and in development in general. The need to maintain safety gains dominance over the need to gain pleasure, and indeed the conflict between these different needs is probably the forerunner of neurotic conflict in general. An activity that leads to pleasure may be inhibited if it lowers the level of safety feeling. From the point of view of learning, it would seem that the maintenance of safety feeling is the most potent reinforcing agent after a certain level of development has been reached.

An important consideration will now be introduced. We have said that structures are intrinsically nonconscious. But the experiential content of the representational world is also largely unconscious (Chapter 16). However, it can become conscious if attention is directed towards it, provided it has not, for any reason, been made inaccessible to consciousness. All this implies a process of knowing, recognizing, thinking, and feeling outside consciousness. Evidence is accumulating to substantiate this assumption in spite of the philosophical objection that may be raised against such concepts as unconscious feelings.

What we have tried to do so far is to prepare the foundations on one side of the theoretical bridge between psychoanalysis and learning theory: we shall now attempt some of the bridge building itself.

1. Learning can be defined as progressive structural modification. If we take the view that no structure is ever lost, then unlearning, or extinction, would imply a process of inhibition. This allows us to explain both the reappearance of extinguished responses in experimental learning situations and the clinical phenomenon of regression.

2. The elements that become linked in processes of learning are not stimulus and response but rather one ideomotor representation and another. Such learning can occur outside consciousness, but learning only takes place through (conscious or unconscious) changes in the experiential content of the individual's representational world.

3. The reinforcing agents in the linking of one ideomotor representation with another are changes in feeling states. Gaining pleasure leads to reinforcement, as does the avoidance of pain or unpleasure, but dominant over this is the process of increasing or maintaining the safety feeling.*

*The relevance of this to masochistic behavior is apparent. An activity that leads to correctly anticipated pain may be pursued if it leads to concealed sexual pleasure. But it may also be instituted if, in spite of the pain created by it, it leads to a heightening of the level of safety feeling.

4. There is a process of scanning of the unconscious area of the representational world; in other words, of evaluating the ideomotor representations in terms of the feeling states or feeling signals associated with them. This occurs extremely rapidly, and a representation is normally only permitted discharge if the feeling state that accompanies it is not too disruptive of safety and well-being.

5. Some structures may evolve in order to solve ongoing inner conflict. But they may persist and be utilized in order to maintain safety feeling even though the original impulses that entered into their formation are no longer operative in the same way. It is likely that the latter structures are those that are most amenable to change through behavior therapy. Thus a neurotic symptom (and the structures that subserve it) may be directed towards solving, for example, an ongoing conflict between an instinctual wish and the internal (superego) standards of the individual. But it may equally function at a later date as a method of producing safety feeling, and if other methods of providing safety feeling are available, then a different and more comfortable solution may be created and utilized, and the employment of the older symptom structure inhibited.*

6. Although the processes of adaptation described above have an immediate "here-and-now" quality, the capacity to manipulate trial actions in thought (as is evident in man) within or outside consciousness and to assess the feeling signals associated with these trial ideomotor representations leads to the function of anticipation and prediction through thought. This, in turn, provides a further dimension to the learning process.

CONCLUSIONS

We have been guilty of gross oversimplification in this presentation, but this is because we believe simplification to be an essential part of the ongoing construction of theory. The processes referred to are complex and continuous—every time one sees or does something new, a new structure is formed. We hope that our presentation may have contributed in some small part to those processes of structure formation that constitute development in our various fields.

---

*All systems and techniques of psychotherapy (including behavior therapy) abound with potential alternative safety-giving solutions that can be adopted by the patient. It would be instructive to examine such procedures as desensitization in this light.

18

Theoretical and Clinical Aspects of Transference

Joseph Sandler, Alex Holder, Maria Kawenoka-Berger, Hansi Kennedy, and Lily Neurath

Some of the difficulties and contradictions inherent in the current use of the concept of transference are examined in this chapter. The examination of relevant material from the Hampsted Index resulted in the formulation of a "multidimensional" approach to transference. The argument is put forward that transference is essentially a clinical concept, but that various aspects of transference can also be seen as dimensions of object relationships in general.

The content of this chapter is relevant to the theme of this volume, as object relationships play an important part in the conceptualization of the "basic model" (although they are only briefly referred to in Chapter 17). The paper reproduced in this chapter was published in *The International Journal of Psychoanalysis* in 1969.

> The analytic situation is a variant of . . . human transference relationship.
>
> HOFFER (1956)

I

Like many other psychoanalytic concepts, that of transference is one that has developed from the clinical situation of psychoanalytic practice. When we come to integrate it into our general psychoanalytic metapsychology, we find—as with other concepts—that difficulties of conceptualization and definition may arise.

264

In this chapter we should like to present some of the difficulties that arise in connection with the integration of a clinical concept into our general psychoanalytic psychology, to illustrate some of the problems with examples drawn mostly from analytic work with children, and to suggest a possible direction in which further research may proceed. No attempt will be made to present a systematic review of the literature, and this chapter should be regarded as presenting a line of thought that has been stimulated by our work and that will certainly require further elaboration and extension.

It is nearly three-quarters of a century since Freud first described the phenomenon that he called "transference." It appeared as a source of resistance to the analytic process, based on what he called "a *false connection*" between the person of the physician and "the distressing ideas which arise from the content of the analysis" (Breuer & Freud, 1893–1895, p. 302). Ten years later, Freud was referring to transferences as "new editions or facsimiles of the impulses and phantasies which are aroused and made conscious during the progress of the analysis; but they have this peculiarity, which is characteristic for their species, that they replace some earlier person by the person of the physician" (1905b, p. 116). He pointed out that *past* experiences are revived as applying to the physician *in the present*, and remarked that "some of these transferences have a content which differs from that of their model in no respect whatever except for the substitution" (1905b, p. 116). Using the analogy from publishing, he continued by saying that such transferences are merely *reprints* or *new impressions* of the old. But other transferences "are more ingeniously constructed . . . and they may even become conscious, by cleverly taking advantage of some real peculiarity in the physician's person or circumstances and attaching themselves to that. These . . . will no longer be new impressions, but revised editions" (1905b, p. 116).

Freud later (1910a) pointed out that "transference arises spontaneously in all human relationships just as it does between the patient and the physician" (p. 51). It is not *created* by psychoanalysis, but psychoanalysis merely *reveals* it and guides the psychical processes towards the desired goal. In 1912 Freud remarked that "unconscious impulses . . . endeavour to reproduce themselves in accordance with the timelessness of the unconscious and its capacity for hallucination." The patient seeks "to put his passions into action without taking any account of the real situation" (p. 108). In the *Introductory Lectures* (1916–17) he comments that transference is present from the beginning of treatment, and is "for a while, the most powerful motive in its advance. We . . . need not bother about it so long as it operates in favour of the joint work of analysis. If it then changes into a resistance, we must turn our attention to it . . ." (p. 443).

In his "Autobiographical Study" (1925d), Freud stressed again that transference "is a universal phenomenon of the human mind . . . and in fact dominates the whole of each person's relations to his human environment" (p. 42).

Freud included under transference what we might perhaps call the transference of *authority* (Chapter 3). In his last work, *An Outline of Psycho-Analysis* (1940), Freud speaks of the "relation of transference" bringing with it two further advantages. One of these is that the patient reproduces part of his life story by "acting it before us . . . instead of reporting it to us."* The second advantage to the analysis of the relation of transference is described as follows: "If the patient puts the analyst in the place of his father (or mother), he is also giving him the power which his super-ego exercises over his ego, since his parents were, as we know, the origin of his super-ego. The new super-ego now has an opportunity for a sort of *after-education* of the neurotic" (p. 175).

It would appear that Freud saw transference as being predominantly a transfer of feelings about important objects from the past to the person of the analyst in the present, and believed that they are experienced as real *in the present*. They may appear in their original form or they may be disguised and distorted. They may include the transfer of *images* from the past as well as feelings, so that they influence the perception or apperception of the analyst by the patient, the altered perception integrating into it revived memory images. Transference of authority is seen as being within the framework of transference of feelings towards, and about, the parents. Moreover, transferences develop not only in the analytic situation and towards the person of the analyst but also in normal life.

The motive forces of transference are allocated, in all of this, primarily to the unconscious (we would nowadays say the id) in accordance with its blind thrust towards repetition, its domination by what Freud referred to as the "repetition-compulsion." It is a corollary of Freud's remarks about what has been referred to earlier as the "transference of authority" that to the extent that superego functions as the internal representative of the parents, the superego introjects are invested with *feelings* of respect and authority, and the superego exercises its authority, in part at any rate, via such feelings (Chapter 3).

The advances in our understanding of the transference *since* Freud have, for the most part, been in the field of psychoanalytic

---

*He refers here to the patient's transformation of present reality so that the past is reexperienced in the patient's perceptions and feelings in regard to the analyst in the present, as if they are emerging anew in the "here-and-now."

technique. There has perhaps been an increase in our sensitivity to transference phenomena, so that, for many analysts, transference appears to have replaced the dream as the "royal road to the unconscious."* We are more sensitive too to the ways in which the patient may attempt to manipulate or to provoke the analyst to react in a particular way, attempting to *make him behave* in the present in the way in which the patient's infantile objects were seen (or fantasied) to behave in the past.

We are perhaps more aware of the ways in which patients defend against transference impulses, and more skilled in noticing transference manifestations *in statu nascendi*. Here the growing awareness of the role of the ego, particularly in regard to its defensive functions, has played a decisive part. But, in general, the contributions to the study of transference after Freud have not led to any fundamental advances on his views. This is particularly true in regard to what we can refer to as the metapsychology of transference, and this is perhaps surprising in view of the substantial developments that have taken place in ego psychology, and our increasing realization that object relationships belong as much to the ego as to the id. True, there have been a number of major clarifying contributions, such as that of Nunberg (1951), Hoffer (1956) and, of course, Anna Freud's *The Ego and the Mechanisms of Defence* (1936).

When one reads the literature on transference and on transference neurosis, one cannot help but have the feeling that there is something that is being searched for, some elusive, slippery quality, inherent in the whole topic, and that this possibly provides one of the motive forces for our continuing preoccupation with the subject. Incidentally, with regard to transference neurosis (that intensification of the transference in which the patient's major conflicts become centered around the person of the analyst, so that his neurosis has become an analytic neurosis, so to speak, with a corresponding lessening of neurotic manifestations outside the analysis), Kepecs has recently shown (1966), in a review of the literature, that a great deal of confusion exists as to the precise distinction between "transference" and "transference neurosis." The terms are often used interchangeably or in such a way that any differences in meaning may become obscured.

---

*See Anna Freud (1965). We take the view, with Anna Freud, that there are indeed many "royal roads to the unconscious"; but there is no doubt that the analysis of transference phenomena has become an increasingly important part of psychoanalytic technique.

It is of interest to note at this point Hoffer's lucid account of the dynamics of the transference neurosis. He suggests that it

> is not a reactive, but an active manifestation; it is not created by reality but by the spontaneous pressure of the Id. The infantile object relationships become intensified in the transference neurosis and remain there at first unrecognized. If the subsequent emergence of a transference neurosis is not interfered with by too brisk transference interpretations, symptomatic-neurotic suffering changes into feelings of inferiority and of mental pain due to frustrated infantile love (transference neurosis proper). Interpretations lead to the transformation of these transference feelings and actions into memories. Mental energy, invested in the repressed and disguised infantile object relations, is thus at first drained into the transference situation and then into memories of those relations . . . The painful actuality in the transference situation becomes transformed into memories of the past, and with it the patient's actual infantile relation towards his analyst will gradually become past as well and will relieve him from much actual suffering (1950a, p. 195).

Many of the difficulties in regard to the concept of transference arise from the fact that most workers have approached the subject from a frame of reference that is essentially related to clinical technique and that although they may *appear* to be considering aspects of the metapsychology of transference, their formulations are either implicitly or explicitly related to the analytical situation, and in particular to the analytical situation when the patient is an adult, that is, to so-called adult analysis.

This problem is not one specific to the area of transference. It is probably true that a great many analysts use a slightly different model (or at best a different frame of reference) when they are considering technical matters from that which they use when they consider theory. One has only to think of the extent to which the topographical model is used in connection with clinical work and technique, and to compare it with the use made of the structural model when theoretical issues are considered.

The importance of the fame of reference is evident when we come to examine the various definitions of transference. Consider, for example, the following definition given by Waelder (1956): "Transference may be said to be an attempt of the patient to revive and re-enact, in the analytic situation and in relation to the analyst, situations and phantasies of his childhood. Hence transference is a regressive process" (p. 367).

He goes on to say: "Transference develops in consequence of the conditions of the analytic experiment, viz. of the analytic situation and the analytic technique" (p. 367). This is, of course, also a view expressed by many others, and although we are sure that Waelder would have agreed with Freud that extraanalytic transferences exist, the way in which he has related his definition to the analytic situation and to the analytic process makes it sound like a special analytic phenomenon, with the implication that it ultimately differs from relationships outside the analysis in aspects of quality as well as quantity. He (deliberately we believe) uses here a "technical" frame of reference. One can have no quarrel with this, but such a technically oriented definition raises problems if we set our sights towards making psychoanalysis into a general psychology, an aim that Hartmann has so often stressed. Definitions of analytic concepts, from this point of view, should ideally be applicable to extraanalytical phenomena as well as to those that arise in the clinical situation, unless, of course, we specifically maintain, as some have done, that a concept such as transference is a clinical or technical one only. However, Freud himself extended his notion of transference outside the analytic situation, and our social experiences, as well as our clinical experience with nonanalytic types of therapy, must surely tend to force us to do the same.

Consider a further definition, one recently given by Greenson (1965), which appears to be *more* general.

> Transference is the experiencing of feelings, drives, attitudes, fantasies and defenses toward a person in the present which are inappropriate to that person and are a repetition, a displacement of reactions originating in regard to significant persons of early childhood. I emphasize that for a reaction to be considered transference it must have two characteristics; It must be a repetition of the past and it must be inappropriate to the present. (p. 156)

Although such a definition does not mention the analytic situation and can, on the face of it, be taken to apply to aspects of all relationships, analytic or otherwise, its use of the criterion "appropriate–inappropriate" suggests that here again we have a frame of reference that is a technical one, for it is in the special analytic situation where appropriateness or inappropriateness can best emerge (although here again it is a question of the judgement of the analyst, not always infallible). Moreover, the differentiation between what is appropriate and what is inappropriate in ordinary *nonanalytic* relationships (in marriage, for example) must be at best be an extremely arbitrary matter.

We may consider yet another example, this time from a British analyst. In a paper in 1930, Ella Freeman Sharpe commented on transference as follows: "Transference begins with the very first analytical session . . . just because everyone has thoughts about another human being when brought into close contact . . ." (p. 54).

She goes on to describe the special conditions of the analytical situation:

> In analysis, through the specially conditioned contact, we have potentially the freest field for phantasy concerning the analyst. . . . From the first hour the patient will have thoughts and opinions about the analyst as in ordinary contacts, but the very fact of the phantasy-situation, the detachedness and isolation of the hour, the unknownness of the analyst, activates phantasy; and this, with the stimulus of dream-life and recollections of the past, brings about a very special relationship with the analyst. This relationship is the transference. (p. 54–55)

Anna Freud (1936) has given a definition of transference that is also in terms of the special analytic situation:

> By transference we mean all those impulses experienced by the patient in his relation with the analyst which are not newly created by the objective analytic situation but have their source in early—indeed, the very earliest—object relations and are now merely revived under the influence of the repetition compulsion. (p. 18)

Interestingly, Anna Freud here contrasts transference with new relationships, as she puts it, "created by the objective analytic situation"—showing here perhaps the influence of her experience with the analysis of children.

Instances of the sorts of definition that we have quoted can be multiplied many times over (e.g., Glover, 1949, 1955; Hendrick, 1934; Klein, 1952; Menninger, 1958; Silverberg, 1948). However, a number of authors have emphasized strongly that transference should be regarded as a general phenomenon, and that its appearance and use in the psychoanalytic situation is a special, albeit highly intensified, case of a more general process. Orr (1954), in a historical survey, echoes Freud in remarking that "Transference in its widest sense is regarded as a universal phenomenon in interpersonal relationships. In its most restricted sense, however, transference implies a specific relationship of patient to psychoanalyst" (p. 621).

Fenichel (1945), among others, spells out what distinguishes the more specific transference of the psychoanalytic situation from the more general and universal phenomenon. Speaking first of the transference situations of everyday life, he says that "it is a general human trait to interpret one's experiences in the light of the past. The more that repressed impulses seek expression in derivatives, the more hampered is the correct evaluation of the differences between the present and the past, and the greater is the transference component of a person's behaviour" (p. 30).

In contrast to such transferences in everyday life, the psycho-analytic situation

> promotes the production of transference in two ways: (1) The
> environment which is reacted to has a relatively uniform and con-
> stant character and therefore the transference component in the
> reactions becomes much more pronounced. (2) Whereas in other
> situations people react to a person's actions and words—thus
> provoking new reactions and creating new realities all of which
> obscures the transference character of the original action—the an-
> alyst, in contrast to this, provides no actual provocation to the
> patient and responds to his affective outbursts only by making the
> patient aware of his behaviour. Thus the transference character of
> the patient's feelings becomes clearer. (p. 30)

Similarly, Greenacre (1954) comments: "First as to the nature of the transference relationship itself: If two people are repeatedly alone together, some sort of emotional bond will develop between them" (p. 671). She then describes the special developments in the artificial situation of the analytic relationship.

> Now in the artificial situation of the analytic relationship, there
> develops early a firm basic transference, derived from the mother–
> child relationship but expressed in the confidence in the knowl-
> edge and integrity of the analyst and the helpfulness of the method;
> but in addition the non-participation of the analyst in a personal
> way in the relationship creates a "tilted" emotional relationship,
> a kind of psychic suction in which many of the past attitudes,
> specific experiences and fantasies of the patient are reenacted in
> fragments or sometimes in surprisingly well-organized dramas with
> the analyst as the main figure of significance for the patient. This
> revival of past experiences with the full emotional accompaniment
> focused upon the analyst, is not only more possible but can be
> more easily seen, understood, and interpreted if the psychic field
> is not already cluttered with personal bits from the analyst's life.
> This of course is the work with the neurotic symptoms and patterns
> as they occur in the transference; i.e. projected directly upon the
> analyst. (p. 674)

In a more recent paper, Greenacre (1966) comments that the phenomenon of transference is omnipresent in human relationships and is based on two essential psychological ingredients, "first, the difficulty of the individual to exist long in emotional isolation; and second, the capacity to shift or transfer patterns of emotional rela-tionship from one person to another, provided there is a connecting link between them" (p. 193).

She reiterates her view that the transference has its roots in the
early and necessary relationship of infancy, and goes on to say:
"However, in therapy, communication through bodily contact and
direct gratification . . . is replaced as much as possible by verbal
communication." (p. 195–196)

Similar points have been made by a number of other analysts,
including Glover, Bornstein and Hoffer. Thus Hoffer (1956) sees the
specific transference of the analytic relationship as a variant of human
transference relationships in general and links it in particular to
infantile experiences. He states:

> The term "transference" refers to the generally agreed fact that
> people when entering into any form of object-relationship and
> using objects around them for instinct gratification and for pro-
> tection against anxieties (as a defence) *transfer* upon their objects
> those images which they encountered in the course of previous
> *infantile* experiences, and experienced with pleasure or learned to
> avoid (pleasure–pain principle). The term "transference," stressing
> an aspect of the influence our childhood has on our life as a whole,
> thus refers to those observations in which people in their contact
> with objects, which may be real or imaginary, positive, negative
> or ambivalent, "transfer" their *memories* of significant previous
> experiences and thus "*change the reality*" of their objects, invest
> them with qualities from the past, judge them and try to make
> use of them in accordance with their own past.
>
> The analytic situation is a variant of such human transference
> relationship. (p. 377)

With the exception of a handful of authors, little work has been
done on the psychological nature of the special bond that constitutes
transference, other than to stress the fact that it involves a repetition
of the past in the present, that it is in some way irrational, and that
it can have an important social and adaptive function. Moreover, the
assumption is often made that we are dealing with a *unidimensional*
or unitary phenomenon, the differences between various types of
transference phenomena, both within and without the analytic situation, being largely a matter of specific content, and of variations
in the degree of complexity and intensity.

As with many other analytic concepts introduced by Freud, what
appeared to be relatively simple in the beginning now turns out to
be very complicated indeed.

We have suggested earlier that the problem of integrating the
technical with the metapsychological frames of reference is an important one, and it arises in heightened form in relation to material
derived from psychoanalytic work with children. Here the differences

in the analytic setting, in the ways in which the patient communicates, in the therapeutic forces at work (for not all improvement during the course of child analysis can be attributed to the development of insight), together with the fact that the child's relationship to the analyst may at times be indistinguishable from extraanalytic relationships, and many other factors, all serve to make the differentiation between what is transference and what is not extremely difficult. Freud remarked in 1933 that, in the analysis of children as opposed to adults, "Transference (since the real parents are still on the spot) plays a different part."

But precisely *because* of the difficulties in distinguishing and defining transference in child analytic work (and a great deal has been written on the subject in recent years), the investigation of material from child analysis offers perhaps a most useful starting point for investigating both theoretical and technical aspects of transference in general—one can start by jumping in at the deep end, as it were. Accordingly we would like to present some of the results of the examination of relevant child analytic material from one of the studies conducted as part of the Hampstead Index project.

II

We should like to preface this part of the chapter with a few remarks about the role of transference in child analysis.

In Anna Freud's "Introduction to the Technique of Child Analysis" (1926), she expressed the view that although transference occurs in child analysis in the form of what she called transference reactions, a transference *neurosis* in the form in which it is seen in adults does not occur.* An exception to this might be the case in which the child was living away from the real parents, for example in an institution. Anna Freud later altered her views on this, attributing the change to the developments that have occurred in the technique of child therapy, in particular the elimination of the introductory phase and the deliberate use of defense analysis. She now

*Bornstein (1945) expresses a very similar view. In child analysis "the analyst may become the target of many of the child's sexual or aggressive impulses, and occasionally and within a limited scope he may play the part of one of the parents. And yet, as a rule, no transference neurosis in the proper sense of the term arises. The symptoms are not centered around the analyst's person nor around happenings during the analytic session. There is a good reason why the child does not develop a transference neurosis, in the strict sense. There is no need for him to repeat his reaction vicariously since he still possesses his original love-objects, his parents, in reality."

believes it possible for the child's transference reactions to develop into a transference neurosis.

In *Normality and Pathology in Childhood* (1965), she states:

> I have modified my former opinion that transference in childhood
> is restricted to single "transference reactions" and does not develop
> to the complete status of a "transference neurosis." Nevertheless,
> I am still unconvinced that what is called transference neurosis
> with children equals the adult variety in every respect (p. 36).*

In *The Ego and the Mechanisms of Defence* (1936), Anna Freud had distinguished different types of transference phenomena according to the degree of their complexity. These are: (1) *transference of libidinal impulses*, in which instinctual wishes attached to infantile objects break through or attempt to break through towards the person of the analyst; (2) *transference of defense*, in which former defensive measures against the drives are repeated; and (3) *acting in the transference*, in which the transference intensifies and spills over into the patient's daily life.

Anna Freud has always maintained that in child analysis the analyst can be used by the child for multiple purposes—to play multiple roles—and only one of these is transference. Thus she has written of the analyst functioning as a "new object" for the child, the healthy part of the child's personality displaying a "hunger" (as she put it) for new objects, in contrast to the neurotic part of the child that uses the analyst for purposes of repetition. She also emphasizes the importance of the "treatment alliance" (a concept that has come to replace that of the earlier "introductory phase" in treatment). In addition, the analyst can also function as an object for externalization, externalization being a *subspecies* of transference that should nevertheless be kept separate from transference proper. She put it in the following way:

> Not all the relations established or transferred by a child in analysis
> are object relations in the sense that the analyst becomes cathected
> with libido or aggression. Many are due to externalizations, i.e.,
> to processes in which the person of the analyst is used to represent
> one or the other part of the patient's personality structure. (1965,
> p. 41)

Thus the child restages in analysis his internal (intersystemic) conflicts as external battles with the analyst. Transference proper would be regarded as the repetition, by way of regression in the analysis, of the child's object relations from all levels of development.

All of this draws attention to the fact that distinctions can be

*Similar views have been expressed, for instance, by Kut (1953), Brody (1961), and Fraiberg (1966).

made between various types of relationship to the analyst, some of which may be regarded as transference and others not. Here the definition of transference is one that is essentially related to the analytical situation and to the technique of analysis, and we are dealing with formulations that are basically within a technical frame of reference. This also applies to formulations regarding transference that have been put forward by other child analysts. The problem of integrating the clinical and theoretical frames of reference still remains.

In an attempt to investigate this problem further, a research group was set up within the framework of the Hampstead Index project some years ago. It specific task was to examine the accumulated child analytic material from the point of view of the clinical classification of those manifestations in analysis that could possibly be called transference, and then to consider these from a more theoretical, that is, metapsychological, standpoint.

We had at our disposal in this project a mass of information collected in the Index under various headings that were relevant to the concept of transference. This material was examined in some detail, and in consequence a number of conclusions as to their classification were reached. We shall attempt to summarize some of these under a few broad headings, that are by no means mutually exclusive.

1. It very quickly became clear that the clinical and technical usage of the term "transference" covered a very broad spectrum of phenomena. It became apparent, too, that this was not due to failure on the part of our therapists to apply what they had learned, but was connected with an intrinsic difficulty in regard to the definition of what was transference and what was not. However, we could group the material under a number of headings.

First we have all those manifestations that could be understood in terms of the way in which past experiences, impulses, fantasies, and conflicts were *revived* in the course of the analysis, and that now relate to the person of the analyst in their manifest or latent content. We see here in particular how a repressed unconscious wish emerges as a new derivative of the unconscious, and that may combine with present reality (including the person of the analyst) in the expression of a revived wish, memory, or fantasy (for example, the wish for the exclusive possession of the therapist, representing a revival, in the analysis, of a boy's oedipal or preoedipal wish for the exclusive possession of the mother). The particular content of such a transference from the past is influenced not only by present preconscious and conscious content but also by content derived from past memories and fantasies.

From a metapsychological point of view, transference of this sort could be considered as a derivative of the repressed unconscious— or, from a structural point of view, as a derivative of the id. (Fenichel (1941) has elaborated the notion of transference as a derivative—a point, of course, originally made by Freud.)

2. We had no doubt that a relationship that corresponds to the transference neurosis as it has been described in adult psychoanalytic work also occurs in a considerable number of child cases. The whole question of the occurrence of transference neurosis in the analysis of children is a controversial one, and, of course, much turns on the definition that one uses.

Our own definition of transference neurosis was arrived at after a considerable amount of thought and discussion, and we mean by it here the concentration of the child's conflicts, repressed wishes, fantasies, and so on on to the person of the analyst, *with the relative diminution of their manifestations elsewhere*. With this definition in mind, an examination of indexed instances of transference neurosis showed that, in some cases of what could appear to be a transference neurosis, the mechanism involved was not simply a concentration of the child's instinctual impulses on to the person of the analyst. Rather, the permissive attitude of the therapist allowed the child to express impulses that had to be restrained elsewhere, and this was accompanied by symptomatic improvement outside the analysis. The changes within the analytic situation were connected with changes in the direction of obtaining a more realistic ideal self-image.

3. We come now to the various forms of *externalization*. As mentioned earlier, Anna Freud has drawn our attention to the way in which the various major structures can be externalized during the course of the analysis, and although she suggests that this is a subspecies of transference that should be distinguished from transference proper, it worked out in practice to be impossible to avoid bringing externalization under the major heading of transference. Thus a patient may externalize his superego so that the analyst comes to bear for the patient the characteristics of the patient's own conscience, and is reacted to by the patient as if he were the patient's superego—an internal conflict has become an external one in the analysis. But it becomes extremely difficult to draw a dividing line between the externalization of the superego as a structure and the externalization of the introjects that form the basis of the superego, in which case we have the revival of a past object relationship (we mean here a psychic object relationship, not necessarily the real one that existed between patient and parents in the past); and we would very definitely have to call this a form of transference.

We have mentioned earlier Freud's remark that the analyst can take over the power of the patient's superego—here the *authority* of the introject is transferred rather than its content. The analyst does not reflect the superego introject—indeed one might say that the introject has not been externalized, but rather that there has been a transfer or displacement of authority (Chapter 3). This is, of course, of great importance as part of the mechanism of the therapeutic process.

Similarly, we might talk of externalization of the id—as, for example, when the patient sees the analyst as a seducer. But here again, how do we differentiate between externalization of the id and a projective defense against a revived instinctual impulse directed towards the person of the analyst in the present, as it was directed towards an object in the past?

Under the heading of "externalization" we can also include all those various forms that relate to the externalization of one or other aspect of the patient's own self-representation. This includes what we ordinarily understand by projection, in which an impulse of the patient towards the analyst is felt by the patient as being directed by the analyst towards him. But externalization of the self-representation includes far more; aspects of the patient's *ideal self* may be externalized, and this includes both positive and negative ideals. Or we may see the complicated but highly important mechanism in which the patient externalizes an aspect of his self-representation on to the analyst and at the same time identifies with a superego introject. This is sometimes loosely called "projection," but it is in fact a rather more complicated mechanism—for example, when the patient feels *guilty* about an impulse of one sort or another, he may accuse the analyst of it, gaining at the same time a feeling of virtue through his own identification with his superego.

We can also get "splitting" of the self-representation between analyst and patient in specific forms, as in the revival of the fantasy of having a twin, and so on. The range of possible externalizations is infinite, and it is often extremely difficult to divorce externalization from the types of transference described earlier, for every libidinal or aggressive impulse carries with it some form of self-representation as well as some form of object representation—and, of course, some form of relation between the two. Thus an unconscious exhibitionistic impulse carries with it an unconscious representation of the person exhibiting himself, some representation of the person exhibited to, and a representation of the act of the person exhibiting to the object.

Externalizations of aspects of the self-representations are, of course, paralleled by internalizations of various sorts, and the identifications and introjections that occur in the analytic situation belong in this category.

4. We come now to what we can call "displacements and extensions of other relationships." Perhaps more noticeable in analytic work with children than with adults is the occurrence of displacements of *current* wishes, conflicts, or reactions to persons outside the analysis into the analytic situation, or onto the person of the analyst. With children it is most frequently aspects of the relationship to the parents that are displaced or extended into the analysis in this manner. These current preoccupations may be largely reality-related (e.g., the child's reaction to real rejection by the parent); or they may be a product or manifestation of the child's current level of functioning (e.g., the appearance of oedipal strivings as a consequence of the child's progressive development).

There can be little doubt that the interpretation and working through of these current preoccupations of the child extended into the analysis is one of the most important aspects of analytic work with children. It is perhaps of some interest that therapists vary in the degree to which they take up such material as relating specifically to the analytical situation. These displacements and extensions, which have been discussed in the literature (e.g., by Fraiberg), are what one could call "transferences in breadth" as opposed to "transferences in depth."

5. The phenomena to which we have just referred bring us into the related field of what we might perhaps refer to as "character transference." Here we see reactions, attitudes, and relations manifested towards the therapist that can be considered to be habitual and characteristic for the patient concerned. Of importance in this connection is that these aspects of the patient's relationship to people (or to specific groups of people) are not in any way specific to the therapist, but are rather in the nature of character traits. Such reactions may be seen, and indeed very often are seen, in the *earliest* sessions of treatment, and may involve feelings of *the greatest intensity*. Typical of such manifestations is the occurrence in the analysis of a habitual tendency to placate or appease, or habitual demandingness, or a sadomasochistic tendency. From a purely technical point of view, it may be correct and valuable to take these habitual or character transferences up in the analytic work as if they were specifically related to the analytical situation. However, there are occasions when the interpretation of such reactions of the patient (and we are thinking here of certain types of cases with a so-called character disturbance) in terms of the intra-analytic situation is technically quite inappropriate.

6. We can comment briefly on certain other aspects of the analytic relationship. One of these is the so-called relationship to the

analyst as a real person—of particular importance in children who have suffered severe deprivations in their object relationships, but also seen, of course, in certain adult patients who may have had such early deprivations or who may be suffering from defects in the capacity to make full object relationships.

Another role of the analyst is his function, in certain cases, of being what has been referred to as an "auxiliary ego"—something that we see particularly in borderline and psychotic cases, or in children with an organic defect, in blind children, and so on.

To these we can add the function of the analyst in those instances in which the patient relates to him simply on the basis of his being a person who can satisfy a need. What is significant here is that the analyst as a real and specific person plays no part—if the need arises then the demand is there for any person to satisfy it, and the analyst happens to be the person present. This is characteristic for certain patients who have not progressed far in their level of object relations and in whom the need-satisfying components of their object relationships predominate.

7. We come now to an aspect of the relationship to the analyst that has been much discussed in regard to both adult and child analysis. This is what has been called the "therapeutic alliance" or the "working alliance." It is usually *contrasted* with transference— and refers to the treatment alliance between therapist and patient, based on the patient's conscious or unconscious wish to co-operate, and his readiness to accept the therapist's aid in overcoming internal difficulties. This is not the same as attending treatment simply on the basis of getting pleasure or some other form of gratification. In the treatment alliance, there is an *acceptance* of the need to deal with internal problems, and to do analytic work in the face of internal or (particularly with children) external (e.g., family) resistance.

Although it is clear that we can distinguish between the treatment alliance and what we normally call transference, there can be little doubt that the success or failure of a treatment alliance depends, among other things, on the existence of what Greenacre (1954) has called a "basic" or "primary" transference. She considers that the basic transference originates from a primary need for sensory contact, for the warmth of contact with another body. Greenacre stresses, incidentally, the need for a full adherence to the rules of analysis in order for the analytic process to develop within the matrix of the "basic" or "primary" transference.

The point we wish to emphasize here is that even though we may (and from a technical point of view *should*) contrast the treatment alliance with transference, a form of transference itself appears to be an essential ingredient of the treatment alliance. Indeed, the phrase "positive transference" has often been used to denote the establishment of the basic transference to which Greenacre refers.

8. To conclude this section we would like to mention only briefly the whole host of fantasies and expectations that the patient may bring to treatment. These again have been referred to at times as transference manifestations, "ready-made" transferences, and the like; yet at the same time they are always contrasted with the forms of transference that develop as a consequence of regressive processes within the analytic situation.

It is perhaps of interest to hark back here to Greenson's two essential elements of (1) repetition of the past and (2) inappropriateness to the present—for these will on the whole apply also to the initial fantasies and expectations with which the patient comes to treatment. In contrast, a definition of the sort given by Waelder would not apply. Let us give an example recorded in the Index (a child who started analysis at the age of 3):

> Sara played many games in which she showed that she saw the treatment situation as a repetition of her hospitalization, with the therapist as the doctor. When her fears about treatment were interpreted, she said to the therapist: "You are a doctor." She then took the role of the doctor and put plaster on the therapist's hand, saying it was bleeding.

We have spent some considerable time so far in describing some of the types of clinical phenomena that could conceivably be brought together under the general heading of transference, but we should like to emphasize at this point that we are not claiming that all these clinical manifestations *are* in fact transference. What we are saying is rather that it is extremely difficult to draw the line and to define transference in such a way that we can satisfactorily categorize our material into what is transference and what is not. If we start, as Freud did, from the view that transference represents the transferring of an impulse directed towards an infantile object, towards a new object—the analyst—in the present, we are limiting ourselves to a very narrow field, and excluding much of what is, in present-day usage, considered to be transference. The reader will recall that it was Anna Freud who, in 1936, spoke of *transference of defence* and who later referred to *externalization* as a *subspecies* of transference.

We should also like to emphasize that the problem in regard to transference is not necessarily a clinical one—we can assume that practising psychoanalysts know what they mean by transference— or the exact meaning of the term may not be important as long as one understands what the patient is doing, what mechanism is operating, and so on. The problem is basically a conceptual one, but as such, it is also a problem in psychoanalytic communication and consequently an important one in psychoanalytic teaching. When psychoanalysts speak to one another of transference, or teach their candidates about when to take up the transference or when to leave it alone, they may be in an area of pseudocommunication, unless they are sure that others understand the same thing by the term as they do. Indeed many avoidable technical errors are made by beginning analysts because they have been given "rules of thumb" about when and when not to interpret material in the transference.

The objection may be raised at this point that the types of relationship that develop in analytic work with adults have a special quality and are more restricted in scope than those that can be discerned in analytic work with children, and that this is brought about because of the special structure of the adult psychoanalytic situation. We are accustomed to taking this special situation and the technique of adult analysis as our basic model and to consider departures from the basic process as necessary variations in technique forced upon us by the needs of the patient. In this context, Eissler (1953) has spoken of parameters of technique, referring here to necessary temporary deviations from the standard analytic procedure. From this point of view, the technique of child analysis is one that appears to involve parameters of the grossest sort, but although the differences between adult and child analysis have always been stressed, there are also marked similarities. In both, for example, we aim at creating a situation in which we allow the patient's material to develop and unfold, a situation in which internal and internalized conflicts can be externalized, interpreted and so on. Whereas in the adult analytic situation we have a set of rules that are appropriate to the fact that material can be brought in the form of free association, in child analysis we have a more flexible set of rules aimed in particular at providing suitable *modes of expression* to the child so that he too can bring and develop his analytic material. We believe that child analysis has shown us that it is possible for the child analyst to step out of one role into another—for example, to initiate a game with a young child and at the same time to take sufficient distance in order to give an appropriate interpretation.

A great deal of adaptation to the limits, peculiarities, and needs of the child goes on in child analysis, but even in the analysis of adults we often do something similar, except on a much more microscopic scale. Perhaps we should distinguish here between micro- and macroparameters of technique, the macroparameters being more characteristic of analytic work with children than with adults.

The point of saying all of this is to emphasize the conclusion, which is evident from the instances quoted earlier, that the types of relationship and the content of the material that emerge in child analysis do not essentially differ from that with which we are familiar from work with adults (although of course the technical procedures may be very different). All the instances we have referred to can be found in work with adults as well, but the child-analytic situation, operating as it does on a broader beam, with more flexible rules than adult analysis, enables us perhaps to see the range of relationships (which in the analytic situation could be called transference) in a more comprehensive way than we might otherwise do.

The concept of transference is one that has been developed from within psychoanalytic work—it derives historically from the understanding of particular types of resistance to the analytic process—and it has been extended outside the psychoanalytic situation into the general sphere of the psychology of interpersonal relationships. Freud himself did this when he referred to transference as a universal phenomenon. It is an inescapable conclusion that we have to view "transference"—the term is now used in a broad sense—as a *multidimensional* rather than as a unitary or unidimensional phenomenon. And if we want to conceptualize these dimensions from the point of view of psychoanalytic metapsychology, it is also evident that we need to consider the metapsychology of object relationships rather than that of transference as such. The term "object relationship" is used here with the qualification that it includes much more than the libidinal or aggressive cathexis of another person, but that it also refers to such things as the use of objects for externalizations and internalizations of all sorts, or as objects of displacement, or as objects to whom the relationship is entirely connected with reality matters. Thus there would appear to be as many dimensions to relationship as there are to transference in its broadest sense, and indeed the study of the one is, we believe, the study of the other. Freud, it will be remembered, spoke of "the relation of transference." Thus we are perhaps at a point at which we can proceed from psychoanalytic general psychology, from the more general field, to the study of the specific analytic phenomena—even though it may be that the analytic situation gives us the best insights into the general psychology of object relationships. But there is no doubt that there are other techniques—child observation, to cite but one example—that will also serve us well in this connection.

If we adopt this point of view, we should then *not* ask ourselves what is and what is not transference in the analytic situation, but rather *what dimensions of relationship enter into the special and artificial analytic situation, and how are these involved in the process of treatment?*

We have used the term "dimensions of relationship" in order

to emphasize something that may become obscured when we view the development of object relationships in terms of the stages and phases that the child passes through in the course of his development. From a descriptive point of view, we do see the replacement of an earlier type of relationship by different, more mature, forms. We see the replacement of the psychological reflection of the biological mother–infant relationship by anaclitic, so-called need-fulfilling, relationships, these in turn leading to further developments, and so on. But in fact we probably do not ever get a real replacement of one type of relationship by another. What we see is rather the addition of various new types of object relationship developing collaterally, being integrated with and dominating the old, but not necessarily replacing them. Thus even in the person who has attained the most mature type of object love, the infantile aspects, for example the purely need-satisfying aspects, remain, although they may be subordinated to the higher level developments. Sex is never entirely transformed into object love, but the same object may come to serve both aspects of the relationship. Included in the concept of relationship here are all those bonds that involve indentification, externalization, and the like, and here too we have the development of parallel lines, so that even the most primitive state of primary identification, or primary confusion as it is better called, persists alongside the more mature capacity to make secondary identifications once ego boundaries have been developed and are capable of being imposed. It has been suggested (Chapter 14) that the first automatic response to the perception of another person is to be confused with him, but that normally this primary confusion or identification is dealt with by the rapid setting of self and object boundaries. Thus we have as part of normal development the attainment of the capacity to *disidentify*, a process that represents the inhibition of a genetically earlier state. Indeed, we would take the view that in normal ego functioning the ego has to expend a considerable amount of effort inhibiting earlier tendencies and solutions.* Thus so-called phase-dominance is only descriptively a replacement of earlier forms of functioning by developmentally later ones. Dynamically, it involves a *subordination* of developmentally earlier trends that persist in the present in unconscious "trial" form.

In normal life the elements of the past that enter into relationships may repeat themselves over and over again in the present. Or

---

*The relaxation of this effort or constraint on the part of the ego in the analytic situation probably contributes in a substantial way to "the return of the repressed" in the special (adult) psychoanalytic situation, in the forms that have been discussed in this chapter.

some degree of stability may be reached in an ongoing interpersonal relationship. The analytical situation, for both children and adults, owes its uniqueness and special properties to the fact that by means of a set of rules, conditions, and procedures, the patient is enabled to re-create (among other things) the important aspects of his present and past internal and external object relationships in the analysis— all of which provides material for the ongoing analytic work. As a consequence of the analyst's interpretations, confrontations, recon- structions, and other interventions, a process of further development within the analysis occurs, material shifts to a different level, and so on. We would like to stress the *process* aspect of analysis, for the analysis of resistances permits a development—including the rela- tionships that we call transference—in a way and to a degree that would not be possible in normal life. Infantile impulses, fantasies, object relationships, conflicts, and solutions become alive in the pre- sent, and with the co-operation of that part of the patient that is in alliance with the work of analysis, successful analytic work may ensue.

CONCLUSIONS

Transference is a clinical rather than a metapsychological concept. The concept as it has come to be used encompasses a whole variety of elements, all of which enter into object relationships in general. The special psychoanalytic situation may facilitate the emergence of particular aspects of relationships, especially aspects of past rela- tionships, but it is technically of the greatest importance to distin- guish between these various elements ("dimensions" of transference) rather than to regard *all* aspects of the patient's relationship to the analyst as being a repetition of past relationships to objects.* In other words, "transference," in the diluted sense in which it tends to be used today, should not be understood as only reflecting transference in the narrow sense in which it was originally conceived. The psy- choanalyst must be ready to distinguish between the repetition of past relationships to objects, defenses against this, the various forms of externalization, the displacements and extensions of other current relationships, so-called character transferences, and the like. Work with children shows the differences between these various elements most clearly, but they emerge as well, although in different propor- tions, in psychoanalytic work with adults.

*As does Melanie Klein (1952).

19

The Role of Affects in Psychoanalytic Theory

Joseph Sandler

This chapter is concerned with tracing some of the vicissitudes of the concept of affect in psychoanalytic theory, with presenting some of the difficulties that arise in relation to the concept because of changes that have taken place in that theory, and with offering some tentative formulations that may be of theoretical and clinical relevance.

Before 1897 the concept of affect was a crucial one in Freud's theory of pathogenesis, being related to trauma on the one hand and to the production of symptoms on the other. In the next phase of Freud's thinking, affects were relatively neglected, but they were to some extent reinstated after 1923 when Freud introduced the structural theory (1923a). This chapter discusses some historical aspects of the confusion with regard to affects in psychoanalytic theory, and the view is developed that the distinction between somatic changes and subjective experience is a necessary one if the theoretical problems involved in emotions are to be clarified. The role played by conscious and unconscious feeling states in psychological functioning is discussed, as well as some aspects of the interaction between psychological processes and somatic disturbances.

This chapter was presented as a contribution to a symposium held by the CIBA Foundation and published in *Physiology, Emotion and Psychosomatic Illness* (Sandler, 1972).

In the first part of what follows, the term "affect" will be used in a relatively broad sense, for reasons that I hope will become apparent. Later in this paper a differentiation will be made between the physical and somatic processes involved in emotional states on the one hand, and *feelings* on the other.

The most exhaustive treatment of the history of the psychoanalytic theory of affect has been given by Rapaport (1953). His scholarly paper is of substantial value, not only for its detailed exploration of the problems that surround the theory of affect, but also because it shows the degree of confusion and uncertainty that exists in connection with the place of the concept of affect in psychoanalytic theory. Rapaport found it convenient to divide the history of psychoanalysis into a number of phases, and it is possible to make use of this approach with benefit here. However, in my view, Rapaport unfortunately failed to clarify the conceptual problems sufficiently because of his adherence to a unitary theory of affect—that is, one that encompassed the physical, energic, and experiential aspects within the same concept. A number of other authors (e.g., Brierley 1937; Jacobson 1953b; Lewin 1965; Schur 1953) have addressed themselves to the same theoretical problems, and although feelings are frequently distinguished from instinctual drives and also from bodily changes in emotion, the single overall concept of affect has been maintained. As a consequence, the subject appears to remain as confused as ever. This is partly due to the tendency of psychoanalytic theorists to retain all previous formulations, discarding none, and to attempt to formulate theoretical propositions in a way that would be consistent with previously accepted formulations, especially those of Freud. Unfortunately it is often forgotten that Freud himself discarded certain of his own theories when he found them to be inadequate.

At this point an account of the major phases of development in Freud's own writings is appropriate. Freud was always aware that his psychological formulations and models were essentially theoretical constructs, to be adhered to as long as they proved useful, and to be modified as necessary. The account of the developmental phases in psychoanalysis that follows is based on a modification of Rapaport's description (1953).*

THE FIRST PHASE

Four years after qualifying in medicine, Freud visited Charcot in France and attended his demonstrations at the Salpêtrière for some months in 1885–1886. The patients demonstrated by Charcot could be made to lose their physical symptoms by psychological interventions, particularly suggestion and hypnosis. Freud was impressed

*The description of the three phases in the development of Freud's psychoanalytic theories is taken in large part from a paper on the historical context and phases in the development of psychoanalysis (Sandler et al., 1972a).

by the link that the French had shown between the mental "disso-ciation" induced by hypnosis, and the apparently similar dissociation between a conscious and unconscious part of the mind that seemed to occur in patients with hysterical symptoms. Freud was profoundly impressed by his experience with Charcot, and this led him to the belief that mental disturbances could have psychological origins. He was later able to elaborate the notion of dissociation further in his theories of repression and defense.

On his return to Vienna, Freud began a collaboration with Josef Breuer (Breuer & Freud 1893–95) and was led to the conclusion that the patient's symptoms could be seen as the irruption, in a distorted form, of *charges of affect* that had been kept in a pent-up state, dis-sociated from consciousness. This dissociation was (contrary to the view of Charcot and Janet) regarded by him as an active process of *defense*. Freud also became convinced that the barrier between the conscious and unconscious parts of the mind occurred in normal as well as in neurotic subjects. Symptoms arose when the quantity of affective energy was too great to be absorbed in the normal way, and was forced to find some form of indirect expression. The pent-up or "strangulated" affects were thought of as having been aroused by *real* traumatic experiences.* The memories associated with these emotions were not acceptable to the patient's moral and ethical stand-ards and, being no longer under voluntary control once they had been repressed, found their concealed expression through, for ex-ample, being "converted" into hysterical symptoms. Thus conversion hysteria (as well as the other psychoneuroses) was seen as a way in which traumatically induced affect could be "discharged." It is im-portant to remember that in this phase Freud equated affect with energy, and saw psychoneurotic symptoms as being brought about by the need for the mind to rid itself of abnormally large quantities of such affective energy (to restore "constancy"). From the point of view of therapy, the central aim was to release such emotions by bringing them (and the associated memories) into consciousness, with subsequent abreaction or catharsis and a resulting assimilation into consciousness of those mental contents that had previously been rejected.

---

*This was regarded as true of the psychoneuroses, but Freud also considered con-ditions (in the first phase) that were thought to be due to "pent-up" affective energy that had accumulated for reasons other than psychological traumas. Typical of these was the "anxiety neurosis," thought to be a manifestation of undischarged affective excitation due to sexual frustrations of one sort or another. The "anxiety neurosis" was not, at that time, thought to be a psychoneurosis, but rather an "actual" (in German *Aktual*, meaning "current" or "present-day") neurosis.

It is evident that in the first phase, the concept of affect played a central role in psychoanalytic theory. The evocation of a "charge of affect" by traumatic experiences was thought to be an essential step in the development of pathology (particularly hysteria and obsessional neurosis). If the affect could be dealt with in "normal" ways ("wearing away," "discharge" through associative pathways, etc.), pathology would not ensue. In this phase, the arousal of affective energy was thought of as being predominantly in response to external stimulation, although charges of affect could also arise from the internal needs of the individual. An abnormally strong charge of energy could be a direct result of early sexual trauma, or an emotional reaction (of disgust, anxiety, guilt, etc.) to the later revival of early sexual memories. The model of the "mental apparatus" in this phase was a very simple one, and no theoretical distinction was made between feelings and "charges of energy."

THE SECOND PHASE

This phase lasted from 1897 until the publication of *The Ego and the Id* (Freud, 1923a). Freud's orientation now shifted completely from an emphasis on *real* traumatic experiences to instinctual drives arising from within. His change of viewpoint was a consequence of his realization that the memories that had been uncovered in his work with hysterical patients were often not real memories, but rather memories of early fantasies. His own self-analysis also played a significant part in his change of viewpoint. At the beginning of this phase, he was paying special attention to the analysis of his own and his patients' dreams, and found dream analysis to be the most useful way of conducting psychoanalytic exploration. In *The Interpretation of Dreams* (1900), he put forward a new conceptual framework that was to form the basis for the theories of the second phase. This has come to be known as the "topographical" model of the mind. In 1901, in *The Psychopathology of Everyday Life*, he published the results of his studies on "symptomatic acts" (such as slips of the tongue), seeing them as expressions of unconscious instinctual wishes. In 1905 he elaborated further the so-called instinct, or more properly, the *drive* (Freud used the German word *Trieb*) theory of psychoanalysis in the *Three Essays on the Theory of Sexuality* (1905a). Instinctual drives were seen as the basis for a whole range of sexual (and later, aggressive) wishes in childhood and adult life. Psychoanalysis was now unequivocally a drive psychology. Although in the first phase Freud had concentrated on adaptation to events in the external world, his orientation and interests now shifted to the way in which the person adapts to internal forces.

In the first phase, Freud had differentiated between conscious and unconscious aspects of the mind, and this distinction is elaborated in the topographical model. He now described two main sorts of unconsciousness. The first was characteristic of the processes in the system *Unconscious*, the reservoir of instinctual wishes that if allowed to emerge to the surface would constitute a threat to consciousness. The strivings in the Unconscious were regarded as being constantly propelled towards "discharge," but being allowed to reach consciousness and motility only in a disguised and censored form. The second sort of unconsciousness was that which was attributed to the system *Preconscious*, conceived of as containing knowledge, thoughts, and memories that were not defended against and that could enter consciousness relatively freely. The contents of the preconscious were utilized by instinctual wishes for purposes of disguise in their path from the depths to the surface. The instinctual wishes in the system Unconscious were thought to represent infantile sexual impulses derived from all the phases of the child's psychosexual development. A review of the changes that Freud made in his theory of instinctual drives during the second phase is given in the classical work by Bibring (1941).

The system Unconscious was regarded as being characterized by a primitive mode of functioning that Freud referred to as the "primary process." Logical and formal relations between elements in the Unconscious are regarded as absent, and simple rules of primitive association apply. Drives and wishes in the Unconscious function according to what Freud termed the "pleasure principle"—that is, they seek discharge, gratification, and relief of painful tension at all costs. The systems Preconscious and Conscious were considered as being in direct opposition to this. Here secondary processes—logic, reason, and the knowledge of external reality, as well as conscious ideals and standards of conduct—predominate. In contrast to the Unconscious, the other two systems attempt to follow what Freud called, "Formulations on the Two Principles of Mental Functioning" (1911), the "reality principle"—that is, to take anticipated consequences into account.

In 1914 Freud introduced the concept of "narcissism" in an attempt to clarify the problem of the person's relation to his love objects and to himself in both normal and pathological states. Here Freud was also concerned with the formation of ideals, on the basis of the parents as models, and introduced the concept of the "ego ideal," adumbrating the later concept of the "superego." In all his discussions of self- and object love, descriptions of feelings are given, but the theoretical discussion is couched in terms of the disposition of "libidinal energy."

In all this, the concept of "energy" was taken over from the first phase, although it was now seen as instinctual energy, rather than as a "charge" of affect. Ideas and feelings, as well as emotional tensions within the body, were seen predominantly as drive derivatives. Affects were no longer regarded as main motivators in behavior but rather as secondary and surface manifestations of drive impulses finding their way from the depths of the system Unconscious. Thus, for example, anxiety was regarded as transformed "libido" (the term given to the energy of the sexual drives—aggression was added to the instinctual drives relatively late in the second phase, and no specific term was coined for aggressive energy).

The pleasure (or pleasure–unpleasure) principle related to the tendency of the apparatus to experience tension (or to be in a state of tension) when instinctual drives were aroused, and to experience a reduction of tension (with associated pleasure) when the drives were gratified ("discharged"). Although Freud's formulations during this phase were often couched in affective experiential terms (e.g., pleasure–unpleasure), affects were relatively neglected, and the theoretical model was formulated predominantly in terms of energic tensions. The homeostatic "pleasure principle" was little different from the "principle of constancy" that Freud had adopted from Fechner in the first phase. Although Freud described many different feeling states, in his theoretical explanations we find, for example, that "to love" becomes "to cathect (invest) with libido," and so on. Feelings were all explained in terms of the vicissitudes of charges of libidinal energy.

THE THIRD PHASE

In this phase, beginning with the publication of *The Ego and the Id* (1923a) and *Inhibitions, Symptoms and Anxiety* (1926), a major theoretical shift occurred. Freud now put forward his *structural* theory in order to deal with certain inconsistencies that had begun to be apparent in his view of the mental appartus and its functioning. While he introduced this theory in 1923 partly in order to postulate the existence of an unconscious sense of guilt, it can be added that his formulations during the second phase in regard to narcissism and the clinical conditions of melancholia, paranoia, and hypochondriasis, all contributed to the strain imposed on the explanatory potential of the topographical model.

In the structural theory, Freud put forward a model that represented a threefold division of the mental apparatus into major *structures:* the "id," "ego," and "superego."

The id corresponds approximately to what had been encompassed by the unconscious in the second phase. It can be conceived of as the area containing primitive instinctual drives, dominated by the pleasure principle, and functioning according to the primary process. During development a portion of the id is modified, under the influence of the child's interaction with the external world, to become the ego. The primary function of this latter agency is that of self-preservation and the acquisition of means whereby a simultaneous adaptation to the demands of the id and of reality can be attained. It gains the function of delaying and controlling instinctual "discharge," using a variety of mechanisms, including the mechanisms of defense. The third agency, the superego, was seen as a sort of internal precipitate of the child's early conflicts, especially in relation to his parents. The superego is regarded as the vehicle of the conscience and of the individual's ideals, and functions predominantly outside consciousness, as does a large part of the ego and all of the id. Consciousness was now seen as a "sense organ" of the ego, and the latter structure was described as an organization attempting to serve three masters at one time—the id, the superego, and the external world. Anxiety could be aroused by threats from any one of these three sources. Instead of anxiety being regarded as the way in which a threatening instinctual wish showed itself in consciousness (by means of a "transformation" of libido), it was now seen in *Inhibitions, Symptoms and Anxiety* (1926) as an affective signal, a response of the ego, indicating the likely occurrence of a danger situation that, in turn, indicated the possibility of the ego being traumatically overwhelmed.

In the third phase, the ego was seen as essentially a problem-solving apparatus and the importance attached to it as an organization with strength and forces of its own gradually increased.

Although Freud now put the *experiencing* of affects into the mental structure that he called the ego, he still made no formal theoretical distinction between the somatic aspects of emotion—which were still seen as drive derivatives—and associated feeling states. The energy concept, which can be traced back to the first phase, and which was retained in an altered form in the second phase, still remained as an essential part of psychoanalytic theory in the third phase. The ego was seen as operating with "desexualized" energy, originating in the id, as well as possessing energies of its own. In this phase psychoanalysis was left with a muddled situation with regard to affects. On the one hand, the distinction between energies and affects, between instinctual and affective "tensions," was not made. Although clinical psychoanalytic work operated via the understanding of affects as well as of ideas, theoretical explanations still focused on the hypothetical drives and their vicissitudes (Freud pointed out that the instinctual drives were never directly observable but were explanatory constructs). On the other hand, the introduction of the new theory of anxiety implied that a feeling—anxiety—could act as a *signal*, mobilizing adaptive and defensive behavior on the part of the ego; and, moreover, that it could occur outside consciousness.

By pointing out, in 1926, that anxiety or fear could also arise as a consequence of the perception of dangers in the real world (i.e., not only because of the threatening nature of drive-linked impulses) Freud took a fundamental step in divorcing affects from drives. Unfortunately he never pursued this differentiation and for many, if not most, psychoanalysts, affects are still seen as secondary drive manifestations and as a form of psychic energy, a view that has remained more or less unmodified for three-quarters of a century. Attempts to reconcile new ideas about affects with the theory of energy disposition and energy transformation have resulted in, at times, the most tortuous theoretical acrobatics.

In what follows, an outline will be given of a view of affects that may perhaps go some way towards solving certain of the difficulties surrounding this topic in psychoanalytic theory. However, before proceeding further, it may be useful to discuss one of the basic hypotheses of psychoanalysis, that is, the existence of a "mental apparatus." The account that follows is based, in large part, on a discussion of the basic assumptions in psychoanalytic psychology given elsewhere (Sandler *et al.*, 1972b).

THE MENTAL APPARATUS

The asumption of a mental apparatus implies the existence of a stable, or relatively stable, psychological organization in the individual. Although psychological processes can be assumed to be a function of the nervous system, psychoanalysis supposes, for the purposes of its theories, that psychological phenomena can be conceptualized as involving a psychological "apparatus." This concept parallels, in effect, the physiologist's concepts of the cardiovascular, nervous, digestive, and other bodily systems. It is an added "system" that is a psychological rather than an organic one, although it is influenced by and has effects on the other systems. From the psychoanalytic viewpoint, psychology can be regarded as including the study of the mental apparatus and its functioning, just as physiology, anatomy, and biochemistry study the physical systems and their functions. The notion of a mental apparatus carries the implication of processes involving psychological "structures"—psychological organizations with a slow rate of change—but the field of psychoanalytic psychology includes not only behavior in terms of psychological structures and functions but also the study of subjective experience.

The mental apparatus is regarded as relatively simple early in life, increasing in complexity as time goes on. Thus the apparatus is capable of modification, and its development is a function both of maturation of the external and internal forces acting on it, and of the responses that subserve psychological adaptation.

In this context, the term "adaptation" is related to the assumption that the apparatus functions (among other things) to maintain a "steady state" (comparable to the physiological notion of homeostasis) in the face of constant disturbances of that hypothetical state. Such disturbances may arise from outside the individual as well as from within. In the first phase, the major source of disequilibrium was regarded as the external environment, but in the second phase, the major source of disturbance was thought to be stimuli arising from the instinctual drives. In the third phase, the external world was again given a place as a major source of disturbance of psychological homeostasis, and the apparatus was seen as having to cope with disruptions of the notional "steady state" arising from the drives, from the external world, from the superego, and from within the ego itself. Processes of adaptation in turn bring about changes in the structure and in the mode of functioning of the mental apparatus. It should be noted that this approach to adaptation is radically different from the one that emphasizes adaptation to the social environment only. From the psychoanalytic standpoint, even the grossest self-destructive behavior, completely maladaptive from a social point of view, can be considered to be the outcome of attempts at psychological adaptation.

The progressive development of the mental apparatus can be regarded as a consequence of the interaction between an individual's biological tendencies and his external environment. The high degree of complexity of the apparatus reached in the human is probably related to his capacity to make decisions, including decisions that take into account the long-term effect of his actions. The apparatus can be considered to be a psychological system that functions as a superordinate system controlling (primarily by means of evaluation, delay, and facilitation) the automatic innate and learned psychological responses of the individual (Chapter 16). It has as its main function adaptation to all the inputs into it, from inside the body and from outside, and to forces arising from within the apparatus itself. In what follows I shall suggest that the relation of such adaptation to affect, and in particular to *feeling states*, is a crucial one.

While both the bodily changes occurring in emotion and qualities of *feeling* have been subsumed under the heading of "affect," and while physiological processes may be associated with feelings, it is important to distinguish between the two. The neurohumoral and metabolically caused changes in the body, commonly referred to as emotions, can be regarded as biologically based adaptive bodily responses to disturbances of physiological homeostasis, and can be thought of as having various functions in regard to the mobilization of responses, to preparation for "fight" and "flight," and so on. They can be initiated by psychological cues, and consideration of the actual physiological processes involved can safely be left in the hands of other contributors to this symposium, who will doubtless discuss aspects of them in detail.

As far as the mental apparatus is concerned, the only information on which judgments can be made is *experiential*. Although maturational and physical factors play an important part, the full development of the apparatus and its progressive modification is based firmly on its relation to experiential input. The child's progressive control over himself and over the external world depends entirely on the contents of experience. While these contents must be rudimentary at first, the sensations, feelings, images, and ideas progressively experienced by the child gradually become differentiated as he builds up what might be called his "representational world" (Chapters 4 and 5).

The actions of the child, more or less automatic at first, alter his experiential feedback, and it is the interaction between subjective experience and the mental representations of action that is critical in the progressive development of the mental apparatus. I should like to emphasize that although physical events may give rise to various types of subjective experience (ultimately via processes in the nervous system), all the apparatus can "know" are the contents of subjective experience. This applies even in regard to the "real world," which is never known *in itself*—only experiential representations are known. And it follows that the control of reality is in essence the control of the subjective experience that we assume to be a representation of that reality. Even the "purest" scientist, with the most sophisticated instruments, is working with experiential reflections of reality. From this we can go on to say that the function of the mental apparatus is to deal with changes in the realm of experience, to handle mental contents, whether these arise from perception, mem-

ory, the imagination, or any other source. These contents are both
the input and output data to which the mental apparatus adapts,
even though the apparatus itself can be considered to be a function
of the nervous system.

In order for experiential content to be assessed, it must have
significance and *meaning*, and I should like to suggest that such meaning and significance is closely related to feeling states, even though
these may be restricted to the merest trace in the form of a feeling
signal of one sort or another. The crudest forms of such meanings
(which we assume to exist in the very young infant) are pleasure
and pain, "nice" and "nasty," comfort and discomfort. Naturally
such "meanings" become progressively refined as development proceeds, but it is likely that even the most abstract experiential content
only has significance for the mental apparatus through a connection
with some form of feeling signal. The behavior of the child and the
functioning of the mental apparatus are guided by the feeling states
and feeling signals embedded in its experience. While this is usually
referred to as the pleasure principle (or "pleasure–unpleasure principle"), it is clear that this "principle" has a number of different
aspects to it. One of these refers to needs, drives, and the bodily
changes associated with these, and this aspect of the "pleasure principle" is connected with the regulation of bodily homeostasis, particularly in relation to disturbances brought about by instinctual drives.

Chapter 16 contained a discussion of the way in which the feeling
states aroused by drive stimuli (as well as those that accompany
drive-reducing activities) bring about the regulation of the drives. It
was pointed out that feelings reflect much more than the state of
the drives, and in the course of development attach themselves to
the ideational content reflecting self and outer world. Emphasis was
placed on the differentiation of feelings during development and on
the fact that the source of changes in feeling states is external as well
as internal. The feeling of safety (Chapter 1) was given particular
importance in regard to intrapsychic adaptation. In Chapter 16 the
point was made that we can speak of an economics of feeling states,
and we can consider the mental apparatus to function to maintain
a dynamic *feeling homeostasis*. Normally this is "in step" with the
maintenance of bodily homeostasis. By this is meant that the restoration of a feeling homeostasis (with its associated feeling of safety
and well-being) is perfectly correlated with the restoration of homeostasis in the physical systems of the body. The infant who is hungry
has a bodily need, with corresponding physiological disequilibrium,
and through sucking at the breast temporarily does away with the
need, with equilibrium being restored. At the same time we may say

that he experiences a feeling of unpleasure as a consequence of the bodily need, obtains a form of sensual pleasure through the act of sucking, and experiences a feeling of well-being after the feed.*

It has been pointed out (Chapter 16) that "in the assessment of the contents of the experiential field a process of rapid *scanning* of the field by the apparatus is involved, and we can make use of the concept of a scanning function that operates to guide the apparatus to some sort of action. Such action includes the organization of experience arising from stimuli from the outside world as well as experience prompted by drive stimuli. This scanning function is the internal sense organ of the apparatus. It is part of the nonexperiential realm, but a major part of its function is to scan the material of the experiential realm *before it reaches consciousness.*"

From the point of view put forward in the present chapter it would follow that the prime motivators, *from the point of view of the mental apparatus,* are changes in feeling states. While drives, needs, emotional forces, and other influences arising from within the body are highly important in determining behavior, from the point of view of psychological functioning, they exert their effect *through changes in feelings.* The same is true for stimuli arising from the external world. This approach removes feelings from their total conceptual tie to the instinctual drives alone, and gives them a central position in psychoanalytic psychology.

It should be noted that it has been found necessary to postulate the somewhat paradoxical notion of "unconscious" feelings (or their equivalent), and that the mental apparatus (or the part of it that is usually referred to as the ego) can scan its field of experiential input and associated feeling signals extremely rapidly before experience is permitted to enter consciousness. If the experience carries with it a threat that consciousness might be overwhelmed by painful sensations, the mechanisms of defense may be called into play to *alter* the content of experience before the content is allowed access to consciousness.

The experiential field contains perceptual, memory, and imaginative products, as well as symbolic representations. These include, as a significant aspect, representations of self and of objects, and of the interaction between these. In addition, ideal or "wished-for" states of the self are included, and the discrepancy between an "actual" or "present" state (as represented experientially) and an "ideal" or "wished-for" state may be accompanied by a painful feeling experience. In general we can say that the ideational content of the

---

*It has been suggested that a psychoanalytic learning theory can be written in terms of the reinforcing action of changes in feeling states (Chapter 17).

experiential field is embedded in a matrix of feelings, and these feelings are the essential basis upon which the nature and direction of the adaptive action of the mental apparatus is taken.

Although normally the mental apparatus and the physical apparatuses function "in step," and the regulation of homeostasis in the realm of the body goes parallel with the regulation of feeling homeostasis in the mental apparatus, the possibility exists for the two to get "out of step." Mental conflict may, for example, cause the mental apparatus to find an adaptive solution that restores a feeling of safety, at the same time interfering with normal physiological affective regulatory processes—that is, preventing so-called affective discharge. If we assume that an aggressive impulse causes affective changes in the body, or that a person has an unconscious reaction of rage against an irritating or threatening figure, the mental apparatus may (because of, say, guilt feelings) prevent the activity that would normally restore physiological affective homeostasis. The body may, as a consequence, remain in a state of chronic physiological imbalance because of the defensive activity of the mental apparatus. The person may consciously *feel* well, but may, for example, have an elevated blood pressure or other changes that, in the course of time, may lead to irreversible organic changes in the body. To put it another way: Because of guilt or anxiety, the mental apparatus may find a solution that restores a feeling homeostasis, but does so at the expense of physiological adaptation. The body is thrown out of balance, so to speak, because the normal behavioral processes that lead to the disappearance of temporary and normal affective states are not permitted to take place. This leads to abnormal chronic affective physiological states, which may in turn lead to organic pathology. This is one possible pathway for the development of certain forms of psychosomatic disturbance.

20

Varieties of "Aggression Turned Against the Self"

Rose Edgcumbe and Joseph Sandler

This short chapter has emerged from the work of a study group of the Hampstead Index project concerned with the clarification of problems of aggression directed against the self. A major stimulus to the work of the group came from the discussions on aggression at the International Psycho-Analytical Congress in Vienna in 1971, where it was abundantly clear that, to say the least, a great amount of work remains to be done in regard to the clarification of the concept of aggression (cf. Heimann & Valenstein, 1972; Lussier, 1972). A further important stimulus came from the fact that when we examined the material loosely grouped under the heading "aggression directed against the self" in the Hampstead Index, we found a wide variety of clinical phenomena. These ranged from the young infant's scratching his own face to various forms of self-denigration, self-condemnation, and guilt feelings, and included such phenomena as the older child's head banging, hair pulling and nail biting, major and minor accidents of all sorts, deliberate self-injury and mutilation, suicide, psychosomatic illness, various forms of masochistic behavior, and the inhibition or undermining of one's own potential achievements and capacities, as well as a number of other forms.

This paper was first published in *The International Journal of Psycho-Analysis* in 1974.

After many attempts to find a basis for distinguishing and explaining these phenomena, it became clear to those of us working on the Index project that the use of the *descriptive* concept of aggression must be rigorously avoided. What might appear to the observer to be aggressive need not reflect a destructive or aggressive impulse in the child. We recognized the importance of postulating a point in development at which we could properly talk of aggression; and this point was that at which an *aggressive wish* could be assumed to be in existence. We felt that we had to place ourselves on firm psychological ground in considering aggression to be in existence only when the infant had developed the capacity for intentionality, and when some sort of representation of self, object, and aggressive aim could exist in the mind of the child. This aim includes anything that represents destruction, hurt, damage, and so on directed towards the object. Our basic unit, then, became the *aggressive wish;* and capacities such as motility and activity could be regarded as resources that can be called upon for purposes of implementing the aggressive wish.

Further advantages followed from this decision. If the wish were not regarded purely as an instinctual one, but rather as one that could be aroused by a variety of stimuli from inside or outside the individual, including drive impulses and affects such as rage or anxiety, the problem of distinguishing between "instinctual" and "reactive" aggression disappeared. The wish could be considered as representing a sort of "final common pathway," obtaining its impetus from different sources. The individual could then make use of a variety of capacities, devices, ways and means in order to enact or express the wish. Finally, we had the advantage, in taking this point of view, of not being involved in questions of the nature and vicissitudes of aggressive energies.

Returning to the problem of aggression directed against the self, we had therefore to consider the hypothetical vicissitudes of the aggressive wish; and we should like to discuss two of these (selected from many others). The two chosen are: the directing of the aggression against the self (especially the body) where the self represents a substitute for the object; and the directing of aggression against the self as a punishment for *any* act or thought (sexual, aggressive, or other) that has aroused guilt feelings. These two have been chosen because we found that they have been consistently confused both in the literature and in the discussion of case material derived from psychoanalytic treatment.

In the first class of reactions, we can postulate an aggressive wish in the mind of the child that the child *deflects* from the object to himself. The observation of such deflections of aggression towards the self in the consulting room is a frequent phenomenon. The child begins to punch the therapist, for example, but instead turns the blow towards himself. The wish can be an entirely unconscious one, but given sufficient evidence, the therapist can interpret that the child had intended to do to the therapist *precisely what he did to himself.* For example, a latency boy tripped and fell down the stairs, hurting himself, but was able to recall, following interpretation, that he had indeed had the fleeting thought of pushing the therapist down the stairs, but had cleared his mind of this idea as he felt it to be reprehensible. He then did to himself what he had wished to do to the therapist. The crucial element in this type of reaction is that the content of the child's attack on himself is identical with the content of what he wanted to do to the therapist. The motives for deflecting the aggressive wish from the object to the self are found to include, besides guilt, such feelings as shame, embarrassment, fear, or a conflicting wish to protect the loved or needed object.

In marked contrast are other cases, superficially similar, in which the child also damages himself or his possessions. He may fall, hurt himself in a variety of ways, or inflict pain involuntarily on himself. However, in these cases, analysis has shown that the child's aggressive attack on himself is a form of punishment, intimately related to guilt feelings. The aggression he employs on himself is mobilized *by the need to punish himself* for a guilty thought, wish, or deed. One could say that he punishes himself in expiation. But the crucial and distinguishing characteristic in this type of case is the fact that the content of the punishment need not be similar to that of the guilty impulse. For example, a child expressed affectionate feelings towards the therapist and, it transpired, unconsciously felt acutely guilty at what he thought was an act of disloyalty to his mother. As a consequence of the guilt feeling, he spoiled the toy model he was making so that it was damaged beyond repair. It would be quite wrong to conclude that he directed against himself an aggressive impulse originally intended towards his mother or therapist. In this particular case such a conclusion would not only have been a gross oversimplification but would have led to an incorrect interpretation. A young adolescent boy piled up furniture into a screen through which he peered at his therapist, then contrived to make the pile collapse on himself so that he was bruised. Analysis showed that he was punishing himself not for any aggressive wish but for a forbidden wish to watch his parents having intercourse. Interpretation of guilt over *hostile* oedipal impulses would have been inappropriate at this point in treatment when scopophilic wishes were the prime source of conflict.

In conclusion, the general approach we have taken has led to a distinct possibility of creating, for the first time, a viable and useful classification of different forms of aggression directed against the self, two examples of which have been given. There are many other forms that require clarification, for example, those that raise questions concerning faulty development of self–object differentiation, those that represent a reproach to a neglectful object or compliance with a hostile object, and, in particular, those that involve a component of masochistic sexual suffering.

21

The Psychoanalytic Concept of Orality

Joseph Sandler and Christopher Dare

Problems of definition and the particular problems of changes in meaning of concepts are not exclusive to psychoanalysis. They occur in all sciences, but perhaps particularly in those that rely not on mathematical symbolization but almost entirely on verbal description. The general biological problem of "instinct" is an example of this (Fletcher, 1968). There is a tendency to keep the same terms in making theoretical statements even though the theories may have evolved. This is particularly true of psychoanalytic theories (Sandler *et al*, 1970), in which the situation has been further complicated by the application of psychoanalytic concepts outside the classical psychoanalytic situation. This has led to many ambiguities of meaning and to the proliferation of relatively idiosyncratic usages of particular technical or conceptual terms. Moreover, as we believe will be evident in this discussion of the concepts of orality, the same psychoanalytic term may have different meanings at different levels of abstraction. Thus, for example, the notion of "aggression turned against the self" may be used to *describe* overtly self-damaging behavior and to explain such complicated manifestations as feelings of guilt (Chapter 20). The failure to distinguish between descriptive and explanatory concepts has led to much confusion in psychoanalysis. In the history of the development of psychoanalytic theory, alternative and overlapping conceptual systems have used the same words to describe nonidentical concepts. A classical example of this is the use of the term "ego" (Allport, 1943; Hartmann, 1964). We have for these reasons had to become accustomed to exploring the *history* of terms and concepts in psychoanalysis in order to determine their meaning, status, and utility (Sandler, 1969). Thus in order to understand psychoanalytic concepts of orality, we need to place them, to some extent, in a historical context. It will be seen that although some of the confusion surrounding the term "orality" has arisen from the use of the term outside the psychoanalytic framework, psychoanalysts have themselves caused the bulk of the confusion.

The material that follows was published in 1970 in the *Journal of Psychosomatic Research.*

For the purpose of presentation and discussion, we propose (somewhat artificially) to designate a number of separate areas of use of the term "oral." The first of these is that of the idea of oral erotism and its place in theories of psychosexual development. The second area to be considered is that of the concept of oral character formation. The third is the role of the mouth and the associated ingestive functions in the psychoanalytic theory of processes of identification and ego formation. In this last section, we will also discuss "oral fantasies" and their relation to mental mechanisms.

Before going on to examine these three areas in detail, it is worth noting that the adjective "oral" has been applied:

1.   Descriptions denoting behavior, thoughts, or sensations relating to or involving the mouth. Thus the term "oral" could apply to delivering learned papers, even though such an activity may, from a psychoanalytic point of view, have many nonoral components (for example, sublimated sexual exhibitionism of a primitive sort!)
2.   Phenomena associated with the period of infancy when the mouth is the predominant organ of sensual and aggressive satisfaction, or even to describe all activity characteristic of the first year of life. A number of authors (e.g., Bowlby, 1958) have shown convincingly that such a use is far too wide to be useful and is indeed misleading. It is clear that although mouth activity and satisfactions gained via the mouth play an important part in early developmental processes, many other psychological processes occur during the first year of life that it would be an error to call "oral."
3.   Descriptions of adult manifestations and processes that, in psychoanalytic reconstruction, appear to derive from the earliest relationship between the infant and its mother or have been taken to represent indirect manifestations of covert oral strivings, even though the mouth is not directly involved (e.g., "omnivorous" reading, "demandingness," needs for comfort, etc.

It is clear that these three usages represent differing levels of abstraction from observable data. The first usage "denoting behavior, thoughts, or sensations relating to or involving the mouth" is phenomenological or descriptive. The second, specifying "the period of infancy when the mouth is the predominant organ of sensual and aggressive satisfaction" is a developmental usage. The third, referring to "psychoanalytic reconstruction" is at a more abstract theoretical level.

We hope that this preliminary outline of the complexity of the field we are discussing will show both the breadth and the importance of the meanings of the word "oral," and will also show the need for an attempt at some clarification.

THE CONCEPT OF ORAL EROTISM AND THE ROLE OF THE MOUTH IN SEXUALITY

Infantile Oral Erotism

Freud's first use of the word *oral* occurred in his extensive correspondence with Wilhelm Fliess (an ear, nose, and throat surgeon who was one of the first to apply psychoanalytic concepts to somatic diseases). Freud suggested in 1896 that, "During childhood sexual release would seem to be obtainable from very many parts of the body." In the following year he identifies "the oral sexual system" as an example of this (Freud, 1887–1902). This idea became more clearly formulated later when he wrote, "Now, the zones which no longer produce a release of sexuality in normal and mature human beings must be the regions of the anus and of the mouth and throat." This is a formulation that later found its most extensive development in *Three Essays on the Theory of Sexuality* (1905a). Freud was presumably influenced in his thinking by a consideration of the perversions. He developed the view that the organs that become so important in sexual perversions are those that give sexual pleasure in childhood. The idea that he put forward was that the instinctual drive that is a precursor to adult (so-called genital) sexuality can be identified in earliest childhood in the pleasurable, sensual sucking of babies. This is an experience that accompanies, yet is separate from, the need for nourishment (see the observations of Engel and Reichsman, 1956, the experiments of David Levy, 1934, and those of Hunt, 1941). In childhood the mouth is an "erotogenic zone . . . being the organ whose excitation lends the instinct a sexual character" (Freud, 1905a). Thus sensual sucking of the breast (and of the thumb and fingers) can be regarded as the first manifestation of infantile sexuality. It is of interest that, in his last work, Freud reiterated these themes, and commented on what he meant by sexuality in such a context: "The baby's obstinate persistence in sucking gives evidence at an early stage of a need for satisfaction which, though it originates from and is instigated by the taking of nourishment, nevertheless strives to obtain pleasure independently of nourishment and for that reason may and should be termed *sexual*" (1940, p. 154). Thus Freud clearly distinguished between what we might refer to as nutritional urges and a sexual drive that has as its aim the gaining of oral erotic satisfaction through stimulation of the erotogenic zone of the lips and mouth. This distinction has on the whole been maintained in subsequent psychoanalytic writings, although at times the need to gain nourishment has been confused with oral instinctual aims of a sexual or aggressive sort.

Another derivative of the importance of mouth activities and associated experiences in the sexual life of infants postulated by Freud was presented in his paper "On the Sexual Theories of Children" (1908b). He pointed out that "there is the significant theory that a baby is got by a kiss—a theory which obviously betrays the predominance of the erotogenic zone of the mouth (p. 223)." What is suggested is that the little child interprets adult sexuality, and its reproductive outcomes, in terms of its memories of experiences during previous phases of its own sexual development. Belief in oral impregnation is implied in a number of myths and is also consistently found in patients with anorexia nervosa (see Waller et al, 1940 and Blitzer et al., 1961). The existence of oral sexual theories does not imply, however, that such theories were developed during the oral phase of development that is, during the first year of life. There is no evidence at all that the infant of only a few months of age can construct theories of any sort, and it is clear that organized thinking (and thus the construction of organized fantasies) can at best only begin to be in evidence towards the end of the first year. This does not mean that *experiences* during the first year are not important. Memory traces of sensory experiences of motor and other activities probably begin to be laid down very early and almost certainly influence the infant's psychological development to a profound degree. Such memories are, it would appear, readily absorbed into later fantasy life which may then, because of "oral" elements, be thought of as having occurred much earlier.

Adult Oral Erotism

In mature, adult sexuality there are "sexual uses of the mucous membranes of the lips and mouth" (Freud, 1905a), and contact of the mucous membranes of the mouth as a sexual act is "held in high sexual esteem among many nations." We may regard this form of "oral erotism" as relating to sexual satisfaction derived from the mucosa of the mouth or from sucking. It seems clear, however, that in adult sexuality, mouth activities may not be a simple persistence of infantile sucking, biting, or mouthing. Fellatio, for example, has been found to have many features of a displacement from breast to penis as an object to suck (see Freud, 1909b), but fellatio may also represent a displacement from vagina or anus to mouth as a consequence of, for example, anxieties about anal or urethral soiling and contamination. Thus an erotic, manifestation that may be *descriptively* oral may represent the unconscious fulfillment of repressed wishes to return to a "sucking" relationship with the loved person, but also (or alternatively) may represent a compromise between feminine wishes for penetration, and fears of contamination more appropriate to the later phase. Thus the developmental and ontogenetic viewpoints may have to be taken into account even in what appear to be straightforward oral erotic activities. This shows itself clearly in the analyses of certain obese persons who, in their obesity, bring about an unconscious identification with a pregnant mother, and the fact that the oral mode is used is of secondary, rather than of primary psychopathological significance. The role of the attempt to reduce secondary sexual characteristics in anorexia through self-starvation is probably seen more constructively from the point of view of the fight against oedipal feminine wishes (represented by the idea of remaining a prepubertal, nonmenstruating little girl) than as a manifestation of oral self-denial.

Similarly, in the course of psychoanalytic treatment of a patient with a proclivity for fellatio, the wish to suck the penis may be found to represent an unconscious fantasy of sucking at the breast. Equally, however, in other patients (for example in certain cases of male homosexuality) fellatio may serve the purpose of maintaining an illusion of employing a vagina. It follows from this that if we are investigating the psychopathological elements in psychosomatic disturbances involving the mouth (or ingestion) we cannot immediately conclude that these elements derive from pathological disturbances of oral erotism simply because the mouth is involved. Disturbances involving the mouth and the proximal gut may not represent pathological disturbances of what we can, for short, call "oral sexuality." Conversely, psychopathological elements in functional disturbances of organs far removed from the mouth may involve oral sexuality. Thus some forms of frigidity and impotence have been shown to be associated with the well-known fantasy of the vagina dentata (Fenichel, 1931, 1945).

Sucking and "Safety"

We may turn to another problem in evaluating the concept of orality. An activity, such as a nonnutritive, apparently sensual sucking may have psychodynamics other than those of the satisfaction of a sexual

drive (whether it be oral in nature or not).* We are referring here to
such things as "comfort sucking." In Chapter 1, Sandler has written
of "the background of safety." Under stress (e.g., in conflict situations producing anxiety), reversion to an activity that *looks like* an
instinctual drive-satisfying process may occur. This may be resorted
to because it provides the child with a repetition of an earlier feeling
of comfort, for example that associated with sucking at the bottle or
the breast. This distinction, between reversion to a safe "comfort"
situation and the revival of earlier sexual drives and wishes, is insufficiently made in the psychoanalytic literature. It is all too easy
to ascribe smoking or thumbsucking to oral sexual or aggressive
instinctual drive activity when the they can equally represent an
attempt, in feelings and in fantasy life, to establish the safe, secure
psychological relationship with the comforting object of earliest childhood.

Bringing this into line with a more recent formulation (Chapter
6), we can say that a comfort–sucking activity may have to do with
"the wish to attain 'ideal' states previously experienced in reality or
in fantasy." Although the original "ideal" state, with its accompanying special affective value, may have originally provided a state
of comfort because of the gratification of oral sexual drives, the return
to an apparently erotic oral activity may not be a direct manifestation
of an oral erotic instinctual drive.†

The point we are attempting to establish in all of this is that
what may be descriptively *oral* is not necessarily always, from a
psychodynamic point of view, a reflection of underlying oral wishes.
This is of the greatest relevance to the understanding of neurotic
disturbances that are descriptively "oral" (e.g., in some cases of
psychogenic stammering) and must, it seems, be equally true of
certain psychogenic psychosomatic disorders.‡ Simply because the
disturbance involves oral function, it should not be inferred that the

---

*In general we believe, with many others, that "instinct" is an unsatisfactory and
misleading translation of the German *Trieb* (employed by Freud), and that "instinctual
drive" is preferable. Instinctual drives can be conceptualized as being aroused by
stimuli derived from intraorganismic biological states impinging on the psychological
apparatus.

†The distinction between reversion to sexual activities for the gaining of feelings of
safety on the one hand, and the regressive revival of past instinctual drives on the
other, probably applies to all forms of sexual activity, and is not restricted to oral
sexuality. Thus the compulsive sexuality of the "Don Juan" is very often motivated
by the need to reduce anxiety or feelings of inadequacy rather than by an over-
abundance of sexual drives.

‡This is exemplified by a case treated by one of the authors in which an ulcer that
developed in the mouth was found to represent an identification with a fantasied
venereal lesion in the mother's genitals (Sandler, 1959a).

psychopathology of the disturbance either represents the revival of infantile oral drives or originated in early infancy. Conversely, oral impulses and fantasies of a sexual or an aggressive kind may manifest themselves in dysfunctions of other organs.

ORAL CHARACTER FORMATION

We have outlined some of the links between infantile and adult oral erotism as well as some of the connections between adult manifestations and infantile wishes (and associated fantasies) relating to the mouth. In this section we should like to take the discussion further, with particular reference to the connection between so-called oral character traits and early development.

The relation of infantile sexuality to later character was first traced by Freud in regard to *anal* erotism (1908d). Although in the same paper he commented on the mouth as an erotogenic zone, he made no comment on the influence of oral sexuality on character development. However, in the "Fragment of an Analysis of a Case of Hysteria" (1905b), he had linked the patient's symptoms of throat irritation and of coughing to reactions to fantasies of oral intercourse, although the origin of such fantasies in childhood was not suggested. The subject of the "oral character" had its first full exposition in 1924 when Abraham and Glover published their separate papers (Abraham, 1924a; Glover, 1924). Their analysis of the subject depended upon a subdivision of the oral phase of development that Abraham had elaborated in his description of manic–depressive states and schizophrenia (1916, 1924b). Abraham had drawn specific conclusions from the analyses of a number of patients that led him to postulate that the oral stage of the development that Freud had outlined, was in fact *two* phases. He said: "We are thus obliged to assume that there is a differentiation within the oral phase of the libido, just as there is within the anal–sadistic phase. On the primary level of that phase the libido of the infant is attached to the act of sucking. This act is one of incorporation, but one which does not put an end to the existence of the object. . . . The secondary level of this phase differs from the first in that the child exchanges its sucking activity for a biting one. . . . It is in this stage that the ambivalent attitude of the ego to its object begins to grow up" (1924b, p. 450–451).

Part of the importance of Abraham's formulations at this time lay in the integration of the ideas of *aggressive* instinctual drives and the more established and previously more strongly emphasized sexual drives. Having developed these conceptualizations by reconstructions within the psychoanalytic treatment situation, Abraham described (and his description was amplified by Edward Glover) two main groups of *character traits* thought of as related to these two divisions of the oral activities of the infant. He pointed out that some adult oral traits or tendencies could be regarded as direct carryovers from the infantile form of oral sexual gratification, and instanced adult pleasures in sucking, chewing, and licking in this connection (1924*a*). He not only postulated a link between experiences in the oral stage and later character traits, but also postulated some of the factors that could cause such a persistence of oral tendencies into adulthood. Thus he remarks, for example: "In the child who has been disappointed or over-indulged in the sucking period the pleasure in biting . . . will be especially emphasized . . . [and] the development of character expresses itself in pronounced characteristics of hostility and dislike. It accounts for the presence of the abnormally over-developed envy which is so common" (p. 398). Besides the development of envy as an "oral" characteristic, other character traits can be associated with oral tendencies. Abraham remarks: "In certain other cases the person's entire character is under oral influence . . . we are here concerned with persons in whom the sucking was undisturbed and highly pleasurable. They have brought with them from this happy period a deeply rooted conviction that everything will always be well with them. They face life with an imperturbable optimism which often does in fact help them to achieve their aims." He points out that the outcome of overindulgence in the sucking period can be inactivity and that: "they expect the mother's breast to flow for them eternally, as it were" (p. 399).

Both Abraham's and Glover's descriptions of the oral character emphasize a basic polarity between two opposing character types or sets of character traits. Broadly speaking, traits relating to *oral gratification* can be distinguished from those connected with experiences of *oral frustration*.

Glover describes the orally gratified type as being the possessor of an "excess of optimism which is not lessened by reality experience" (1925). This is associated with generosity, sociability, accessibility to new ideas, as well as ambition accompanied by the optimistic expectation that all will work out well. The orally frustrated or ungratified character has a characteristically pessimistic outlook on life that may be associated with moods of depression, attitudes of withdrawal, passive–receptive attitudes, feelings of insecurity with a need for constant reassurance, an intense ambition linked with feelings that disappointment or failure must inevitably occur, feelings of injustice and of having been cheated, sensitivity to competitiveness, a dislike of sharing, and a general feeling of demanding coupled with

*See Joffe (1969) for a full discussion of the psychoanalytic theory of envy, with special reference to its supposedly oral roots.

dissatisfaction. We would also see marked traits of hostility, dislike, envy, and maliciousness. The ambivalence related to the second oral phase would be extremely pronounced in such oral characters.

Various other authors (e.g., Bergler, 1934 and Fenichel, 1945) have elaborated the various elements in so-called oral characters. There is no doubt that the formulations stemming from Abraham have had far-reaching influence. Subsequent accounts of oral characterology have tended to lean heavily on his beautifully documented and persuasive accounts. However, it is often forgotten that Abraham himself emphasized that there can be no "pure culture" of oral characteristics (1927), as there will always be an admixture from subsequent phases of development. It is worth noting that experimental attempts to demonstrate connections between the nature of the early feeding situation and character development have been inconclusive or contradictory (see Caldwell, 1964, for a detailed review). However, psychoanalytic experience has enriched and elaborated Abraham's and Glover's accounts of the processes relating the character structure to early experiences. Rado (1926) and Fenichel (1945) among others, pay attention to the intensity of stimulation around the sucking, feeding process in determining the so-called oral fixation that is thought to be the basis of oral character traits. Both, too, stress the alimentary connections of the mouth, so that Fenichel suggests that the phase is more correctly seen as an "intestinal stage" than an "oral" one. He stresses the importance of instinctual satisfaction in associating character traits with orality: "Most frequently, however, fixations are rooted in experiences of instinctual satisfaction which simultaneously gave reassurance in the face of some anxiety or aided in repressing some other feared impulse ['orality' as a defense against anxiety]. Such simultaneous satisfaction of drive and of security is the most common cause of fixations" (1945, p. 66). Rado too was impressed by the relaxation and satiation after eating that he hypothesized as having an analogy to genital sexual orgasm. "It is only too plain that the oral organization of the sucking infant culminates in alimentary orgasm. Since the somatic processes on which this orgastic pleasure is based take place within the body, and are thus unperceived by the infant, his interest must be displaced onto the tangible oral zone, the excitation of which, as a fore-pleasure mechanism, sets in motion the process of gratification" (1926). While we acknowledge the relation of orality to other experiences involving the gastrointestinal tract that may bring about fixation with its resulting influence on character formation, we wish here to emphasize the role of a high level of oral stimulation, especially when it is accompanied by anxiety reduction, in the determination of the form of the influence of oral events on subsequent character development.

Erikson, in a series of publications (1937, 1946a, 1946b, 1968) has

elaborated a scheme relating early development and subsequent relations to the world. He says of the newborn infant: "At this point
he lives through, and loves with, his mouth, and the mother lives
through, and loves with, her breasts or whatever parts of her coun-
tenance and body convey eagerness to provide what he needs. . . .
To him the mouth is the focus of a general first approach to life—
the incorporative approach" (1968). Erikson emphasizes the relative
passivity of this phase, and points out that Abraham's second oral
phase, in which biting develops, is also associated generally with
more active "holding" and "taking in." Erikson's viewpoint moves
towards a critique of the emphasis that Freud put upon the essentially
dependent nature of the oral phase, a topic that we will discuss later
in this section. Erikson suggests that the phrase that should be employed to describe the importance of the oral stage in regard to
subsequent personality, is that of "basic trust."

What is given by Erikson is a statement about the pattern of
relationship between the child and the external world that obtains
in the stage in which oral sensuality is dominant. It is suggested
that this pattern will tend to show its effect in the course of subsequent development.

The general point that early experiences and modes of functioning and relating to the external world have an influence on later
character and attitudes is one that has been made by many psychoanalytic authors. The mechanism whereby such early patterns
and experiences can have an enduring effect has been related to the
unchanging presence, and hence the potential influence, of fantasies
supposedly elaborated in the earliest phase of life. This notion poses
problems. Those psychoanalysts who attach great significance to the
role of experiences and fantasies during the earliest months in later
development have tended to attribute a complexity of functioning to
the infant that runs against all other knowledge of psychological
development. Thus it is often assumed (particularly by those psychoanalysts who adhere to the theories of Melanie Klein) that the
infant has a very early knowledge of the boundaries between itself
and the outside world, that it is capable of having fantasies involving
such complicated notions as those of "devouring," of "scooping out"
and even of parental intercourse while it is still in the first year of
life (see Segal, 1973). Nevertheless, it is likely that gross patterns of
experience in the first weeks or months of life may have an effect
on later development. We see this in the case of children who have
been severely traumatized or deprived in their earliest life. However,
the elaboration of oral fantasies* occurs, in our view, for the most

---

*We are using the term "fantasy" in the sense in which it was used by Freud, that
is, as a wish-fulfilling product of the imagination that can, when it is conscious, be
distinguished from perception of reality.

part *after* the first year of life, and their existence may lead to false assumptions regarding the influence of experiences during the oral phase on further normal or pathological development.

At this point it seems worthwhile to state our own position in regard to what may be an apparent paradox in our presentation. There seems to be considerable evidence that experiences during the first months of life have a profound effect on later development. At the same time we take the view that the child is, at that age, incapable of constructing fantasies involving his own relationship to others (in particular his parents), if only because it takes some considerable time for him to learn to differentiate between what belongs to his own self and what belongs to the outside world. Thus, although it is extremely tempting to consider fantasies of, for example, being back at the breast, as having arisen in the oral phase, it would seem proper to consider them as having their origin later in the infant's life, even though earlier psychobiological experiences may have predisposed to their formation. In other words, we find ourselves in profound disagreement with those psychoanalytic authors who readily perceive and explain all later experiences in terms of the repetition or persistence of supposed early oral fantasies. We would say, rather, that early experiences have an effect on the development of psychological mechanisms and structures. To put it in an oversimplified way: We do not subscribe to the idea that such things as the "oral" character traits mentioned earlier represent persisting fantasies about the infant's relation to his mother (or parts of her) that have been created in the oral phase. We would agree, on the other hand, that experiences of frustration in the early months can lead, for example, to a bitter and pessimistic outlook on the world, and that the elaboration of fantasies of being cared for and fed develop subsequently as a consequence of further experiences of frustration.

It seems appropriate to refer to the specific attribute that is commonly called "oral dependence" in the present context, as it is so often invoked in discussions of the psychopathology of various psychosomatic disturbances (e.g., Alexander, 1950). Dependence as a psychological characteristic tends, because the tiny infant is biologically dependent on its mother, to be considered by many psychoanalysts as essentially "oral" in nature. It is often equated with the wish to return to the breast (or even to the womb), but this is based on the unwarranted assumption that the young infant who, to the observer, can be seen to be dependent, is aware of his state of dependence. It does not seem to be justifiable to regard all later demandingness and wishes to be dependent and cared for as being a wish to regain the particular remembered state of being fed at the breast. From a psychological, as opposed to a biological point of view, the stimulus to longings for dependence on the object as a provider is probably at its greatest intensity during the second year of life, during the anal phase as described by Freud, or the separation–individuation phase of Margaret Mahler.

Much of the psychoanalytic literature on psychosomatic medicine seems, to us, to use concepts of orality that are muddled by the sort of confusion we see implicit in such a phrase as "oral dependence." In the writings of the Chicago school on the character traits of patients with peptic ulcer, the equation of the unconscious wish for a passive, dependent relationship, with the patient's real experiences in the breast-feeding period, is always made (see e.g., Levey, 1934). A quotation from a recent work emanating from this school exemplifies our point. Alexander, French, and Pollock, writing on duodenal ulcer in the book *Psychosomatic Specificity* (1968) say: "The central dynamic feature in duodenal peptic ulcer is the frustration of dependent desires originally oral in character. The craving to be fed appears later as a wish to be loved, to be given support, money and advice. This fixation on early dependent situations of infancy comes in conflict with the adult ego and results in hurt pride. . ." It seems to us that the origin of "dependent desires" cannot uniformly be considered as originating in the first year of life. It may be that towards the end of the first year, an infant develops a form of awareness that it is dependent. But the longing for dependence must come from a much more sophisticated understanding that may give rise to a wish to return to what it conceives of as the earliest relationship. Bowlby's (1958) discussion of dependence is useful in this connection. It is of interest that Glover commented in 1924 that "the system of word presentation essential to direct psychical remembering is not developed until the primacy of the mouth is over."

All the character traits that have been described as "oral" (and this applies to character traits in general) can also be considered from the point of view of object relationships. By "object relationships" in this context we do not only mean the overt ways in which an individual behaves towards others, but also the internal relationships between self and others that exist in the individual's conscious and unconscious fantasy life. Thus the trait of "demandingness" may be looked at from the point of view of the inner wish to be given everything by others and a deep expectation that satisfaction will never be provided by another person. This could certainly be described in terms of the infant's longing to suck at his mother's breast, which he feels can never satisfy him. But, as we have implied, the particular "sucking" internal relationship to the mother does not arise when the sucking is dominant, but afterwards, when the child becomes aware of his separateness from the mother and longs to be one with her again.

The role of inner object relationships is a vital one, not only in the consideration of character traits but also in many other areas, including the area of psychosomatic disturbance. Psychosomatic symptoms, insofar as they have a psychogenic element, may represent an attempt to fulfill an unconscious wish to relate to an object in a particular way. This is reflected in those disturbances of eating in which the relationship to food becomes the concrete expression of some inner wished-for relationship to an important figure in childhood.

THE DEVELOPMENT OF THE EGO AND THE FIRST YEAR OF LIFE

The third area in which concepts of orality are used in psychoanalysis is one that we consider to be of considerable importance to psychosomatic theorizing in general, as it relates to the initiation of psychological processes at a time in life when they have the closest possible link to body processes. Again the first comments in this area of conceptualization are to be found in Freud. He writes (1905a) of the "oral or, as it might be called, cannibalistic pregenital sexual organization" and indicates that the sexual activity of that time cannot be separated from food ingestion. The sexual "*aim* consists in the incorporation of the object—the prototype of a process which, in the form of identification, is later to play such an important psychological part." It is important to remember, in this context, that Freud was referring to the aim of the oral drive from a biological point of view, as such an aim could not conceivably exist as a psychological one in the mind of the infant until self–other differentiation had taken place. Mouth activity and associated mouth sensations certainly contribute to ego development (Hoffer, 1949, 1950b, 1950c). The clear descriptions of Gesell *et al.* (1949) are of interest here. He says of the 20-week-old child: "Should he seize an object of interest, it goes avidly to his mouth and he tries to regard it even while he mouths it. The whole eye–hand–mouth episode is surcharged with optical implications. This mouthing may be interpreted as a form of tactual–spatial exploitation, which contributes a nucleus to the visual perception of form and substance."

The point we are attempting to bring out is that early mouthing behavior not only serves feeding needs and provides other, sensual, gratifications, but also is a mode of experiencing and apprehending the world. In exploring the world with its mouth and eyes, the child builds up a model of its environment. This first model is imparted an "oral" quality, just as, later in the first year, visual perceptual qualities become crucial. Hoffer (1950c) pointed out that "with the help of the hand the oral–sucking drive undergoes a transformation from an instinctual demand to an ego-controlled activity. In the course of this process the hand, like the mouth, is perceived as part of the self and the differentiation between self and not-self has been carried forward" (p. 21). Spitz (1965), in his volume reporting an investigation of the first year of life, makes the same point: "Our contention is that the oral cavity with its equipment of tongue, lips, cheeks and nasopharynx is the first surface in life to be used for tactile perception and exploration." In his phrase, the mouth is "the cradle of perception."

Observation of children in the first year of life has shown that the biological function of "grasping" is transferred, as development proceeds, to both the hand and the eye. Thus visual "taking in" may have a direct psychobiological connection with earlier oral incorporation (A.-M. Sandler, 1963) and, indeed, the term "introjection" has been used to describe the perceptual processes that follow the biological oral incorporative activities of the infant. This does not mean to say, however, that the process of visual perception is accompanied by, or is derived from, infantile fantasies of incorporating the mother's breast, although the impression that this is so may be gained from some of the psychoanalytic literature.

It probably *is* true, on the other hand, that the pleasures gained by the infant in his developing perceptual and motor achievements are developmentally related to the pleasures of eating, and this is a field well worth exploring further.

CONCLUSIONS

In this chapter we have attempted to explore some of the many meanings and implications of the various psychoanalytic concepts of orality. If we were to draw a single conclusion from this review, it would be that great care is to be used before ascribing later manifestations (be they character traits or symptoms) to the simple repetition, in later life, of the experiences and attitudes of the infant, and his relations to his biological objects (in particular the mother), during his first months of life, during the so-called oral phase of psychosexual development.

Appendix

The Hampstead Index as a Method of Psychoanalytic Research

Joseph Sandler

The research project known as the Hampstead Index was initiated in the mid-1950s. Quite apart from the concrete results obtained in this project, many of which are documented in this volume, work with the Index has prompted the consideration of a number of problems of research methodology in psychoanalysis. One outcome of this was the conclusion that the technique of "indexing" can provide the basis for a method of research in psychoanalysis that fulfills the requirements of a scientific method.

The paper that follows was an early one, and was presented in the Symposium on Research at the International Psycho-Analytical Congress in 1961. It was published in *The International Journal of Psycho-Analysis* (1962b).

I

One of the duties of psychoanalytic child therapists and analysts who have cases in daily analysis at the Hampstead Clinic is documentation, for the psychoanalytic material collected there is the property of the Clinic as a whole, and is meant to be available for research. Therapists write detailed weekly reports, and further reports every 2 months.

With the accumulation of this material, the Clinic was faced with the problem of using the recorded data for the purposes of research. The mere accumulation of records, however accurate and illuminating, does not constitute research. A solution to this problem came about through a suggestion by Mrs. Dorothy Burlingham that an index to the case material be constructed, that would make the material more accessible for research, teaching, and reference purposes, and that would suggest new lines of research by assembling the

315

analytic data in such a way as to facilitate comparison between cases.

In order to construct this Index, which was directed by Mrs. Burlingham from its outset, a working group classified the analytic and other material of 50 cases that they had in daily treatment. The aim was to provide a comprehensive system of classification, at the same time retaining the flexibility of the therapists' reports. Therapists (with the help of advisers) were asked to break down the material in their reports according to the way in which the therapist saw the case, and to draw upon psychoanalytic theory for constructing the necessary categories.

On the basis of this pilot study, it was possible to draw up a preliminary set of common categories, a common framework of classification, that would eventually contain much of the case material. The principle was followed throughout that therapists should order and classify their material according to those categories that they considered most satisfactory, and although the common set of categories could be drawn on as necessary, it is clear that any single piece of material could be approached from any one of a number of conceptual paths.

The data that were to be classified can be located under one of two main headings. The first refers to "general case material," containing factual information and data relating to the external reality and early history of the child. The second, and by far the greatest division of the Index, contains the "psychoanalytic material." This division is further subdivided into a number of clinically or metapsychologically meaningful sections and subsections, such as object relationships, instinctual material, fantasies, defenses, other ego material, superego, symptoms, treatment-situation, and technique.

The outcome of indexing a case is a set of typed cards, and to this set comprehensive cross-references are added, so that the research investigator can find the relevant material without too much difficulty. Each typed card contains a piece of material—a so-called unit of observation—and a reference to the appropriate pages in the patient's case notes from which it was extracted, or that it summarizes. In addition, there is the name of the patient, his age at the time of indexing, and so on.

An essential part of the Index project has been the construction of a number of manuals to help the therapists in their work. These do not lay down a formal set of headings, but rather present a list, derived from actual experience of indexing cases, with comprehensive definitions. As time has gone on, the manuals have been modified, and various research projects and interests in special types of cases have had the secondary effect of causing new headings to appear.

Although the original aim of the Index project was to provide an index to the case material, this aim has proved more difficult to attain than was at first realized. The voluminous minutes of the various Index committees show very clearly that one difficulty after another was encountered. At first there was the question of what constituted the "unit of psycho-analytic observation." The moment therapists began to make assessments of their material in metapsychological terms, the problem of defining theoretical units emerged. As these were clarified, so was there a corresponding change in the "units of observations," Therapists had at times to break down the material on one card into several segments that could then be indexed under appropriate headings. The interaction of the clinical observations and the theoretical framework was much more extensive than had been anticipated, and when it was found necessary to modify or amplify the accepted definition of, say, a mechanism of defense, it was equally necessary to give more precise definitions in order to avoid confusion. Much of the work of the Index committees has been taken up with theoretical discussion, discussion that was always related to an actual set of indexed observations. This has led to a number of new formulations, for those that were available in the literature were at times inadequate, imprecise, or contradictory. Such new formulations are, for example, certain of the definitions of the defenses, with special references to the distinction between defense mechanisms and other defensive measures; or the definitions relating to superego functions (Chapter 3) formulated after it was found that certain distinctions generally accepted in the past did not enable us to categorize the actual observations of the therapists at all precisely—distinctions between such concepts as ego and superego identification. Research groups, stimulated by the problems that have arisen in indexing, are examining such topics as the mechanisms for self-esteem regulation, and the problem of regression.

The process of index making has had a number of secondary gains, not the least of which has been an increase in theoretical precision among those students and therapists who have indexed cases, and this has inevitably had corresponding repercussions on their clinical formulations.

From this it can be seen that what began with a limited aim has in fact achieved rather more than was bargained for in the beginning. Moreover, it has become apparent that the construction of an Index to the case material is a continuous process, a sort of progressive spiral, for as the definitions we use are elaborated and modified, so are the observations that they seek to encompass refined in turn, with corresponding increase in acuity of observation and conceptualization.

II

I should now like to consider, from a purely theoretical viewpoint, some aspects of scientific procedure, and in the final section of this paper, to link these comments up with the technique of indexing.

For many years the physical scientist and the philospher have exercised their proprietary rights over the methods of science. Yet these methods are psychological in nature, for they deal with the discrepancy between perceptions of reality on the one hand, and theories about that reality, constructed within the mind of the scientist, on the other. Perception is an ego function, the scientific theories that scientists construct to account for their perceptions are, *par excellence*, the product of secondary thought processes of the ego, and all the instruments of scientists are no more than specialized aids to normal ego functions. Moreover, as the content of perception, memory, and thought is so susceptible to influence by unconscious distorting factors, much of scientists' activities represent, of necessity, forms of reality testing.

If we take an ego-psychological point of view, the assumption can be made that the processes of science are the same as those that occur in the child in the course of progressive adaptation. On this basis one can argue that a close study of the methods used by the child in the course of such adaptation can suggest formal techniques of investigation that fulfill all the requirements of a scientific method and yet have a special application to psychoanalytic observations and theory.

An integral part of the child's progressive adaptation is the construction of increasingly complex inner representations and organizations of experience (Chapter 5). This proceeds on the basis of the child's widening range of sensorimotor activities, his interaction with the real world, and within the child's reality we must include the models of reality transmitted to the child by his parents and educators. These inner organizations or frames of reference are used by the child to perceive and comprehend those aspects of the world that are significant for him, but they are of course much influenced by his wishes and fantasies. As time goes on, they provide the child with an increasingly accurate picture of the real world, although both the child's and the scientist's picture of the world will always remain approximate and distorted.

The child's organized frames of reference are essential not only to perception but to secondary-process thinking as well. All perception is apperception, but this is apperception that is controlled and limited by the ego. If it were not so, and primary process functioning were allowed full play, our perceptions of reality would be as distorted and hallucinatory in quality as they are in early infancy. The hallmark of organized perception is the ability to select from the whole range of stored memories those that are relevant to the immediate apperception and that facilitate progressive adaptation. The selection of reality-appropriate elements for apperception is the ego function of *reality testing*. (Bellak, 1958) Similarly, organized thinking involves the mental manipulation and integration of appropriate "trial" actions and "trial" perceptions (and of symbols that are derivatives of these) with a high degree of selection of what is appropriate and suppression of the inappropriate. This can be referred to as the ego's function of "concept testing." I need hardly add that in creative thinking the ability to permit and make use of a certain amount of primary-process activity is all-important.

The ego makes use of its organized internal frames of reference to structure and control both perception and thinking, and these activities in their turn can modify the child's internal world. In normal progressive ego development, the child deals with contradiction and incongruity between aspects of perception and thought by reconstructing his inner perceptual and conceptual models, and this restructuring facilitates adaptation. There is a fundamental tendency within the ego to resolve such contradictions, to synthesis and integration. If the outcome of this tendency to integration increases the child's ability to predict and control events more successfully, we speak of successful reality testing, and in this context we may speak of successful concept testing as well.

Adaptive reorganization of the internal world does not always occur. The ego may, and indeed often does, show great resistance to such reorganization. This resistance has a number of sources. One is the natural resistance of the ego to change, slight in childhood, and usually increasing in old age. Another is that any reorganization of the internal world may constitute a threat to the narcissistic integrity of the ego, evoking anxiety through the promise of forbidden instinctual gratification, or by bringing about superego conflict. This is the resistance that motivates otherwise discerning adults to deny so vehemently the existence of infantile sexuality even when its manifestations occur under their very noses. All the defense mechanisms of the ego can be brought into play in order to deal with such conflict, and of those that deserve mention in connection with perception, denial and splitting are of special note.

These considerations are directly applicable to scientific research. Scientists have a theoretical model of part of the external world, and modify this model on the basis of their observations, predictions, and thought processes. Their techniques are specialized forms of reality and concept testing, and their scientific attitude is directed against the use of non-reality-adaptive measures for the resolution of perceptual and conceptual discrepancies. We know, however, from the history of science, that scientists are not immune to the use of the ordinary defenses against the awareness of resolution of perceptual and conceptual conflict. Where scientists differ from the man in the street is that they have evolved certain *formal* techniques for heightening and focusing discrepancies between expectations based on their theoretical model and their actual observations, as well as contradictions between different aspects of their theoretical models.

Psychoanalysts, like other scientists, are concerned with the modification of inner theories on the basis of their experiences, and their methods are essentially scientific, whether they are concerned with the progressive testing of their theories about one patient or with psychoanalytic theory as a whole. Their special training should serve to make the components of their own and the patient's apperceptive processes more readily available to them, to reduce their resistance to new ideas, and to enable them to tolerate and examine contradictions in perceptions and thoughts. Their knowledge of mental processes in general and of their own in particular, together with their understanding of transference and countertransference, their capacity to observe with free-floating attention, to suspend judgement, to tolerate surprises, and to influence the content of the patient's material through interpretation are all scientific aides to their work.

Against these advantages we must place certain disadvantages. Any single fragment of psychoanalytic material may be grossly over-determined, and in our psychoanalytic perception and assessment of that material we must, willy-nilly, be involved in processes of selection according to our inner model of the patient. We shall be faced with the constant temptation to perceive and understand those aspects of the material that conform to our model. It cannot be otherwise, and we have to be on our guard not to use various parts of our preconceived theory to "explain" everything. (We all know that there is a tendency for certain patients to enter into collusion with the analyst in such "explanations".) A consequence of this necessity to select certain aspects of the material and to suppress others is that our need to evaluate our own internal models critically by means of reality and concept testing may be hindered, for the very abundance of material produced by a patient may make our established theories and conceptions work *too* well. The fact that they work well may in turn lead to an undue resistance to the progressive integration and modification of our concepts, so necessary for scientific development. This resistance can partly be overcome by the cultivation of a critical attitude towards our ideas, by the cultivation of a critical attitude towards our ideas, by discussion with colleagues, and by honest reading of the literature, but unless we are *directly* confronted with contradictions in our thinking, resistance to change due to secondary gains may prove too great.

III

The Index was first seen as a method of ordering psychoanalytic material for later research, and the difficulties that were met within its construction were for some time regarded as obstacles to the production of a finished piece of work. These difficulties were substantial, and I have alluded to some of them earlier. For the most part they are centered around two major problems. The first was that of making the Index sufficiently comprehensive and detailed for any research worker to be able to find enough material to provide answers to his questions. Time and time again those who used the Index to look for answers to specific questions would return with the complaint that instead of finding answers they found further questions. Any small segment of the material collected in the Index, when looked at microscopically, was found to be full of holes, for unless the therapist indexing the case had a special interest in the particular problem, he was liable to report insufficient detail, or to index the relevant material in some other way.

The second major problem was the constant need to modify the definitions in the manuals so that they were more precise and meaningful in terms of the therapists' observations. The modifications brought with them the need for the reindexing of large parts of the case material, and this in turn had repercussions on the formulations in the Index manuals.

These two areas of difficulty were a source of much frustration, and at times despondency, on the part of all concerned with the Index. However, as the manuals gradually took shape, it was realized that what had originally seemed to be by-products of the Index were in themselves substantial contributions to psychoanalytic theory. We had been doing research without knowing it! With this realization, the formation of a number of research groups to investigate theoretical problems thrown up by the indexing process was a matter of course.

If we examine the processes involved in constructing the Index, they can be seen to fall into a number of interconnected stages. The first was the request that therapists conceptualize and categorize their material in terms of their own knowledge of psychoanalytic theory. This had the effect of tying theory and observation more closely together in the minds of individual therapists. It also resulted in an increased sharpness of perception, due to the need to break down masses of material into units of observation that corresponded to units of theory; gaps in the material and indeed inaccuracies in the understanding were revealed.

The second stage involved the refinement of our internal psychoanalytic models so that they accorded more precisely with the observations. Concepts and perceptions were brought into juxtaposition and the theoretical model became more coherent, accurate, and integrated. Theoretical anomalies were highlighted and attempts to resolve these anomalies were made.

A third stage consisted in the reevaluation of the analytic observations in terms of the revised theoretical formulations. This corresponds to the first stage on a different level, and as more and more cases were indexed, so the effects of this "to-and-fro" process could be seen. These processes are quite analogous to the "to-and-fro" processes of perceptual and conceptual development both in the child and in the scientist. The procedure of constructing an Index then falls into line with other scientific methods as a special technique of reality and concept testing.

From this it is not a great step to the application of the procedure of index construction to other types of psychoanalytic observation, to the material of adults as well as of children, or to special areas within psychoanalysis; and it is as a scientific technique of potentially wide application that it is commended to analysts.

REFERENCES

ABRAHAM, K. (1907). The experiencing of sexual traumas as a form of sexual activity. In *Selected Papers*. London: Hogarth Press, 1927.

ABRAHAM, K. (1916). The first pregenital stage of the libido. In *Selected Papers*. London: Hogarth Press, 1927.

ABRAHAM, K. (1924*a*). The influence of oral erotism on character formation. In *Selected Papers*. London: Hogarth Press, 1927.

ABRAHAM, K. (1924*b*). A short study of the development of the libido, viewed in the light of mental disorder. In *Selected Papers*. London: Hogarth Press, 1927.

ADLER, A. (1907). *Studie über Minderwertigkeit von Organen*. Berlin, Vienna: Urban & Schwarzenberg.

ADRIAN, E. D. (1946). The mental and the physical origins of behaviour. *Int. J. Psychoanal.*, 27, 1–6.

AICHHORN, A. (1925). *Wayward Youth*. New York: Viking Press, 1935.

ALEXANDER, F. (1950). *Psychosomatic Medicine*. New York: Norton.

ALEXANDER, F., FRENCH, T.M., & POLLOCK, G.H. (1968). *Psychosomatic Specificity*. Chicago: Chicago University Press.

ALLPORT, G. W. (1943). The ego in contemporary psychology. *Psychol. Rev.*, 50, 451–478.

ARLOW, J. A. (1955). Report of Panel on Sublimation. *J. Am. Psa. Assn.*, 3, 515–527.

BALINT, M. (1932). Character analysis and new beginning. In *Primary Love and Psycho-Analytic Technique*. London: Hogarth Press, 1952.

BALINT, M. (1937). Early developmental stages of the ego. In *Primary Love and Psycho-Analytic Technique*. London: Hogarth Press, 1952.

BALINT, M. (1952). New beginning and the paranoid and the depressive syndromes. In *Primary Love and Psycho-Analytic Technique*. London: Hogarth Press, 1952.

BALINT, M. (1959). *Thrills and Regressions*. New York: International Universities Press.

BALINT, M. (1963). The benign and malignant forms of regression. In DANIELS, G.E., ed., *New Perspectives in Psychoanalysis*. New York: Grune and Stratton, 1965.

BARTLETT F. (1931). *Remembering*. Cambridge: Cambridge University Press.

BELLAK, L. (1958). *Schizophrenia*. New York: Logos Press.

BERES, D. (1958). Vicissitudes of superego functions and superego precursors in childhood. *Psychoanal. Study Child*, 13, 324–351.

BERES, D. (1962). The unconscious fantasy. *Psa. Quart.*, 31, 309–328.

BERES, D. (1965). Structure and function in psycho-analysis. *Int. J. Psychoanal., 46,* 53–63.

BERGLER, E. (1934). Zur Problematik des 'oralen' Pessimisten. *Imago, 20,* 330–376.

BIBRING, E. (1941). The development and problems of the theory of instincts. *Int. J. Psychoanal., 22,* 102–131.

BIBRING, E. (1953). The mechanism of depression. In GREENACRE, P., ed., *Affective Disorders.* New York: International Universities Press.

BLITZER J. R., ROLLINGS, N., & BLACKWELL, A. (1961). Children who starve themselves: anorexia nervosa. *Psychosom. Med., 23,* 369.

BORNSTEIN, B. (1945). Clinical notes on child analysis. *Psychoanal. Study Child, 1,* 151–166.

BOWLBY, J. (1954). Psychopathological processes set in train by early mother–child separation. In SENN, M.J.E., ed., *Infancy and Childhood.* New York: Josiah Macy Foundation, 1954.

BOWLBY, J. (1958). The nature of the child's tie to his mother. *Int. J. Psychoanal., 39,* 350–373.

BOWLBY, J. (1960a). Separation anxiety. *Int. J. Psychoanal., 41,* 89–113.

BOWLBY, J. (1960b). Grief and mourning in infancy and early childhood. *Psychoanal. Study Child, 15,* 9–52.

BOWLBY, J. (1960c). Ethology and the development of object relations. *Int. J. Psychoanal., 41,* 313–317.

BOWLBY, J. (1961a). Separation anxiety: A critical review of the literature. *J. Child Psychol. & Psychiat., 1,* 251–269.

BOWLBY, J. (1961b). Processes of mourning. *Int. J. Psychoanal., 42,* 317–340.

BOWLBY, J. (1962). Pathological mourning and childhood mourning. *J. Amer. Psa. Assn., 11,* 500–541.

BOWLBY, J. (1965). Personal communication.

BOWLBY, J. (1969). *Attachment and Loss, Vol. 1: Attachment.* London: Hogarth.

BOWLBY, J. (1973). *Attachment and Loss, Vol. 2: Separation.* London: Hogarth.

BRENNER, C. (1953). An addendum to Freud's theory of anxiety. *Int. J. Psychoanal., 34,* 18–24.

BREUER, J. & FREUD, S. (1893–1895) *Studies on Hysteria.* In *Standard Edition of the Collected Works of Sigmund Freud, 2.*

BRIERLEY, M. (1937). Affects in theory and practice. *Int. J. Psychoanal., 18,* 256–268.

BRODY, S. (1961). Some aspects of transference resistance in prepuberty. *Psychoanal. Study Child, 16,* 251–274.

BRUNER, J. S., BRUNSWIK, E., FESTINGER, L., HEIDER, F., MUENZINGER, K. F., OSGOOD, C. E., & RAPAPORT, D. (1957). *Contemporary Approaches to Cognition.* Cambridge, MA: Harvard University Press.

BÜHLER, K. (1924). *Die geistige Entwicklung des Kindes.* 4th ed., Jena: Fischer.

BÜHLER, K. (1927). *Die Krise der Psychologie.* Jena: Fischer.

CALDWELL, B. M., (1964). The effects of infant care. In HOFFMAN, M. L. & HOFFMAN, L. W., eds., *Review of Child Development Research.* New York: Russel Sage Foundation.

CHAPMAN, J., FREEMAN, T., & McGHIE, A. (1959). Clinical research in schizophrenia—the psychotherapeutic approach. *British J. Med. Psychol., 32,* 75.

DEVEREUX, G. (1950). In Panel: The interaction of social and deep–psychological factors. *Bull. Amer. Psa. Assn.*, 6.

DUNCKER, K. (1945). *On problem solving.* New York: International Universities Press.

EDGCUMBE, R. & SANDLER, J. (1974). Some comments on 'aggression turned against the self': A brief communication. *Int. J. Psychoanal.*, 55, 365–367.

EISSLER, K. R. (1953). The effect of the structure of the ego on psychoanalytic techinque. *J. Am. Psychoanal. Ass.*, 1, 104–143.

ENGEL, G. L. & REICHSMAN, F. (1956). Spontaneously and experimentally induced depressions in an infant with a gastric fistula. A contribution to the problem of depression. *J. Am. Psychoanal. Ass.*, 4, 428–452.

ERIKSON, E. H. (1937). Configurations in play. *Psychoanal. Q.*, 6, 139–214.

ERIKSON, E. H. (1946a). *Childhood and Society.* New York: Norton.

ERIKSON, E. H. (1946b). Ego development and historical change. *Psychoanal. Study Child*, 2, 359–396.

ERIKSON, E. H. (1968). *Identity.* London: Faber and Faber.

FENICHEL, O. (1926). Identification. In *The Collected Papers of Otto Fenichel, Vol. 1.* New York: Norton, 1953.

FENICHEL, O. (1931). *Perversionen, Psychosen, Charakterstörungen.* Vienna: Int. Psychoanal. Verlag.

FENICHEL, O. (1941). *Problems of Psychoanalytic Technique.* New York: Psychoanalytic Quarterly Inc.

FENICHEL, O. (1945). *The Psychoanalytic Theory of Neurosis.* New York: Norton.

FERENCZI, S. (1925). Psycho-analysis of sexual habits. In *Further Contributions to the Theory and Technique of Psycho-Analysis.* London: Hogarth Press, 1927.

FLAVELL, J. H. & DRAGUNS, J. (1957). A microgenetic approach to perception and thought. *Psychol. Bull.* 54, 197–217.

FLETCHER, R. (1968). *Instinct in Man* (revised ed.). London: Allen & Unwin.

FORDHAM, M. (1958). *The Objective Psyche.* London: Routledge & Kegan Paul.

FOULKES, S. H. (1937). On introjection. *Int. J. Psychoanal.*, 18, 269–293.

FRAIBERG, S. (1966). Further considerations of the role of transference in latency. *Psychoanal. Study Child*, 21, 213–236.

FRANKL, L. (1963). Self-preservation and the development of accident-proneness in children and adolescents. *Psychoanal. Study Child*, 18, 464–483.

FREUD, A. (1926). Introduction to the technique of child analysis. In *The Psycho-Analytical Treatment of Children.* London: Imago, 1946.

FREUD, A. (1936). *The Ego and the Mechanisms of Defence.* London: Hogarth.

FREUD, A. (1945). Indications for child analysis. *Psychoanal. Study Child*, 1, 127–149.

FREUD, A. (1946). *The Psycho-Analytical Treatment of Children.* London: Imago.

FREUD, A. (1951a). A connection between the states of negativism and of emotional surrender (Hörigkeit). *Int. J. Psychoanal.*, 33, 265.

FREUD, A. (1951b). Observations on child development. *Psychoanal. Study Child*, 6, 18–30.

FREUD, A. (1962). Assessment of childhood disturbances. *Psychoanal. Study Child, 17,* 149–158.

FREUD, A. (1963*a*). Regression as a principle in mental development. *Bull. Menninger Clinic, 27,* 126–139.

FREUD, A. (1963*b*). The concept of developmental lines. *Psychoanal. Study Child, 18,* 245–265.

FREUD, A. (1965). *Normality and Pathology in Childhood.* New York: International Universities Press.

FREUD, A. (1970). *Research at the Hampstead Child-Therapy Clinic and Other Papers: 1956–1965.* London: Hogarth.

FREUD, S. (1887–1902). *The Origins of Psychoanalysis.* New York: Basic Books, 1954.

FREUD, S. (1891). *On Aphasia.* London: Imago, 1953.

FREUD, S. (1892). Sketches for the preliminary communication of 1893. In *Standard Edition, 1.*

FREUD, S. (1892–1894). Preface and footnotes to the translation of Charcot's *Tuesday Lectures.* In *Standard Edition, 1.*

FREUD, S. (with BREUER, J.) (1893–1895). *Studies on Hysteria.* In *Standard Edition, 2.*

FREUD, S. (1895). A reply to criticisms of my paper on anxiety neurosis. In *Standard Edition, 3.*

FREUD, S. (1900). *The Interpretation of Dreams.* In *Standard Edition, 4–5.*

FREUD, S. (1901). *The Psychopathology of Everyday Life.* In *Standard Edition, 6.*

FREUD, S. (1905*a*). *Three Essays on the Theory of Sexuality.* In *Standard Edition, 7.*

FREUD, S. (1905*b*). Fragment of an analysis of a case of hysteria. In *Standard Edition, 7.*

FREUD, S. (1907). *Delusions and Dreams in Jensen's 'Gradiva'.* In *Standard Edition, 9.*

FREUD, S. (1908*a*). Hysterical phantasies and their relation to bisexuality. In *Standard Edition, 9.*

FREUD, S. (1908*b*). On the sexual theories of children. In *Standard Edition, 9.*

FREUD, S. (1908*c*). Creative writers and day-dreaming. In *Standard Edition, 9.*

FREUD, S. (1908*d*). Character and anal erotism. In *Standard Edition, 9.*

FREUD, S. (1909*a*). Some general remarks on hysterical attacks. In *Standard Edition, 9.*

FREUD, S. (1909*b*). Analysis of a phobia in a five-year-old boy. In *Standard Edition, 10.*

FREUD, S. (1909*c*). Notes upon a case of obsessional neurosis. In *Standard Edition, 10.*

FREUD, S. (1910*a*). Five lectures on psycho-analysis. In *Standard Edition, 11.*

FREUD, S. (1910*b*). Leonardo da Vinci and a memory of his childhood. In *Standard Edition, 11.*

FREUD, S. (1911). Formulations on the two principles of mental functioning. In *Standard Edition, 12.*

FREUD, S. (1912). The dynamics of transference. In *Standard Edition, 12.*

FREUD, S. (1913a). The disposition to obsessional neurosis. In *Standard Edition, 12.*

FREUD, S. (1913b). The claims of pycho-analysis to scientific interest. In *Standard Edition, 13.*

FREUD, S. (1914). On narcissism: An introduction. *Standard Edition, 14.*

FREUD, S. (1915a). Repression. In *Standard Edition, 14.*

FREUD, S. (1915b). The unconscious. In *Standard Edition, 14.*

FREUD, S. (1915c). Instincts and their vicissitudes. In *Standard Edition, 14.*

FREUD, S. (1916–1917). *Introductory Lectures on Psycho-Analysis.* In *Standard Edition, 15–16.*

FREUD, S. (1917a). Mourning and melancholia. In *Standard Edition, 14.*

FREUD, S. (1917b). A metapsychological supplement to the theory of dreams. In *Standard Edition, 14.*

FREUD, S. (1918). From the history of an infantile neurosis. In *Standard Edition, 17.*

FREUD, S. (1920). *Beyond the Pleasure Principle.* In *Standard Edition, 18.*

FREUD, S. (1921a). *Group Psychology and the Analysis of the Ego.* In *Standard Edition, 18.*

FREUD, S. (1921b). Introduction to J. Varendonck's *The Psychology of Day-Dreams.* In *Standard Edition, 18.*

FREUD, S. (1922). Some neurotic mechanisms in jealousy, paranoia, and homosexuality. In *Standard Edition, 18.*

FREUD, S. (1923a). *The Ego and the Id.* In *Standard Edition, 19.*

FREUD, S. (1923b). Remarks on the theory and practice of dream-interpretation. In *Standard Edition, 19.*

FREUD, S. (1923c). Two encyclopaedia articles. In *Standard Edition, 18.*

FREUD, S. (1924a). The economic problem of masochism. In *Standard Edition, 19.*

FREUD, S (1924b). The loss of reality in neurosis and psychosis. In *Standard Edition, 19.*

FREUD, S. (1925a). A note upon the 'mystic writing-pad.' In *Standard Edition, 19.*

FREUD, S. (1925b). Negation. In *Standard Edition, 19.*

FREUD, S. (1925c). Some additional notes on dream-interpretation as a whole. In *Standard Edition, 19.*

FREUD, S. (1925d). *An Autobiographical Study.* In *Standard Edition, 20.*

FREUD, S. (1926). *Inhibitions, Symptoms and Anxiety.* In *Standard Edition, 20*

FREUD, S. (1927). *The Future of an Illusion.* In *Standard Edition, 21.*

FREUD, S. (1930). *Civilization and its Discontents.* In *Standard Edition, 21.*

FREUD, S. (1931). The expert opinion in the Halsmann case. In *Standard Edition, 21.*

FREUD, S. (1933). *New Introductory Lectures on Psycho-Analysis.* In *Standard Edition, 22.*

FREUD, S. (1939). *Moses and Monotheism.* In *Standard Edition, 23.*

FREUD, S. (1940). *An Outline of Psycho-Analysis.* In *Standard Edition, 23.*

FRIES, M. E. (1946). The child's ego development and the training of adults in his environment. *Psychoanal. Study Child, 2,* 85–112.

FROMM, E. (1941). *Escape from Freedom.* New York: Rinehart.

FURST, S., ed. (1967). *Psychic Trauma*. New York: Basic Books.

GARDNER, R., HOLZMAN, P. S., KLEIN, G. S., LINTON, H., & SPENCE, D. P. (1959). *Cognitive Control: A Study of Individual Consistencies in Cognitive Behavior*. New York: International Universities Press.

GESELL, A., ILG, F. L., & BULLIS, G. E. (1949). *Vision: Its Development in Infant and Child*. London: Hamish Hamilton.

GILL, M. (1963). *Topography and Systems in Psychoanalytic Theory*. New York: International Universities Press.

GLOVER, E. (1924). The significance of the mouth in psycho-analysis. *Br. J. Med. Psychol.*, 4, 134–155.

GLOVER, E. (1925). Notes on oral character information. *Int. J. Psychoanal.* 6, 131–154.

GLOVER, E. (1945). Examination of the Klein system of child psychology. *Psychoanal. Study Child, 1*, 75–118.

GLOVER, E. (1949). *Psycho-Analysis* (2nd ed.). London: Staples Press.

GLOVER, E. (1955). *The Technique of Psycho-Analysis*. London: Bailliere, Tindall & Cox.

GREENACRE, P. (1952). *Trauma, Growth, and Personality*. New York: Norton.

GREENACRE, P. (1954). The role of transference: Practical considerations in relation to psychoanalytic therapy. *J. Am. Psychoanal. Ass., 2*, 671–684.

GREENACRE, P. (1966). Problems of overidealization of the analyst and of analysis: Their manifestations in the transference and countertransference relationship. *Psychoanal. Study Child, 21*, 193–212.

GREENSON, R. R. (1954). The struggle against identification. *J. Am. Psychoanal. Ass., 2*, 200–217.

GREENSON, R. R. (1965). The working alliance and the transference neurosis. *Psa. Quart., 34*, 155–181.

HARTMANN, H. (1939). *Ego Psychology and the Problem of Adaptation*. New York: International Universities Press, 1958.

HARTMANN, H. (1947). On rational and irrational action. In *Essays on Ego Psychology*. New York: International Universities Press, 1964.

HARTMANN, H. (1950). Comments on the psychoanalytic theory of the ego. *Psychoanal. Study Child, 5*, 74–96.

HARTMANN, H. (1955). Notes on the theory of sublimation. *Psychoanal. Study Child, 10*, 9–29.

HARTMANN, H. (1956). The development of the ego concept in Freud's work. *Int. J. Psychoanal. 37*, 425–438.

HARTMANN, H. (1964). *Essays on Ego Psychology*. New York: International Universities Press.

HARTMANN, H. and KRIS, E. (1945). The genetic approach in psychoanalysis. *Psychoanal. Study Child, 1*, 11–30.

HARTMANN, H., KRIS, E., & LOEWENSTEIN, R. M. (1949). Notes on the theory of aggression. *Psychoanal. Study Child, 3–4*, 9–36.

HARTMANN, H., KRIS, E., & LOEWENSTEIN, R. M. (1964). *Papers on Psychoanalytic Psychology*. New York: International Universities Press.

HARTMANN, H. & LOEWENSTEIN, R. M. (1962). Notes on the superego. *Psychoanal. Study Child, 17*, 42–81.

HEAD, H. (1926). *Aphasia and Kindred Disorders of Speech.* New York: Macmillan.

HEIMANN, P. & VALENSTEIN, A. F. (1972). The psychoanalytical concept of aggression: An integrated summary. *Int. J. Psychoanal., 53,* 31–35.

HENDRICK, I. (1934). *Facts and Theories of Psychoanalysis.* New York: Knopf, 1958.

HENDRICK, I. (1942). Instinct and the ego during infancy. *Psa. Quart., 11,* 33–58.

HENDRICK, I. (1943). Work and the pleasure principle. *Psa. Quart., 12,* 311–329.

HENDRICK, I. (1951). Early development of the ego: Identification in infancy. *Psa. Quart., 20,* 44–61.

HOFFER, W. (1949). Hand, mouth and ego-integration. *Psychoanal. Study Child, 3 & 4,* 49–56.

HOFFER, W. (1950*a*). Three psychological criteria for the termination of treatment. *Int. J. Psychoanal., 31,* 194–195.

HOFFER, W. (1950*b*). Oral aggressiveness and ego development. *Int. J. Psychoanal., 31,* 156–160.

HOFFER, W. (1950*c*). Development of the body ego. *Psychoanal. Study Child, 5,* 18–23.

HOFFER, W. (1952). The mutual influences in the development of ego and the id: Earliest stages. *Psychoanal. Study Child, 7,* 31–41.

HOFFER, W. (1955). *Some Current Problems of Psychoanalytic Training and Research.* Baltimore: Williams & Wilkins.

HOFFER, W. (1956). Transference and transference neurosis. *Int. J. Psychoanal., 37,* 377–379.

HOLT, R. T. (1965). Ego autonomy re-evaluated. *Int. J. Psychoanal., 46,* 151–167.

HOLZMAN, P. S. (1962). Repression and cognitive style. *Bull. Menninger Clin., 26,* 273–282.

HUNT, J. McV. (1941). The effects of infant feeding-frustration upon adult hoarding in the albino rat. *J. Abnorm. Soc. Psychol., 36,* 338.

ISAACS, S. (1948). The nature and function of phantasy. *Int. J. Psychoanal., 29,* 73–97.

JACOBSON, E. (1953*a*). Contribution to the metapsychology of cyclothymic depression. In GREENACRE, P., ed., *Affective Disorders.* New York: International Universities Press.

JACOBSON, E. (1953*b*). The affects and their pleasure–unpleasure qualities in relation to the psychic discharge processes. In LOEWENSTEIN, R. M., ed. *Drives, Affects, Behavior,* Vol. 1. New York: International Universities Press.

JACOBSON, E. (1954*a*). Contribution to the metapsychology of psychotic identifications. *J. Am. Psa. Assn., 2,* 239–262.

JACOBSON, E. (1954*b*). On psychotic identifications. *Int. J. Psychoanal., 35,* 102–108.

JACOBSON, E. (1954*c*). The self and the object world: Vicissitudes of their infantile cathexes and their influence on ideational affective development. *Psychoanal. Study Child, 9,* 75–127.

JACOBSON, E. (1964). *The Self and the Object World*. New York: International Universities Press.

JAMES, W. (1890). *The Principles of Psychology*. New York: Henry Holt & Co.

JOFFE, W. G. (1969). A critical review of the status of the envy concept. *Int. J. Psychoanal.*, *50*, 533–545.

JOFFE, W. G. & SANDLER, J. (1965). Notes on pain, depression, and individuation. *Psychoanal. Study Child*, *20*, 394–424.

JOFFE, W. G. & Sandler, J. (1967a). On some conceptual problems involved in the consideration of disorders of narcissism. *J. Child Psychother.* *2*, 56–66.

JOFFE, W. G. & SANDLER, J. (1967b). On the concept of pain, with special reference to depression and psychogenic pain. *J. Psychosom. Res.*, *11*, 69.

JOFFE, W. G. & Sandler, J. (1968). Comments on the psychoanalytic psychology of adaptation, with special reference to the role of affects and the representational world. *Int. J. Psychoanal.*, *49*, 445–454.

JONES, E. (1926). The origin and structure of the superego. *Int. J. Psychoanal.*, *7*, 303–311.

JONES, E. (1935). Psycho-analysis and the instincts. In *Papers on Psycho-Analysis* (4th ed.). London: Balliere, Tindall & Cox, 1938.

JUNG, C. G. (1923). *Psychological Types*. London: Kegan Paul.

KAPLAN, A. (1964). *The Conduct of Inquiry*. San Francisco: Chandler.

KAPLAN, S. & WHITMAN, R. (1965). The negative ego ideal. *Int. J. Psychoanal.*, *46*, 183–187.

KEPECS, J. G. (1966). Theories of transference neurosis. *Psychoanal. Q.*, *35*, 497–521.

KHAN, M. MASUD R. (1963). The concept of cumulative trauma. *Psychoanal. Study Child*, *18*, 286–306.

KLEIN, G. S. (1959). Consciousness in psychoanalytic theory. *J. Am. Psa. Assn.*, *7*, 5–34.

KLEIN, M. (1927). Symposium on child analysis. In *Contributions to Psycho-Analysis, 1921–1945*. London: Hogarth Press, 1948.

KLEIN, M. (1933). The early development of conscience in the child. In *Contributions to Psycho-Analysis, 1921–1945*. London: Hogarth Press, 1948.

KLEIN, M. (1948). *Contributions to Psycho-Analysis, 1921–1945*. London: Hogarth Press.

KLEIN, M. (1952). The origins of transference. *Int. J. Psychoanal.*, *33*, 433–438.

KLEIN, M. (1957). *Envy and Gratitude*. London: Tavistock.

KLEIN, M. (1958). On the development of mental functioning. *Int. J. Psychoanal.*, *39*, 84–90.

KNIGHT, R. P. (1940). Introjection, projection, and identification. *Psychoanal. Quart.*, *9*, 334–341.

KÖHLER, I. (1951). *Über Aufbau und Wandlungen der Wahrnehmungswelt*. Vienna: Rohrer.

KÖHLER, I. (1953). Umgewöhnung im Wahrnehmungsbereich. *Die Pyramide*, *5*, 92–95; *6*, 109–113.

KÖHLER, I. (1964). *The Formation and Transformation of the Perceptual World*. New York: International Universities Press.

KOHUT, H. (1971). *The Analysis of the Self.* New York: International Universities Press.

KOHUT, H. (1977). *The Restoration of the Self.* New York: International Universities Press.

KRIS, E. (1947). Problems in clinical research: Discussion remarks. *Amer. J. Orthopsychiat., 17,* 210.

KRIS, E. (1955). Neutralization and sublimation. *Psychoanal. Study Child, 10,* 30–46.

KRIS, E. (1956). The recovery of childhood memories in psychoanalysis. *Psychoanal. Study Child, 11,* 54–88.

KRIS, M. (1957). The use of prediction in a longitudinal study. *Psychoanal. Study Child, 12,* 175–189.

KUT, S. (1953). The changing pattern of transference in the analysis of an eleven-year-old girl. *Psychoanal. Study Child, 8,* 355–378.

LAMPL-DE GROOT, J. (1936). Hemming und Narzissmus. *Int. Ztschr. Psa., 22,* 198–222.

LAMPL-DE GROOT, J. (1947). On the development of the ego and superego. *Int. J. Psychoanal., 28,* 7–11.

LAMPL-DE GROOT, J. (1957). On defense and development: Normal and pathological. *Psychoanal. Study Child, 12,* 114–126.

LAMPL-DE GROOT, J. (1962). Ego ideal and superego. *Psychoanal. Study Child, 17,* 94–106.

LAMPL-DE GROOT, J. (1965). *The Development of the Mind.* New York: International Universities Press.

LEVEY, H. B. (1934). Oral trends and oral conflicts in a case of duodenal ulcer. *Psychoanal. Quart., 3,* 574–582.

LEVY, D. M. (1934). Experiments on the sucking reflex and social behavior of dogs. *Am. J. Orthopsychiat., 4,* 203.

LEWIN, B. (1965). Reflections on affect. In SCHUR, M., ed., *Drives, Affects, Behavior,* Vol. 2. New York: International Universities Press, 1965.

LIND, J. (1965). Personal communication.

LUSSIER, A. (1972). Panel report on "Aggression." *Int. J. Psychoanal., 53,* 13–19.

MAHLER, M. S. (1952). On child psychosis and schizophrenia. *Psychoanal. Study Child, 7,* 286–305.

MAHLER, M. (1957). On two crucial phases of integration concerning problems of identity: Separation–individuation and bisexual identity. Abstract in Panel on Problems of Identity, reported by D. Rubinfine. *J. Amer. Psychoanal. Assn., 6,* 131–142.

MAHLER, M. (1958). Autism and symbiosis: Two extreme disturbances of identity. *Int. J. Psychoanal., 39,* 77–83.

MAHLER, M. (1961). On sadness and grief in infancy and childhood: Loss and restoration of the symbiotic love object. *Psychoanal. Study Child, 16,* 332–351.

MAHLER, M. (1963). Thoughts about development and individuation. *Psychoanal. Study Child, 18,* 307–324.

MAHLER, M. & FURER, M. (1963). Certain aspects of the separation–individuation phase. *Psychoanal. Quart., 32,* 1–14.

MENNINGER, K. (1958). *Theory of Psycho-Analytic Technique.* New York: Basic Books.

NOVEY, S. (1955). The role of the superego and ego ideal in character information. *Int. J. Psychoanal., 36,* 254–259.

NUNBERG, H. (1932). *Principles of Psychoanalysis.* New York: International Universities Press, 1955.

NUNBERG, H. (1951). Transference and reality. *Int. J. Psychoanal., 32,* 1–9.

ORR, D. W. (1954). Transference and counter-transference: A historical survey. *J. Am. Psychoanal. Assn., 2,* 621–670.

PIAGET, J. (1936). *The Origins of Intelligence in Children.* New York: International Universities Press, 1952.

PIAGET, J. (1937). *The Construction of Reality in the Child.* New York: Basic Books, 1954.

PIERS, G. & SINGER, M. B. (1953). *Shame and Guilt: A Psychoanalytic and a Cultural Study.* Springfield, Ill.: Charles C. Thomas.

POLLOCK, G. H. (1961). Mourning and adaptation. *Int. J. Psychoanal., 42,* 341–361.

PROVENCE, S. & LIPTON, R. C. (1962). *Infants in Institutions.* New York: International Universities Press.

RADO, S. (1926). The psychic effects of intoxicants: An attempt to evolve a psycho-analytical theory of morbid cravings. *Int. J. Psychoanal., 7,* 396–413.

RADO, S. (1928). The problem of melancholia. *Int. J. Psychoanal., 9,* 420–438.

RANGELL, L. (1963a). The scope of intrapsychic conflict: Microscopic and macroscopic considerations. *Psychoanal. Study Child, 18,* 75–102.

RANGELL, L. (1963b). Structural problems in intrapsychic conflict. *Psychoanal. Study Child, 18,* 103–138.

RAPAPORT, D. (1951a). The conceptual model of psychoanalysis. *J. Personal., 22,* 56–81.

RAPAPORT, D. (1951b). The autonomy of the ego. *Bull. Menninger Clin., 15,* 113–123.

RAPAPORT, D. (1953). On the psycho-analytic theory of affects. *Int. J. Psychoanal., 34,* 177–198.

RAPAPORT, D. (1957). Cognitive structures. In BRUNER, J. S. *et al., Contemporary Approaches to Cognition.* Cambridge, MA: Harvard University Press, 1957.

RAPAPORT, D. (1958). The theory of ego autonomy: A generalization. *Bull. Menninger Clin., 22,* 13–35.

RAPAPORT, D. (1959). A historical survey of ego psychology. In ERIKSON, E. H., Identity and the Life Cycle. New York: International Universities Press, 1959.

REICH, A. (1954). Early identifications as archaic elements in the superego. *J. Am. Psychoanal. Assn., 2,* 218–238.

REICH, A. (1960). Pathologic forms of self-esteem regulation. *Psychoanal. Study Child, 15,* 215–234.

RIBBLE, M. (1944). *The Rights of Infants.* New York: Columbia University Press.

ROBERTSON, J. (1953a). Film: *A Two-Year-Old Goes to Hospital*. London: Tavistock Child Development Research Unit.

ROBERTSON, J. (1953b). Some responses of young children to loss of maternal care. *Nursing Times, 49,* 382–386.

ROBERTSON, J. & BOWLBY, J. (1952). Responses of young children to separation from their mothers. *Courrier de Centre International de l'Enfance, 2,* 131–142.

ROSEN, I. (1954). The clinical significance of obsessions in schizophrenia. *J. Ment. Sci., 103,* 773–785, 1957.

SANDER, F. (1927). *Experimentelle Ergebnisse der Gestaltpsychologie.* Jena: Fischer.

SANDLER, A. -M. (1963). Aspects of passivity and ego development in the blind infant. *Psychoanal. Study Child, 18,* 343–360.

SANDLER, J. (1959a). The body as phallus. *Int. J. Psychoanal., 41,* 191–198.

SANDLER, J. (1959b). On the repetition of early childhood relationships in later psychosomatic disorder. In *The Nature of Stress Disorder.* London: Hutchinson, 187–195.

SANDLER, J. (1960a). The background of safety. *Int. J. Psychoanal., 41,* 352–365.

SANDLER, J. (1960b). On the concept of superego. *Psychoanal. Study Child, 15,* 128–162.

SANDLER, J. (1962a). Psychology and psychoanalysis. *Brit. J. Med. Psychol., 35,* 91–100.

SANDLER, J. (1962b). The Hampstead Index as an instrument of psychoanalytic research. *Int. J. Psychoanal., 43,* 287–291.

SANDLER, J. (1965). The Hampstead Child-Therapy Clinic. *W.H.O. Public Health Papers, 28,* 109–123.

SANDLER, J. (1967). Trauma, strain and development. In FURST, S. ed., *Psychic Trauma.* New York: Basic Books, 1967.

SANDLER, J. (1969). *On the Communication of Psychoanalytic Thought.* Leiden: University Press.

SANDLER, J. (1970). Sexual fantasies and sexual theories in childhood. In *Studies in Child Psychoanalysis: Pure and Applied.* New Haven: Yale University Press.

SANDLER, J. (1972). The role of affects in psychoanalytic theory. In *Physiology, Emotion and Psychosomatic Illness.* Ciba Foundation Symposium 8 (New Series). Amsterdam: Elsevier.

SANDLER, J. & DARE, C. (1970). The psychoanalytic concept of orality. *J. Psychosom. Res., 14,* 211–222.

SANDLER, J., DARE, C., & HOLDER, A. (1970). Basic psychoanalytic concepts: I. The extension of clinical concepts outside the psychoanalytic situation. *Br. J. Psychiat., 16,* 551–554.

SANDLER, J., DARE, C., & HOLDER, A. (1972a). Frames of reference in psychoanalytic psychology: II. The historical context and phases in the development of psychoanalysis. *Br. J. Med. Psychol., 45,* 133–142.

SANDLER, J., DARE, C., & HOLDER, A. (1972b). Frames of reference in psychoanalytic psychology: III. A note on the basic assumptions. *Br. J. Med. Psychol., 45,* 143–147.

SANDLER, J., DARE, C., & HOLDER, A. (1973). *The Patient and the Analyst.*

New York: International Universities Press.

SANDLER, J. & HAZARI, A. (1960). The 'obsessional': On the psychological classification of obsessional traits and symptoms. *Brit. J. Med. Psychol.*, 33, 113–122.

SANDLER, J., HOLDER, A., KAWENOKA, M., KENNEDY, H., NEURATH, L. (1969). Notes on some theoretical and clinical aspects of transference. *Int. J. Psychoanal.*, 50, 633–645.

SANDLER, J., HOLDER, A., & MEERS, D. (1963). The ego ideal and the ideal self. *Psychoanal. Study Child*, 18, 139–158.

SANDLER, J. & JOFFE, W. G. (1965a). Notes on obsessional manifestations in children. *Psychoanal. Study Child*, 20, 425–438.

SANDLER, J. & JOFFE, W. G. (1965b). Notes on childhood depression. *Int. J. Psychoanal.*, 46, 88–96.

SANDLER, J. & JOFFE, W. G. (1966). On skill and sublimation. *J. Am. Psa. Assn.*, 14, 335–355.

SANDLER, J. & JOFFE, W. G., (1967a). On the psychoanalytic theory of autonomy and the autonomy of psychoanalytic theory. *Int. J. Psychiat.*, 3, 512.

SANDLER, J. & JOFFE, W. G. (1967b). The tendency to persistence in psychological function and development, with special reference to fixation and regression. *Bull. Menninger Clin.*, 31, 257–271.

SANDLER, J. & JOFFE, W. G. (1968). Psychoanalytic psychology and learning theory. In *The Role of Learning in Psychotherapy* (Ciba Foundation Symposium). London: Churchill, 274–287.

SANDLER, J. & JOFFE, W. G. (1969). Towards a basic psychoanalytic model. *Int. J. Psychoanal.*, 50, 79–90.

SANDLER, J., KAWENOKA, M., NEURATH, L., ROSENBLATT, B., SCHNURMANN, A., & SIGAL, J. (1962). The classification of superego material in the Hampstead Index. *Psychoanal. Study Child*, 17, 107–127.

SANDLER, J. & NAGERA, H. (1963). Aspects of the metapsychology of fantasy. *Psychoanal. Study Child*, 18, 159–194.

SANDLER, J. & NOVICK, J. (1968). Some recent developments in child psychoanalysis at the Hampstead Clinic. In HOWELLS, J. G., ed., *Modern Perspectives in International Child Psychiatry*. Edinburgh: Oliver & Boyd, 1968.

SANDLER, J., & ROSENBLATT, B. (1962). The concept of the representational world. *Psychoanal. Study Child*, 17, 128–145.

SCHAFER, R. (1960). The loving and beloved superego in Freud's structural theory. *Psychoanal. Study Child*, 15, 163–188.

SCHILDER, P. (1920). On the development of thoughts. In RAPAPORT, D., ed. and tr., *Organization and Pathology of Thought*. New York: Columbia University Press, 1951.

SCHILDER, P. (1935). *The Image and Appearance of the Human Body*. London: Routledge, & Kegan Paul.

SCHILDER, P. (1942). *Mind: Perception and Thought in Their Constructive Aspects*. New York: Columbia University Press.

SCHUR, M. (1953). The ego in anxiety. In LOEWENSTEIN, R. M., ed., *Drives, Affects, Behavior*, Vol. 1. New York: International University Press, 1953.

SCHUR, M. (1960). Discussion of Dr. John Bowlby's paper. *Psychoanal. Study Child*, 15, 63–84.

SCHUR, M. (1966). *The Id and the Regulatory Principles of Mental Functioning*. New York: International Universities Press.

SEGAL, H. (1973). *Introduction to the Work of Melanie Klein*. London: Hogarth.

SHARPE, E. F. (1930). *Collected Papers on Psycho-Analysis*. London: Hogarth, 1950.

SILVERBERG, W. V. (1948). The concept of transference. *Psychoanal. Quart.*, 17, 303–321.

SPIEGEL, L. A. (1959). The self, the sense of self, and perception. *Psychoanal. Study Child*, 14, 81–109.

SPITZ, R. A. (1945). Hospitalism: An inquiry into the genesis of psychiatric conditions in early childhood. *Psychoanal. Study Child*, 1, 53–74.

SPITZ, R. A (1946). Hospitalism. A follow-up report. *Psychoanal. Study Child*, 2, 113–117.

SPITZ, R. A. (1950). Anxiety in infancy: A study of its manifestations in the first year of life. *Int. J. Psychoanal.*, 31, 138–143.

SPITZ, R. A. (1957). *No and Yes: On the Genesis of Human Communication*. New York: International Universities Press.

SPITZ, R. A. (1958). On the genesis of superego components. *Psychoanal. Study Child*, 13, 375–404.

SPITZ, R. (1965). *The First Year of Life*. New York: International Universities Press.

STENGEL, E. (1945). A study of some clinical aspects of the relationship between obsessional neurosis and psychotic reaction-types. *J. Ment. Sci.*, 91, 166–187.

TOMKINS, S. S. (1963). *Affect, Imagery, Consciousness*, Vol. 2, *The Negative Affects*. New York: Springer.

ÜXKÜLL, J. VON (1920). *Theoretical Biology*. New York: Harcourt Brace, 1926.

WAELDER, R. (1933). The psychoanalytic theory of play. *Psychoanal. Quart.*, 2, 208–224.

WAELDER, R. (1956). Introduction to the discussion on problems of transference. *Int. J. Psychoanal.*, 37, 367–368.

WALLER, J. V., KAUFMAN, M. R., & DEUTSCH, F. (1940). Anorexia nervosa: A psychosomatic entity. *Psychosom. Med.*, 2, 3.

WEISS, E. (1950). *Principles of Psychodynamics*. New York: Grune & Stratton.

WERNER, H. (1940). *Comparative Psychology of Mental Development*. New York: International Universities Press, 1957.

WERNER, H. (1956). Microgenesis and aphasia. *J. Abnorm. Soc. Psychol.*, 52, 347–353.

WERNER, H. (1957). The concept of development from a comparative and organismic point of view. In HARRIS, D. B., ed., *The Concept of Development*. Minneapolis: University of Minnesota Press, 1957.

WERNER, H. & WAPNER, S. (1955). The Innsbruck studies on distorted visual fields in relation to an organismic theory of perception. *Psychol. Rev.*, 62, 130–138.

WINNICOTT, D. W. (1954). The depressive position in normal emotional development. In *Collected Papers*. London: Tavistock, 1958.

WINNICOTT, D. W. (1956). On transference. *Int. J. Psychoanal.*, 37, 386–388.

WINNICOTT, D. W. (1958a). Psycho-analysis and the sense of guilt. In SUTHERLAND, J. D., ed., *Psycho-Analysis and Contemporary Thought.* London: Hogarth Press, 1958.

WINNICOTT, D. W. (1958b). A note on normality and anxiety. In *Collected Papers.* London: Tavistock, 1958.

WINNICOTT, D. W. (1964). The value of depression. *Brit. J. Psychiat. Soc. Work*, 7, 123–127.

WULFF, M. (1951). The problem of neurotic manifestations in children of preoedipal age. *Psychoanal. Study Child*, 6, 169–179.

ZETZEL, E. R. (1960). Introduction to the symposium on "depressive illness." *Int. J. Psychoanal.*, 41, 476–480.

Index

Abraham, K., 164, 307–309
Abstraction, 302
Acting out, transference, 274
Activity cathexis, as replacement for object
    cathexis, 202–206
  cf. sublimation, 206
Adaptation, 239–240
  Balint on, 164–165
  defenses and, 223–224
  dissociation as, 222
  Freud on, 221–222
  and frustration, 172–173, 230–231
  growth in importance, 46
  and homeostasis, 293–297
  to inner forces or states, 225
  and narcissism, 222–223
  to pain, 172–176
  and persistence, 232
  and strain, 139–141
  structure cf. experience, 225
  and superego, 228
  and trauma, 133–134, 138
Adualism (Piaget), 219
Affect, 285–297
  charge, 290
  and defense, 222–223
  and depression, 155
  distancing, 149
  cf. drives, 292
  and fantasy, 113
  cf. feeling-states, 223–226, 261, 285, 286,
      294–297
  and meaning, 295
  mental apparatus, 292–297
    development, 293–294
  pathogenesis, and catharsis, 221–222
  phases, historical view
    first (trauma/cathexis), 286–287
    second (drive/topographical), 288–290
    third (structural), 290–292
  Rapaport, 285–286
  and representations, 189
  somatic aspects, 243
  sublimation as defense against, 204, 206

Aggression
  and depression, 160–163, 169
  developmental course, 70, 298–299
  instinctual cf. reactive, 299
  and longing, 169–172
  projection, 160
  against the self, 298–300, 301
    self- cf. object-directed, 299–300
  and superego, 21–23
  see also Sadism
Aggressor, identification with, 87
Alcohol, 41
Alliance, therapeutic/treatment, 274
Ambivalence, 151, 169
  and depression, 176
  and fantasy, 157
  and object loss, 170
  obsessional, 143, 151
  towards self, 171
Anaclitic objects, 158, 201–202
Anal erotism, 307
Analization, Oedipal relations, 144
Anal phase, 213, 312
  and development, 150–153
  disturbance in, and obsessional manifesta-
      tions, 152–153
  ego development in, 150–151
  sphincter morality, 29
  and trauma, 132
Anal-reactive character, cf. obsessional, 146,
    148, 151, 153
Anal sadism, 143, 145, 151, 213
Anorexia, 304, 305
Anus, 15
  birth through, fantasies of, 124
  and fellatio, 305
Anxiety, 245–246, 297
  and fantasy, 110–111
  cf. guilt, 39
  persecutory, 28, 160
  transformed libido, 222
  and trauma, 134–135
Aphasia, 216
Art and creativity, 106–107

337